A Unified Theory of Party Competition

This book integrates spatial and behavioral perspectives – in a word, those of the Rochester and Michigan schools – into a unified theory of voter choice and party strategy. The theory encompasses both policy and nonpolicy factors, effects of turnout, voter discounting of party promises, expectations of coalition government, and party motivations based on policy as well as office. Optimal (Nash equilibrium) strategies are determined for alternative models for presidential elections in the United States and France, and for parliamentary elections in Britain and Norway. These polities cover a wide range of electoral rules, numbers of major parties, and governmental structures. The analyses suggest that the more competitive parties generally take policy positions that come close to maximizing their electoral support, and that these vote-maximizing positions correlate strongly with the mean policy positions of their supporters.

James F. Adams is Associate Professor of Political Science at the University of California, Santa Barbara. His primary research interest is the application of spatial modeling to real-world elections and the insights this approach can provide into theories of political representation. He is the author of *Party Competition and Responsible Party Government: A Theory of Spatial Competition Based upon Insights from Behavioral Voting Research* (2001) as well as articles in the *American Journal of Political Science*, the *Journal of Politics*, the *British Journal of Political Science*, and *Public Choice*.

Samuel Merrill III is Professor Emeritus of Mathematics and Computer Science at Wilkes University. He received his Ph.D. in mathematics from Yale University. His current research involves mathematical and statistical modeling, particularly in political science. He is the author (with Bernard Grofman) of *A Unified Theory of Voting* (Cambridge University Press, 1999) and *Making Multicandidate Elections More Democratic* (1988) and has published in a number of journals, including the *American Political Science Review*, the *American Journal of Political Science*, and the *Journal of the American Statistical Association*. He has been a visiting professor at Yale University and a visiting scholar at the University of Washington.

Bernard Grofman is Professor of Political Science (and adjunct Professor of Economics) at the University of California, Irvine. He received his Ph.D. in political science from the University of Chicago in 1972. He is an expert on comparative election systems and models of voting, and on social choice theory. He has published more than 200 articles in journals such as the *American Political Science Review*, the *American Journal of Political Science*, *Electoral Studies*, and *Public Choice*, and he has authored or coedited seventeen books. He has been a Fellow of the Center for Advanced Study in the Behavioral Sciences at Stanford University; a visiting professor at the University of Michigan, the University of Washington, and the University of Mannheim; and a scholar-in-residence at the University of Bologna, Kansai University (Osaka), the German Science Center (Berlin), Pompeu Fabra University (Barcelona), and the Brookings Institution. He is a past president of   lic Choice Society and a Fellow of the American Academy of A

A Unified Theory
of Party Competition

A Cross-National Analysis Integrating Spatial and Behavioral Factors

JAMES F. ADAMS
University of California, Santa Barbara

SAMUEL MERRILL III
Wilkes University

BERNARD GROFMAN
University of California, Irvine

CAMBRIDGE
UNIVERSITY PRESS

CAMBRIDGE UNIVERSITY PRESS
Cambridge, New York, Melbourne, Madrid, Cape Town, Singapore, São Paulo

Cambridge University Press
40 West 20th Street, New York, NY 10011-4211, USA

www.cambridge.org
Information on this title: www.cambridge.org/9780521836449

First published 2005

Printed in the United States of America

A catalog record for this publication is available from the British Library.

Library of Congress Cataloging in Publication Data

Adams, James, 1962–
A unified theory of party competition : a cross-national analysis integrating spatial
and behavioral factors / James F. Adams, Samuel Merrill III, Bernard Grofman.
    p. cm.
Includes bibliographical references and index.
ISBN 0-521-83644-1 (hardback : alk. paper) –
ISBN 0-521-54493-9 (pbk. : alk. paper)
1. Political parties. 2. Democracy. 3. Elections. 4. Comparative government.
5. Voting research. I. Merrill, Samuel, 1939– II. Grofman, Bernard. III. Title.
JF2051.A34 2005
324.2′01 – dc22   2004054561

ISBN-13 978-0-521-83644-9 hardback
ISBN-10 0-521-83644-1 hardback

ISBN-13 978-0-521-54493-1 paperback
ISBN-10 0-521-54493-9 paperback

Contents

Tables and Figures

Tables

Acknowledgments

Several different strands of literature have influenced our work, which integrates the perspectives of spatial modeling and behavioral research in an effort to understand the real-world policy behavior of political elites. Our analyses of office-seeking politicians have been directly influenced by the extensive spatial modeling literature extending Downs's work, particularly that of Enelow, Hinich, Munger, and Schofield. Our work on policy-seeking candidates has been similarly influenced by Wittman's seminal work, and also by the important recent extensions developed by Groseclose, Londregan and Romer, and Roemer. Finally, our thinking about how to apply survey data to the analysis of elite behavior in real-world elections has been enriched by the empirical and theoretical work of Schofield and his coauthors, Erikson and Romero, Dow, and Alvarez and Nagler.

We particularly thank Barry Burden, Jay Dow, Roy Pierce, Norman Schofield, and Anders Westholm for general discussions and for correspondence that has advanced our thinking about the topics covered in this book. Jay Dow kindly provided us with some of the statistical estimates of survey respondents' voting behavior that we used in the analyses we report in Chapter 8. At Cambridge University Press, we thank Lew Bateman, Russell Hahn, and Sarah Gentile. We owe special thanks to Florence Sanchez of the UCSB Political Science Department, whose tireless copyediting greatly improved the presentation of our ideas.

The data sets used in our study were made available by the Interuniversity Consortium for Political and Social Research (ICPSR), the Norwegian Social Science Data Services (NSD), and the Centre for Research into Elections and Social Trends (CREST) and are acknowledged with appreciation. Berndt Aardal and Henry Valen were the Principal Investigators of the 1988 Norwegian Election Study, Roy Pierce was the Principal Investigator of the 1988 French Presidential Election Study (FPES), and Anthony Heath, Roger Jowell, J. K. Curtice, and Pippa Norris were the Principal Investigators of the 1997 British General Election Study. The ICPSR, the NSD, CREST, and the Principal Investigators of these studies are not responsible for the analyses presented here.

Portions of the following chapters are based on previously published work of the authors: Chapter 4, on Merrill and Adams (2001, 2002); Chapters 7 and 8, on work presented in Adams and Merrill (2003a); and Chapter 10, on Merrill, Grofman, and Adams (2001). The analyses in Chapters 5 and 6 are sequels to related analyses in Adams and Merrill (2000) and Adams and Merrill (1999b), respectively. Material adapted from Merrill and Adams (2001) is used with permission from Oxford University Press; that adapted from Adams and Merrill (2003a) is used with permission from the *Journal of Politics*.

A Unified Theory of Party Competition

CHAPTER 1

Modeling Party Competition

1.1. Introduction to the Unified Theory of Party Competition

Despite the insights provided by the standard models of party competition, these models have failed to account for some fundamental empirical regularities found throughout the democratic world. Regardless of electoral system, political parties tend to be located across a wide ideological spectrum, and parties tend to exhibit considerable consistency in their ideological locations. Many models of party competition – particularly, spatial models that emphasize electoral incentives – generate predictions that are at variance with empirical observation. Either these theories predict convergence of party positions to similar, centrist positions (Enelow and Hinich 1984; de Palma, Hong, and Thisse 1990; Hinich and Munger 1994; Lin, Enelow, and Dorussen 1999), or they predict instability in party positions and the absence of an equilibrium (Schofield 1978; McKelvey 1986). With important exceptions to be discussed later,[1] models that follow the tradition of Anthony Downs (1957) highlight centripetal forces in party competition – forces that draw party positions toward the center of the policy spectrum. On the other hand, the main alternative approaches to spatial models – sociological models that are driven by voter demographics, and social psychological theories that rest entirely on notions of partisan loyalties – customarily fail to take into account the importance of policy issues and campaign strategies.

---

[1] See, e.g., Garvey (1966); Coleman (1971); Snyder and Chang (2002); Miller and Schofield (2003); Grofman (in press); Moon (in press).

At the heart of this book is a desire to reconcile theory and evidence: to explain the theoretical puzzle of party divergence and to identify the factors that most strongly affect the extent of that divergence.[2] In order to address this puzzle, we offer a unified theory that implies that centrifugal as well as centripetal forces affect party competition, and we show that the theory accounts for much of the divergence of party policy strategies observed in a wide range of countries. Empirically, we investigate the strategic aspects of party locational choices vis-à-vis policy issues in four countries: the United States, Britain, France, and Norway. These countries differ both in their institutional arrangements – for example, parliamentary versus presidential democracies, plurality versus proportional representation voting systems – and in the number of competing parties, ranging from two-party competition in the case of the United States to seven-party competition in the case of Norway, with Britain and France representing intermediate cases.

Throughout most of the book (Chapters 2–10), we assume that parties are engaged in vote-maximizing behavior. Using only this assumption, we show that three factors, each linked to voter choice, can generate strong centrifugal pressures on the positioning of parties: (1) the existence of nonpolicy considerations in voter decision making – most especially, party loyalty; (2) the capacity of voters to discount the claims of parties or candidates concerning the policy changes they could achieve; and (3) an unwillingness of citizens to participate in the electoral process when they find that none of the competing parties or candidates are sufficiently attractive (abstention due to alienation). We refer to models incorporating these three factors as our *unified theory of party competition*.[3] In later chapters, we will explicate exactly why each of these factors can be expected to promote party divergence.

In illuminating the theoretical importance of centrifugal factors, we show how to bridge the gap between two major schools of thought. On the one hand are spatial models in the tradition of Anthony Downs, which emphasize policy-oriented voters who support parties based on ideological or issue proximity to party platforms. On the other hand are voter-choice models that emphasize the existence and persistence of strong partisan loyalties or that view voting as rooted in class, ethnicity, or other sociodemographic

---

[2] The view that theory construction can often be helped by trying to account for empirical puzzles that are not adequately dealt with by existing theory is developed at length in Grofman (2001).

[3] A review of the literature that provides a theoretical background for this analysis is provided in Appendix 1.1.

factors. To put it simply (in terms familiar to many political scientists), in this book we show how to reconcile the spatial-modeling traditions of the University of Rochester with the behavioral traditions of the University of Michigan and Columbia.

We believe that a unified theory of party competition, which integrates the behavioralist's perspective on voting into the spatial-modeling framework, provides insights into party/candidate policy positioning and policy representation that neither approach provides by itself. For example, although spatial modelers increasingly recognize the critical role that voters' non-policy-related motivations can play in shaping party strategies, we believe that the extent of this impact on spatial strategies and mass–elite policy linkages is still imperfectly understood. We argue that when we incorporate voters' measured non-policy-related motivations into the spatial model, this changes the strategic logic of spatial competition in an important way: namely, it shows that *parties and candidates have electoral incentives to appeal on policy grounds to voters who are biased toward them for nonpolicy reasons.*

Because voters' non-policy-related characteristics often correlate with their policy beliefs (so that, for instance, working-class voters tend to support more liberal policies than do middle-class voters), this strategic incentive tends to draw vote-seeking parties and candidates to divergent regions of the policy space. Thus voters' non-policy-related considerations – even if parties cannot manipulate them in the course of an election campaign – are nonetheless crucial for understanding party strategies. A second, related argument is that because parties have electoral incentives to appeal to voters who support them for nonpolicy reasons, we should expect a strong connection between the policy positions that parties present and the beliefs of their supporters, even if voter support for a given party is only in part due to policies.

For each of the four countries we examine, we find that the policy positions projected by the unified theory – based only on the assumption of vote maximization by parties – correlate well with the observed data; and in two of these countries (Norway and France), our projections also anticipate the actual configurations of the parties' policy positions. However, we find that the policies of major parties and candidates in real-world elections in the other two countries (Britain and the United States) are similar to, but more extreme than, their vote-maximizing positions as computed using our unified models of party competition.

In order to complete our theory, in Chapters 11 and 12 we move beyond the effects of voter-centered influences on party strategy to incorporate a crucial missing link: political elites' policy-seeking motivations. We show that by incorporating reasonable assumptions about elites' policy preferences and the uncertainty associated with national election outcomes, we can explain the distinctly noncentrist policies that British and American parties and candidates have proposed in recent elections.

Because it sheds light on the puzzle of mass–elite linkage, our work also has normative implications. The *responsible party* model specifies that parties' policies should reflect the views of the voting constituencies that support them (see Sartori 1968; Dalton 1985). In the theoretical chapters, we present results showing that parties have electoral motivations to reflect their supporters' beliefs – expectations that are confirmed by our empirical analyses.

Elections plausibly provide a vehicle through which citizens influence the policy behavior of governments only if (1) the parties present a diverse array of policy positions that reflect the spectrum of public opinion and (2) citizens base their voting decisions in significant part on a comparison of these policy platforms. Neither the spatial modeling nor the behavioral approach alone, however, supports the expectation of strong mass–elite policy linkages. If voters are purely policy oriented, as pure spatial modeling assumes, then we should expect that the policies of every party will be similar, so that voters are not afforded the option of choosing between truly distinct policy visions. If voters deemphasize policies, as behavioral researchers suggest, then it would appear that there is little reason to expect election outcomes to reflect public opinion, even that of the supporters of a winning party.

The unified theory of party competition also portrays the impact of turnout decisions on party competition in a fashion quite different from what is commonly taken to be the main Downsian insight about turnout – namely, that few will be interested enough in political outcomes to be willing to bear the cost of voting. If this view were right, or if, for whatever reason, a substantial number of citizens failed to vote, it is hard to see why elections would necessarily reflect citizens' policy preferences. It would appear, on the face of it, that a citizen who does not cast a ballot would have no influence on the choice of parties and hence on the policies that they might advocate while seeking election or implement if elected. To the contrary, by emphasizing the role of alienated voters, we will show how the implicit threat of a refusal to vote can lead parties to be more faithful to their own supporters.

1.2. Data and Methodology

The primary data sources that combine information on voters' policy preferences and data relevant to their non-policy-related motivations are national election studies. Such studies are available from only a relatively small number of countries. As noted earlier, we will employ our unified theory of party competition to analyze party/candidate strategies and mass–elite policy linkages in historical elections in Britain, France, Norway, and the United States. We employ survey data drawn from national election studies in these countries to estimate the distributions of voters' policy preferences and the parameters of our unified models of party competition in each election. These empirical estimates are used to compute the electoral effects of possible changes in the parties'/candidates' policy positions. Such computations form the basis for analyzing the strategic policy decisions of parties and candidates in these elections.

The four countries we have chosen to study permit us to apply and test the unified theory of party competition in diverse settings. These polities differ along a variety of important dimensions, including their institutional features, their electoral laws, the number of major parties, and the party composition of their governments. Britain and Norway are parliamentary democracies, while the United States features a presidential system and France a mixed presidential-parliamentary system. In comparing the two parliamentary democracies, we find that the British "two-and-a-half" party system, in conjunction with the plurality-voting rule, typically awards a single party a parliamentary majority.[4] By contrast, the seven significant parties of the Norwegian system, in which seats are awarded via proportional representation, typically produce a splintered seat allocation that creates incentives for coalition governments. In comparing presidential elections in France and the United States, we find that U.S. presidential contests typically feature only two major candidates (the Democratic and Republican Party nominees) but also feature a large proportion of nonvoting citizens. The outcome depends on a single stage, with the winner determined by electoral votes, which in turn depend on plurality voting by citizens in each state. By contrast, French presidential elections typically feature several competitive candidates, with outcomes determined over two ballots, the winner being

---

[4] In Britain, the Liberal Democratic Party competes against the dominant Labour and Conservative Parties, one of which typically wins a majority of seats in parliamentary elections.

selected by direct popular vote.[5] By applying our methodology in these diverse settings, we explore whether the unified theory of party competition can provide a general explanation for party behavior and mass–elite policy linkages that applies both to two-party and to multiparty systems, to parliamentary and to presidential democracies, and to single-party and to coalition governments.

Our analyses have both empirical and theoretical components. We present results on the optimal policy strategies that parties and candidates should pursue under each of several versions of the unified model for the actual voting model parameters (and the distributions of respondents' policy preferences) estimated from election survey data. Specifically, in each case we seek a Nash equilibrium – a set of positions that vote-seeking or policy-seeking candidates/parties would present in order to win elections and that would be stable in the sense that no party would have an incentive to deviate unilaterally from its position. These analyses are developed in Chapters 2–10 using only the assumption of vote-maximizing parties, but later, in Chapters 11 and 12, we incorporate alternative assumptions about policy-seeking motivations. The optimal strategies obtained are compared to observed strategies. Such comparisons permit us to ask: In these real-world elections, were the candidates/parties simply vote maximizers, or did their behavior reflect both vote-maximizing and policy-seeking motivations?

1.3. Justifying Our Theoretical Focus: Why Assume a Unified Model of Party Competition with Vote-Maximizing Parties?

Although our theoretical focus entails integrating the behavioral and spatial-modeling perspectives, we retain the Downsian assumption that politicians seek to maximize votes in the general election. Of course, we recognize that there are many alternative explanations for the phenomenon of party divergence, which invoke factors falling outside the scope of our model (we will discuss these factors later). This raises the questions: Why do we emphasize the importance of integrating behavioral models of the vote into spatial-modeling theory? Why do we omit numerous alternative factors that plausibly illuminate party behavior? A clearly relevant concern is the need

---

[5] French presidential elections feature a two-stage system in which the two top candidates in the first round advance to a runoff election held two weeks later.

to develop a parsimonious theory, and by focusing our attention on the implications of behavioral voting research for party strategies, and by focusing in particular on our three central variables – party identification, voter discounting of the parties' positions, and voter abstention – this is exactly what we have done.

Our modeling is intended to be applicable over a wide range of cases without the need to build in special institutional features of particular political systems and, perhaps most importantly, without the need, at least initially, to assume any motivation on the part of candidates or parties other than winning elections. In addition, we believe that in exploring the implications of our three key variables, we highlight factors that are quite important for understanding party strategies and that are underemphasized in the existing spatial-modeling literature. Simply put, we believe that our unified approach highlights strategic considerations that are extremely important to politicians, considerations that in and of themselves go a long way toward illuminating parties' and candidates' policy strategies in real-world elections.

The preceding observations do not imply that we discount spatial-modeling work that explores the many alternative considerations that plausibly influence politicians' policy strategies. Indeed, we believe that these models – many of which have been developed in the past five years – identify numerous factors that illuminate party competition and, in particular, the strategic factors that may motivate party divergence. These factors include:

- *The possibility of strategic entry by new parties.* Theoretical work by Palfrey (1984) and Callander (2000) shows that existing parties in two-party systems may be motivated to present divergent policies in order to deter entry by new competitors who might siphon off votes from the existing parties. The threat of new parties – particularly small ones – is related to the threat of abstention, which we study extensively in Chapters 7 through 9. In either case, the potential loss of support by alienated citizens affects party positioning.
- *The role of nomination processes* – for example, the potentially polarizing effects of primary elections in the United States (see, e.g., Coleman 1971; Aranson and Ordeshook 1972; Fiorina 1973, 1974; Polsby 1980; Owen and Grofman 1995; Gerber and Morton 1998; Burden 2000a; Grofman and Brunell 2001).

- *The influence of party activists and campaign donors.* Theoretical and empirical work by Aldrich (1983a,b; 1995) and Baron (1994) suggests that, even in the absence of party primaries, policy-motivated party activists (and donors) often pressure party elites to present divergent, noncentrist policy positions. McGann (2002) develops theoretical results suggesting that similar processes operate in multiparty systems. Important recent papers by Moon (in press) and Schofield (2003; see also Miller and Schofield 2003) on U.S. and British elections present theoretical and empirical arguments that candidates gain scarce campaign resources (notably, campaign funds and increased efforts from party activists) by presenting noncentrist policies, and that these resources can be used to enhance the candidates' images along "valence-related" dimensions of evaluation (competence, integrity, etc.). These papers suggest that when a mixture of valence-related and policy-related considerations moves voters, especially those most concerned with policy outputs, candidates maximize votes by diverging from the center of the policy space.
- *Information-centered models of elections.* Recent papers by Snyder and Chang (2002) and Callander and Wilkie (2002) argue that in certain circumstances, candidates and parties can decrease voter uncertainty about their policy positions – thus rendering their platforms more attractive to risk-averse voters – by presenting noncentrist policies. There is a related theoretical literature that explores the implications of restrictions on candidate positioning in terms of movement from previously announced positions (Kramer 1977; Wuffle, Feld, and Owen 1989; Kollman, Miller, and Page 1992; see also Downs 1957: 107–13).
- *Studies on the geographic distribution of party loyalties and voter ideologies across constituencies* (see, e.g., Austen-Smith 1986; Grofman et al. 2000; Grofman in press). For plurality-based competition, when there are multiple constituencies and these constituencies differ in the location of their median voter, a risk-averse party may opt for positions that make it nearly certain to win some given set of constituencies (say, those where the median voter in the constituency is considerably to the left of the overall median voter), rather than taking moderate positions that may render the party more widely competitive but that do not give it a decisive advantage in any given set of constituencies. The latter option bears the risk that, given unfavorable national trends favoring the other party (caused by exogenous factors, such as differences in the popularity

of the parties' candidates for national office, or times of national crisis that might favor the incumbent), a party might be largely shut out of the legislature.[6]

- *Studies on the role of electoral laws.* There is a voluminous literature on contrasts between list proportional representation (PR) and plurality or runoff methods in matters such as the incentives for party proliferation and proportionality of seats–votes relationships (see, e.g, Taagepera and Shugart 1989; Lijphart 1994). Here the most important finding is that electoral rules that favor multiple parties, such as list methods of proportional representation, also foster a wider ideological range among the parties. Only a limited number of studies have looked directly at the relationship between electoral rules and ideological differences among parties (see, e.g., Dow 2001). In this context, Gary Cox has made many of the most important contributions (see, especially, Cox 1990, 1997). Some of the most interesting recent work has been done by Anthony McGann. For example, McGann has shown that when ideological distributions are non-symmetric, sequential elimination runoffs that require a majority vote for a candidate to win tend to elect candidates who are more extreme than the median voter – candidates located between the median and the mode of the ideological distribution (McGann, Koetzle, and Grofman 2002; McGann, Grofman, and Koetzle 2003; see also McGann 2002).

- *Politicians' policy motivations.* There is extensive theoretical work (Wittman 1977, 1983; Cox 1984; Calvert 1985; Chappel and Keech 1986; Londregan and Romer 1993; Roemer 2001; Groseclose 2001; Schofield 1996) suggesting that policy-motivated politicians – that is, politicians who are seeking office as a means of enacting their proposed policies rather than proposing policies as a means of attaining office – may propose divergent, noncentrist policies. A key theoretical result derived from this approach is that policy divergence emerges only when the competing politicians are uncertain about the election outcome, a condition that is quite plausible in real-world elections. We investigate policy-seeking motivations in depth in Chapters 11 and 12 .

---

[6] On the other hand, candidates might be only lightly "tethered" to the national party position (as if by a flexible rubber band) and therefore able to adapt their platforms in order to bring them closer to the views of the constituency median (or the median party voter in the constituency). Grofman (in press) claims that for two-party competition, the greater the stretch in the rubber band at the constituency level, the more alike the two parties will be at the national level.

We believe that the studies just cited identify important determinants of candidate/party strategies. However, in this book our primary goal is to determine how much progress we can make toward understanding politicians' policy strategies *without* recourse to any of these explanations except the last one. We hope to convince the reader that the progress we can thereby achieve, relying entirely on the unified theory with vote-maximizing parties, is considerable. But as noted earlier, in order to complete our theory we will incorporate political elites' policy-seeking motivations – an augmentation of the model that is particularly pertinent in our explanation of the distinctly noncentrist policies offered by British and American parties and candidates.

1.4. Plan of the Book

Chapters 2 though 4 introduce the general theoretical ideas that are the foundation of this volume.

Chapter 2 provides the statistical framework for the unified, conditional logit model for voter choice that is used throughout the book – a (multivariate) random-utility model that incorporates policy dimensions, measured nonpolicy factors such as partisanship and voter and candidate characteristics, and a random component representing unmeasured factors that render the vote choice probabilistic. The development begins with the traditional proximity model of voter choice, after which discounting of party positioning is introduced. Appendix 2.1 discusses alternatives to the conditional logit model – in particular, the generalized extreme value (GEV) model and the multinomial probit (MNP) model. Appendix 2.2 discusses the empirical status of party identification as an explanatory variable in empirical voting research, while Appendix 2.3 discusses the status of policy-discounting theory as an alternative to the standard proximity model and the link between the discounting model and directional voting.

In Chapter 3, we present four simple, nontechnical examples designed to convey the logic of party competition under successively more complex versions of the unified theory of party competition. When only policy is included in a deterministic model, parties are drawn toward the center. When a partisan component is added, however, policy divergence may occur as long as there are three or more parties. Specifically, we present reasons why parties have electoral incentives to present policies that reflect the beliefs of voters who are biased toward them in part for nonpolicy reasons. Incorporating the response of candidates to voter discounting of their claimed platforms substantially increases divergence of party strategies. Finally, adding a probabilistic component reflecting unmeasured components of voter utility to a model that also incorporates measured nonpolicy factors leads to a more completely specified model and, as in the case of a comparable deterministic model, to divergence of party strategies. Not only is voter choice more realistic under a probabilistic model, but also – unlike the results of a deterministic approach, in which there are dramatic differences in the one-dimensional and multidimensional cases – the results under a probabilistic model are similar for one and more than one dimension.

Next, the concept of Nash equilibrium is introduced – a set of stable strategies toward which the parties may gravitate over a period of time and from which vote-maximizing parties would have no incentive to deviate. We discuss the advantages of the Nash equilibrium approach and a condition for the uniqueness of such an equilibrium along with a method for computing it, with the details given later in Appendix 4.1. Application of the model in this simple form is made to survey data from a real-world election (the 1988 French presidential election).

Chapter 4 presents a quantitative analysis of the degree to which a number of structural factors affect the divergence of optimal party strategies, with most factors exerting centrifugal influences. We show that parties have greater electoral incentives to shift away from the center of the voter distribution as each of the following factors increases: the number of parties; the salience of nonpolicy factors, such as party identification; the salience of policies; the variance in locations among partisan groups; the variance of the voter distribution; and, for each party, the size of the party's partisan constituency (i.e., large parties have stronger centrifugal incentives than small parties). The number of independents, on the other hand, exerts a centripetal force on party positioning. Specific formulas are developed (in Appendices 4.2, 4.3, and 4.4) for computing approximate equilibrium locations incorporating many of these factors.

Chapters 5 through 9 represent country-specific analyses of the modeling ideas introduced in Chapters 1–4.

In Chapter 5, equilibrium strategies are presented for successively more complex probabilistic models for the 1988 French presidential election. We begin with a four-dimensional, policy-only model that involves voter and party locations on an ideological scale and three policy scales. This framework is then extended to a unified model that includes a number of sociodemographic characteristics of the voters, especially partisanship. For at least the three major candidates, the equilibrium strategies correlate with the perceived locations of parties and with the partisan mean locations of the voters but are considerably more centrist. Although this association indicates some support for the responsible party model, further agreement with supporters' positions is explained by a third extension of the model that employs discounting of candidate positions by the voters – the unified discounting model. (A further alternative explanation based on policy-seeking motivations of the candidates is developed in Chapters 11 and 12.)

Empirical results are presented in Chapter 6 for the 1989 Norwegian parliamentary election, which involved seven major parties, providing the most detailed test of the Nash equilibrium procedure. Here the voting is directly for parties in a PR system, but the pattern of the equilibria is similar to the pattern found in France, with greater dispersal of party positions when discounting occurs. In particular, we find that if each voter – in determining her vote choice – focuses on the likely compromise position of the parliament she helps to create rather than simply the location of the nearest party, the parties' vote-maximizing strategies will be substantially more dispersed. Finally, because typically no one party receives majority support in Norway, we consider optimal strategies for parties that are concerned not just to maximize the size of their own vote share but also to ensure that the coalition with which they are traditionally associated forms the government. We find that equilibrium strategies for such parties whose office-seeking motivations are coalition-oriented are remarkably similar to those obtained under simple vote-maximizing assumptions. We also find that the computed Nash equilibrium in Norwegian parties' strategies (whether for vote-seeking or coalition-oriented parties) that we obtain for the unified model with voter discounting closely matches the actual distribution of party policies observed in the 1989 parliamentary election.

Chapters 7 and 8 deal with the United States. With only two major parties in the United States, we cannot expect any divergence between optimal candidate strategies without additional centrifugal forces not introduced in earlier models. But abstention – a factor that is especially salient in United States elections – has such an effect. We model both abstention due to alienation and abstention due to indifference and find that the threat of abstention due to alienation (but not indifference) exerts a centrifugal influence leading to divergent party strategies at equilibrium, with each candidate shifting away from the mean voter position in the direction of his partisan supporters. In Chapter 8, empirical applications are made to the United States presidential

elections of 1980, 1984, 1988, 1996, and 2000 that support the theoretical expectations, although the divergence that results from the threat of abstention
is modest. Consistent with the Chapter 7 results, we find that the candidates'
equilibrium positions are shaded in the direction of their partisan supporters.

Chapter 9 deals with the 1997 British election. Even though the British
election is for members of Parliament rather than for a president as in France,
and is a first-past-the-post system rather than a PR system as in Norway, the
equilibria for these three countries are similar, although the British equilibrium is less dispersed. Because there are only three major parties (sometimes
interpreted as only two and a half), this empirical finding is consistent with
our theoretical expectation that the degree of divergence depends on the
number of parties. Because turnout was unusually low in the 1997 election,
we apply the turnout model developed in Chapter 7, obtaining equilibrium
party locations more dispersed than those obtained without the effects of
abstention. The dynamics of a positive feedback loop as studied by Nagel
(2001) are reported, which suggest long-term swings back and forth in the
degree of divergence between Labour and Conservative positions. Nagel
finds that as Liberal Democratic strength waxes, Labour and the Conservatives diverge (the occupied-center thesis), permitting the Liberal Democrats
to gain even more strength (the vacated-center thesis) – a process that is
likely to continue until reversed by exogenous forces.

Chapters 10 through 13 provide further theoretical extensions and applications of our basic approach to understanding party strategies for optimal
policy locations and offer cross-national comparisons among the four countries whose elections we are studying.

In Chapter 10, we consider the tendency of voters to project their own
views onto the candidates of parties they prefer (an *assimilation effect*) and
to describe the views of the candidates of parties they dislike as further
away from their own views than may actually be the case (a *contrast effect*).
We show theoretically that such effects have consequences for party location
that are similar to those of party identification – namely, generating pressures
for party divergence. Empirically, the degree of assimilation and contrast is
assessed for each of the four countries discussed in earlier chapters.

In Chapters 11 and 12, we shift from a focus on voter motivations to a
focus on party motivations. Heretofore we have attempted to explain parties'
strategies by assuming only their responses to voter behavior. Yet, while our
country-specific applications suggest that this latter approach illuminates the
parties' observed policies in Norway and France, in the United States and

Britain the parties' actual policies are similar to, but more dispersed than, their vote-maximizing positions as computed in our model. We account for this discrepancy in part by including in the model of two-party competition the policy-seeking motivations of the parties, as well as a valence advantage[7] of one of the candidates and uncertainty about the extent of that advantage. We find, both theoretically and empirically, that policy-seeking motivations generate greater divergence of candidate positions and that – for the range of parameters that can be expected in national elections in developed democracies – the valence-advantaged candidate is motivated to move away from the voter center toward his or her own preferred position, whereas the valence-disadvantaged candidate is motivated to take a more centrist position.[8]

In Chapter 13, we review and summarize our theoretical results and summarize and synthesize our empirical findings for the four nations whose electoral politics and party strategies we have studied. We also discuss topics for future research.

---

[7] Candidates' valence advantages typically revolve around voters' comparative evaluations of the competing candidates' levels of competence, honestly, or charisma (see Appendix 3.1). From the perspective of spatial modeling, these considerations differ from the voter-specific non-policy-related motivations discussed in this chapter – such as partisanship and voters' sociodemographic characteristics – in that valence evaluations are typically modeled as being identical across voters. As we shall argue in subsequent chapters, voter-specific nonpolicy variables motivate policy divergence between candidates in ways that valence issues do not.

[8] These results, which are applied to the 1988 French and American elections and the 1997 British election, obtain both for our model – based on uncertainty about the valence advantage – and for Groseclose's (2001) model, which is based on uncertainty about the location of the voter distribution. The Extremist Underdog effect reported by Groseclose – in which it is the valence-disadvantaged candidate that takes the more extreme position – occurs only for a range of parameter values outside what we can reasonably expect for high visibility elections that are forecast by frequent, scientifically credible polls.

CHAPTER 2

How Voters Decide

The Components of the Unified Theory of Voting

2.1. Introduction

As discussed in Chapter 1, behavioral researchers and spatial modelers have quite different perspectives on how voters decide. Spatial modelers typically assume that voters are entirely (or at least chiefly) motivated by the policies that the competing parties or candidates present in the current campaign, and, in their empirical applications, policy factors are the chief (if not the only) influences that are incorporated into their models. Behavioral researchers, by contrast, emphasize that voter choices are affected by a variety of considerations besides the parties' current policies, including voters' party identifications and sociodemographic characteristics, their perceptions of economic conditions, and retrospective evaluations of incumbent performance.

Furthermore, while spatial modelers typically posit that voters employ a *proximity metric* to evaluate parties' policies – that is, that voters prefer parties whose positions are close to their own positions along salient policy dimensions – some research, both theoretical and empirical (see Grofman 1985; Fiorina 1994, 1996; Lacy and Paolino 1998, 2001; Merrill and Grofman 1999; Kedar 2002; Adams, Bishin, and Dow 2004; Lewis-Beck and Nadeau 2004), suggests that this behavior is modified by voters' realization that parties/candidates will probably not be able to implement the full extent of the policies that they advocate. Hence, a proximity model with *discounting* may be appropriate. As we argue beginning in Chapter 3, both of these perspectives contribute to our understanding of party policy strategies and the nature of mass–elite policy linkages.

In this chapter, we compare the spatial-voting model to the behaviorist's perspective on voting, developing the various components of the unified multivariate voting specification that we use in subsequent chapters to analyze elections in the four countries we study.

2.2. The Policy-Only Model

2.2.1. Deterministic Policy Voting

Although spatial modelers and behavioral researchers have profoundly different perspectives about how voters decide, the two camps agree that policies matter, at least to some voters. In order to introduce the way in which the policies of candidates and parties enter the voter's decision calculus in both behavioral and spatial models, we begin with a simple model in which policy debates revolve around a single overarching issue dimension. For simplicity, we speak about candidates, not parties, although the model applies equally well to party-centered elections.

We assume that voters and candidates are located at ideal points on some continuum, representing their preferred positions along a single issue or ideological dimension. While the measured range of variation along this continuum may, in principle, be either finite or infinite, we will normally employ a finite interval from 1 to 7 (or a similar finite interval) in order to conform to the options presented to respondents in many national election studies. The 1–7 Left–Right scales that we use to place the voters, parties, and candidates in Figures 2.1 and 2.2 later in this chapter are typical of such intervals. Normally, the value 1 on such a scale represents a strongly liberal or leftist position on the issue, whereas the value 7 represents a strongly conservative or rightist position, with intermediate values representing intermediate positions.

Given the voter and candidate positions, the voter's utility (evaluation) of the candidate may employ this information in various ways. Spatial modelers typically posit that voters evaluate candidates according to their proximity along the policy interval, so that left-wing voters prefer left-wing candidates, centrist voters prefer centrist candidates, and so on. The most common way to implement this definition is via *quadratic proximity utility*, specified as the negative of the squared distance between the voter i at location x_i on the scale and a candidate k at location s_k:

$$V_i(k) = -(x_i - s_k)^2, \tag{2.1}$$

where $V_i(k)$ represents voter i's utility for candidate k's position.[1] The negative sign is used so that utility declines with distance. This proximity model has been the cornerstone of most empirical analyses of voting behavior (see Markus and Converse 1979; Page and Jones 1979; Alvarez 1997; Dow 2001).

Incorporating multiple policy dimensions. So far, we have restricted the development to a single issue. More realistically, however, voters arrive at preferences on the basis of more than one issue. Suppose that there are J issues, that the voter's position on the jth issue is x_{ij}, and that the candidate's position on the jth issue is s_{kj}. Multidimensional utility functions are obtained by summing the corresponding one-dimensional utilities over the various issue dimensions. Thus the voter's utility for the candidate's policies becomes

$$V_i(k) = -\sum_j a_j (x_{ij} - s_{kj})^2, \tag{2.2}$$

where a_j denotes the policy-salience parameter for the jth issue.

2.2.2. *Unmeasured Voter Motivations: Probabilistic Voting Models*

Many spatial modelers employ the specifications given in equations 2.1–2.2; that is, they assume that voters evaluate the candidates entirely on the basis of their positions along important policy dimensions. This implies that voters

---

[1] An alternative to quadratic utility is *linear utility*, in which the utility of a voter i for candidate k is given by $V_i(k) = |x_i - s_k|$. It is difficult to distinguish empirically whether quadratic or linear utility (or some other function of distance) better represents voters' relative evaluations of candidates. There is evidence that linear utility gives a better fit to thermometer scores interpreted as utilities, such as those solicited from respondents in the American National Election Studies and other national election studies (Westholm 1997: 876; Merrill and Grofman 1999: 173–5; Berinski and Lewis 2001). Inferring that the utility scale itself is linear from such evidence is, however, problematic, because both the policy scales from which distance is measured and the thermometer scores are constrained to specified finite intervals (typically 1–7 or 1–10 for the policy scales and 0–100 for the thermometer scales), whereas the utility scale need not be so constrained. On the other hand, quadratic utility is more convenient mathematically for most applications and has frequently been the preferred choice (Erikson and Romero 1990; Alvarez and Nagler 1995). We will use quadratic utility in our analyses unless otherwise stated. In our empirical applications, the policy optima that we determine for quadratic and linear losses are fairly similar (see, for instance, Table 1 in Merrill and Adams 2001), so that our substantive conclusions do not depend on the utility function we use.

invariably support the candidate who best reflects their policy beliefs – that is, that voters employ a *deterministic policy-only model*. While this assumption simplifies theorizing about candidate strategies, empirical voting studies find that unobservable factors – which may stem from voters' evaluations of the candidates' personal qualities, retrospective evaluations of incumbent performance, or from policy motivations that are not accurately measured in voter surveys – can motivate voters to support a particular candidate even when some rival candidate better reflects these voters' measured policy beliefs (Campbell et al. 1960; Alvarez 1997; Schofield et al. 1998). These factors – unobserved both by researchers and, in general, by the candidates themselves – are best modeled as random variables. Accordingly, we extend the utility formula given in equation 2.2 by incorporating a voter-specific random utility term X_{ik}, which represents unmeasured components of the voter i's utility for candidate k. Thus the formula for a random utility model becomes

$$U_i(k) = V_i(k) + X_{ik} = -\sum_j a_j (x_{ij} - s_{kj})^2 + X_{ik}. \tag{2.3}$$

Note that we have retained the notation $V_i(k)$ to refer to the deterministic component of the random utility model – here, the voter's evaluation of the candidate's policies. The utility of the full random utility model is denoted by $U_i(k)$. The random term X_{ik} in equation 2.3 renders the voter's choice indeterminate from measured policy components alone, so that this choice is probabilistic from the candidates' (and the analyst's) perspectives.

We label the specification given in equation 2.3, in which voters employ the proximity metric and policies are the only measured influence on the vote, the (probabilistic) *policy-only model*. Because probabilistic models will be our default, for simplicity we omit the term "probabilistic" in specifying this and similar models. According to this model, the voter supports the candidate who maximizes his combination of measured policy-related utilities and his unmeasured utilities. In this model, the vote probability depends on the distribution of X_{ik}. One plausible assumption, which we employ in subsequent chapters, is that the values of X_{ik} are generated independently from a type I extreme-value distribution – the assumption that characterizes the *conditional logit* (CL) model, which has been used extensively by behavioral researchers in empirical voting studies (Endersby and Galatas 1997; Adams and Merrill 1999a,b) and by spatial modelers (Coughlin 1992;

Adams 1999a,b).[2] Given a random-utility model for a K-candidate election, a CL model specifies that the probability that voter i chooses candidate k is proportional to the exponential of the deterministic component of utility and that the sum of these probabilities over candidates is one. Thus, the probability that a voter i votes for candidate k is given by

$$P_{ik} = \frac{\exp[V_i(k)]}{\sum\limits_{j=1}^{K} \exp[V_i(j)]}, \tag{2.4}$$

where $V_i(k)$ is defined by equation 2.2. It follows that in an election in which n voters cast votes, the expected vote share for candidate k is given by

$$EV(k) = \frac{1}{n} \sum_{i=1}^{n} P_{ik}. \tag{2.5}$$

It is the straightforward nature of formula 2.4 for the choice probabilities – a formula that follows logically from the definition of utility in the model specification (see Train 1986) – that makes the conditional logit model so convenient to use.

In Appendix 2.1, we discuss alternatives to the conditional logit model – in particular, the generalized extreme value (GEV) model and the multinomial probit (MNP) model – and argue that the greater specificity obtained in these more complicated models usually does not outweigh the disadvantages inherent in their complexity.

2.3. Nonpolicy Factors: The Unified Model

2.3.1. A Unified Specification That Incorporates Measured Nonpolicy Variables

Probabilistic policy-voting models have been employed extensively by spatial modelers in their theoretical work on both two-candidate elections (Enelow and Hinich 1984; Coughlin 1992; Hinich and Munger 1994) and multicandidate elections (Lin, Enelow, and Dorussen 1999; Adams 1999a,b;

---

[2] The cumulative distribution function for a type I extreme value distribution is $F(x) = \exp[-\exp(-x)]$. The distribution has a variance of $\pi^2/6$ and a mean equal to Euler's constant. We note that this distribution is similar to the normal in shape but has the advantage that the choice probabilities have a simple, tractable form. See Alvarez and Nagler (1998a) for a comparison of conditional logit and related models.

Schofield 2002). Yet empirical voting studies suggest that without further modifications, these models are only marginally more realistic than the deterministic policy-voting model of equations 2.1–2.2. The reason is that voters' candidate preferences are also influenced by a number of non-policy-related factors that are measured in voter surveys and that are arguably observable by the candidates during the election campaign. Some of these factors, such as partisanship, sociodemographic traits (race, gender, class, income, education, and the like), and retrospective evaluations of party performance, are voter-specific. Others, such as voters' impressions of the candidates along evaluative dimensions of character such as integrity and leadership ability, vary not only across voters but also across candidates. These nonpolicy attributes, commonly available in national election studies, are often referred to as *measured* nonpolicy variables, as opposed to random variables (which may be either non-policy-based or policy-based).

Distinguishing between the effects of policies and measured nonpolicy factors is by no means easy, and there are ongoing scholarly controversies about the relative influence of policy-related and nonpolicy factors on the vote. In particular, the electoral impact of party identification is a subject of debate (see Appendix 2.2 for a summary of this issue). For our purposes, however, it is important only that both policy and nonpolicy factors do influence voter choice. We are concerned in this book with the joint effects of both types of factors and less concerned with their relative degree of contribution.

Central to our analysis is the claim that both policy and nonpolicy motivations influence voter choice. We illustrate the effects of liberal–conservative ideology and partisanship in the 1988 American National Election Study (ANES).[3] Figure 2.1 plots the proportion of validated voters in the 1988 ANES who voted for the Democratic candidate (Michael Dukakis) versus voters' liberal–conservative self-placement. The separate plots for Democratic and Republican identifiers show that self-identified Democrats were significantly more likely to vote for the Democratic candidate than self-identified Republicans, regardless of the voter's ideological location.[4]

---

[3] The 1988 election is the primary American election that we study in this book because it is the most recent presidential election for which validated voting is available in the ANES study. The latter is important because of the central use we make of voter turnout decisions in our model of U.S. party competition. However, in Chapter 8 we present additional empirical applications to the 1980, 1984, 1996, and 2000 U.S. presidential elections.

[4] This plausibly occurs in part because party identity is used as a cue or proxy for party policy; alternatively, partisan voters may be persuaded to adjust their policy preferences in response to the appeals of party elites (see Appendix 2.2). But our objective in this book is to show

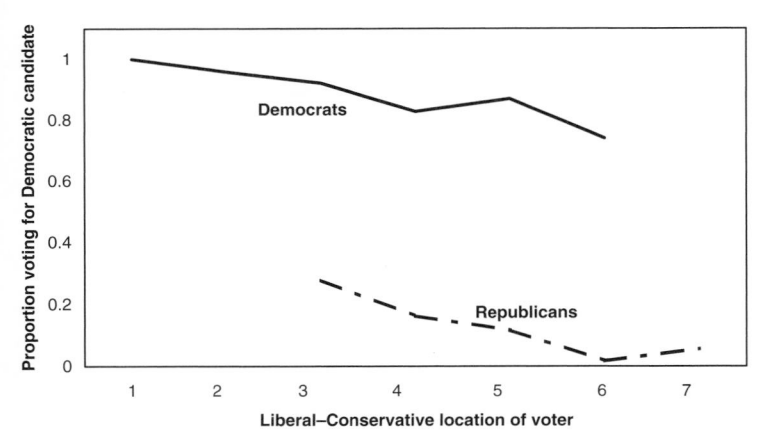

Figure 2.1. Proportion of validated voters voting for the Democratic candidate, stratified by party identification and liberal–conservative locations: United States, 1988. ($N = 701$)

Note: Strong and weak Democrats and others leaning toward the Democrats were classified as Democrats (0, 1, and 2 on the ANES party scale); strong and weak Republicans and others leaning toward the Republicans were classified as Republicans (4, 5, and 6 on the ANES party scale).

Moreover, the downward slope of each of the plots shows that self-identified conservative voters were less likely to vote Democratic, regardless of party identification, than liberal voters were. These relationships suggest that policy (ideology) and partisanship together have greater influences on voter choice than either factor alone.

Second, our analysis depends on the fact that nonpolicy factors, such as party identification, are correlated with voters' policy positions. This is illustrated for the 1988 ANES in Figure 2.2, which shows that although the two sets of partisans are spread over wide, overlapping ranges, self-identified Democrats are, not surprisingly, significantly more leftist than self-identified Republicans. This separation of partisan distributions is typical, and is even more distinct in European electorates than in the United States (see Figures 3.3 and 6.1A in later chapters).

We note that the contribution of each nonpolicy factor to voter utility – whether this contribution is large or small – may be modeled by introducing

that policy and nonpolicy factors together have certain effects on party positioning and that neither should be omitted from a fully specified model; it is less important, for our purposes, to determine the exact mix of these effects or the reciprocal influences between them.

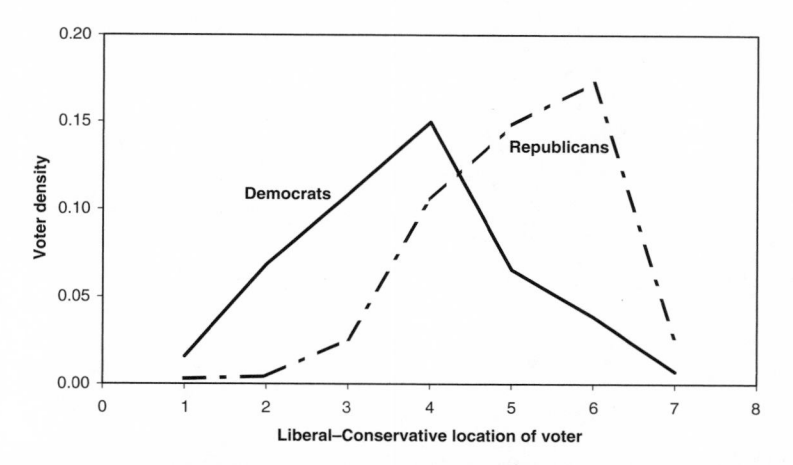

Figure 2.2. Distribution of self-identified Democrats and Republicans by liberal–conservative location: United States, 1988. (N = 701; validated voters only)
Note: Strong and weak Democrats and others leaning toward the Democrats were classified as Democrats (0, 1, and 2 on the ANES party scale); strong and weak Republicans and others leaning toward the Republicans were classified as Republicans (4, 5, and 6 on the ANES party scale).

a variable t_{ik}, which specifies a characteristic of voter i in relation to candidate k. For example, for the partisanship variable, t_{ik} might equal 1 if voter i identifies with candidate k's party and zero otherwise. This variable is then multiplied by a salience parameter b_k, which is estimated from the data and which represents the importance or contribution of the corresponding variable in determining voter utility. In order to model the influence of several nonpolicy factors – partisanship, sociodemographic characteristics, retrospective evaluations of incumbent performance, and so on – we introduce a vector $\mathbf{t}_{ik}$ of nonpolicy variables with coordinates t_{ikl} for the kth candidate and the lth nonpolicy variable, and a vector $\mathbf{b}_k$ of parameters with coordinates b_{kl}.[5] Combining policy factors and nonpolicy factors (both measured and unmeasured) in the same model, we obtain

$$U_i(k) = V_i(k) + X_{ik} = - \sum_j a_j (x_{ij} - s_{kj})^2 + \mathbf{b}_k \mathbf{t}_{ik} + X_{ik}, \quad (2.6)$$

[5] In general, the nonpolicy contribution to voter utility is given by

$$\mathbf{b}_k \mathbf{t}_{ik} = \sum_l b_{kl} t_{ikl}.$$

where a_j is the policy-salience parameter for the jth issue to be estimated from the data, and, as before, $V_i(k)$ denotes the deterministic component of utility.

Note that in equation 2.6, $V_i(k)$ now represents *all* measured elements – both policy-related and non-policy-related – of the voter's utility. We label equation 2.6, which represents the behavioral researcher's typical specification for analyzing voting, the *unified model* (see Markus and Converse 1979; Page and Jones 1979; Erikson and Romero 1990; Alvarez and Nagler 1995; Dow 1999). However, we caution the reader that this singular designation does not imply that there is a single, universally accepted explanation for how voters decide! Rather, behavioral researchers have advanced many alternative theories of voting, which can be captured using differing specifications of equation 2.6. That is, one can capture alternative behavioral voting models by varying the set of explanatory variables included on the right-hand side of equation 2.6 as well as the variable parameters. We elaborate on this point in the following discussion.

2.4. The Unified Discounting Model

Heretofore, we have assumed that in a Downsian or proximity model, voters take their notion of candidate/party location at face value – that is, they evaluate the parties as if they will implement the policies they are perceived to advocate. Downs himself (1957: 39) notes, however, that "[the voter] cannot merely compare platforms; instead he must estimate in his own mind what the parties would actually do were they in power."

There are several reasons why we may expect that parties or candidates may be unable to implement the full extent of the policies that they advocate. The effect will be most pronounced in nations in which power is shared between an executive and a legislature, which are frequently controlled by different parties. Notable examples are the United States, in which either or both houses of Congress may be controlled by other than the president's party, and France, in which a similar cohabitation between different parties may occur. Empirical work by Lacy and Paolino (1998, 2001) documents that U.S. voters in both presidential and gubernatorial elections distinguish between the policies that candidates propose and the policy outcomes that voters expect from each candidate in government, and furthermore, that voters' proximities to the expected position of the government under each candidate influences the vote more strongly than proximity to the candidates' policy proposals.[6] In a multiparty parliamentary system, as in Norway, the governing party frequently holds a minority of seats or is part of a formal coalition. In either case, compromise is required to implement policies. Empirical work by Merrill and Grofman (1999) and Kedar (2002) supports the hypothesis that voters in multiparty parliamentary democracies account for these expected policy compromises when casting their votes.[7] Even in a country such as Britain, where normally a single party holds a majority of seats in Parliament, the government does not have totally free rein because of the constraints of shifting public opinion (see Kedar 2002).

Grofman (1985) suggests the following implementation of the discounting idea: Voters perceive a status quo point in the spatial model and judge that the candidates'/parties' capacity to move that status quo to the location that they appear to advocate must be discounted. For example, suppose that, on a 1–7 Left–Right scale, the status quo is at 5; party L is perceived to advocate a position at 1, while party R appears to advocate a position at 6 (see Figure 2.3A). If voters discount both parties' ability to move the status quo to their respective advocated locations by, say, 50 percent, then they would expect party L to implement policy at 3.0 and R to implement policy at 5.5. Note that under deterministic voting, such discounting would change the vote choice of a voter located at 4 on the scale. Because 4 is closer to 6 than to 1, such a voter who does not discount would choose party R. However, the discounted location of L, namely 3.0, is closer to this voter than the discounted location of R (5.5), so a discounting voter would choose party L.

Hence we might expect that optimal party strategies will be affected if discounting takes place. Because, relative to the advocated policies, discounting will tend to draw the expected policies to be implemented toward the center, we would expect that voters would vote for parties that advocate relatively extreme policies in an attempt to obtain implemented policies that they favor. Accordingly, we expect that parties – anticipating such discounting – may

---

[6] Fiorina's (1994, 1996) work on divided government, which posits that citizens cast their votes based on policy expectations rather than candidate positions, is a well-known version of this thesis (see also Alesina and Rosenthal 1995; Adams, Bishin, and Dow 2004; Lewis-Beck and Nadeau 2004).

[7] McCuen and Morton (2002) report experimental support for this proposition. In addition, we note that Iversen's (1994a,b) Representational Policy Leadership Model – in which voters prefer parties presenting policies that are similar to but more extreme than the voters' own beliefs – is consistent with the logic that voters project likely government policy outputs when casting their ballots (see also Adams and Merrill 1999a,b, 2000).

2.3A. Potential effect of discounting on voter choice

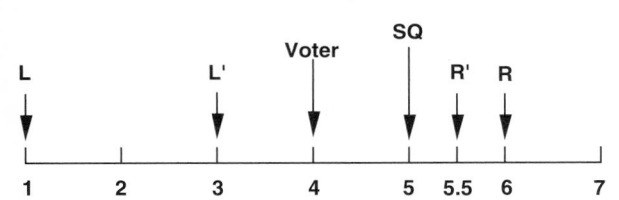

2.3B. Example of discounted position for _d_ = 0.25

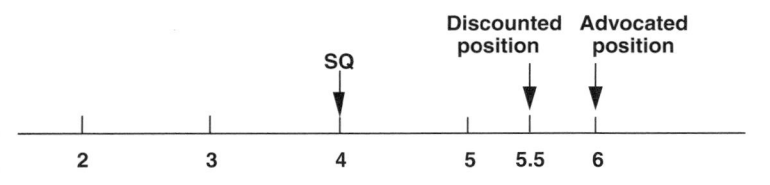

Figure 2.3. Candidate location under the discounting model.
Note: For 2.3A, advocated positions are **L** and **R**, discounted positions are **L'** and **R'**.

advocate policies that are more extreme than those they would advocate if discounting did not occur.

In order to implement the Grofman discounting model, we denote by d_k the discounting factor for party k, which, for simplicity, we will assume is the same for all voters and for each issue dimension. The factors d_k all lie between 0 and 1. When we say, for example, $d_k = 0.25$, we mean that the voters discount candidate k's capacity to draw the status quo to her advocated position by 25 percent.[8] In effect, voters multiply the distance from the status quo to the candidate's advocated position by one minus the discount factor – that is, by 0.75. Thus if the status quo is at 4.0 and the candidate advocates a policy at 6.0, the voters anticipate implementation at 5.5 (see Figure 2.3B). In general, if SQ denotes the status quo point, the voters anticipate that candidate k, who advocates policy at s_k, will implement policy at location $SQ + (1 - d_k)(s_k - SQ)$. If $d_k = 0$, there is no discounting; if $d_k = 1$, then there is complete discounting and the status quo will be implemented.

---

[8] Note that the discounting factor d_k as defined here is equal to $(1 - d_k)$, as defined in Merrill and Grofman (1999).

There is a simple relationship between the level of discounting, specified by the value of d, and the policy position that must be advocated by a candidate if voters are to anticipate policy implementation at a specific position. For example, if $d = 0.5$, $SQ = 4$, and voters are to expect policy implementation at 5.0, then the candidate must advocate policy at 6.0 – that is, at $4.0 + (5.0 - 4.0)/(1 - d) = 6.0$. Thus if voters discount candidates' capacities to implement the policies they advocate, the candidates can be expected to advocate policies that are more extreme than those the voters actually want – in fact, more extreme by approximately the factor $1/(1 - d)$. For example, if discounting is 25 percent, policy advocacy can be expected to be about 33 percent more extreme; if discounting is 50 percent, policy advocacy can be expected to be about 100 percent more extreme, and so on.

Thus, under the Grofman discounting model, the voter's utility function given in equation 2.6 is replaced by

$$U_i(k) = V_i(k) + X_{ik} = \sum_j a_j \left[x_{ij} - \left(SQ + (1 - d_k)(s_{kj} - SQ) \right) \right]^2$$
$$+ \mathbf{b}_k \mathbf{t}_{ik} + X_{ik} \tag{2.7}$$

where, again, a_j is the policy-salience parameter for the jth issue, $V_i(k)$ is the deterministic component of utility, and $\mathbf{b}_k\mathbf{t}_{ik}$ represents the measured nonpolicy utility components. We label the specification given in equation 2.7 the *unified discounting model* of voting. Appendix 2.3 presents a discussion of the relationship between our discounting formulation and the directional voting model proposed by Rabinowitz and Macdonald (1989). Appendix 6.1 presents a similar discussion for the outcome-oriented model of Kedar (2002).

2.5. Discussion

In this chapter, we have presented a range of increasingly complex models so as to be able to incorporate a wide range of motivations in voter decision making. We began with a spatial model based on one or more policy dimensions and then incorporated both measured and unmeasured (random) components representing nonpolicy factors affecting voting decisions. Finally, we returned to policy considerations and explored alternative voter metrics (direct proximity, discounted proximity) for evaluating candidates' associations with policies.

A question that has arisen in connection with empirically assessing the relative contributions of the proximity and discounting (and directional) utilities is whether to use voter-specific placements of candidates or mean placements when computing the distance between voters and candidates (see Rabinowitz and Macdonald 1989; Merrill and Grofman 1999). We believe that conceptually idiosyncratic placement is preferable because, unlike mean placement, it is known to each voter. For the voter-choice models used in this volume – as opposed to regression models using a thermometer scale as dependent variable – use of mean or voter-specific placements yields very similar parameter estimates and equilibrium positions. Hence, for simplicity, we report results based on mean placements throughout the book.

These models of voting – the policy-only model, the unified model, and the unified discounting model – will be used throughout the book to assess candidates' and parties' responses to voter behavior in historical elections in four countries exemplifying a range of electoral rules and circumstances. In particular, for elections in each of these four countries, we will determine the strategies (i.e., policy positions) that parties might choose to maximize their vote shares, and, in order to assess the *responsible party model*, we will compare each party's vote-maximizing location with the mean location of its supporters. The effects of nonvoting will be investigated primarily in the context of American elections – in which this phenomenon is particularly prominent – although the effect of abstention will also be analyzed for Britain. Because there are only two major parties in the United States, abstention is crucial to our arguments for party divergence in America. For these reasons, technical discussion of the extension of the model to accommodate the effects of nonvoting on party positioning will be delayed until Chapter 7.

In addition to their responses to voters, however, parties have their own motivations concerning policy. In Chapters 11 and 12, we will see how these latter motivations, coupled with uncertainty about the expected vote, lead to significant modifications of the parties' optimal strategies. We begin the process of investigating alternative models in Chapter 3 via illustrative arguments about the ways in which different degrees of partisan voting affect candidates' policy strategies.

Linking Voter Choice to Party Strategies

Illustrating the Role of Nonpolicy Factors

3.1. Introduction

Our objective in this chapter is to analyze how nonpolicy considerations – such as partisanship, candidate characteristics, and the sociodemographic characteristics of voters – affect parties' policy strategies. Our goal here is not to develop formal theorems about party strategies (such theorems are presented in Chapter 4), but to convey the strategic logic of party competition in the unified model via simple, nontechnical examples. We present a series of heuristic arguments that illustrate how, in multiparty or multicandidate elections, incorporating nonpolicy variables into a spatial model can alter the strategic calculus of vote-maximizing candidates, as compared to using the policy-only model in which policies are the only measured influence on the vote. After considering what happens when voters are motivated only by policies and vote in a deterministic fashion, we consider what happens when voters are motivated by a mixture of policy and nonpolicy considerations but still vote in a deterministic fashion. Then we introduce discounting by voters of the platforms presented by candidates as well as probabilistic voting. Finally, we illustrate the central intuitions on party strategies that grow out of the unified spatial model with empirical applications to one national survey – that of the 1988 French presidential election.

Each of our initial illustrations of the importance of nonpolicy factors and other aspects of voter choice involves only a one-step optimal strategy – that is, the vote-maximizing location of a focal candidate when the positions of the other candidates are fixed. Each candidate, however, can be expected to react to the locations of all the other candidates. In other words, all candidates move in a minuet, each seeking his or her own best position in relation to all the others. In this context, the key concept in specifying jointly optimal party strategies to which the parties may settle down is that of a *Nash equilibrium* – that is, a configuration of party locations such that no candidate can improve his or her vote share by further movement. We revisit the illustrative examples, indicating the party locations constituting Nash equilibria – when such configurations exist – and comparing the results to those of one-step optima.[1]

Our examples suggest that while the policy-only spatial model typically motivates candidates to present similar, centrist policies, the unified spatial model can motivate parties to diverge from one another. Specifically, we argue that candidates have electoral incentives to present policies shaded away from the center, in the direction of voters who are favorably disposed toward them for nonpolicy reasons that are related to such factors as party identification and sociodemographic characteristics. This intuition is important not only for understanding party strategies, but also for what it implies about representation: namely, that parties have electoral incentives to faithfully represent the policy beliefs of their partisan constituencies, the mass–elite linkage that underlies the responsible party model of representation.

As discussed in Appendix 2.2, behavioral researchers disagree sharply about what the most important factors in the voter's decision calculus are, and they also disagree about how to integrate nonpolicy motivations into the voter calculus. When we shift from seeking to understand voter choice to seeking to understand party strategies, however, with few exceptions (e.g., Chapman 1967, 1968; Erikson and Romero 1990; Adams 1999a,b; Schofield 2002) spatial modelers have omitted voters' measured nonpolicy motivations when theorizing about parties' policy strategies.

In addition, we note that almost without exception, the spatial-modeling studies that do incorporate voters' measured nonpolicy motivations focus on one specialized context: namely, two-candidate elections in which one

---

[1] In Appendix 4.1 to Chapter 4 , we present a statistical methodology that allows us to compute parties' vote-maximizing policy positions efficiently and to determine if they constitute a Nash equilibrium. The heart of Chapter 4 presents theoretical results that relate these policy optima to the estimated parameters of the unified voting model – that is, our theorems illuminate how vote-seeking parties' strategies (especially the congruity between party positions and the faithfulness of parties to their own electorates) depend upon the policy and nonpolicy factors that significantly influence voter choice. In later chapters, we apply these methods and theorems to survey data from real-world elections in Britain, France, Norway, and the United States, and we assess whether our unified model of party competition – in conjunction with the assumption of vote-maximizing politicians – illuminates parties' policy strategies in these countries.

candidate enjoys a *valence* advantage – that is, an advantage accruing to a candidate due to voters' comparative evaluations of the competing candidates' perceived competence, integrity, leadership ability, and so forth (see, e.g., Londregan and Romer 1993; Macdonald and Rabinowitz 1998; Ansolabehere and Snyder 2000; Groseclose 2001; Miller and Schofield 2003; Moon [in press]). A key aspect of this specialized spatial-modeling literature – which we review in Appendix 3.1 – is that candidates' valence advantages are assumed to be identical across voters. Here we note that while we incorporate across-the-board valence issues into our analyses of policy-seeking motivations in Chapters 11 and 12, we are primarily concerned in this book with non-policy-related motivations that vary *across* voters, such as partisanship, class, education, religion, and race. This is because our empirical applications to multiparty election data for vote-maximizing parties (reported in Chapters 4–6 and 9) suggest that, when we account for such voter-specific nonpolicy motivations, incorporating valence dimensions of evaluation does not significantly enhance our ability to explain parties' policy strategies.[2]

Although the omission of nonpolicy motivations – in particular, voter-specific variables – is due in part to a desire for parsimony, some spatial modelers believe that nonpolicy variables, although they influence voters, are irrelevant to party positioning. Thus Iversen argues, "While other factors such as class background and candidate personalities enter into the determination of the voters' choices, these are arguably not important for explaining party *strategy* (since they cannot easily be manipulated)" (1994a: 49).

To the extent that Iversen's intuition is correct, spatial modelers can safely ignore the controversies that swirl around behavioral voting research, and this book, which attempts to unify the spatial and behavioral perspectives, could be expected to provide disappointingly few insights into parties' policy strategies! But our analyses show that modeling in the Downsian tradition that omits non-policy-related voting considerations may be misleading, particularly in the context of multiparty elections. Even though parties and

---

[2] In note 19 to Chapter 4 on the 1988 French presidential election, we compare the party equilibrium configurations we obtain for empirical voting specifications that include valence dimensions of evaluation to the equilibrium configurations obtained for voting specifications that omit valence dimensions. These comparisons show that incorporation of valence issues does not significantly alter party strategies. In Chapters 11 and 12, we consider the implications of valence advantages for *policy-seeking* candidates' strategies, where valence evaluation plays a very significant and qualitatively different role.

candidates cannot necessarily manipulate them, nonpolicy considerations can strongly affect the nature of optimal strategies. Moreover, failing to take nonpolicy effects into account yields empirically misleading predictions about how parties can be expected to behave.

3.2. The Logic of Policy Competition in the Unified Spatial Model: Illustrative Examples of How Nonpolicy Considerations Matter

In developing our heuristic arguments, we analyze four stylized election contexts that allow us to isolate how voters' nonpolicy motivations affect vote-seeking parties' strategic calculus, and also to see how parties' strategic incentives differ under probabilistic voting models as opposed to deterministic models. For all of our examples, we posit that three parties compete for votes: a liberal party, L, and two conservative parties, R and Q. We consider a one-dimensional model with an electorate in which voters are motivated only by Left–Right ideology and (starting in example 2) partisanship. Examples 1–3 are deterministic; example 4 introduces a probabilistic component. Using the notation introduced in Chapter 2 (see equation 2.6), for the three deterministic examples we represent voter i's utility for each party k as

$$U_i(k) = -a(x_i - s_k)^2 + bt_{ik}, \tag{3.1}$$

where s_k is the position of party k, and x_i and t_{ik} represent the voter's ideological position and partisanship, respectively. The parameter a represents the salience of ideology to the voter, while b represents the salience of partisanship, which we assume to be identical for all three parties. For our illustrative example, we set the policy salience parameter to $a = 1$, and we set t_{ik} to $+1$ if the voter identifies with party k and to zero otherwise.

We analyze the hypothetical electorate pictured in Figure 3.1, which shows the distribution of voters' policy preferences along a Left–Right scale stratified by partisanship. Specifically, we assume that the electorate is composed of three groups of voters: those who identify with parties L, R, and Q. We further assume that the set of ideal points (on a 1–7 Left–Right scale) of each partisan constituency is normally distributed, with the mean for party L set at 3.0 (to the left of the midpoint of the scale) and the means for R and Q both set at 5.0 (to the right of the midpoint), with a common standard

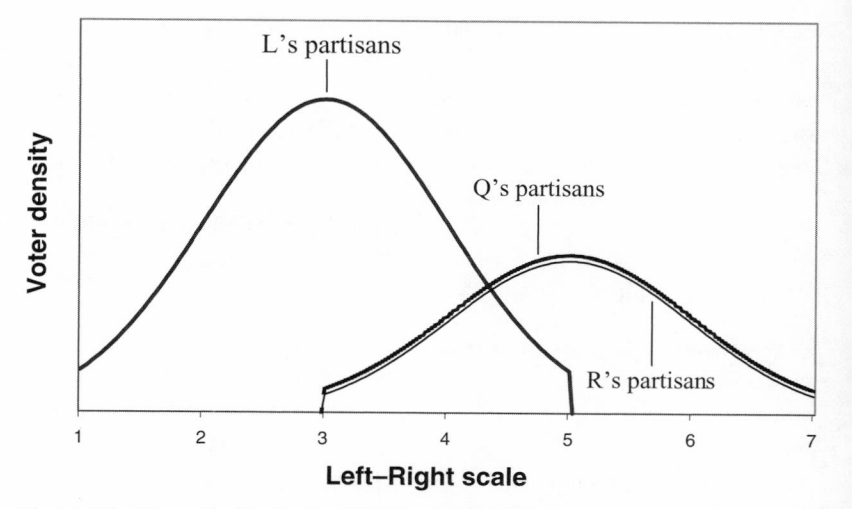

Figure 3.1. Voter distribution stratified by partisanship.

deviation of 1.0 for each of these partisan distributions.[3] Finally, we suppose that 25 percent of the electorate identifies with R and 25 percent identifies with Q, while 50 percent identifies with party L. As we will show, this example roughly corresponds to the situation in French politics, in which the three dominant parties are the conservative Union for French Democracy (UDF) and Rally for the Republic (RPR) and the leftist Socialists, and where the size of the Socialists' partisan constituency roughly equals the combined constituencies of the UDF and the RPR.

We initially locate party L at $s_L = 3$, the position of the median partisan of L, and party R at $s_R = 5$, the location of the median partisan of R. For this scenario, we examine four questions concerning Q's strategic calculus: What are Q's strategic motivations under the standard spatial model, which omits nonpolicy motivations (example 1)? How does Q's strategic calculus change if we account for partisan-based voter biases (example 2)? What is Q's strategic calculus if voters discount the claimed Left–Right positions of the parties (example 3)? What is Q's strategic calculus if we account for both partisan biases and for unmeasured voter motivations, which

---

[3] For convenience in this example, we suppose that each partisan distribution is truncated two standard deviations away from its mean – that is, the distribution of the partisans of L extends over the policy interval [1, 5], and the distributions of partisans of R and Q extend over the interval [3, 7].

render their voting decisions probabilistic from the parties' perspectives (example 4)?

3.2.1. *Illustrative Example 1: Spatial Competition for the Policy-Only Voting Model: The Parties Are Drawn toward the Center*

In a policy-only spatial model, voters are entirely policy motivated, so that partisanship does not influence their decisions. In order to explore the implications of this model, we initially set $b = 0$ in equation 3.1; that is, we assume that partisanship has no independent influence on the vote. Thus for all voters,

$$U_i(k) = -(x_i - s_k)^2. \tag{3.2}$$

Figure 3.2A, which plots Q's vote share (the vertical axis) against its Left–Right position (the horizontal axis), shows that for this policy-only model, Q maximizes support by presenting the centrist position 4.0 (location Q^* in Figure 3.2A), which attracts all voters who are located in the heavily populated interval [3.5, 4.5]. This constitutes slightly more than 25 percent of the electorate. Of course, if Q presents this centrist ideology, then the rival parties L and R have electoral incentives to converge toward Q's position so as to attract additional support from centrist voters. This reflects the centripetal incentive that typically operates under the policy-only model:

Strategic Proposition 1: When voters choose according to the policy-only voting model, vote-seeking parties typically have incentives to present centrist policies that are widely shared by the electorate.

3.2.2. *Illustrative Example 2: Policy Divergence in a Deterministic Voting Model with Partisan Components*

Next, we consider how the introduction of partisan loyalties alters the parties' strategic calculus. We let s_L denote the position of party L, s_R the position of party R, and s_Q the position of party Q. Specifically, in equation 3.1 let the partisan-salience parameter $b = 2$ so that for partisans of L, equation 3.1 can be written as:

$$U_i(L) = -(x_i - s_L)^2 + 2; \quad U_i(R) = -(x_i - s_R)^2;$$
$$U_i(Q) = -(x_i - s_Q)^2, \tag{3.3}$$

3.2A. *Q*'s vote, for the policy-only model

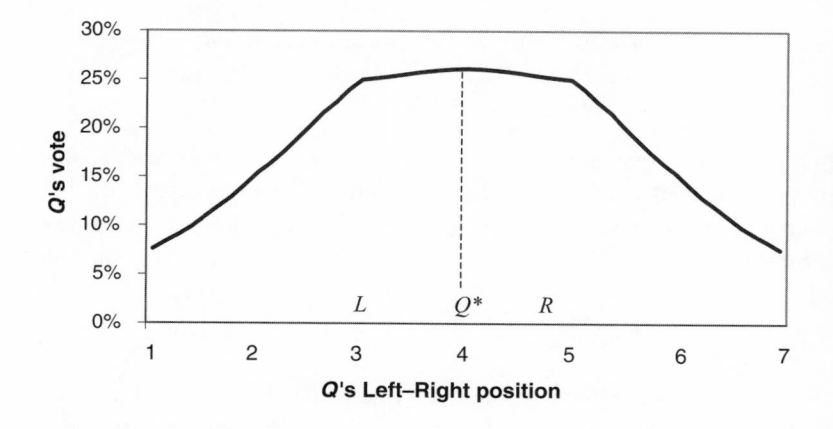

3.2B. *Q*'s vote, for the partisan-voting model

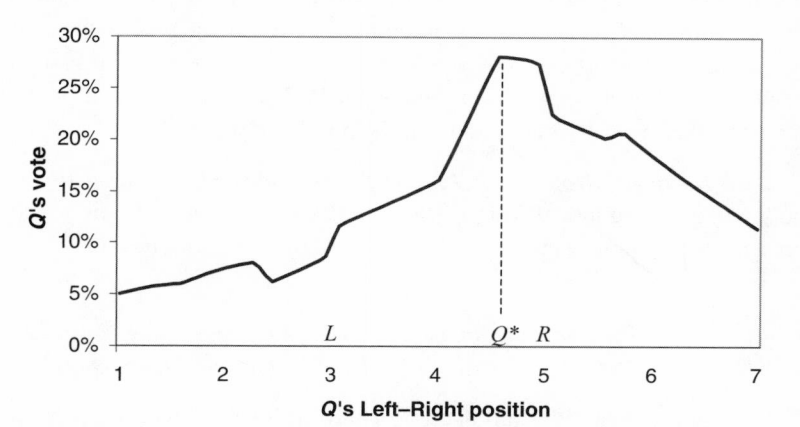

Figure 3.2. Party *Q*'s expected vote as a function of policy position, for alternative voting models.

Note: Q* represents *Q*'s vote-maximizing position.

3.2C. *Q*'s vote, for the discounting model with partisan component

3.2D. *Q*'s vote, for the probabilistic voting model with a partisan component

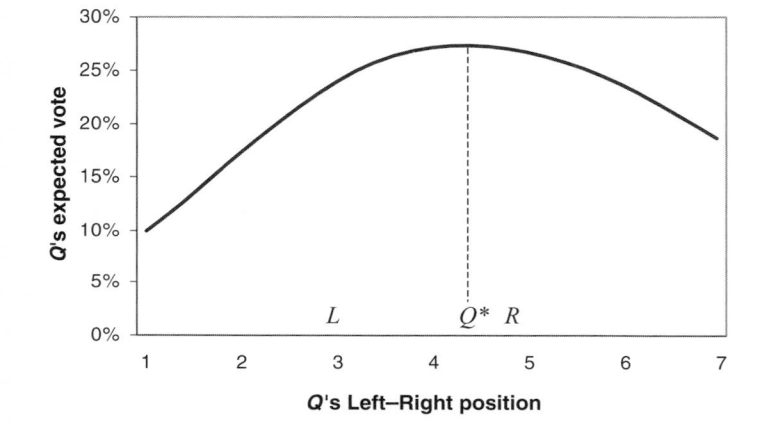

Figure 3.2. (*continued*)

while for partisans of R, equation 3.1 becomes

$$U_i(L) = -(x_i - s_L)^2; \quad U_i(R) = -(x_i - s_R)^2 + 2;$$
$$U_i(Q) = -(x_i - s_Q)^2, \tag{3.4}$$

and for partisans of Q, equation 3.1 becomes

$$U_i(L) = -(x_i - s_L)^2; U_i(R) = -(x_i - s_R)^2;$$
$$U_i(Q) = -(x_i - s_Q)^2 + 2. \tag{3.5}$$

Given these parameters, partisans of L grant a nonpolicy advantage to party L, partisans of R grant a nonpolicy advantage to party R, and so on.[4]

Now consider party Q's strategic calculus under this alternative voting model, with L and R again located at $s_L = 3$ and $s_R = 5$. If Q locates at 4, it attracts support from all of its own partisans who locate in the policy interval [2.5, 5.5];[5] collectively, these partisans represent approximately 18 percent of the electorate. The reason Q receives such extensive support from its partisan constituency – including support from many partisans who prefer a rival party on policy grounds – is that these voters' partisan loyalties to Q outweigh their policy preference for one of the rival parties (see note 5). However, if Q locates at 4, similar arguments show that it attracts *no* support from voters who identify with L or R. This is because the centrist partisans of these rival parties – who prefer Q on policy grounds – nevertheless vote for their own party because their partisan loyalties outweigh their policy preferences. Hence, for this partisan voting model, centrist positioning by Q attracts support only from a subset of its own partisans, about 18 percent of the electorate.

---

[4] Later in this chapter, we report an empirical analysis of the 1988 French presidential election that suggests that this is a plausible value of the partisan voting parameter. In addition, in subsequent chapters we report sensitivity analyses suggesting that the intuitions we develop here on party strategies do not depend on the specific values of the partisan voting parameter (see Chapter 4, section 4.5, and note 7 to Chapter 6).

[5] To see this, note that given the voting specifications in equation 3.5 and for $s_Q < s_R$, a voter i who identifies with Q has a positive utility differential for Q versus R if

$$-[(x_i - s_Q)^2 + 2] - [-(x_i - s_R)^2] = (s_R^2 - s_Q^2) + 2x_i(s_Q - s_R) + 2 > 0,$$

that is, if

$$x_i < \frac{s_R + s_Q}{2} - \frac{1}{s_Q - s_R}.$$

If $s_Q = 4$ and $s_R = 5$, then $x_i < 4.5 + 1 = 5.5$. A similar calculation shows that given $s_L = 3$ and $s_Q = 4$, all partisans of Q located to the right of 2.5 prefer Q to L.

Now consider the consequences if Q presents the right-wing position $s_Q = 5.0$, a position that reflects the preferences of the median voter in its partisan constituency. For this position, Q receives votes from all partisans of Q located in the policy interval [3.5, 7.0] (this can be verified using the computational approach outlined in footnote 5). This represents virtually every member of Q's partisan constituency, about 23 percent of the electorate in all. Of course, the reason why Q's support increases among its own constituency, for right-wing positioning as compared to centrist positioning, is that the former better reflects this constituency's policy preferences. And if Q attracts only 18 percent of the vote when located at 4.0 but attracts 23 percent of the vote from its partisan constituency alone when located at 5.0, then the strategic imperative is clear: *Q has electoral incentives to shift away from the center, in the direction of its partisan constituency.*

Figure 3.2B shows Q's vote as a function of policy position, with L and R located at $s_L = 3$ and $s_R = 5$. We see that Q maximizes support by presenting the center-right position $s_Q = 4.56$ (location $Q*$ in Figure 3.2B).[6] For this position, Q attracts support from all of its partisans located in the policy interval [3.14, 7.00], as well as support from the center-right partisans of party L located in the interval [4.42, 4.78] – approximately 28 percent of the vote in all. By contrast, Q's vote drops sharply if Q locates to the left of center.

We emphasize that the intuition that drives party Q's strategic calculus revolves around the fact that voter characteristics that bias their vote choices (here partisanship) correlate with their policy beliefs. (Later we will document this correlation in the case of the French electorate.) In this scenario, so long as the leftist-based party L presents a leftist policy that is broadly acceptable to its constituency, rival parties cannot easily capture these voters' support. Hence rightist-based parties, such as Q, have electoral incentives to present right-wing policies that reflect the beliefs of their own voting constituencies. This suggests a second strategic proposition:

Strategic Proposition 2: When voters' partisan loyalties influence their voting decisions, and these loyalties correlate with their policy preferences, then parties are motivated to appeal on policy grounds to voters who are attracted to them in part for nonpolicy reasons.

---

[6] The erratic nature of the support curves pictured in Figures 3.2B and 3.2C is an artifact of deterministic voting that is cleared up by the use of a probabilistic model (see, e.g., Figure 3.2D).

One caveat we emphasize is that, Strategic Proposition 2 notwithstanding, parties typically maximize votes by presenting policies that are similar to, *but more moderate than*, their partisan constituencies' beliefs. This is especially true in situations where parties' partisan constituencies hold distinctly noncentrist preferences. The reason is that vote-seeking parties usually have opportunities to siphon off some (typically small) degree of support from rival parties' partisans, and, in situations where these rival partisans hold more moderate positions than the party's own constituency, party elites have incentives to moderate their policies in order to appeal jointly to their own partisan constituency *and* to neighboring constituencies that constitute targets of opportunity. Example 2 given earlier illustrates this strategic logic: Note that Q's optimal location at $s_Q = 4.56$ is similar to but more moderate than the median position of Q's partisan constituency (5.0), and that this center-right positioning allows Q to siphon off support from a limited number of party L's partisans located in the policy interval [4.42, 4.78].

3.2.3. Illustrative Example 3: Voter Discounting of Candidate Positions

In our third example, we suppose that voters discount the candidates' ability to implement policies at the locations they advocate (see Chapter 2, section 2.4). Specifically, we assume that there is a status quo point, SQ, located at 4 on a 1–7 scale, and that all voters discount by 50 percent the capacity of candidates to move policy from SQ to their advocated location. Thus, for example, a candidate advocating policy at 6.0 would be judged by the voters to be able to implement policy at halfway between 4.0 and 6.0, that is, at 5.0. Accordingly, a voter who desires government policy outputs at 5.0 might support a candidate whose campaign position is at 6.0. Anticipating such behavior by voters, parties might advocate policies more extreme than those they would advocate if discounting did not occur.

For this example, we locate candidates L and R at $s_L = 2$ and $s_R = 6$, so that voters project that these candidates would implement policies at 3 and 5, respectively, as in the previous illustrative examples. For this scenario, the third candidate Q is motivated to move to a more extreme position than he would take without discounting, in order to compensate for the expected voter response. In fact, Q maximizes support by assuming the position 5.12, substantially more extreme than Q's optimal position in example 2 ($s_Q = 4.56$), in which no discounting occurs. Candidate Q's vote as a function of policy position is presented in Figure 3.2C. We are led to a third strategic proposition:

Strategic Proposition 3:   When voters discount the abilities of the candidates to implement the policies they proclaim, candidates and parties are motivated to position themselves further away from the status quo – and typically in more extreme policy locations – than they would under the unified model without discounting.

3.2.4. Illustrative Example 4: Incorporating Probabilistic Choice into the Partisan Voting Model

In the preceding examples, we assumed that party elites could predict voters' decisions with certainty, based upon knowledge of these voters' ideologies and partisanship. In actual elections, however, voters are also moved by unmeasured considerations, so that neither party elites nor the researcher can be certain of voters' choices. As discussed in Chapter 2 (see section 2.2.2), we model this uncertainty by incorporating a random variable into voters' party evaluations, which renders voting decisions probabilistic from both the parties' and the analyst's perspective.[7] Here we re-examine the partisan scenario discussed earlier – without policy discounting – using the conditional logit model of probabilistic choice, yielding the voting model:

$$U_i(k) = -0.2(x_i - s_k)^2 + 2\mathbf{t}_{ik} + X_{ik}, \tag{3.6}$$

where X_{ik} represents unmeasured components of voter i's evaluation of party k, which are assumed to be independently distributed according to a type I extreme value distribution (see Chapter 2, section 2.2.2). Note that in equation 3.6, we introduce one other change in our voting specification – namely, we specify that the policy salience coefficient is $a = 0.2$, rather than $a = 1$ as in the previous examples. We introduce this modification because the empirical analyses of survey data from the 1988 French presidential election, to be

---

[7] Not only is voter choice better specified under a probabilistic model, but the complexity and instability of party competition in a multidimensional setting under a deterministic model is avoided, as well, since results under a probabilistic model are similar for one or more dimensions. Insofar as equilibria exist under deterministic models, however, they are generally similar to those obtained under probabilistic models. In this sense, the locations of equilibrium configurations are robust to the choice of models.

reported later, suggest that this is a realistic value for the policy salience parameter, under a probabilistic voting model. Logit probabilities for choosing various candidates were given in Chapter 2 (see equation 2.4).

For this probabilistic voting scenario, Figure 3.2D presents party Q's expected vote as a function of Left–Right position, with parties L and R again fixed at 3.0 and 5.0. Q's vote-maximizing position is approximately 4.35, which is similar to Q's optimal position for the deterministic model: that is, party Q once again has electoral incentives to present a center-right policy that is similar to but less extreme than the mean position of Q's partisan constituency.[8] Thus the introduction of unmeasured voter motivations, which renders the vote choice probabilistic, does not alter Q's incentive to present right-wing policies that reflect the beliefs of its partisan constituency.

3.3. Party Competition and the Concept of Equilibrium in Policy Strategies

3.3.1. Policy Equilibrium: Definitions and Illustrative Examples

To this point, we have considered how a specific vote-seeking party (Q in our illustrative examples) chooses its policy strategy in scenarios where the policies of rival parties are fixed at arbitrary positions. This focus on a party's one-step optimum may be unrealistic, because, in real-world elections, the policies of rival parties are *not* typically set in stone; instead, rival politicians typically have some leeway to adjust their policy images in response to their competitors' policy strategies. Hence the following questions arise with respect to our illustrative examples: What policy strategies maximize electoral support for party R and for party L when party Q presents its vote-maximizing position? If L and R were to shift to these vote-maximizing positions, what would be Q's optimal response to such policy shifts? As this process proceeds, if all parties seek to maximize votes and each party updates its strategy in response to rivals' policy shifts, will the parties ever converge to a stable configuration of policy positions, such that no party has incentives to further change its strategy? As we have indicated, such a set of stable strategies, if it exists, is called a Nash equilibrium.

---

[8] For a probabilistic voting model with voter discounting of 50 percent of the candidates' capacity to move policy from the status quo point at 4 (as in illustrative example 3), Q's vote-maximizing position is at approximately 4.70.

We now revisit several of our three-party illustrative examples, comparing in each case the Nash equilibrium – if one exists – to the one-step optima noted earlier.[9] Our first example was a policy-only, deterministic model. In such a model, in which each voter always votes for the party that maximizes his or her policy-determined utility, there is no Nash equilibrium. The two most extreme of the three candidates always have incentives to move toward the central candidate in order to increase their vote shares.[10] But as the central candidate is squeezed out of support, he or she has an incentive to leapfrog one of the others in order to avert the squeeze. The new central candidate then has a similar incentive to leapfrog, and so forth, ad infinitum. Although leapfrogging appears to be uncommon in practice (Budge 1994: 460), only minor movement is required to avert a squeeze, so that instability would be expected under a pure deterministic, policy-only model with three candidates.[11] Such instability is, however, an artifact of the unrealistic assumptions of this model.

If, however, we add both partisanship and a probabilistic component to the model (as in illustrative example 4, given earlier), we obtain a Nash equilibrium with nonidentical strategies.[12] To illustrate how such an equilibrium may come about as parties jockey for position in response to each other, we continue with example 4, but this time allow the parties, one at a time, to shift to their vote-maximizing positions, successively updating their policies in response to the rival parties' positioning. This process is continued until, if possible, no further movement is needed – that is, until an equilibrium configuration is reached.

Recall that with parties L and R fixed at 3.0 and 5.0, respectively, party Q maximizes support by locating at 4.35 (see Figure 3.2D). Now, with R again fixed at 5.0 and Q fixed at 4.35, we vary L's position until L's vote share

---

[9] Recall that the algorithm for this calculation will be presented as Appendix 4.1 to Chapter 4.

[10] We are assuming here that the voter distribution is continuous and that the probability density is nonzero. In this case, a three-party Nash equilibrium does not exist regardless of the voter distribution for deterministic voting.

[11] In a deterministic model with four candidates, under special conditions a Nash equilibrium may occur with one pair of candidates at identical positions on the left and one pair at identical positions on the right (Eaton and Lipsey 1975; Cox 1990). Such pairing, however, does not appear to be observed in real electorates, and intuitively it is rather implausible.

[12] In general, in order to obtain a Nash equilibrium with nonidentical strategies in a probabilistic model with a nonpolicy component, it is necessary to have three or more candidates. With only two candidates, a Nash equilibrium typically occurs, but with both candidates at the center unless additional centrifugal influences – such as the threat of abstention due to alienation – are added to the model (see Chapters 7 and 8).

is maximized. This occurs at the slightly left-of-center policy 3.81 (with no leftist rival, party L can afford to approach the center more than Q can). Next, with L and Q fixed at 3.81 and 4.35, respectively, party R – in order to maximize its vote share – shifts to the center-right position 4.24, to which party Q's best response is the position 4.25.

Following a further succession of minor policy adjustments, party L locates at 3.74, while R and Q pair at the center-right position 4.26. For this policy configuration, no party can improve its expected vote by modifying its position; hence, so long as circumstances do not change, the parties will converge to this stable policy configuration, which therefore constitutes a Nash equilibrium. Figure 3.3A displays the parties' vote shares as a function of their positions, with the rival candidates fixed at their equilibrium positions. Note that the optimal strategies at equilibrium are not all identical. Thus, the parties *are motivated to appeal on policy grounds to voters who are attracted to them, in part, for nonpolicy reasons.* Note, however, that the degree of policy dispersion between the rightmost and leftmost parties at equilibrium – which amounts to 0.52 policy units – is less than the dispersion between the mean position of L's partisan constituency (3.0) and the mean positions of R's and Q's partisans (5.0). As discussed earlier, this occurs because while the parties have electoral incentives to appeal to their own partisans, they also have opportunities to attract some limited support from rival partisan constituencies, which prompts them to attach moderate weights to these rival partisans' policy preferences.

Finally, Figure 3.3B displays the equilibrium configuration for the unified model with probabilistic voting and voter discounting of the candidates' positions. Assuming that all voters discount by 50 percent the capacities of candidates to move policy from the status quo point 4.0 to the announced positions, this equilibrium configuration finds candidate L locating at 3.48, while R and Q pair at the right-wing position 4.52. As expected, this equilibrium finds the candidates at considerably more dispersed positions than they would occupy when voters do not discount the candidates' promises.

3.3.2. Applying Equilibrium Analysis to Real-World Elections: A Methodology Based upon an Iterative Algorithm

Two potential problems arise when using equilibrium analysis to understand party strategies. First, in some situations the parties may not converge to a

3.3A. Equilibrium for the proximity model (*a*=0.2, *b*=2)

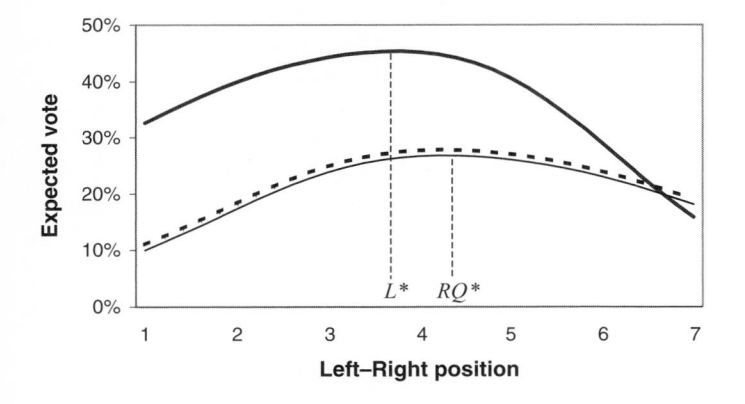

3.3B. Equilibrium for the discounting model (*a*=0.2, *b*=2, 50% discounting)

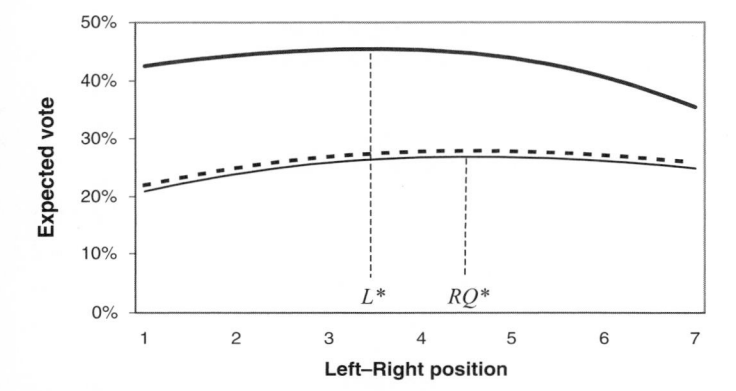

Figure 3.3. Equilibrium configurations for probabilistic voting models.
Note: The support curves represent the parties' expected votes as a function of their positions, with the rival parties located at their equilibrium positions. These illustrative examples are based on the voter distribution pictured in Figure 3.1.

policy equilibrium. For instance, recall that in our earlier example involving deterministic voters who choose according to the policy-only voting model, the parties *L, R*, and *Q* can be expected to continually leapfrog each other, never reaching an equilibrium configuration. In this scenario, equilibrium analysis generates no clear prediction about party policies beyond the prediction that these policies will be unstable. Second, in some election scenarios, *multiple* equilibria may exist – that is, there may be more than one stable configuration of party strategies.[13] In such situations, the particular equilibrium configuration that the parties eventually reach may depend on arbitrary factors, such as the order of party movement and the parties' initial positions.

In order to address these problems, we derive formal conditions that guarantee a unique Nash equilibrium (see Appendix 4.1). The practical importance of this result is that when the equilibrium conditions are satisfied – which, as we show in subsequent chapters, is usually the case in our analyses of historical elections for models involving a nonpolicy component – the parties are guaranteed to converge to a unique configuration of policies. Hence in our empirical applications to historical elections, we can typically employ equilibrium analysis to derive a unique prediction – that is, an explanation – of parties' policy proposals.

3.3.3. Equilibrium Analysis Versus Analysis of Parties' One-Step Policy Strategies

While spatial modelers emphasize the search for policy equilibrium in their theoretical work, the question arises: Is equilibrium analysis the best way to understand party strategies in *real-world* elections? In particular, empirically oriented scholars may question the central assumption that underlies equilibrium analysis: namely, that party elites have the leeway to continuously readjust their policy proposals in response to their competitors' policy strategies. While this assumption plausibly captures the dynamics of party

---

[13] In a probabilistic, policy-only model, a Nash equilibrium does exist, but with all three parties located at identical positions at the center. For quadratic utility, the equilibrium occurs at the voter mean; for city-block utility, it occurs at the voter median (Lin, Enelow, and Dorussen 1999). This centrist Nash equilibrium is unique as long as the policy-salience parameter *a* remains below a certain threshold (whose value depends on the number of parties, the voter distributions, etc.). Above this threshold, however, many different Nash equilibrium configurations occur. The question of the uniqueness of a Nash equilibrium in the unified model will be dealt with in Chapter 4.

systems over a period of years (assuming no external "shocks" to the party system, such as the formation of new parties or the collapse of existing parties), it is not clear that it is optimal for analyzing the dynamics of candidate strategies over the course of a single election campaign. If a candidate actually switched policies several times over a period of weeks or months, as equilibrium analysis implies, might not voters dismiss this candidate due to confusion about her policies and concerns about her sincerity?[14] Thus in real-world elections, vote-seeking candidates may have incentives to limit their policy switches, and therefore a focus on candidates' "one-step" policy optima – that is, the policies that maximize a candidate's vote given his competitors' actual positions – may illuminate candidates' behavior as effectively as equilibrium analysis does.

These considerations notwithstanding, in this book we focus on equilibrium analysis, for the following reasons.

First, equilibrium policy locations for each candidate do not depend on specified locations for the other candidates, whereas one-step values must be estimated from observed locations of the other candidates or set arbitrarily. Thus determination of one-step values is to some extent circular, because estimates of the locations of (some of) the candidates are used to determine the optimal locations of others, and vice versa. This is akin to using the same variables on both sides of an equation. Furthermore, the one-step optimum for a focal candidate assumes, somewhat arbitrarily, that one candidate can move but that the others remain fixed. But then, when the identity of the focal candidate changes, who can move and who cannot is reversed – a reversal that is difficult to justify.

Secondly, at a Nash equilibrium no candidate can improve his or her vote share by changing policy, so that such an equilibrium represents stability for the party system. One-step optima, on the other hand, are computed separately for each party and hence have no correspondence with overall stability.

---

[14] However, recent work by Stokes (1999) on presidential elections in Latin America suggests that once they attain office, politicians have the leeway to alter their policies quite dramatically, and even to renege on their central policy commitments, without suffering significant electoral penalties. To the extent that Stokes's conclusions extend to elections held outside of Latin America (we are unaware of comparable research on North American or European elections), they suggest that it is feasible for politicians to readjust their policies continually in the course of election campaigns, and therefore that equilibrium analysis may be the appropriate prism through which to analyze candidate strategies.

Finally, in our empirical applications to real-world elections, we find that *candidates' and parties' one-step policy optima are usually quite similar to their equilibrium positions* (later we illustrate this similarity in the case of the 1988 French presidential election). In other words, in typical situations, vote-maximizing candidates would move in a single step most of the way toward their eventual equilibrium locations, given any reasonable configuration of the other candidates. For this reason, our substantive conclusions about candidate/party strategies are similar whether we base them on analyses of equilibrium positions or on one-step optima.

In order to avoid needless repetition, we will typically report the equilibrium positions of candidates/parties in historical elections, not their one-step optima. However, in the (rare) cases where these two measures differ substantially, we report both equilibrium and one-step optimum positions.

3.4. Empirical Application to the 1988 French Presidential Election

We now investigate vote-maximizing candidates' policy strategies and the configuration of the candidates' equilibrium positions in a real-world setting: the first round of the 1988 French presidential election.[15] We shall base our computations on the probabilistic version of the policy-only model, the unified model with partisan components, and the partisan model with policy discounting. Our data on French voters' partisan identities, ideological self-placements, and voting behavior are derived from Pierce's (1996) 1988 French Presidential Election Study (FPES), using self-placements on the Left–Right scale for voter ideal points ($N = 748$) and respondents' mean candidate placements for the candidates' actual positions.[16] The major candidates were the Communist Andre Lajoinie; the Socialist Francois Mitterrand, the incumbent president; Raymond Barre, the nominee of the center-right UDF; Jacques Chirac, the incumbent prime minister and the leader of the

---

[15] French presidential elections provide for two rounds of voting, with the two top vote getters in the first round advancing to a runoff election held two weeks later. If one of the candidates wins a majority of the first round vote, then this candidate is elected without recourse to a runoff; however, this has never occurred in practice.

[16] Our analysis focuses on the subsample of 748 respondents (out of 1,013) who reported voting for one of the five candidates in the first round and who could place themselves on the Left–Right dimension.

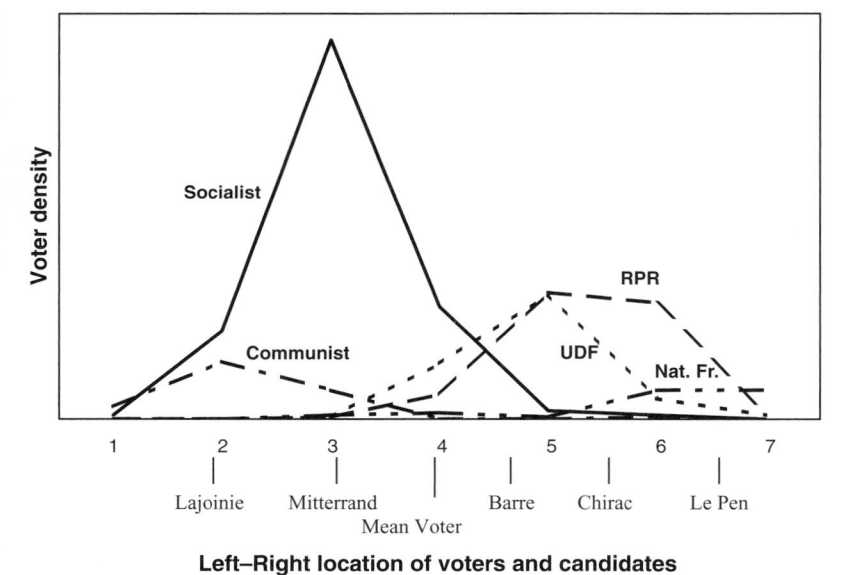

Figure 3.4. Voter distribution by party in the 1988 French Presidential Election Study.

right-wing RPR; and Jean-Marie Le Pen, the leader of the extreme right-wing National Front.[17]

Figure 3.4 shows the distribution of the FPES respondents' Left–Right self-placements, stratified by partisanship (see also Table 3.1, column 2). The presidential candidates' (mean perceived) positions are also shown, as is the mean voter self-placement. Note that these partisan distributions conform to our illustrative examples in that they are centered at quite different locations along the Left–Right scale: partisans of the Communist and Socialist Parties take predominantly left-wing positions, while partisans of the UDF, the RPR, and the National Front are centered on the right. Also consistent with our illustrative examples is the fact that the partisan constituency of the Socialists, the major left-wing party, is roughly the same size as the combined constituencies of the two major right-wing parties, the RPR and the UDF. Previous voting research suggests that Left–Right ideology is

[17] Four additional candidates contested the first round of the 1988 French presidential election, but none of these candidates reached 4 percent of the vote; therefore, we have omitted them from this analysis.

Table 3.1. *Nash equilibrium strategies under the conditional logit model for the 1988 French Presidential Election Study*

Candidate	Vote Share (1)	Mean Position of Partisans[a] (2)	Equilibrium Strategies		One-step Strategies
			Policy-only Model[b] (3)	Partisan Model (4)	Partisan Model (5)
Lajoinie	6.6%	2.24	3.98 (.005)	3.69 (.02)	3.64
Mitterrand	39.2%	3.08	3.98 (.005)	3.52 (.01)	3.58
Barre	13.5%	4.85	3.98 (.005)	4.24 (.02)	4.14
Chirac	18.0%	5.36	3.98 (.005)	4.44 (.02)	4.38
Le Pen	4.5%	6.03	3.98 (.005)	4.23 (.02)	4.24
Other[c]	18.2%	4.02	–	–	–
Parameter estimates:					
a (policy salience)			0.414	0.204	0.204
b (partisan salience)			0.00	2.14	2.14

[a] *Partisans* are defined as identifiers of the parties represented by the candidates indicated.

[b] This centrist equilibrium is not unique, i.e., there are other sets of strategies that constitute equilibria under the policy-only model. See Chapter 5.

[c] The category *other* includes identifiers of other parties as well as those respondents who did not identify with any party.

the dominant dimension in French politics; it has also been found to reflect primarily economic preferences (see, e.g., Converse and Pierce 1986, 1993; Fleury and Lewis-Beck 1993).

3.4.1. Candidate Strategies for the Policy-Only Voting Model

We first analyzed candidate strategies for a policy-only voting model, in which voters' utilities are influenced solely by their evaluations of the candidates' Left–Right positions, plus an unmeasured probabilistic component. For the 1988 French presidential election, we estimate the policy-salience parameter for this model (under conditional logit) as $a = 0.414$ (see Table 3.1, column 3). We ask the question: Given this model parameter, and the distribution of French voters' ideologies shown in Figure 3.4, does an equilibrium configuration exist, and, if so, what are the candidates' equilibrium positions?

Indeed, for this election scenario a Nash equilibrium exists in which all five candidates locate at the center (see Table 3.1, column 3). This set of strategies, however, does not constitute the only Nash equilibrium under the policy-only model; there are many others that are not centrist! Thus, the policy-only model can easily lead to an indeterminate result, as we will see again in Chapters 5 and 6.

3.4.2. Incorporation of Partisanship: A Unified Model

Incorporation of a nonpolicy component can resolve the indeterminacy of the policy-only model. As in our hypothetical examples, the nonpolicy component of the model is limited to party identification.[18] For the 1988 French presidential election, the parameter estimates for the unified model of equation 3.1 are $a = 0.204$ and $b = 2.14$, parameters that are quite similar to the ones we used in our earlier illustrative example with probabilistic voting ($a = 0.2$, $b = 2.0$).[19] Application of our algorithm yielded the determination that for this election scenario, a unique Nash equilibrium exists (see Appendix 4.1) in which the candidates assume five distinct optimal locations. These equilibrium positions are reported in Table 3.1 (column 4) and are illustrated in Figure 3.5, which shows the candidates' expected votes as a function of their Left–Right positions (with the rival candidates fixed at their equilibrium positions).

---

[18] Converse and Pierce (1993) argue that respondents' reported party identification is not equivalent to their current vote intention, a conclusion that is supported by Lewis-Beck and Chlarson's (2002) analysis of French presidential voting. In fact, 19 percent of the respondents who reported voting for one of the major candidates and reported a party identification voted for a candidate of a rival party. This is in addition to the 18 percent of respondents in our data set who identified with other than one of the five major parties or who reported no party identification at all. Adams and Merrill (2000: Table 3A) show that additional nonpolicy variables (class, income, religion, economic perceptions, etc.) had relatively small effects upon the 1988 French presidential vote, when controlling for partisanship. Equilibrium analysis based upon these more fully specified voting models produced results similar to those reported here.

[19] When a nonpolicy factor that correlates with policy preference – such as partisanship – is included in the model, the value of the policy-salience parameter a is reduced (in this case, from 0.414 to 0.204). This occurs because in a policy-only model, the policy-salience parameter not only reflects policy but also serves as a proxy for correlated nonpolicy parameters such as partisanship. Of course, in the unified model, partisanship is determined in part by policy, at least in the long term – that is, partisanship is in part endogenous. Hence the parameter estimate for partisan salience may be an overestimate. However, our equilibrium values are quite robust to changes in the partisan-salience parameter, b. If, for example, we divide the value of b in half, so that $b = 1.07$, and re-estimate ($a = .300$), the party positions at equilibrium are almost unchanged and are in fact slightly more spread out. Some insight into this nonlinear effect of changes in b on equilibrium strategies is given in Chapter 4.

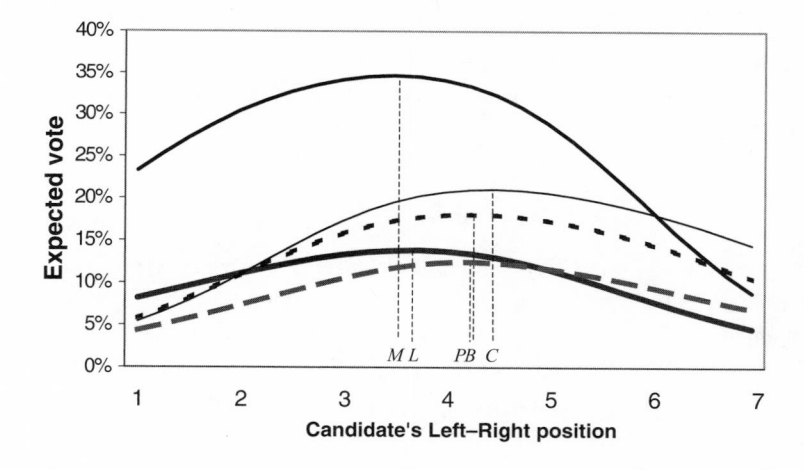

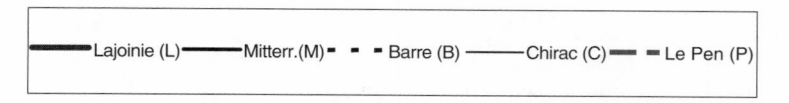

Figure 3.5. Equilibrium configuration for the presidential candidates in the 1988 French Presidential Election, for the unified model.

Note: The support curves represent the candidates' expected votes as a function of their Left–Right positions, with the rival candidates fixed at their equilibrium locations. These expected votes were computed using the estimated parameters for the unified model (which are reported in Table 3.1), for the voter distribution pictured in Figure 3.4.

These equilibrium configurations are consistent with our illustrative arguments that candidates maximize votes by presenting policies that are similar to, but less extreme than, the mean preferences of their partisan constituencies. We see that Lajoinie and Mitterrand, the candidates who have left-wing partisan constituencies, locate to the left of center on the ideological spectrum, while Barre, Chirac, and Le Pen each locate to the right of center, in the direction of their right-wing partisan constituencies. Furthermore, note that the candidates' positions under the partisan model are all relatively centrist: the maximum separation of the candidates occurs between Mitterrand and Chirac, who are separated by 0.92 on the 1–7 scale. This separation is significantly less than the distance between the mean locations of their parties' partisans, which is 2.28. This feature of the equilibrium configuration is consistent with our illustrative arguments, which suggested that when voters display partisan loyalties and do not discount the candidates' policy promises, candidates have electoral incentives to present policies that are similar to but more moderate than the policy preferences of their partisan constituencies.

Finally, we ask the question: What are the candidates' one-step policy optima, and how do these compare with their equilibrium positions? The candidates' one-step optima for the unified voting model are reported in Table 3.1, column 5. A comparison to their equilibrium positions (column 4) shows that for every candidate, the one-step optimum and the equilibrium position are extremely similar. Thus in this empirical application to the 1988 French presidential election, we conclude that our substantive conclusions about candidate strategies do not depend on the distinction between one-step optima and equilibrium positions.

CHAPTER 4

Factors Influencing the Link between Party Strategy and the Variables Affecting Voter Choice

Theoretical Results

4.1. Introduction

In this chapter, we formalize the intuitions developed in the illustrative examples presented in Chapter 3 by analyzing how changes in both policy and nonpolicy variables affect vote-seeking candidates' incentives to present centrist versus extreme policy positions in multicandidate elections. A technique that can calculate Nash equilibria for our fully specified unified model, as well as the proof of a uniqueness theorem for Nash equilibria, are presented in Appendix 4.1. This algorithm is used to calculate Nash equilibria throughout this volume. Theorem proofs for other results described in this chapter and simulation results are found in Appendices 4.2–4.4. The relatively technical material in this chapter[1] may be skipped by readers who wish to focus on the empirical analyses in Chapters 5–9 and beyond.

Following Cox (1990), we define *centripetal* incentives as those that motivate candidates and parties to present centrist policies, and *centrifugal* incentives as those that reward more extreme positions (we will later define the terms "centrist" and "extreme" more precisely). We restrict ourselves here to a model in which voters are influenced only by policies and party identification, and we first present a theorem on the configurations of candidates' vote-maximizing positions in situations where policies have low salience to the electorate. We then develop, for scenarios in which policies are more salient to voters, a combined theoretical and simulation analysis that expresses each candidate's Nash equilibrium position as a function of

---

[1] Chapter 4 is based on Merrill and Adams (2001, 2002).

the election parameters. Although our analyses can be extended to multidimensional spatial models – and/or to models incorporating abstention – we present our work in the context of a single (Left–Right) dimension in order to focus on the basic effects of election parameters on candidates' centrifugal (and centripetal) incentives.

4.2. The Model

We assume that voters choose according to the probabilistic version of the partisan voting model given in equation 3.1 – that is, that each voter i's utility for each candidate k is given by

$$U_i(k) = -a(x_i - s_k)^2 + bt_{ik} + X_{ik}, \tag{4.1}$$

where x_i represents the voter's ideal location; s_k is party k's strategic location; t_{ik} is a dummy variable that equals 1 if the voter identifies with party k and zero otherwise; and X_{ik} is a voter-specific random utility term, which we assume is generated independently from a type I extreme value distribution (the assumption used in conditional logit analysis). The parameter a represents the policy-salience coefficient, while b represents the partisan-salience coefficient.

We assume that the election involves $K \geq 3$ candidates – that is, that this is a multicandidate election – and that a proportion m_k of all voters identify with candidate k's party (to be called *partisans* of candidate k, for short). A proportion, m_0, of voters are *independent*; their utilities have no partisan component. Thus $\sum_{k=0}^{K} m_k = 1$. Suppose further that the partisans of the various candidates have spatial locations, which follow continuous distributions with means μ_k and probability density functions f_k. The overall mean voter location μ_V is thus equal to $\sum_{k=0}^{K} m_k \mu_k$. We refer to the location μ_V as the *center* of the voter distribution. Thus each partisan shift $\mu_k - \mu_V$ represents the policy distance (positive or negative) between the candidate's partisans and the overall voter mean. We also assume that the mean location of independent voters μ_0 is the same as the overall voter mean. Although this assumption apparently limits the generality of our model, a comparison of the overall voter means to the mean placements of independent voters in the elections we study later suggests that the assumption is approximately satisfied (see Chapters 5–9).

4.2.1. Theoretical Results on Candidates' Vote-Maximizing Strategies

The expected vote share of candidate k is given by

$$EV_k(\mathbf{s}, a) = \sum_i P_{ik}(\mathbf{s}, a),$$

where, as before, $P_{ik}(\mathbf{s}, a)$ denotes the conditional logit probability that voter i votes for party k (this probability function was given in equation 2.4) and $\mathbf{s}$ is the configuration (vector) of candidate positions. The partial derivative of $EV_k(\mathbf{s}, a)$ with respect to a, evaluated at $a = 0$, achieves a maximum when s_k assumes the value

$$s_k(0) = \frac{\sum_i P_{ik}(\mathbf{s}, 0)[1 - P_{ik}(\mathbf{s}, 0)]x_i}{\sum_j P_{jk}(\mathbf{s}, 0)[1 - P_{jk}(\mathbf{s}, 0)]}, \qquad (4.2)$$

where $P_{ik}(\mathbf{s}, 0)$ denotes the probability that voter i chooses candidate k when the policy parameter, a, is zero – that is, when candidate choice is determined entirely by voter-specific nonpolicy attributes and the random components of voter utility.[2]

In other words, as a policy component is introduced into the model, the candidate's expected share of the vote increases most rapidly for the strategy $s_k(0)$. It turns out that the values $s_k(0)$, although seemingly only tangentially related to policy considerations, form the primary basis for determining optimal (Nash equilibrium) strategies when policy motivations are present.

This relationship between optimum strategies when policy salience is low and the corresponding strategies when it is more realistic occurs for the following reason. As we will see from computer simulations, the configuration of equilibrium strategies varies continuously as the policy parameter a varies over the range suggested by analysis of real-world elections. Furthermore, as $a \rightarrow 0$, it is observed that each candidate k's equilibrium strategy $s_k(a) \rightarrow s_k(0)$, where the latter is given by equation 4.2. Accordingly, the configuration of the $s_k(0)$ is a good guide to the configurations when a is substantially above zero.

Note that the $s_k(0), k = 1, \ldots, K$, do not specify equilibrium values; rather, each $s_k(0)$ will be shown to be a component of the equilibrium position $s_k(a)$ of the kth candidate when the policy salience coefficient is not zero. We will provide an explicit algebraic formula for $s_k(0)$ and an approximate

---

[2] Note that $P_{ik}(\mathbf{s}, a)$ is independent of $\mathbf{s}$, when $a = 0$.

formula for the residual component of $s_k(a)$, that is, for the difference $s_k(a) - s_k(0)$.

The values $s_k(0)$ are given in Theorem 4.1 by a formula that involves exactly five determinants: (1) the mean ideal location μ_k of the candidate's partisans; (2) the proportion m_k of all voters who identify with the candidate's party; (3) the proportion m_0 of independent voters; (4) K, the number of candidates; and (5) the value of the partisan salience parameter b. As we will see, this result permits us – under rather general conditions – to approximate Nash equilibrium strategies in terms of a small number of parameters and to delineate the nature of the effect of each determinant on the optimal strategy.

Theorem 4.1. If the mean μ_0 of the independent voters is the same as the overall mean μ_V, then

$$s_k(0) = \mu_V + c_k(\mu_k - \mu_V) \tag{4.3}$$

where

$$c_k = \frac{(K-2)(e^b - 1)m_k}{(K-2)(e^b - 1)m_k + (e^b + K - 2) + m_0\left[(e^b + K - 1)^2\left(\frac{K-1}{K^2}\right) - (e^b + K - 2)\right]}. \tag{4.4}$$

Proof. See Appendix 4.2.

We employ computer simulation to investigate the relation between the optimal strategies $s_k(a)$ and the quantities $s_k(0)$ we have just described. We find that the residuals, $s_k(a) - s_k(0)$, increase as a increases and are roughly proportional to $a\sqrt{s_k(0)}$.[3] Thus the optimal strategies at equilibrium – which are distinct from each other, even for a very low degree of policy salience – expand gradually as policy salience increases. Figures 4.1A and 4.1B each depict this expansion of strategies as the policy salience parameter a increases for two five-party simulated electorates. For these examples, the partisan salience parameter b was set at 2.0 – about the value we estimated in our empirical application to the 1988 French presidential election reported in Chapter 3 (see Table 3.1); there are no independent voters; and the mean locations of the candidates' partisan constituencies were set at $\mu_1 = -2$, $\mu_2 = -1$, $\mu_3 = 0$, $\mu_4 = +1$, and $\mu_5 = +2$. In Figure 4.1A, all parties are of equal size; in Figure 4.1B, the center-left and center-right parties are

---

[3] For the special case when $b = 0$, this result holds only for small values of a.

4.1A. Five parties of equal size

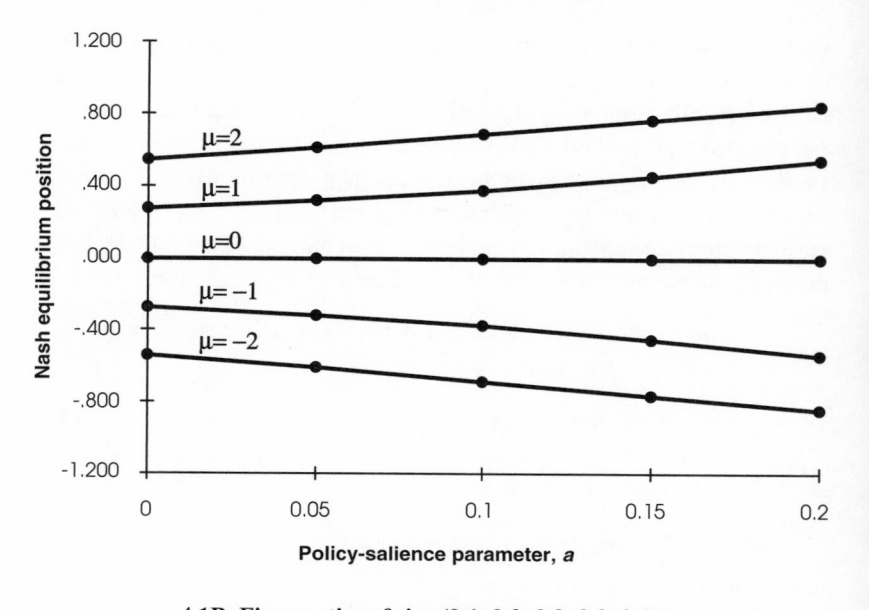

4.1B. Five parties of size (0.1, 0.3, 0.2, 0.3, 0.1)

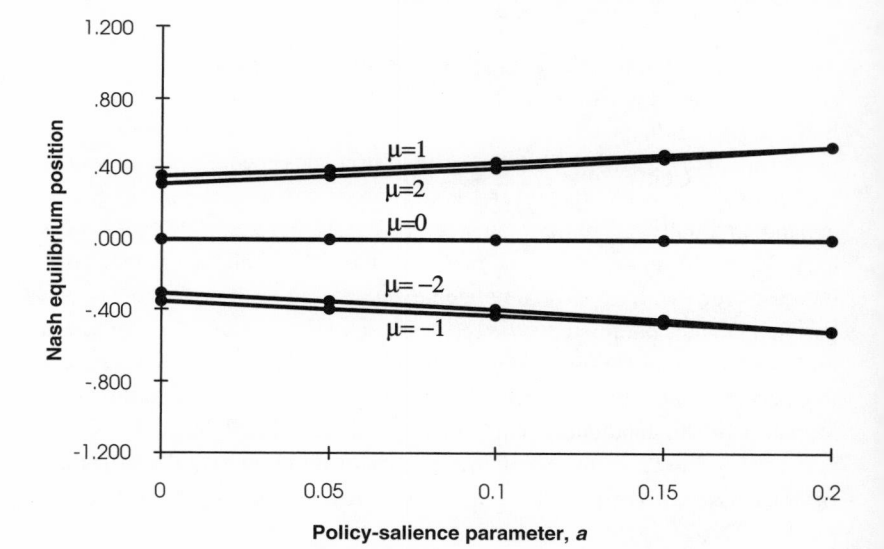

Figure 4.1. Nash equilibrium positions versus the policy-salience parameter, a (simulated data).

substantially larger than the two extreme parties – a pattern that conforms to the empirical distribution of French voters' party identifications to be examined later. Note that in the latter scenarios, the optimal strategies at equilibrium of the two large parties are slightly more extreme than those of the two small extreme parties. This outcome is to be expected from Theorem 4.1, as we will see in section 4.3.1. As will be demonstrated in our empirical analyses in later chapters, when the partisan salience coefficient is incorporated into the voting model, the estimated policy-salience parameter a is typically in the range from 0.1 to 0.2, when voters and candidates are located along the 1–7 policy scales that are often used in voter surveys in France and the United States. For this range, the plots in Figure 4.1B suggest that for a large party, the equilibrium strategy is about one-half as extreme (relative to the voter mean) as the mean location of its partisans; and for a small party, it is on the order of one-quarter as extreme. Thus in either case, we expect that, consistent with the illustrative examples presented in Chapter 3, a party's optimal strategy will be to take an intermediate position between the mean location of all voters and the mean location of that party's partisans.

The simulations also suggest that the residuals are roughly proportional to the variance of the overall voter distribution and to $\ln(K - 1)$, where K is the number of parties. The most important implication of the computer simulations is that the optimal strategies $s_k(a)$ are closely related to the quantities $s_k(0)$, for which we have an explicit formula given by Theorem 4.1. An approximation formula derived from Theorem 4.1 and these simulations is presented in Appendix 4.3.

4.3. Centrifugal Incentives for Candidate Strategies

We are now equipped to consider the question: What does the theorem imply about policy strategies for vote-seeking candidates? We note that for the special case when partisanship does not influence the vote – that is, when $b = 0$ – it follows from equation 4.4 that $c_k = 0$ and hence that the quantity $s_k(0)$ will be μ_V. Therefore, if the policy-salience parameter a is near zero, the candidate optima $s_k(a)$ will be near $s_k(0)$ and thus agglomerated at or very near the center, a result consistent with work by Lin, Enelow, and Dorussen (1999) for multicandidate probabilistic spatial voting (see also de Palma et al. 1989; Adams 1999a). If, however, a is not near zero in such a policy-only model – a likely scenario in a realistic model with no partisanship term – an equilibrium agglomerated at the center may be far from unique, leading to great uncertainty in predicting outcomes (see Chapter 3, note 13).

Although we focus in this chapter on multicandidate competition, a significant implication of Theorem 4.1 is that in two-candidate elections, we can expect convergence of the party positions at equilibrium even if there is a partisanship effect. This conclusion follows from equation 4.4, which implies that for two-candidate elections $(K = 2)$, $c_k = 0$ even if the partisanship parameter $b > 0$. Hence, by equation 4.3, $s_k(0) = \mu_V$. Thus two-candidate equilibria will be agglomerated, a conclusion consistent with results reported by Erikson and Romero (1990) for two-candidate probabilistic spatial voting with measured nonpolicy influences. In Chapters 7 and 8, we will study two-candidate competition and show that in the presence of nonpolicy factors, the threat of abstention may imply divergence of candidate positions at equilibrium.

As we would expect, matters are quite different for the more general case where competition involves three or more candidates and voters display partisan biases (i.e., $b > 0$). In this situation, it is easily verified from equation 4.4 that the shrinking factor c_k is strictly greater than 0 and less than 1,[4] and hence by equation 4.3, $s_k(0)$ lies strictly between the overall mean voter ideal point and the mean position μ_k of the party's partisans. We conclude that for multicandidate competition, *when voters display partisan biases, each candidate's vote-maximizing position is shifted away from the center, in the direction of the mean position of her partisans but not as extreme as that mean*.[5] Recall that this is the same substantive conclusion suggested by our illustrative arguments presented in Chapter 3. Although this result may seem intuitively compelling, a pure spatial model, even with a probabilistic component, does not predict it.

Why, specifically, are vote-seeking candidates motivated to shift away from the center in the direction of their partisans? The reason is that the marginal change in a candidate's probability of attracting her own partisans' votes via policy appeals is higher than is the marginal change in her probability of attracting rival candidates' partisans. To understand why this is true, note that the properties of the conditional logit probability function imply that the weight w_{ik} that a candidate k attaches to a voter i's

---

[4] This is because the denominator in equation 4.4 is equal to the numerator plus two positive terms.

[5] Note, however, that this analysis assumes that voters do not discount the parties' abilities to implement their announced policies. If voters do discount the parties' policy statements, then the parties' optimal positions may be more extreme than their partisans' mean preferences, as in illustrative example 3 in Chapter 3.

policy preference is maximal when the probability that i votes for k is 0.5.[6] In multicandidate competition, the highest of a voter's vote probabilities must be the one nearest to 0.5, and hence the voter is most marginal with respect to the candidate he is most likely to support. Because, ceteris paribus, partisan voters are more likely to vote for their party's candidate than for a rival party's candidate, candidates attach greater weight to their own partisans' beliefs than to the beliefs of rival parties' partisans. Therefore, these candidates' optima will be shaded in the direction of their partisans' preferences.

4.3.1. The Quantitative Effects of Model Parameters

We next consider the question: What factors determine how far candidates' optima diverge from the mean voter position μ_V? We begin by considering the effects of two variables – the policy salience parameter a and the population variance parameter σ_V^2 – whose relationship to party positioning has been analyzed in empirical studies. As we show in Appendix 4.3 (and illustrate in Figure 4.1 and later empirically in Figure 4.2), when voters exhibit partisan biases (i.e., $b > 0$), the candidates tend to shift further away from the center with increases in a and increases in σ_V^2. *Hence the more voters emphasize policies and the more dispersed the electorate's policy preferences, the more extreme the candidates' optimal positions.* The latter result on population variance is consistent with previous theoretical work by Cox (1990) and makes intuitive sense: The more dispersed the distribution of voters' ideal points, the more dispersed we should expect vote-seeking candidates' positions to be at equilibrium. In addition, these theoretical results are supported by two empirical studies on party behavior. Alvarez, Nagler, and Willette's (2000) study of party positioning and voting behavior in four Western European democracies finds that the more voters emphasize policies, the more dispersed the parties' policy positions become.[7] Furthermore, Adams and colleagues' (forthcoming) study of party

---

[6] These weights w_{ik} are given by $w_{ik} = \frac{P_{ik}(s,0)[1-P_{ik}(s,0)]}{\sum P_{jk}(s,0)[1-P_{jk}(s,0)]}$. The statement that the w_{ik} weights are maximal when the probability that i votes for k is 0.5 is also true for the multinomial probit (MNP) probability function, in the general case where the correlations between the error terms associated with voters' candidate utilities are set to zero and the error terms have equal variances.

[7] We note that Alvarez and colleagues interpret their results as implying that dispersed party positioning along a policy dimension motivates voters to attach increased salience to that dimension – that is, that voters change their decision rules in response to parties' policy

positioning in eight Western European democracies reports findings that support our prediction that parties' policy dispersion increases with the dispersion of the voter distribution.

With respect to the partisan mean μ_k, it follows from equation 4.3 and our computer simulations that $s_k(0)$, and hence the $s_k(a)$, expand with μ_k. Therefore, *the more extreme the position of a candidate's partisans, the more extreme the candidate's optimal position.*[8]

The remaining four variables relevant to candidate equilibria – m_k, m_0, K, and b – also influence the candidates' optima through their effect upon $s_k(0)$. Theorem 4.1 establishes that the values $s_k(0)$ are obtained by shrinking μ_k – the mean divergence of candidate k's partisans from the voter mean – by a factor c_k, so that values of c_k near 1.0 indicate that $s_k(0)$ is near μ_k, while values of c_k near zero indicate that $s_k(0)$ is near the overall voter mean μ_V.

Next, we consider the effect of each of the variables m_k, m_0, K, and b upon c_k. First, the shrinkage coefficient c_k given by equation 4.4 increases with m_k, the proportion of candidate k's partisans (see section 4.4.1 in Appendix 4.4 for the proof). Thus *the larger the candidate's partisan constituency, the more extreme the candidate's optimal position.* In particular, small parties that have an extreme constituency may face a quandary. The optimal strategy of such a party, given our model, may be near the center – perhaps nearer the center than the positions of larger, more moderate parties – but such a strategy would seriously undermine the credibility of the small party and would not represent the expressive motivations of its constituents.

Second, the mathematical expression given on the right-hand side of equation 4.4 implies that there is no clear-cut relationship between increases in the partisan-salience parameter b and the degree to which candidates present extreme, as opposed to centrist, policies. If $m_0 = 0$, then c_k increases as b increases throughout the range of b (see item 2 in Appendix 4.4 for the proof). When $m_0 > 0$, however, numerical calculation of c_k for a range of values of b shows that c_k increases with b as long as b does not exceed about 2 or 3 (depending on the values of m_0), but declines thereafter. Since empirical

positioning, rather than vice versa. While it is beyond the scope of our study to parse out the causal relationships in voter–party interactions, the fact remains that the empirical patterns that Alvarez and his colleagues identify are consistent with our theoretical results.

[8] As can be seen from the proof of Theorem 4.1, the values of $s_k(0)$ – but not $s_k(a)$ – depend on the distributions of the partisan constituencies only through their means, μ_k; they do not depend on other aspects of the distributions, such as variance or skewness.

studies suggest that the values of b in historical elections usually fall below this cutoff point, this suggests that *candidate optima typically become more extreme as partisan salience increases.*[9]

With respect to the number K of candidates, for any $b > 0$, c_k increases in value as K increases (see item 3 in Appendix 4.4 for the proof). Thus *the more candidates there are, other things being equal, the more extreme the candidates' optimal positions.* We note that this conclusion is consistent with theoretical results on spatial competition for deterministic policy voting obtained by Cox (1990), who finds that for a variety of electoral systems incentives for policy dispersion increase with the number of competitors.

Finally, simple algebra shows that the coefficient of m_0 (the proportion of independent voters) in the expression for c_k is positive if $b > 0$ and $K \geq 3$. That is to say, *ceteris paribus, optimal strategies become more centrist as the proportion of independents increases.* This is not unexpected, because, as noted earlier, previous results by Lin, Enelow, and Dorussen (1999) have established that if all voters are independents and if the policy component a is sufficiently small, then the overall voter mean is a Nash equilibrium for all candidates.

To our knowledge, no empirical studies have appeared that explore the relationship between the variables μ_k, m_k, m_0, K, b, and party positioning in real-world elections; therefore, previous research does not provide us with an empirical basis for evaluating our theoretical results relating to these variables. However, we shall explore these empirical relationships in the subsequent empirical chapters of this book.

Finally, we emphasize two caveats about our use of the terms "centrist" and "extreme" in the previous discussion. First, these terms are defined relative to the mean position of the electorate rather than against some independent ideological standard. For instance, if the electorate is overwhelmingly Marxist in orientation, then candidates that reflect the electorate's views are considered centrist relative to the voter distribution (see, e.g., Cox 1990: 213). The second, related point is that when we speak of candidates becoming "more extreme" in response to changes in the election variables K, m_k, and

---

[9] While behavioral researchers disagree sharply about the electoral impact of partisanship (see Converse and Pierce 1993; Fleury and Lewis-Beck 1993; Lewis-Beck and Chlarsen 2002), the empirical estimates of b noted earlier typically vary between approximately $b = 1$ and $b = 2.5$, suggesting that, if a remains constant, increases in b will usually be associated with increases in c_k.

Table 4.1. *Characteristics of partisans and equilibrium positions on the Left–Right scale: 1988 French presidential election (N = 748)*

Candidate (1)	Proportion of Partisans (2)	Mean Placement of Candidate (3)	Mean Location of Partisans (4)	Standard Deviations of Partisans (5)	Exact Equilibrium Positions (6)	Approximate Equilibrium Positions (Formula A4.8) (7)
Lajoinie	6.6%	1.90	2.24	0.83	3.69	3.70
Mitterrand	39.2%	3.09	3.08	0.69	3.52	3.48
Barre	13.5%	4.81	4.85	0.68	4.24	4.23
Chirac	18.0%	5.55	5.36	0.71	4.44	4.43
Le Pen	4.5%	6.57	6.03	1.17	4.23	4.21
Other	18.2%	–	4.02	1.01	–	–
a (Policy salience)					0.204	
b (Partisan salience)					2.14	
Log-likelihood					–622.6	

Note: Partisans are defined as identifiers of the parties represented by the candidates indicated. The category *other* includes identifiers of other parties as well as those respondents who did not identify with any party.

so on, this denotes only that the parties are shifting away from the voter mean, not that their positions are extreme in some absolute sense.

4.4. An Empirical Illustration

We illustrate the relationships described in section 4.3 with data drawn from the 1988 French Presidential Election Study (Pierce 1996), first introduced in Chapter 3, section 3.4. Because this election featured five major candidates (Lajoinie, Mitterrand, Barre, Chirac, and Le Pen), it provides a good test of the expected divergence of optimal strategies in the presence of a large candidate field. The study obtained both self-placements and candidate placements from respondents on the Left–Right dimension, which taps into economic policy, as well as partisan self-identifications. Because the French election is a presidential election between candidates rather than between parties (as would be the case in a proportional representation system), partisan identification is not the same as candidate preference and hence represents a partially independent factor affecting voter choice.[10]

Using the respondents' self-placements on the Left–Right dimension (N = 748) for voter ideal points, their mean candidate placements for the candidates' actual positions, their reported vote choices, and their partisan self-identifications, we estimated the policy and partisan parameters a and b from maximum likelihood in a conditional logit model. These and the log-likelihoods are reported in the bottom three rows of Table 4.1. We also computed the mean positions and the standard deviations of each candidate's partisan constituency as well as the proportions of partisans in each constituency (see Table 4.1, columns 2–5).[11] Note that the standard deviations of the partisan constituencies are in the vicinity of 0.5 to 1.0, the range we used in the simulations reported in Appendix 4.3. We computed both the candidates' exact equilibrium positions (using the algorithm presented in Appendix 4.1)[12] and their approximate equilibrium positions

---

[10] In the 1988 French Presidential Election Study, 19 percent of the self-identified French partisans reported voting for a candidate from a different party.

[11] The distribution of these partisan constituencies was pictured earlier in Chapter 3, Figure 3.4.

[12] In order to assess the validity of criterion A4.6 for uniqueness of the Nash equilibrium according to Theorem A4.1 (see Appendix 4.1), the Jacobian norm was evaluated numerically at 100 randomly chosen configurations of potential strategies within the interval from 1 to 7 that encompasses the voter distribution. All but three values were found to be less than 1.0. These three were near the edge of the distribution, far away from likely locations of an equilibrium, suggesting that it is very probable that the criterion for convergence to a unique Nash equilibrium is satisfied in the region of interest.

(as calculated by formula A4.8 in Appendix 4.3). These values are reported in columns 6 and 7 of Table 4.1. As expected from our simulations, we find that the French candidates' equilibrium positions and their approximate equilibrium locations obtained from formula A4.8 are quite similar, with no candidate's actual computed optimum differing from the position predicted by the formula by more than 0.04 units along the 1–7 Left–Right scale.

Each candidate's optimum is similar to but less extreme than the mean position of his partisan constituency, results consistent with our theoretical analysis.[13] Mitterrand's optimum is about one-half as extreme as his partisan constituency, while Chirac's is about one-third as extreme. Note that the optimal policy locations of Lajoinie and Le Pen, the candidates with small constituencies, are substantially closer to the center than are the policy optima for Mitterrand and Chirac, who represent larger constituencies. This is to be expected in light of our theoretical conclusion that larger partisan constituencies exercise greater centrifugal effects on candidate strategies. The more extreme actual positions of Lajoinie and Le Pen suggest, however, that other incentives, such as policy motivations (see Chapters 11 and 12), exert further centrifugal effects on candidate positions.

Figures 4.2A–4.2C show how the candidates' equilibrium positions vary with changes in a, b, and μ_k.[14] Consistent with our previous simulation results, we located equilibria for all values of the parameters that we investigated. This suggests that an equilibrium is to be expected for the 1988 French presidential election, given realistic voting parameters.

Consistent with the simulation results we report in Appendix 4.3, we find that candidate strategies become more extreme as policy voting increases, with the optima expanding roughly linearly with increases in a; that is, the distance from party optima to the voter mean is roughly a linear function of the variable a. We find, also consistent with our theoretical and simulation analyses, that for $b \leq 2$, increases in the electoral salience of partisanship exercise moderate centrifugal effects on candidate strategies, with the candidates adopting more extreme positions as voters become

---

[13] As reported in Chapter 5 (see section 5.5), extension of the model to incorporate voter discounting of candidate positions implies that the optimal strategies of the three major candidates are nearer to the positions of their partisan constituencies.

[14] In these calculations, all election parameters were held constant at their observed values as reported in Table 4.1, except for the single parameter of interest.

4.2A. Equilibrium as a function of the policy-salience parameter

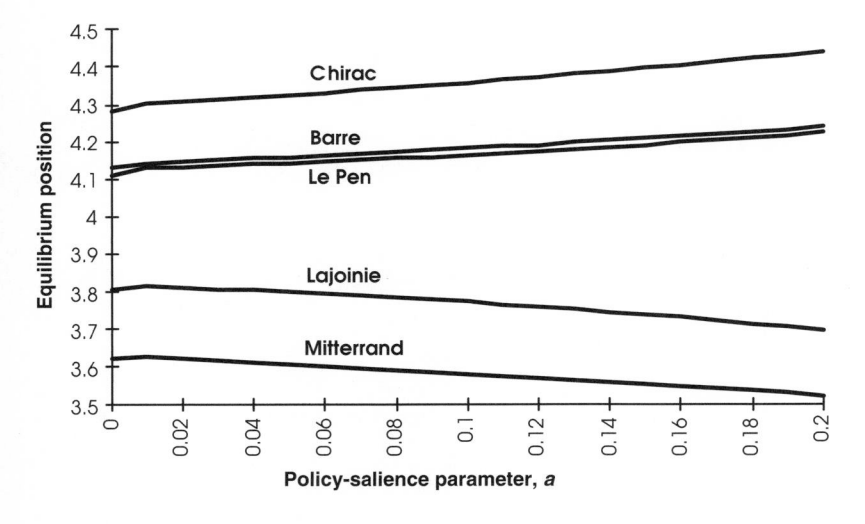

4.2B. Equilibrium as a function of the partisan-salience parameter

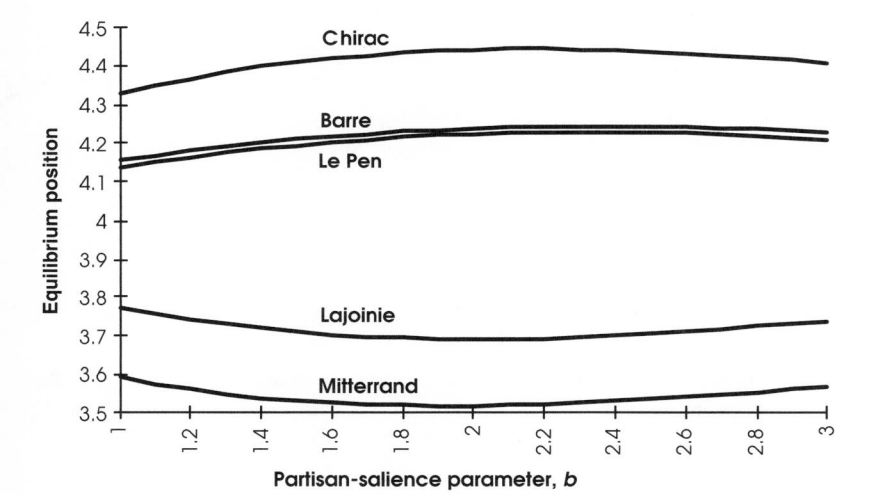

Figure 4.2. Equilibrium positions of candidates in the 1988 French presidential election, as functions of each of the three parameters.

4.2C. Equilibrium as a function of the spread of the voter distribution

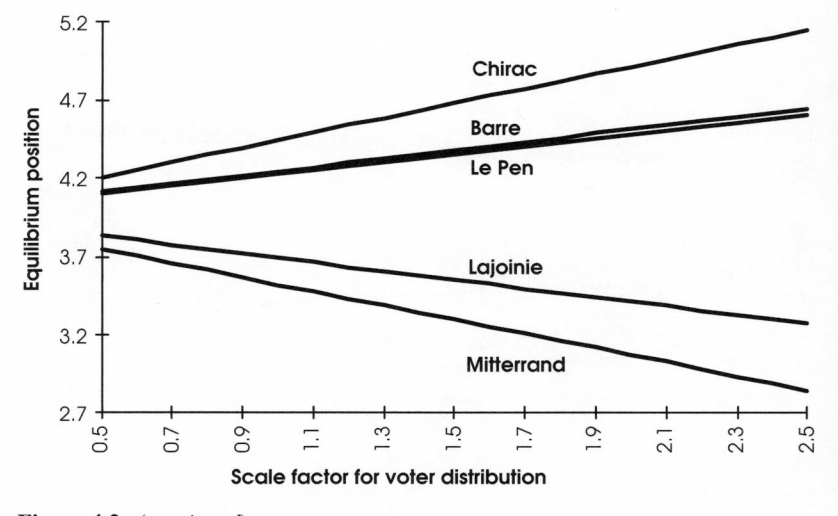

Figure 4.2. (*continued*)

increasingly partisan. The plots in Figure 4.2B, however, show that this effect is nonlinear and that, in particular, in a wide range from about $b = 1$ to $b = 3$ there is very little change in the equilibrium positions. Thus if, for example, our empirical estimates for the partisan effect are unrealistically high, our conclusions about the dispersed nature of equilibrium locations are not affected. These results also support our conclusion that vote-seeking candidates have incentives to shift in the direction of their partisans' beliefs. Figure 4.2C shows how equilibrium configurations vary as a function of the mean positions μ_k of the candidates' constituencies. For this exercise, the positions of all partisan voters were multiplied by a scale factor, which we varied between 0.5 and 2.5.[15] As expected, Figure 4.2C shows that the candidate optima become more extreme with increases in the scale factor. This supports our theoretical conclusion that the more extreme the positions of parties' partisans, the more extreme the parties' vote-maximizing positions.

---

[15] Because $a\sigma_V^2$ is invariant under changes in scale, the policy-salience parameter, a, was varied inversely with the square of the scale factor.

4.5. Robustness of Equilibrium Positions to the Salience of Partisanship

Here we explore whether our substantive conclusions about party strategies are robust to alternative assumptions about the electoral salience of party identification, a variable that is central to our theoretical and empirical analyses. We are aware that our values for the partisan-salience parameter b are subject to measurement and statistical error. Partisanship, furthermore, is endogenous to any analysis of policy effects on voter utility and party competition, because party ID is influenced by long-term policy affinity between voter and party. Still, voters typically give the benefit of the doubt (see Feld and Grofman 1991) to parties and candidates with whom they traditionally identify, particularly on issues with which they are less familiar or on which the party elite may be changing its stand. Thus given these cross-currents, the effects of partisanship on voter utility that are independent of current party policy – although positive – may be substantively lower than the values estimated by our conditional logit model (see Appendix 2.2). We therefore ask the question: If party ID had a significantly smaller impact than we have estimated, would this change our substantive conclusions about vote-seeking parties' policy strategies?

The surprising answer to this question is *no*. Specifically, we find that even if the "true" salience of partisanship is only a fraction of what we estimate it to be, the vote-maximizing equilibrium configuration in the 1988 French presidential election would hardly be changed.[16] Thus we conclude that our substantive findings on parties' policy strategies are indeed robust to alternative assumptions about the electoral salience of party ID.[17]

As reported in Table 4.1, the estimated parameters for the partisan voting model are $a = .204$, $b = 2.14$ for the first round of voting in the 1988 French presidential election. We reestimated the value of a, with b fixed at half its value, obtaining $a = .300$ and $b = 1.07$. The equilibrium positions of the candidates given in Table 4.2 are almost identical to (and in fact slightly

---

[16] Similar analyses for Norway, Britain, and the United States lead to the same conclusion.

[17] We also explored candidate strategies for an alternative voting model that included – in addition to party ID and Left–Right distance – candidate-specific intercepts, which plausibly capture voters' valence-related evaluations of the candidates (see Appendix 3.1). The equilibrium we obtained for this model (based on the empirically estimated vote model parameters) was similar to the equilibrium configuration reported in Table 4.1, although Le Pen's equilibrium position was somewhat more centrist and Lajoinie's somewhat more extreme.

Table 4.2. *Equilibrium configurations for France, for alternative assumptions about the electoral salience of party ID*

Vote Model Parameters	Lajoinie	Mitterrand	Chirac	Barre	Le Pen
$b = .000, a = .414$	3.98	3.98	3.98	3.98	3.98
$b = .535, a = .356$	3.54	3.45	4.25	4.49	4.25
$b = 1.07, a = .300$	3.59	3.46	4.26	4.49	4.25
$b = 2.14, a = .204$	**3.69**	**3.52**	**4.24**	**4.44**	**4.23**

Note: The Left–Right policy salience parameter a was estimated, while the partisan-salience parameter b was held at one-half, one-fourth, and zero times its actual estimated value. The fourth line (in bold) represents the actual estimates.

more extreme than) those for the full value of the partisan-salience parameter $b = 2.14$. Furthermore, this pattern persists even if b is reduced to one-fourth of its value (see Table 4.2 and Figure 4.3). We conclude that even if the true impact of party ID on the vote were much less than that suggested by our empirical estimates, our substantive conclusions on candidate strategies would be unchanged.

Why are equilibrium strategies robust to alternative assumptions about the electoral salience of party ID? Intuitively, our finding that party strategies are similar over a wide range of values of the partisan-salience parameter b appears surprising. Given our theoretical argument that partisan biases motivate vote-seeking parties to shift their policies in the direction of their partisan constituencies, it seems plausible that the degree of policy dispersion should be tied to the strength of voters' partisan biases (see section 4.3.1). Yet our computations do not support this intuition. In fact, we find that as the impact of partisanship decreases to levels 50 percent to 75 percent less than our empirical estimates, equilibrium positions become slightly more *dispersed*. What accounts for this counterintuitive result?

The intuition underlying our finding can be understood by considering the extreme scenario in which every partisan is so strongly biased that she votes for her party regardless of its policy position. For this "party ID dominant" scenario, it is obvious that vote-seeking parties should target independent voters, since independents are the only bloc whose support is truly in play; and with all parties targeting the same voting bloc, the parties can be expected to converge to similar policy strategies. This is the same result we obtain for the policy-only voting model. Thus partisan voting constituencies exert the maximum centrifugal "pull" on their parties' policy strategies when voters

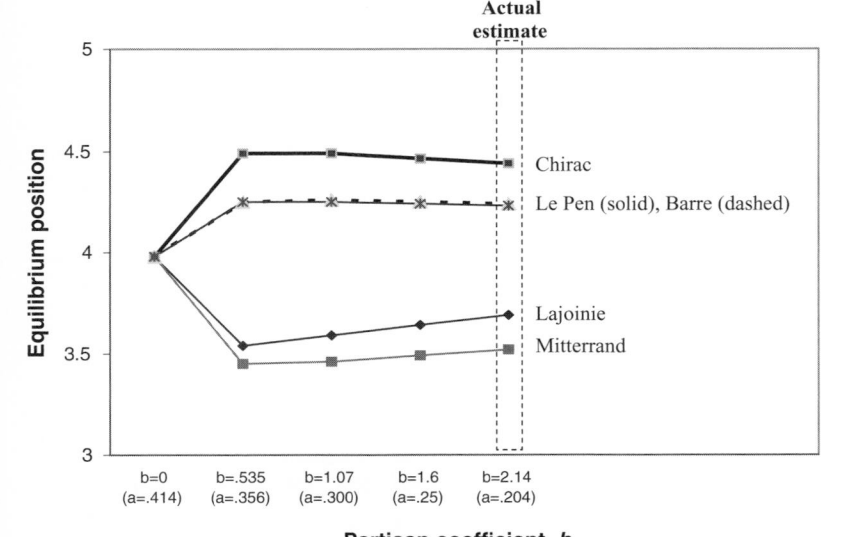

Figure 4.3. Candidate equilibrium in the 1988 French presidential election, with the partisan-salience parameter, *b*, fixed at alternative values.
Note: These parameters were determined by estimating the value of the policy-salience parameter *a* for alternative fixed values of the partisan-salience parameter, *b*. The values ($a = 204$, $b = 2.14$) represent the actual parameter estimates for voting in the 1988 French presidential election, when *b* was not fixed at a specific value.

are influenced by partisanship, but are not so blindly loyal that party elites can take partisans' support for granted.

However, the intuition just outlined is only part of the story. The other part revolves around the connection between the strength of partisanship, as reflected in the value of the partisan-salience coefficient *b*, and the value of the policy-salience coefficient *a*. Specifically, the results reported in Table 4.2 (see column 1) show that the lower the fixed value of *b*, the higher the estimated value of *a* – that is, there is an inverse relationship between the electoral impact of partisanship and the estimated electoral impact of policies.[18] This is important because, as discussed in section 4.2.1 (see also Appendix 4.3), candidate dispersion tends to increase with the electoral salience of policies.

[18] Intuitively, this occurs because survey respondents' partisanship and policy preferences are correlated (though not identical), so that when the partisan-salience coefficient is set at unrealistically low levels, part of the electoral influence that was formerly attributed to party ID is transferred to voters' policy preferences.

Thus when we set the partisan-salience coefficient to a low value and then re-compute the policy-salience coefficient on this basis, the effect is to increase the estimated salience of policies, thereby creating additional incentives for vote-seeking candidates to diverge along the Left–Right dimension. It is for this reason that our computed policy equilibria for France are actually slightly *more* dispersed when we set the partisan salience coefficient to very low levels, compared to the equilibria we obtain when the partisan salience parameter is set at its empirically estimated value.

4.6. Discussion

We conclude that in multicandidate elections, vote-seeking candidates are motivated to shift away from the center in the direction of their partisans' policy beliefs, and that *increases* in the following variables motivate candidates to take more extreme positions relative to the center of the voter distribution: (1) the electoral salience of policies, (2) the electoral salience of partisanship,[19] (3) the dispersion of the electorate's policy preferences, and (4) the size of the candidate field; and, for each candidate, (5) the size of the candidate's partisan constituency, and (6) the extremity of the positions of the candidate's partisans. However, an increase in the number of independent voters provides a centripetal rather than a centrifugal incentive.[20]

While our results on the centrifugal incentives associated with increases in the number of parties and the electoral salience of policies have been anticipated in the spatial modeling literature,[21] our conclusions on the centrifugal

---

[19] We note that these strategic incentives relating to changes in the electoral salience of either policies or partisanship hold, provided that the value of the other of these two variables is fixed. As discussed in section 4.5 in this chapter, if, in empirical applications to election survey data, the electoral salience of partisanship (policies) is increased and the salience of policies (partisanship) is reestimated on this basis, then the candidates may be motivated to take more moderate positions relative to the center of the voter distribution.

[20] We also find that the candidates' equilibrium positions can be predicted with great accuracy from a formula involving seven parameters $(a, b, m_k, m_o, \mu_k, K, \sigma_V^2)$, with the mean error of the predictions in our simulations falling below 0.025 policy units for each candidate along the 1–7 policy scale. This formula is given in equation A4.8 in Appendix 4.3.

[21] As noted earlier, our conclusion on the centrifugal effects associated with increases in the number of parties has been anticipated by Cox (1990; see also Eaton and Lipsey 1975), and our conclusion on the centrifugal effects associated with increases in the salience of policies has been anticipated by Lin, Enelow, and Dorussen (1999; see also de Palma et al. 1989; de Palma, Hong, and Thisse 1990; Adams 1999b). In addition, while we are unaware of previous work on multicandidate elections that explores the effects of increasing the dispersion of the electorate's policy preferences, it strikes us as common sense to expect an increase in voter dispersion to create centrifugal incentives for candidates.

effects associated with increases in the partisan-related variables b, m_k, and μ_k have not.

In general, we find that parties/candidates maximize votes by presenting policies similar to *but less extreme than* their partisans' beliefs. Thus, in real-world multiparty elections, vote-seeking parties and candidates should moderate their policies relative to the views of party supporters. When we do not observe this moderation taking place – as we often do not for smaller parties on the ideological fringe, such as the French Communists and National Front, the German Greens, and the Norwegian Progress Party – we may speculate that these parties are forgoing electoral gains in pursuit of alternative goals, such as policy objectives. (It also may be the case that such parties cannot attempt to maximize their support by moderating their policies without forfeiting both their credibility and the policy goals of their activists.) Alternatively, it is possible that these parties are responding to voter discounting of the parties' ability to implement their announced policies, a factor that we explore in later chapters.

Thus, even though we have developed a seven-variable model, the large number of further potentially complicating factors suggests that we should treat our conclusions on candidate strategies with some caution. In particular, we note again that a complete understanding of parties' or candidates' policy proposals in historical elections must move beyond an exclusive focus on vote maximization to encompass the party elites' policy motivations and the electoral costs involved (in terms of credibility) in changing the party's policy program (see Chapters 11 and 12), their calculations about postelection governing coalitions (see Chapter 6), and the electoral laws in effect in the real-world election of interest (see Cox 1990, 1997; Dow 2001). As noted earlier, we must also consider the strategic implications of voter discounting of the parties' ability to implement their announced policies (see Chapters 5 and 6). These considerations notwithstanding, most analysts believe that because votes are very important to politicians, the electoral incentives we have analyzed in this chapter should be a major factor driving the policy decisions of political elites. Thus our conclusions about the factors affecting centrifugal and centripetal incentives in multiparty elections shed considerable light on the strategic logic of party and candidate competition – and on the observed policy behavior of parties and candidates in actual multiparty elections.

CHAPTER 5

Policy Competition under the Unified Theory

Empirical Applications to the 1988 French Presidential Election

5.1. Introduction

In this chapter, we report further empirical applications to the 1988 French presidential election, which provide tests of the theoretical arguments presented in Chapters 3 and 4. These analyses move beyond the empirical results on France presented earlier, in that here we explore candidate competition under more complex voting models that incorporate multiple policy dimensions and numerous nonpolicy motivations in addition to partisanship. We also discuss whether the French political context plausibly motivated voters to discount the presidential candidates' capacity to implement the policy positions they advocated. Such discounting would lead voters to prefer candidates who proposed policies that were more extreme than the voters' own beliefs – that is, policies that when discounted or moderated would be in line with the voters' preferences. We present empirical results suggesting that French voters did indeed behave as if they discounted candidates' positions in the 1988 presidential election.

For each multidimensional model that we investigate – a policy-only model, a unified model that includes nonpolicy as well as policy factors, and a unified discounting model that includes voter discounting of candidate positions in addition to policy and nonpolicy factors – we report equilibrium analyses, and we compare the candidates' equilibrium positions to their actual advocated policies as perceived by the voters. We also explore whether these alternative voting models gave the candidates electoral incentives to represent faithfully their partisans' policy beliefs, the linkage that underlies the responsible party model of policy representation.

Our results are consistent with the theoretical and empirical results on the 1988 French presidential election presented in Chapters 3 and 4: namely, we find that a multidimensional version of the policy-only voting model motivates the candidates to converge to centrist policies that do not match their actual positioning. By contrast, we find that the unified model that includes measured nonpolicy variables motivates the candidates to diverge from the center in the direction of their partisan constituencies, although the degree of divergence is less than what was actually observed in this historical election. Finally, we find that the unified discounting model provides fairly convincing accounts of the candidates' strategies – and of mass–elite policy linkages – for the candidates of the three largest French parties (Mitterrand, Barre, and Chirac).

5.2. The Context of the 1988 French Presidential Election

The Constitution of the French Fifth Republic, which dates to 1958, specifies a mixed premier-presidential system. As is the case in U.S. politics, in France it is possible for the presidency to be occupied by a representative of one party while the National Assembly, the popularly elected house of the French legislature, is controlled by a rival party or coalition (Pierce 1995). In the period leading up to 1988, French parliamentary politics revolved around the relative strengths of two opposing coalitions: a left-wing bloc consisting of parliamentary representatives of the Socialist and Communist Parties, and a right-wing bloc that included representatives of the Union for French Democracy (UDF) and the Rally for the Republic (RPR). For the two years preceding the 1988 election, the Socialist Francois Mitterrand held the presidency, while the right-wing UDF–RPR coalition controlled the National Assembly. As a result, Mitterrand selected a right-wing prime minister, Jacques Chirac, the leader of the RPR. The resulting period of "cohabitation" from 1986 to 1988 was a first in French politics.

French presidential elections are conducted using a two-stage system, with the top two candidates from the first round advancing to a runoff election held two weeks later.[1] The first round of voting in the 1988 election, held on

---

[1] If a first-round candidate wins a majority of all valid votes cast, then there is no runoff election. However, this has not occurred in the seven presidential elections conducted using the two-ballot system.

April 24, featured five major candidates, four of whom were leaders of the parties that constitute France's major left- and right-wing coalitions: Andre Lajoinie, leader of the Communist Party (Partie Communiste – PC); Francois Mitterrand, leader of the Socialist Party (Partie Socialiste – PS); Raymond Barre, leader of the center-right UDF; and Jacques Chirac, leader of the right-wing RPR. The fifth major candidate was Jean-Marie Le Pen, the leader of the far right National Front, a party that emerged as a significant electoral force in the early 1980s on a platform of opposition to immigration and advocacy of old-fashioned values concerning religion, country, and family (Safran 1998). Le Pen was viewed as qualitatively different from the other major French candidates because of his implicit appeal to anti-Semitism, his hostility to foreigners (particularly North African Muslims), and his rejection of the "compromise politics" of the Socialists, Communists, UDF, and RPR, whom Le Pen collectively dubbed the "gang of four." As a result, many political elites from the major right-wing parties, the UDF and the RPR, consciously distanced themselves from the National Front, seeking to portray Le Pen as outside the mainstream of French politics.[2] In the event, each of the candidates just listed won at least 7 percent of the valid votes cast, and collectively they won over 90 percent of the vote.[3] In the subsequent runoff election, Mitterrand defeated Chirac, 54 percent to 46 percent. Voter turnout was over 80 percent in both the first and second rounds of voting (Table 5.1).

5.2.1. Ideology and Policy Issues in the 1988 Presidential Election

Ideological debates have traditionally structured political competition in France. From the perspective of political elites, Pierce notes that

the terms left and right are the organizing concepts by which French politicians, political commentators, and scholars alike classify the political parties. These politically attentive groups may be intensely interested in some particular political party at any

---

[2] In fact, some UDF and RPR officials adopted a conciliatory tone toward Le Pen and the National Front, hoping to entice Le Pen supporters to vote for a center-right candidate on the decisive ballot in the 1988 presidential election; however, a majority of political elites argued that the UDF and RPR should have nothing to do with the National Front (see Safran 1998: Chapter 4).

[3] The first round also included four minor candidates, all of whom won less than 4 percent of the valid vote (see Table 5.1). Pierce's 1988 French Presidential Election Study (Pierce 1996) did not include items relating to these candidates; consequently, we cannot evaluate their policy strategies in the 1988 election.

Table 5.1. *French presidential election results, 1988*

	First Ballot[a] (April 24, 1988)	Second Ballot (May 8, 1988)
Francois Mitterrand	34.0%	54.0%
Jacques Chirac	19.8	46.0
Raymond Barre	16.5	
Jean-Marie Le Pen	14.6	
Andre Lajoinie	6.9	
Antione Waechter	3.8	
Pierre Juquin	2.1	
Arlette Laguiller	2.0	
Pierre Boussel	0.3	
Voter turnout	82.0%	84.6%

[a] Candidate vote percentages for both rounds are calculated as a percentage of valid votes cast.

given moment, and from one or more points of view, but that party will inevitably be situated in relation both to the other parties of the same moment and to its historical ancestors in left-right terms. (1995: 61)

Prior empirical research also documents that ideology structures French voters' choices, in that leftist voters consistently support the Socialist and Communist Parties, while voters who hold right-wing beliefs overwhelmingly support traditionally conservative parties (see Converse and Pierce 1986, 1993; Frears 1991; Fleury and Lewis-Beck 1993; Pierce 1995; Lewis-Beck and Chlarson 2002).

Figure 5.1 displays the distribution of the respondents' ideological self-placements and the mean positions ascribed to each candidate for the set of respondents who reported voting in the first round of the election and who could self-place on the Left–Right scale. Note that French respondents perceived a wide range of ideological options, in that they placed the Communist Lajoinie on the far left (on average), Le Pen on the extreme right, and Mitterrand, Barre, and Chirac on the left, center-right, and right, respectively. These respondent placements accord well with experts' placements of the parties' positions (see Huber and Inglehart 1995: 97), thereby supporting Pierce's conclusion (1995: 67–73) that French voters had sharp-edged perceptions of the candidates' ideologies at the time of the 1988 presidential election.

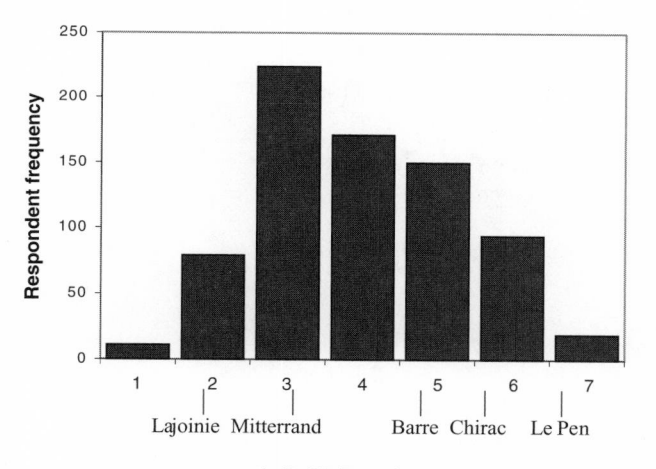

Figure 5.1. Distribution of respondents' ideological self-placements, and their candidate placements, in the 1988 French presidential election.
Note: The distribution of respondents' Left–Right self-placements is given for the 748 respondents in Pierce's 1988 French Presidential Election Study who reported voting for one of the five major candidates and who could place themselves on the Left–Right scale. The positions assigned to the five candidates (Lajoinie, Mitterrand, etc.) represent the mean placements ascribed to these candidates by the respondents.

In addition to Left–Right ideology, the 1988 FPES contained questions on three specific policy dimensions that the candidates debated in the presidential election. The first was an *immigration scale*, which ran from 1 ("We should integrate immigrants into French society") to 7 ("Immigrants should return to their native country"); as mentioned earlier, opposition to immigration was a central theme of Le Pen's National Front. The second dimension was a *public sector scale*, running from 1 ("Supports a large public sector") to 7 ("The role of the state in the economy should be reduced"). This issue represents a long-standing source of disagreement between the left-wing and right-wing parties and was particularly salient in the years leading up to 1988, since in the early 1980s the leftist governing coalition had nationalized dozens of enterprises, many of which were subsequently denationalized by the UDF–RPR coalition that was returned to power in 1986. The third policy dimension was captured via a *church schools scale*, running from 1 ("The state should not subsidize church schools") to 7 ("The state should increase subsidies for church schools"). Approximately 20 percent

Table 5.2. *Candidates' ideological and policy positions on a 1–7 scale, as perceived by the French electorate, 1988* (N = 748)

	Left–Right	Immigration	Public Sector	Church Schools
Mean voter position	3.97	3.76	3.88	4.66
Lajoinie	1.90	2.29	1.93	2.34
Mitterrand	3.09	2.43	2.89	3.57
Barre	4.81	4.07	5.06	5.08
Chirac	5.55	4.54	5.75	5.34
Le Pen	6.57	6.80	5.55	5.16

Source: 1988 French Presidential Election Study.

of French schoolchildren (kindergarten through secondary school) attend parochial schools, and the issue of government subsidies for these schools has long been salient in French politics, with right-wing parties typically favoring generous government funding (see Safran 1998: Chapter 2).[4]

Table 5.2 shows the respondents' mean positions, as well as their mean candidate placements, for the subsample of 748 respondents who reported voting for one of the five major candidates in the first round of the election and who could place themselves on the Left–Right scale. Note that the French public appears centrist (on average) on each dimension, and that the candidates were perceived as taking divergent positions, with the Communist Lajoinie placed on the far left along each dimension, and Le Pen placed at the extreme right on the Left–Right and immigration scales. Mitterrand was viewed as center-left along each dimension, while Barre and Chirac were seen as center-right.

5.3. Candidate Competition under the Policy-Only Model

Table 5.3A, column 1 presents parameter estimates for a policy-only voting specification, with voters' candidate utilities specified as a function of their (squared) distances from each candidate along the ideology and policy scales included in the FPES. Consistent with previous empirical studies of French voting behavior, the Left–Right scale emerges as by far the most salient

---

[4] Note that we have reversed the end points of the policy scales so that the most left-wing response is 1 and the most right-wing response is 7. In addition, we note that the survey did not record respondents' placements of Lajoinie on the three policy scales; we report instead their placements of the Communist Party.

Table 5.3A. *Logit equations predicting the first-round vote, 1988 French presidential election* (N = 748)

	Policy-only	Unified	Unified Discounting
Policy parameters			
Left–Right	**.340**	**.159**	**.179**
	(.024)	(.021)	(.023)
Immigration	**.028**	**.018**	**.028**
	(.010)	(.010)	(.011)
Public sector	**.076**	**.055**	**.051**
	(.012)	(.013)	(.013)
Church schools	**.056**	**.033**	**.029**
	(.014)	(.015)	(.015)
Discounting	1.00	1.00	**0.34**
parameter	–	–	(.11)
Party identification	–	**2.07**	**2.15**
		(.11)	(.12)
Sociodemographic variables			
Class (Chirac)	–	**.33**	**.32**
		(.14)	(.14)
Income (Lajoinie)	–	**.20**	**.28**
		(.17)	(.16)
Sex (Le Pen)	–	**.28**	**.23**
		(.17)	(.16)
Log-likelihood	−822.0	−601.5	−597.4

Table 5.3B. *Projected vote shares for alternative models*

	Lajoinie	Mitterrand	Barre	Chirac	Le Pen
Sample vote	8.8%	41.2%	18.0%	19.1%	12.8%
Policy-only	17.5	28.9	24.5	18.7	9.9
Unified	11.2	38.6	20.0	22.0	8.3
Unified discounting	12.3	37.6	18.4	22.0	9.6

Note: The candidates' expected votes are computed using the coefficients reported in Table 5.3A, using the assumption that each candidate was located at its actual (perceived) position along the Left–Right and policy scales.

dimension of candidate evaluation (see Fleury and Lewis-Beck 1993; Pierce 1995: Chapter 7; Dow 1999; Lewis-Beck and Chlarson 2002). Table 5.3B reports the respondents' expected aggregate votes under the policy-only model (row 2), along with the distribution of the respondents' actual reported

votes.[5] The candidates' expected votes do not closely match the sample vote –
particularly for the leftist candidates, Lajoinie and Mitterrand – indicating
that the policy-only model does not fully capture voter decision making in
the 1988 presidential election.

Table 5.4A (p. 81) reports the alternative equilibrium configurations that
we located for the policy-only voting model. The first configuration finds the
five candidates converging into a single bloc that presents identical centrist
locations along each of the four policy dimensions. This is consistent with
the theoretical arguments advanced in Chapters 3 and 4. The second configuration finds the candidates converging into two opposing blocs: a two-party
bloc that takes positions moderately to the left of the mean voter position
along each policy dimension, and a moderately right wing, three-party bloc.[6]
These equilibrium configurations are consistent with previous simulation results obtained by Schofield, Sened, and Nixon (1998) for Israel, and by de
Palma, Hong, and Thisse (1990) and Lomborg (1996) for simulated data,
all of which show that the policy-only model tends to motivate equilibria in
which the parties cluster into blocs. Of course, these computed equilibrium
configurations bear no resemblance to the actual configuration of candidates
in the 1988 French presidential election, nor do these equilibria illuminate
the policy linkages between the candidates and their supporters. We conclude that the policy-only voting model, in conjunction with the assumption
of vote-maximizing candidates, taken alone, does not illuminate candidate
behavior in the 1988 French presidential election.

5.4. Candidate Competition under a Unified Model
with Nonpolicy Factors

Next, we explore the candidates' policy strategies using a unified voting
model that incorporates – in addition to policy distances – voter-specific
attributes not directly tied to the candidates' policies in the current campaign. Using the specification introduced in Chapter 2 (see equation 2.5),

---

[5] See Chapter 2 (equations 2.4 and 2.5) for the calculation of probabilities that a voter votes
for each candidate and the expected vote share for each candidate. Note that in these and all
subsequent calculations, candidates' votes are expressed as percentages of the five-candidate
vote, thereby eliminating from consideration the minor candidates who competed in the first
round of voting.

[6] We note that for this latter configuration, the identities of the candidates in each bloc are
interchangeable (with leftist parties being just as likely to be in the rightist bloc as in the
leftist one, etc.), so that there are actually ten permutations of this equilibrium configuration.

we estimate the effects of respondents' perceptions of national and personal economic conditions, sex, age, and sociodemographic characteristics related to class and income.[7] Also included is the respondent's partisanship, coded 1 if the respondent identified with the candidate's party and zero otherwise.[8] In order to simplify the subsequent simulations on candidate movement, parameter estimates for the nonpolicy variables that are not statistically different from zero in the initial analysis were set to zero, and the remaining parameters were recalculated on this basis.

Table 5.3A, column 2 displays the resulting parameter estimates for this *unified model*. Note that the parameters for partisanship and for ideological distance are quite similar to those estimated for the one-dimensional partisan-voting model that we examined in Chapter 4 (see Table 4.3). Of the additional variables examined (retrospective economic evaluations, income, class, age, and sex), only class, income, and sex were estimated to have statistically significant impacts, and these only with respect to three candidates: class for Chirac (with middle-class respondents most likely to support Chirac), income for Lajoinie (with evaluations declining with income), and sex for Le Pen (with males most likely to support Le Pen).[9] A plausible explanation is that sociodemographic variables indirectly affect the

---

[7] Given that Le Pen's electoral appeal plausibly revolved in part around his rejection of the French political system (see Pierce 1995: Chapter 3) – a system that his main rivals supported – we would have liked to incorporate a measure of respondents' attitudes along some dimension such as system support or political efficacy; however, none was available in the 1988 FPES. In an effort to determine whether French voters viewed Le Pen as a qualitatively different type of presidential candidate, compared to his rivals, we estimated the parameters of an alternative voting specification that permitted the random variables associated with voters' candidate evaluations to be correlated. (For this exercise, we used the generalized extreme value [GEV] model described in Appendix 2.1). The results, reported in Adams and Merrill (1998), suggest that Le Pen was indeed viewed as being qualitatively different from his rivals, perhaps due to his rejection of the political system. However, computations on candidate strategies for this GEV voting specification produced results quite similar to those we obtained for the conditional logit (CL) model that we employ in this chapter.

[8] We note that while there is extensive debate over the electoral impact of partisanship (see Appendix 2.2), Lewis-Beck – a scholar prominently identified with the thesis that partisanship does not substantially influence French voters' behavior compared to ideology (see Fleury and Lewis-Beck 1993) – has recently reported empirical results suggesting that partisanship in fact exerts highly significant effects in the *first round* of voting in two-stage French presidential elections. The parameter estimates that Lewis-Beck and Chlarson (2002: Table 2) report for partisan effects in the first round of the 1995 French presidential election are similar to the magnitudes of the effects reported here, for the first round of the 1988 French presidential election.

[9] The class variable runs from -1 (self-described working class) to $+1$ (self-described middle class). The income variable runs from 1 (less than 5,000 francs per month) to 4 (over 15,000 francs per month). The sex variable is coded 0 for female, 1 for male. Income for Lajoinie and sex for Le Pen were close to significant and were retained in the model.

Table 5.4. *Candidate equilibria for alternative voting models, 1988 French presidential election*

5.4A. *The policy-only model*

	One-bloc Equilibrium			
	Left–Right	Church Schools	Public Sector	Immigration
Lajoinie	3.98	4.66	3.87	3.76
Mitterrand	3.98	4.66	3.87	3.76
Barre	3.98	4.66	3.87	3.76
Chirac	3.98	4.66	3.87	3.76
Le Pen	3.98	4.66	3.87	3.76

	Two-bloc Equilibrium[a]			
	Left–Right	Church Schools	Public Sector	Immigration
Lajoinie	3.49	4.30	3.31	3.43
Mitterrand	3.49	4.30	3.31	3.43
Barre	3.49	4.30	3.31	3.42
Chirac	4.63	5.18	4.65	4.21
Le Pen	4.63	5.18	4.65	4.21

[a] There are ten permutations of this equilibrium configuration (i.e., all possible groupings of the parties into one three-party bloc and one two-party bloc).

5.4B. *The unified model*

	Left–Right	Church Schools	Public Sector	Immigration
Lajoinie	**3.63**	**4.33**	**3.44**	**3.54**
	(.03)	(.06)	(.08)	(.04)
Mitterrand	**3.48**	**4.37**	**3.37**	**3.44**
	(.02)	(.01)	(.02)	(.01)
Barre	**4.25**	**4.96**	**4.25**	**3.95**
	(.02)	(.03)	(.04)	(.02)
Chirac	**4.47**	**5.09**	**4.46**	**4.06**
	(.02)	(.03)	(.04)	(.03)
Le Pen	**4.21**	**4.82**	**4.18**	**4.07**
	(.03)	(.04)	(.06)	(.03)

5.4C. *The unified discounting model*

	Left–Right	Church Schools	Public Sector	Immigration
Lajoinie	**3.16**	**4.29**	**2.81**	**3.03**
	(.27)	(.15)	(.51)	(.28)
Mitterrand	**3.12**	**4.53**	**2.95**	**3.10**
	(.19)	(.08)	(.26)	(.18)
Barre	**4.57**	**5.65**	**4.62**	**4.08**
	(.19)	(.39)	(.27)	(.08)
Chirac	**4.92**	**5.81**	**4.94**	**4.29**
	(.26)	(.40)	(.32)	(.14)
Le Pen	**4.59**	**5.52**	**4.63**	**4.39**
	(.27)	(.42)	(.44)	(.22)

Note: The equilibrium configurations for these alternative voting models were computed using the equilibrium algorithm described in Appendix 4.1, based on the parameter values reported in Table 5.3A. Bootstrap standard errors of the equilibrium estimates are reported in parentheses for the unified voting and unified discounting models.

vote by influencing respondents' partisanship or their policy preferences, as posited in the "funnel of causality" developed by the Michigan Model of voter choice (e.g., Campbell et al. 1960). Table 5.3B reports the candidates' expected aggregate votes for the unified model, which closely match the distribution of the respondents' actual votes.

Table 5.4B reports the unique policy equilibrium that we located when applying the equilibrium algorithm (see Appendix 4.1) to the unified proximity model. Consistent with our earlier theoretical and empirical analyses, this equilibrium finds the candidates presenting dispersed positions along each policy scale, with Lajoinie and Mitterrand consistently shaded to the left and Barre and Chirac to the right. Figure 5.2 displays the candidates' equilibrium configuration along the Left–Right scale, the dimension that emerged as the most salient in our analysis. The figure displays each candidate's expected vote as a function of his Left–Right position, with the rival candidates fixed at their equilibrium positions on the Left–Right scale (and with each candidate fixed at his equilibrium position on the three remaining policy scales). The Left–Right equilibrium configuration is extremely similar to the one obtained for the one-dimensional partisan-voting model examined in Chapters 3 and 4 (see Figure 3.5). As expected, the candidates from the larger parties (Mitterrand, Barre, and Chirac) have less centrist equilibrium positions than do Lajoinie and Le Pen, the candidates from the smaller parties (see Chapter 4, section 4.3.1).

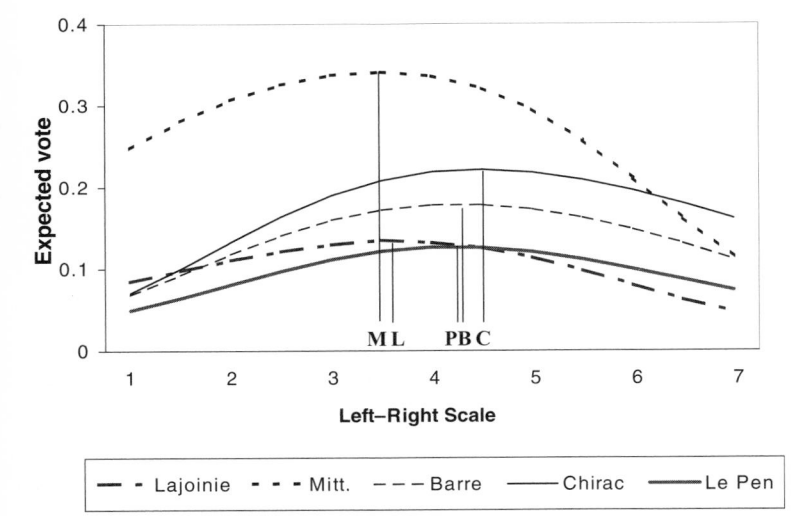

Figure 5.2. Candidates' expected votes with rival candidates at their equilibrium Left–Right positions, as computed for the unified model.

Note: The figure presents the expected vote for each candidate as a function of his Left–Right position, with the rival candidates fixed at their (vote-maximizing) equilibrium Left–Right positions (and with each candidate fixed at his equilibrium position along the additional policy dimensions included in the unified model). The labels "M," "L," "P," "B," and "C" represent the equilibrium positions for Mitterrand, Lajoinie, Le Pen, Barre, and Chirac, respectively. These positions were computed using the equilibrium algorithm and were based on the estimated parameters for the unified model reported in Table 5.3A, column 2.

Figures 5.3A and 5.3B present evidence on the extent to which the computed equilibrium illuminates the candidates' observed policy strategies, and mass–elite linkages, in the 1988 election. Figure 5.3A plots each candidate's equilibrium ideological position against his actual position. The equilibrium positions for Mitterrand, Barre, and Chirac are correlated with their actual positions but are significantly less dispersed. However, Lajoinie's and (especially) Le Pen's actual positions are far more extreme than their vote-maximizing equilibrium positions, so that the unified model does not account well for their observed behavior. One possible explanation is that Le Pen and Lajoinie – neither of whom had a realistic chance of winning – did not seek to maximize their support in 1988, but rather sought to express a different policy perspective. We note that this explanation echoes the argument advanced by Schofield, Sened, and Nixon (1998) in their analysis of party competition in the 1992 Israeli Knesset election. Using a policy-only voting

5.3A. Candidates' equilibrium positions versus their actual (perceived) positions

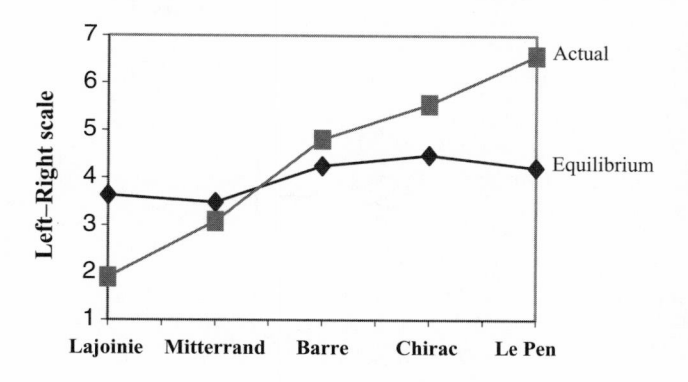

5.3B. Candidates' equilibrium positions versus mean positions of partisan constituencies

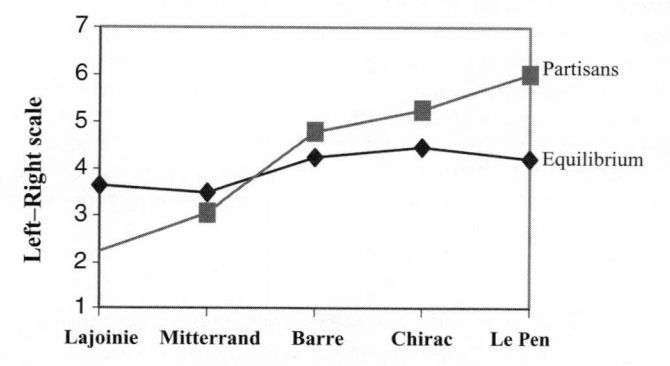

Figure 5.3. The linkages between the parties' equilibrium ideologies and their observed ideologies, for the unified model.

model estimated from election survey data, the authors compute equilibria in vote-maximizing strategies that locate the two major parties (Labor and Likud) at approximately their actual positions, but locate the minor parties at positions far from (and generally more moderate than) their actual positions. Schofield and his coauthors conclude that the two major parties were vote-maximizing, but that the smaller parties were not.[10]

---

[10] Specifically, the authors suggest that in a setting such as Israel's that typically features multiparty coalition government, optimal policy-seeking strategies of smaller parties should be

Figure 5.3B relates to mass–elite linkages by plotting each candidate's equilibrium position against the mean positions of his party's partisans. The figure shows – again, with the exception of Le Pen and Lajoinie – that the candidates' equilibrium positions are correlated with the mean position of their party's supporters, although the candidates' positions are somewhat more centrist than are those of their partisans. Again, this is entirely consistent with the theoretical arguments presented in Chapters 3 and 4, that the unified model motivates vote-seeking candidates to present policies similar to, but more moderate than, their partisans' positions. Thus to the extent that the unified model captures voters' decision processes in the 1988 French presidential election, the candidates had electoral incentives to represent the views of their partisan constituencies, the policy linkage that underlies the responsible party government model of representation.

We conclude that the unified model does a limited job of illuminating the candidates' policy positioning, and mass–elite policy linkages, in the 1988 French presidential election. In addition, our empirical applications suggest that the logic of candidate competition under the one-dimensional partisan-voting model discussed in Chapters 3 and 4 – which assumed a single spatial dimension and only one measured nonpolicy influence, party ID – extends to the more complex unified proximity specification explored here, which incorporates multiple policy dimensions as well as several measured nonpolicy voting influences.

5.5. Candidate Competition under a Unified Discounting Model

5.5.1. Motivations for Citizens to Discount the Candidates' Positions in the 1988 Election

The political situation that French voters confronted in the 1988 presidential election was complex, and it plausibly motivated them to support candidates who advocated policies that were more extreme than the voters' own beliefs.

---

based on the likely effects of these strategies in determining alternative coalition governments. In particular, a small party might choose a more extreme strategy in order to bring about a more desirable compromise policy in postelection negotiations (Schofield, Sened, and Nixon 1998: 12). This argument goes beyond the office-seeking motivations of parties we have considered so far. We will consider such motivations in Chapters 11 and 12, but only for two-candidate contests. Pursuing Schofield's ideas for policy-seeking parties in multiparty contests is a promising area for further research.

As noted in section 5.2, the Constitution of the French Fifth Republic combines features of parliamentary democracies and presidential systems, in that it features both a directly elected president and a government (premier plus cabinet) that is invested by and responsible to the National Assembly. Until the early 1980s, however, the conventional wisdom was that France's "dual executive" system was largely a myth, first because the Constitution of the Fifth Republic grants the president broad powers, and second because the three presidents who held office from 1958 to 1981 – de Gaulle (1958–1970), Pompidou (1970–74), and Giscard D'Estaing (1974–81) – in practice usurped much of the premier's constitutional authority. This was possible because although by strict constitutional interpretation only the National Assembly – not the president – could dismiss the premier, the president's power to dissolve the National Assembly gave him the necessary leverage to bring about the premier's dismissal. Thus the relationship between president and premier was likened to that between a captain and his first mate, with the president setting the broad policy direction and the premier – in the role of first mate – taking responsibility for implementing the president's policy agenda.[11] During this period, French voters might have reasonably inferred that the winning presidential candidate would successfully implement his full policy agenda – that is, that there was little distinction between a candidate's policy proposals and the expected government policy outputs in the event of his election. In this political context, there is scant justification for incorporating policy discounting into the unified voting model.

A series of events during Mitterrand's first presidential term (1981–88), however, undercut the president's reputation for policy preeminence, raising the possibility that voters might discount presidential candidates' policy proposals in the 1988 election. The first such events were a series of policy reversals that Mitterrand and the government undertook beginning in the fall of 1982, a year and a half into Mitterrand's presidency. In 1981, the Socialist government and its premier, Pierre Mauroy, had enacted Mitterrand's leftist policy agenda, which included raising the minimum wage, sharp increases in social spending and taxes on the wealthy, and nationalization of dozens of industries – legislation that reflected the policy vision that Mitterrand had articulated in the 1981 election campaign (see Frears 1991; Pierce 1995). However, in response to the deepening economic crisis of 1981–82, Mitterrand

---

[11] The French president's preeminence during this period gave rise to the label *elective monarchy*, used to describe the political character of the Fifth Republic (see Safran 1998: Chapter 6).

shifted course and directed Mauroy to pursue a "policy of rigor," a series of measures that entailed forced savings, cuts in public sector spending, a retreat from the government's previous nationalization policy, and a fight against inflation (see Safran 1998: Chapter 10). This revised orientation entailed a shift back toward the political center. Although these policy shifts reflected changes urged by Mitterrand's economic advisors – so that Mitterrand's policy preeminence vis-à-vis the premier was unchallenged during this period – the spectacle observed by the French electorate was that of a president who, confronted with difficult economic circumstances, chose to enact policies that were significantly more moderate than the leftist policy agenda he had articulated at the time of the 1981 presidential election campaign.

The second event that plausibly moved voters to discount the candidates' policy pronouncements in 1988 – one that suggested that whoever the public elected might face pressures to compromise on policies – was France's experience with divided government, or cohabitation, from 1986 to 1988. The parliamentary elections of 1986 produced a right-wing majority in the National Assembly, so that for the first time in the history of the Fifth Republic, the president (Mitterrand) confronted a parliament with a different political orientation. In response, Mitterrand nominated a right-wing premier, Jacques Chirac, who was acceptable to the National Assembly. The nature of power sharing in this unprecedented situation had to be determined in an ad hoc fashion. Mitterrand's approach involved ceding important domestic policy-making authority to Chirac – doing little to impede the Chirac government's major domestic initiatives, including the denationalization of some sixty state-owned industries – while Mitterrand retained considerable influence over foreign and defense policy.[12] However, despite Mitterrand's ceding of the domestic policy initiative to Chirac, the latter proved unable (or unwilling) to fully enact his conservative policy agenda. This was in part because of schisms within the right-wing majority in the National Assembly, but public pressures also caused Chirac to modify his government's policy initiatives on such important domestic issue areas as social security, privatization, access to higher education, and the reform of citizenship laws.

---

[12] In fact, Chirac and Mitterrand clashed in the foreign policy domain, with Chirac attempting on several occasions to assert a co-management role. However, the consensus of most observers was that Mitterrand remained preeminent in the fields of foreign and defense policy (see Safran 1998: Chapter 6).

The political events of 1982–88 thus provided grounds for French voters to infer that the winner of the 1988 presidential election would face difficulties in fully implementing his policy agenda. With respect to Mitterrand, the fact that he had modified his domestic policies during the period 1982–86 plausibly motivated voters to discount his policy promises in the 1988 election.[13] Furthermore, the fact that Chirac as premier had been pressured to modify his government's policy proposals might suggest to voters that were they to elect either of the major right-wing presidential candidates (Barre or Chirac), these politicians might face similar pressures to subsequently compromise their policy agendas. Given these expectations, voters might rationally support candidates who proposed policies similar to, but more extreme than, the voters' own beliefs – reasoning that once in office the president would be pressured into policy compromises, producing legislation in line with voters' policy preferences. Indeed, subsequent political events supported this line of reasoning. As we have seen, Mitterrand was elected president in 1988, and despite regaining a parliamentary majority in the National Assembly elections held later that year (see note 13), his subsequent policy course was quite moderate (see Safran 1998: Chapter 10).

Empirical estimates of voters' discounting preferences. In order to determine whether French voters discounted the candidates' positions in the 1988 presidential election, we estimated the parameters using a *unified discounting model*, which incorporated the discounting metric introduced in Chapter 2 as well as measured nonpolicy components. As discussed in section 2.4, this metric specifies that voters prefer candidates who present policies that are more extreme than the voters' own positions (with the degree of preferred candidate extremity to be estimated empirically, as we will describe).

---

[13] From the French electorate's perspective, an additional source of uncertainty in projecting policy outputs in the event of Mitterrand's reelection revolved around the partisan composition of the National Assembly. In the run-up to the presidential election, it was widely anticipated that if Mitterrand were reelected, he would dissolve the National Assembly and call for new elections in hopes of regaining the leftist parliamentary majority he had lost in 1986. (In the aftermath of his reelection, Mitterrand did in fact dissolve the National Assembly and regained a leftist majority in the subsequent parliamentary elections.) However, since Mitterrand had moderated his policy agenda between 1982 and 1986, even while enjoying majority support in parliament, French voters might project that government policy in a second Mitterrand administration would be more moderate than his campaign promises would suggest, regardless of the partisan composition of the National Assembly.

For purposes of statistical analysis, we locate the status quo point SQ, relative to which discounting is computed, at 4 along each dimension, the midpoint of the 1–7 scale. Furthermore, we assume that the discounting factors d_k are the same for each candidate and denote them by the single symbol d. Recall that if, for example, $SQ = 4$, a candidate advocates policy at 6.0, and $d = 0.25$, then the voters anticipate that policy will be implemented not at 6.0 but at 5.5 – that is, that the candidate will move policy 25 percent less than claimed. Thus $d = 0$ corresponds to a pure proximity model (no discounting), whereas $d = 1$ would correspond to total discounting – that is, an assumption by the voters that no candidate could move the status quo at all. Values of d significantly different from 0 and 1 (and that fall between these values) imply that voters prefer candidates whose proposed policies are similar to, but more extreme than, the voters' policy preferences; as discussed earlier, this captures situations where voters project that the winning candidate will succeed in implementing some, but not all, of his policy agenda.

Table 5.3A, column 3 displays the parameter estimates for the unified discounting model. The estimated discounting parameter, $d = 0.34$, is statistically different from 0 and 1 at the .001 level, indicating that voters discounted the candidates' claims, and did so by about a third.[14] This value implies that a voter located at, say, 5 along the Left–Right scale would prefer a candidate located near 5.5, that a voter who locates at 6 prefers a candidate who locates at 7, and so on – that is, that voters prefer candidates who present positions that are similar to, but somewhat more extreme than, the voter's position (see Chapter 2, section 2.4). Substantively, this estimate for d supports the hypothesis that in the 1988 presidential election, French voters projected that the winning presidential candidate would succeed in implementing most – but not all – of his policy agenda. The candidates' expected aggregate votes for the unified discounting model are given in

---

[14] The difference between the log-likelihood for the unified and the unified discounting models is 4.1, significant at the .005 level. Rabinowitz and Macdonald (1998) have shown that estimates of d (or equivalently, of the mixing parameter β for a mixed proximity-directional model) generated from voting data (as opposed to thermometer scores) may be confounded with party-specific intercepts. However, Merrill and Grofman (1999: Appendix 7.1) report the results of Monte Carlo simulations on artificially generated data, which suggest that the magnitude of the bias resulting from the omission of intercepts is manageable as long as there are several candidates. Although the standard error of d is larger in a model without intercepts, the discounting parameter d for the French data set still differs from 0 and 1 at the .05 level, suggesting that discounting occurs.

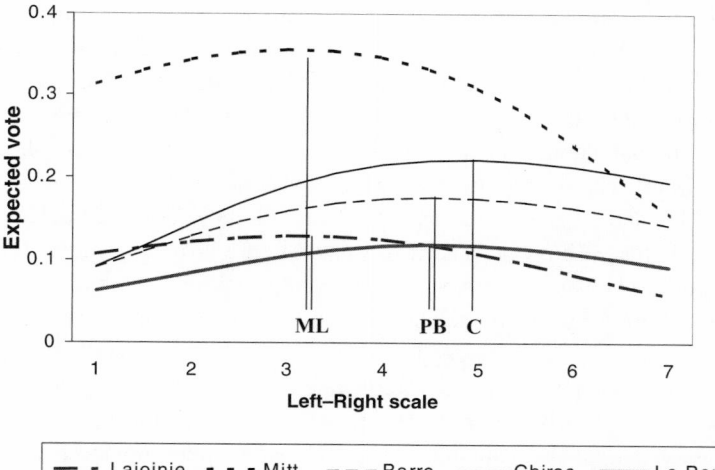

Figure 5.4. Candidates' expected votes with rival candidates at their equilibrium Left–Right positions, computed for the unified discounting model.
Note: The figure presents the expected vote for each candidate as a function of his Left–Right position, with the rival candidates fixed at their (vote-maximizing) equilibrium Left–Right positions (and with each candidate fixed at his equilibrium position along the additional policy dimensions included in the unified model). The Labels "M," "L," "P," "B," and "C" represent the equilibrium positions for Mitterrand, Lajoinie, Le Pen, Barre, and Chirac, respectively. These positions were computed using the equilibrium algorithm and were based on the estimated parameters for the unified model reported in Table 5.3A, column 3.

Table 5.3B (row 4), along with the distribution of the respondents' reported votes (row 1). The projected aggregate vote for this model is similar to the sample vote.

5.5.2. Candidate Equilibrium for the Unified Discounting Model

Table 5.4C reports the unique policy equilibrium that we located when applying the equilibrium algorithm (Appendix 4.1) to the unified discounting model, while Figure 5.4 displays the candidates' equilibrium configuration along the Left–Right scale, with each candidate's expected vote plotted as a function of his ideology (and with the remaining candidates fixed at their equilibrium positions). Consistent with our earlier theoretical and empirical analyses, this equilibrium finds the candidates presenting distinctly dispersed

Table 5.5. *Comparison of candidate equilibria with actual candidate positions and mean partisan positions, 1988 French presidential election*

	Actual Candidate Position	Mean Position of Partisans [a]	Equilibrium Positions	
Candidate			Unified Model	Unified Discounting Model
Lajoinie	1.90	2.24	3.63	3.16
Mitterrand	3.09	3.08	3.48	3.12
Barre	4.81	4.85	4.25	4.57
Chirac	5.55	5.36	4.47	4.92
Le Pen	6.57	6.03	4.21	4.59
Average deviation from actual candidate positions:				
Five candidates			1.22	.83
Three strongest candidates			.68	.30
Average deviation from mean positions of partisans:				
Five candidates			1.02	.62
Three strongest candidates			.63	.25

[a] *Partisans* are defined as identifiers of the parties represented by the candidates indicated.

positions along each policy scale, positions that are more dispersed than those obtained for the unified model without discounting.

Table 5.5 and Figures 5.5A and 5.5B present evidence on the extent to which the computed equilibrium illuminates the candidates' observed ideological positions, and mass–elite linkages, in the 1988 election. The mean distance between the candidates' equilibrium and actual (perceived) positions is 0.83; for the three leading candidates, the mean distance is only 0.30. Figure 5.5A, which plots the candidates' equilibrium positions against their actual positions, also shows that the unified discounting model, in conjunction with the assumption of vote-maximizing candidates, explains ideological positioning quite well for the three competitive candidates – Mitterrand, Barre, and Chirac.

Figure 5.5B relates to mass–elite linkages by plotting each candidate's equilibrium ideological position against the mean positions of his party's partisans. The figure shows that the unified discounting model gives candidates strong incentives to represent the views of their partisans. For every candidate except Le Pen, the candidate optima are within one unit of the partisan means along the seven-point Left–Right scale, and the mean distance between the candidate optima and their voting constituencies' preferences is

5.5A. Candidates' equilibrium positions versus their actual (perceived) positions

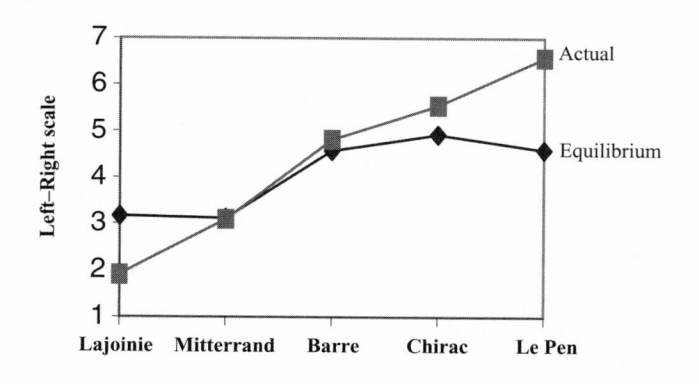

5.5B. Candidates' equilibrium positions versus mean positions of partisan constituencies

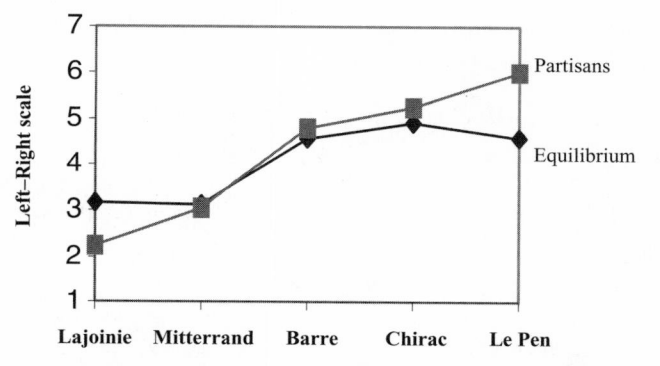

Figure 5.5. The linkages between the parties' equilibrium ideologies and their observed ideologies, for the unified discounting model.

just 0.62 policy units. For the three major candidates, the average deviation between the equilibrium positions and the mean of their voting constituencies' preferences is only 0.25 on the policy scale. We conclude that *in the 1988 French presidential election, the unified discounting model would motivate candidates to present policies that reflected the views of their parties' supporters.*

5.6. Conclusion

We have explored the major French candidates' policy strategies in the first round of the 1988 presidential election for three different voting models: a policy-only model; a unified model that incorporates respondents' retrospective economic evaluations, sociodemographic characteristics, and party identification; and a unified discounting model that incorporates in addition voters' tendencies to discount the candidates' policy promises. Consistent with our theoretical arguments from Chapters 3 and 4, we find that the policy-only model motivates candidate convergence (to either an agglomerated equilibrium or a two-bloc configuration), while the unified voting models – both with and without discounting – motivate divergence, with the candidates shifting away from the center in the direction of their partisan constituencies. The candidates' equilibrium positions for the unified model without discounting correlate with their actual positions, but are distinctly more centrist. Incorporating policy discounting increases the degree of dispersion at equilibrium, so that the policy optima for the three competitive candidates – Mitterrand, Barre, and Chirac – closely resemble their actual (perceived) positions in the 1988 election. In addition, these candidates' equilibrium positions faithfully reflect the beliefs of their partisan constituencies, the key linkage that underlies the responsible party model of representation. By contrast, the unified models (with or without policy discounting) – which depend on the single motivation of maximizing vote share – cannot similarly account for the positions of the Communist Lajoinie and the National Front leader Le Pen, the candidates from the two small, extremist parties that contested the 1988 presidential election.

CHAPTER 6

Policy Competition under the Unified Theory

Empirical Applications to the 1989 Norwegian Parliamentary Election

6.1. Introduction

Unlike France, which has a strong president as well as a governing party or governing coalition in the parliament (the National Assembly), Norway is a pure parliamentary government. Election of this parliament (the Storting), like many similar elections in Europe and elsewhere, is held under proportional representation (PR) and a list system in which each voter votes for a party, not a candidate. Seats in the Storting are assigned roughly in proportion to the vote share received by each party (using a modified Sainte-Laguë system). Again, as in many other polities, some grouping of parties must form a coalition – either explicitly or implicitly – to constitute a government, unless one party can achieve a majority of all the seats, something that has not happened in Norway since 1961.

Not only is Norway the only one of the four countries in our study that has a parliamentary election under PR, it also has a relatively large number (seven) of viable parties that usually secure seats. These parties, in their conventionally conceived order from left to right, are the leftist Socialists and Labor; three center parties – the Liberal,[1] Center, and Christian People's Parties; the rightist Conservative Party; and the ultra-right and maverick Progress Party. Five, and at times six, of these parties partition themselves into two relatively stable blocs that traditionally vie for sufficient seats to form a government (Aardal 1990; Aardal and Valen 1997; Strøm and Svåsand 1997; Urwin 1997). The two leftist parties may form a leftist coalition,

---

[1] The Liberal Party – with its strong environmental stance – may now be classified as center-left.

or Labor may form a minority government with implicit support from the Socialists. Alternatively, the three bourgeois parties (the Center, Christian People's, and Conservative Parties) – and, in earlier periods, the Liberal Party – may form a government. The Progress Party, however, has been considered an anathema by the others, in part because of its anti-immigration stance and unpredictability, and has been excluded from coalition governments. Yet it still has the potential to determine the balance of power between the socialist and bourgeois coalitions, as it did after the 1985 and 1989 elections.

In fact, the competitiveness of the 1989 election makes it an appropriate one for our analysis, because all parties had good reason to maximize their respective vote shares – coalition members in the hope that their coalition would achieve a majority of seats and form an uncontested government, and the Progress Party in the hope that it could hold the balance of power. Nevertheless, the parties other than Progress also had incentives to seek to maximize the vote share garnered not just by themselves but also by their coalitions, while at the same time maintaining a policy position that appealed to decision makers among their prospective coalition partners (see Schofield 1996; Schofield et al. 1998) as well as to policy-seeking elites within their own party. We will treat motivations arising from coalition politics in the Norwegian election in section 6.6.

As we did for the 1988 French presidential election, we will assess optimal strategies for the parties in the 1989 Norwegian parliamentary election using a model that incorporates multiple policy dimensions and numerous nonpolicy motivations, including partisanship. Again, as in the French context, we will consider whether Norwegian voters were plausibly motivated to discount parties' capacity to implement the policy positions they advocated. We present empirical results indicating that Norwegian voters did indeed behave as if they discounted parties' positions, and we investigate the effects such behavior had on the equilibrium positions of the parties. In addition, we will explore the strategic effects of the coalition-seeking and vote-seeking motivations of the parties, comparing each to these parties' actual (perceived) locations.

In the 1989 Storting election, 97.8 percent of those voting cast ballots for one of the seven major parties listed earlier. The percentage of the vote received by each party and the seats allocated to each are presented in Table 6.1.

Table 6.1. *Norwegian Storting election results, 1989*

Party	Vote Share (%)	Seats
Socialists	10.1	17
Labor	34.3	63
Liberal	3.2	0
Center	6.5	11
Christian People's	8.5	14
Conservative	22.2	37
Progress	13.0	22
Others	2.2	1
Total	100.0	165

Note: Voter turnout = 83.2%.

6.2. Ideology and Policy Issues in the 1989 Parliamentary Election

Our data comes from the 1989 Norwegian Election Study conducted by the Norwegian Social Science Data Services (NSD), in which 2,196 respondents were asked to place themselves and each of the seven major parties on several 1–10 scales, which included Left–Right ideology as well as various policy dimensions. We focus on the data subset of 1,786 respondents who reported voting for one of the seven major parties and who could place themselves on the Left–Right scale. Of this group, 1,565 respondents were able to place all seven parties on the Left–Right scale. As in the French electorate, Left–Right ideology defines Norwegian politics and is well recognized by Norwegian voters, as attested by the willingness of most respondents to place themselves and as many as seven parties on the Left–Right scale. Figure 6.1 displays the distribution of the NSD respondents' self-placements on the Left–Right scale, and also displays their mean party placements. These party placements indicate that voters perceived a very dispersed party distribution, running from a mean placement of 2.42 for the Socialists on the left to 9.02 for the Progress Party on the extreme right. The Norwegian respondents' mean party placements, which are also presented in column 3 of Table 6.2, accord well with experts' placements of the parties' positions as compiled in a survey by Huber and Inglehart (1995: 102) and given in column 2 of Table 6.2.

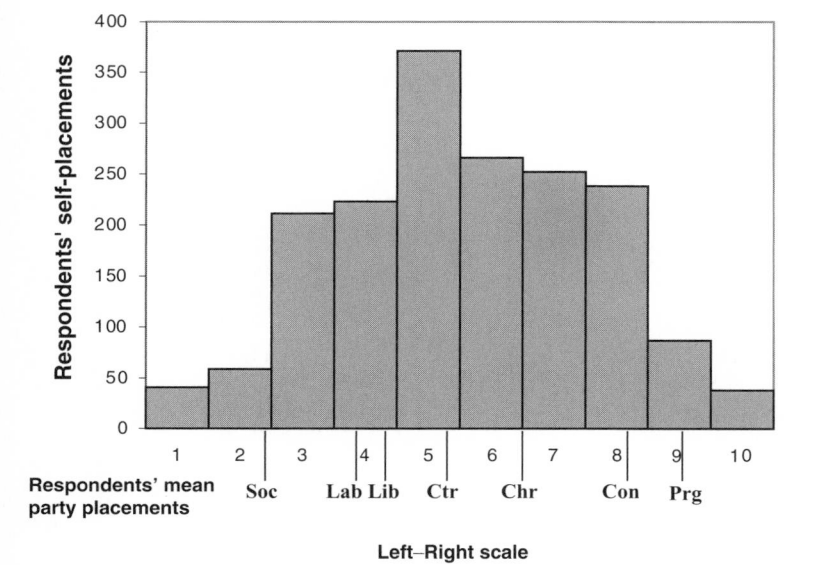

Figure 6.1. Distribution of respondents' Left–Right self-placements and their mean party placements, 1989 Norwegian Storting election.

Note: The voter distribution is from the 1989 Norwegian Storting Election Survey and represents the Left–Right self-placements of all respondents who reported voting for one of the seven major parties and who could place themselves on the Left–Right scale (N = 1,786). The party placements represent the mean Left–Right positions ascribed to each party by these respondents.

Column 1 of Table 6.2 presents the respondents' mean Left–Right self-placements, stratified by their recollections of how they had voted in the previous Storting election, held in 1985. As will be discussed later, we use respondents' recalled votes as a surrogate for party identification in our Norwegian analyses, since there are reasons to believe that reports of party ID are confounded with current vote intentions. To the extent that recalled vote is indeed a surrogate for partisanship, these means indicate that, as expected, the partisans of the Socialists and Labor – the traditional left-wing parties – held leftist beliefs, while partisans of the center and right-wing parties tended to hold centrist and right-wing beliefs, respectively. Given the theoretical and empirical results presented in Chapters 3–5, we should therefore expect that the Socialist and Labor Parties had electoral incentives to maintain their leftist ideologies, while the remaining parties similarly had incentives to

Table 6.2. *Parties' and respondents' policy positions as perceived by the Norwegian electorate and by experts, 1989 (N = 1,786)*

Party	Respondent Self-Placement, Stratified by Previous Vote	Experts' Party Placements[a]	Mean Voter Perception			
	Left–Right (1)	Left–Right (2)	Left–Right (3)	Agriculture (4)	Alcohol Policy (5)	Immigration (6)
Socialist	3.44	2.55	2.42	4.20	4.48	3.29
Labor	4.32	4.13	3.92	3.05	4.52	5.00
Liberal	4.79	5.86	4.36	4.79	4.45	4.55
Center	5.99	5.33	5.36	1.67	4.86	5.52
Christian People's	6.09	6.55	6.54	4.80	1.47	4.73
Conservative	7.23	8.00	8.23	5.66	6.75	6.44
Progress	7.32	9.18	9.02	8.93	9.01	9.38
Mean voter position	–	–	*5.58*	*4.44*	*5.01*	*6.92*

[a] The expert party placements represent the mean positions ascribed to the Norwegian parties, along a 1–10 Left–Right scale, in a survey designed by Huber and Inglehart (1995), which was mailed to the expert respondents in 1993.

present ideologies shaded in the direction of their centrist and right-wing partisan constituencies.

In addition to Left–Right ideology, the 1989 NSD contained questions on three specific policy scales, each of which captured a dimension largely independent of conventional Left–Right ideology (which is usually interpreted as an economic dimension) but particularly salient for one of the seven parties. The first such policy issue was agriculture, the issue on which the Center Party made its case; the second was alcohol policy, the one of greatest interest to the Christian People's Party, whose supporters generally opposed the use of alcohol on religious grounds. The third policy issue involved immigration, fervently opposed by the Progress Party, whose prominent statements about the issue dragged unwilling responses from other party representatives (Aardal 1990). The survey respondents' mean placements of the parties on these three policy issues are given in columns 4–6 of Table 6.2.

6.3. Party Competition in the Policy-only Model

Table 6.3A, column 1 presents parameter estimates for a policy-only voting specification, with voters' party utilities specified as a function of their (squared) distances from each party along the ideology and policy scales included in the NSD. As expected, the Left–Right scale is by far the most salient dimension of party evaluation. Table 6.3B reports the parties' vote shares in the NSD sample (row 1) and their expected vote shares under the policy-only model (row 2).[2] The parties' expected votes do not closely match the sample vote, indicating that the policy-only model does not fully capture voters' decision processes in the 1989 parliamentary election.

Using the algorithm described in Appendix 4.1, we computed equilibrium locations in parties' vote-maximizing strategies along the ideology and policy scales. For these computations, we employed the parameter estimates for the policy-only voting specification reported in Table 6.3, column 1. We found that equilibria for the policy-only voting model are not unique; that is, there are multiple configurations of party locations to which parties might settle over a period of time. One such configuration, given in Table 6.4A, finds the seven parties converging to identical, roughly centrist locations (relative to the voter distribution) along the ideology dimension and each of the three policy dimensions. Alternative equilibrium configurations (see a list of a sample of ten of the many configurations in Table 6.4B) find some

---

[2] Vote shares are expressed as percentages of the seven-party vote.

Table 6.3. *Logit equations and projected votes, 1989 Norwegian Storting election* (N = 1,786)

6.3A. *Logit equations predicting the vote*

	Policy-only (1)	Unified (2)	Unified Discounting (3)
Policy parameters			
Left–Right	**.147**	**.112**	**.238**
	(.007)	(.007)	
Agriculture	**.026**	**.010**	**.038**
	(.003)	(.004)	
Alcohol policy	**.045**	**.021**	**.051**
	(.003)	(.004)	
Immigration	**.068**	**.060**	**.092**
	(.005)	(.005)	
Discounting parameter	.00	0.00	**0.48**
	–	–	(.05)
Party identification	–	**2.08**	**2.17**
		(.07)	(.07)
Sociodemographic variables			
Teetotaler (Christian People's)	–	**.68**	**.53**
		(.12)	(.12)
Agriculture (Center)	–	**.74**	**.65**
		(.11)	(.12)
Urban residence (Liberal)	–	**−0.99**	**−0.66**
		(.21)	(.22)
Urban residence (Center)	–	**−1.68**	**−1.34**
		(.35)	(.35)
Union member (Socialist)	–	**.75**	**.47**
		(.20)	(.20)
Union member (Labor)	–	**.37**	**.45**
		(.14)	(.15)
Income (Socialist)	–	**.72**	**.59**
		(.20)	(.20)
Income (Labor)	–	**.38**	**.54**
		(.14)	(.15)
Religion (Christian People's)	–	**.74**	**.83**
		(.23)	(.24)
Log-likelihood	− 2618.0	− 1676.6	− 1633.4

6.3B. *Projected votes for alternative models with parties at their mean perceived positions*

	Socialist	Labor	Liberal	Center	Christian People's	Conservative	Progress
Sample vote	13.5%	32.7%	5.0%	8.4%	5.6%	23.5%	11.6%
Policy-only	8.8	16.7	16.2	19.0	12.5	17.2	9.5
Unified	11.2	30.2	6.3	9.8	11.8	22.8	7.9
Unified Discounting	12.1	30.0	5.5	8.1	10.9	22.0	11.3

Table 6.4. *Party equilibria for the policy-only model: 1989 Norwegian Storting election*

6.4A. *Example of centrist equilibrium for the policy-only model*

	Left–Right	Agriculture	Alcohol Policy	Immigration
Socialist	5.58	4.45	5.01	6.91
Labor	5.58	4.45	5.01	6.91
Liberal	5.58	4.45	5.01	6.91
Center	5.58	4.45	5.01	6.91
Christian	5.58	4.45	5.01	6.91
Conservative	5.58	4.45	5.01	6.91
Progress	5.58	4.45	5.01	6.91

6.4B. *Left–Right positions for a sample of ten equilibria for the policy-only model*

	Replication									
	1	2	3	4	5	6	7	8	9	10
Party										
Socialist	6.27	6.46	4.91	6.28	6.47	4.70	6.27	4.91	4.70	4.70
Labor	4.70	4.85	4.88	4.70	4.86	6.30	4.70	4.89	6.09	4.70
Liberal	6.27	4.85	6.47	4.70	4.99	4.70	6.27	6.47	6.32	6.26
Center	6.26	6.46	4.91	6.27	4.86	6.30	4.70	4.89	4.70	6.28
Christian	6.27	6.46	4.89	4.70	6.47	4.70	4.70	6.47	4.70	6.26
Conservative	4.70	4.85	6.47	6.26	6.47	6.13	6.27	4.89	6.32	4.70
Progress	4.70	5.06	6.47	6.26	4.88	6.30	6.25	6.47	6.32	6.27

Note: The equilibrium configurations were computed using the algorithm described in Appendix 4.1, based on the parameter values reported in Table 6.3A.

of the parties at a slightly leftist position, in the vicinity of 4.7 along the 1–10 Left–Right scale, while the remaining parties are slightly rightist, in the vicinity of 6.3.[3] But in such an equilibrium, there is no relation between these left and right positions and the traditional leanings of these parties – a finding that is not surprising, as a policy-only model makes no distinctions between the parties. From the perspective of such a model, the labels of the parties are arbitrary. Thus, because of the nonuniqueness of the equilibrium configurations of strategies and the arbitrariness of the association of parties to positions, a policy-only model is not only useless in accounting for specific party strategies, it also fails to account for the rich variation in the positions of the seven parties.

6.4. Party Competition in the Unified Model

We now extend our analysis to the unified model specified in Chapter 2, adding a party identification variable as well as several sociodemographic variables, including teetotaler, association with the agricultural sector, urban residence, union membership, income, and religion. Because voters in Norway express a vote for a party rather than a candidate, we have not used current party affiliation for party identification. Instead, we use recalled vote – that is, the party that the respondent reports voting for in the immediately previous election (that of 1985).[4] Accordingly, a respondent's partisanship for a party was coded 1 if the respondent reported voting for that party in 1985, and zero otherwise.[5] In order to simplify the analysis,

---

[3] For each equilibrium configuration, the same parties are also clumped on the other three dimensions; therefore, each clump of parties represents a single point in multidimensional space.

[4] In the 1989 NSD, only 6.6 percent reported affiliation with a party different from that for which they voted, while 24.5 percent reported switching parties from the previous election in 1985. In any event, analyses using current party affiliation for party identification yield substantive conclusions on equilibrium party strategies that are quite similar to those we report here.

[5] The recalled vote variable has been criticized on the grounds that respondents' memories of their previous votes may be systematically biased (see Himmelweit, Jaeger, and Stockdale 1978). In order to determine whether this drawback applied to our Norwegian sample, we examined the vote transition matrix from 1985 to 1989 constructed from the recalled vote variable and compared it to a 1985–89 transition matrix based upon a smaller panel study of 800 Norwegians who were interviewed in 1985 and again in 1989 (see Aardal 1990: Table 3). The key question is whether the relationship between vote 1985 and vote 1989 changes between the two layers. The p-value for a test based on the three-way interaction of a log-linear analysis of vote 1985, vote 1989, and the two survey layers is .083, indicating that there is no statistically significant difference between the two survey layers. This suggests that in the 1989 Norwegian survey, respondents' vote recollections were not significantly biased. We thank Eric Smith for drawing our attention to this point.

Table 6.5. *Unique party equilibria for the unified model: 1989 Norwegian Storting election*

	Left–Right	Agriculture	Alcohol Policy	Immigration
Socialist	**5.46**	**4.47**	**5.18**	**6.66**
	(.09)	(.04)	(.03)	(.07)
Labor	**4.99**	**4.37**	**4.94**	**6.92**
	(.07)	(.01)	(.01)	(.02)
Liberal	**4.99**	**4.24**	**4.91**	**6.21**
	(.08)	(.03)	(.04)	(.10)
Center	**5.57**	**3.59**	**4.55**	**7.20**
	(.02)	(.06)	(.05)	(.03)
Christian	**5.80**	**4.09**	**4.05**	**6.77**
	(.03)	(.04)	(.11)	(.02)
Conservative	**6.73**	**4.92**	**5.56**	**7.25**
	(.04)	(.02)	(.02)	(.02)
Progress	**6.46**	**4.83**	**5.55**	**7.60**
	(.07)	(.03)	(.03)	(.06)

Note: The equilibrium configurations were computed using the algorithm described in Appendix 4.1, based on the parameter values reported in Table 6.3A. Parametric bootstrap standard errors of the equilibrium estimates are reported in parentheses.

parameter estimates for the nonpolicy variables that were not statistically different from zero in the initial analysis were set to zero, and the remaining parameters were recalculated on this basis. Table 6.3A, column 2 displays the resulting parameter estimates for this *unified model*. Table 6.3B reports the candidates' expected aggregate votes for the unified model (with the parties located at their mean perceived positions), which closely match the distribution of the respondents' actual votes.

Table 6.5 reports the unique policy equilibrium that we located when applying the equilibrium algorithm (Appendix 4.1) to the unified model.[6] Figure 6.2 pictures this equilibrium configuration along the Left–Right dimension and also displays the parties' expected votes as a function of their ideologies, with the rival parties located at their equilibrium positions. Consistent with our earlier theoretical and empirical analyses, this equilibrium finds the parties presenting dispersed positions along each policy

---

[6] In order to assess the uniqueness of this equilibrium configuration, we implemented the equilibrium algorithm with 100 starting configurations, each of which consisted of 7 randomly drawn values from the interval [1, 10]. All runs led to the same equilibrium. This Monte Carlo approach was used because the sufficient condition for convergence of the algorithm specified in Appendix 4.1 is not satisfied (i.e., the Jacobian norm is greater than 1.0).

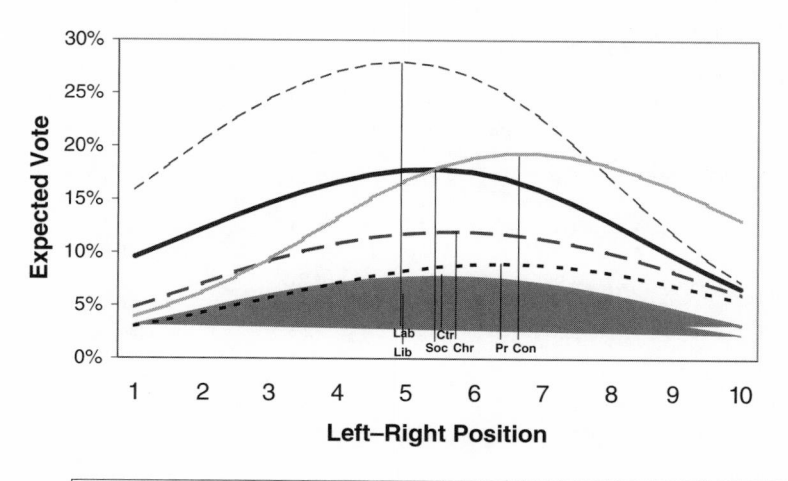

Figure 6.2. Parties' expected votes with rival parties at their equilibrium Left–Right positions, under the unified voting model: Norway, 1989.
Note: The figure presents each party's expected vote as a function of its Left–Right position, with the rival parties fixed at their (vote-maximizing) Left–Right equilibrium positions (and with each party fixed at its equilibrium position along the additional policy dimensions included in the unified model). The labels "Lab," "Lib," "Soc," "Ctr," "Chr," "Pr," and "Con" represent the equilibrium positions for the Labor, Liberal, Socialist, Center, Christian People's, Progress, and Conservative Parties, respectively. These parties' equilibrium positions were computed using the algorithm presented in Appendix 4.1, based on the unified vote model parameters reported in Table 6.3A, column 2.

scale, with the parties' positions shaded in the direction of their supporters' mean preferences.[7] Although the party positions at equilibrium are dispersed and generally conform to expectations, at least for Left–Right ideology, the degree of dispersion falls well short of that empirically observed. Furthermore, the equilibrium Left–Right locations of the two parties perceived to be on either extreme – the Socialists on the left and Progress on the right – are both more centrist than the major center-left and center-right

---

[7] Sensitivity analysis for the value of the partisan-salience parameter b (in a two-parameter model including only Left–Right ideology and partisanship) indicates that the equilibrium locations are at least as dispersed when b is reduced to one-half or even one-fourth of its actually estimated value (while the parameter a is reestimated). Thus, even if the effect of partisanship is substantially smaller than we have estimated, our substantive conclusions about the dispersion of optimal strategies is unchanged. See Chapter 4, section 4.5 for further discussion of this point.

parties – Labor and the Conservatives. These latter relationships, however, are not unexpected – based on Theorem 4.1 in Chapter 4 – because the Socialist and Progress Parties both have smaller partisan constituencies than the Labor and Conservative Parties. But still, overall, these predictions do not account for the observed positions of the seven parties.

6.5. Party Competition in a Unified Discounting Model

6.5.1. Motivations for Citizens to Discount Parties' Positions in Norwegian Elections

Unlike France – which elects both a president and a parliament, leading to the possibility of a divided government or "cohabitation" – Norway has a purely parliamentary form of government. Thus any motivation for voters to discount parties' positions in Norwegian parliamentary elections must be the result of quite different factors than those operating in French presidential elections. Such factors, however, may arise from the need for parties to form governing coalitions.

Party elites of noncentrist parties as well as supporters of such parties are aware that their party is not likely to govern alone but rather will need to enter into a coalition with other parties, especially more centrist parties, in order to achieve a working majority in parliament. This is particularly true of the Socialist Party in Norway – which has no chance of participating in a government without Labor – and the Conservative Party, which typically needs support from the Center and Christian People's Parties in order to approach governing strength. But coalition with more centrist parties leads to implemented policies that are more centrist than could be expected without the compromises such coalitions entail. Thus a voter anticipating this effect may be motivated to support a party that advocates policies more extreme than those of the voter, rather than the party to which the voter is closest. Support for a more extreme party may occur because such a party will help to balance the more centrist elements of any governing coalition that forms, leading to implemented policies more in tune with those of the voter. For example, a mildly conservative voter at location 7 on a 1–10 scale of ideology might prefer a party advocating policies at 9, anticipating that a coalition with a centrist party at 5 will lead to compromises at about 7, which is the voter's preferred policy position. McCuen and Morton (2002) report experimental evidence in support of this "tactical coalition voting" hypothesis, while Kedar (2002) presents theoretical and empirical analyses (to be discussed later) showing that citizens account for parties' probable policy impacts when voting.

In addition to voters' expectations about the effects of coalition government, three other factors could plausibly lead Norwegian voters to infer
that policy outputs will be more moderate than the announced positions of
the governing parties. First, Norway features a relatively "decentralized"
political system, in the sense that a significant share of citizens' taxes are
collected – and spent – by local governing authorities as opposed to the
central government (see Lijphart 1984: Table 10.2). This to some extent
limits the central governing coalition's policy influence. Second, the Norwegian Constitution requires that a two-thirds legislative majority support
amendments to the Constitution, so that even majority governing coalitions
typically require support from parties outside the coalition in order to enact constitutional changes. Finally, Norwegian voters – like those in any
democracy – can expect moderation due to the influence of public opinion.
Regardless of the coalition in power, citizen opinion extends from left to
right and can be expected to pull conservative governments toward the left
and liberal governments toward the right. Thus, as in the case of the French
electorate, the prospect of governmental compromise and the influence of
public opinion plausibly motivate Norwegian voters to discount the parties'
ability to fully implement their policy programs.[8]

Accordingly, we may expect that the discounting model developed in
Chapter 2, section 2.4 may be appropriate for Norwegian elections –
particularly for the election of 1989, in which the contest between potential leftist and rightist coalitions was close. Table 6.3A (column 3) reports
parameter estimates for a unified discounting model including the same
nonpolicy variables used in the unified (nondiscounting) model discussed
earlier. As in the case of France, we locate the status-quo point SQ, relative to which discounting is computed, at the midpoint of the scale. For the
Norwegian Election Study, the midpoint of the 1–10 scale is 5.5. Again as
in the French study, we assume that the discounting factors d_k are the same
for each party and denote them by the single symbol d. The estimate of the

---

[8] We note that there are many additional factors that are relevant to the central governing
coalition's ability to implement policy, including provisions for national and local referenda,
bicameral versus unicameral legislatures, the number of political parties, and electoral system
type. While we will not review these factors exhaustively in the context of Norwegian politics,
we note that Lijphart (1984), in his influential comparative study of Western democracies,
locates Norway at an intermediate position along a continuum running from majoritarian
political systems (in which the central governing coalition can be expected to exert maximal
policy influence) at one extreme to consensual political systems (in which the government's
policy influence is substantially limited) at the opposite extreme. From our perspective, the
central point is that Norwegian voters may rationally anticipate that the postelection governing
coalition will face obstacles to implementing its full policy agenda.

Table 6.6. *Unique party equilibria for the unified discounting model: 1989 Norwegian Storting election*

	Left–Right	Agriculture	Alcohol Policy	Immigration
Socialist	**3.62**	**3.04**	**4.47**	**6.60**
	(.57)	(.30)	(.15)	(.28)
Labor	**3.98**	**3.12**	**4.22**	**7.93**
	(.31)	(.29)	(.18)	(.26)
Liberal	**2.73**	**2.81**	**4.05**	**5.32**
	(.56)	(.33)	(.23)	(.60)
Center	**5.95**	**1.47**	**3.45**	**9.16**
	(.13)	(.55)	(.33)	(.43)
Christian	**6.73**	**2.55**	**2.48**	**8.36**
	(.18)	(.47)	(.61)	(.40)
Conservative	**8.45**	**4.53**	**5.82**	**9.21**
	(.45)	(.10)	(.11)	(.40)
Progress	**8.95**	**4.88**	**6.23**	**10.20**
	(.50)	(.11)	(.21)	(.21)

Note: The equilibrium configurations were computed using the algorithm described in Appendix 4.1, based on the parameter values reported in Table 6.3A. Parametric bootstrap standard errors of the equilibrium estimates are reported in parentheses. Some of the bootstrap runs for the unified discounting model – for immigration for three parties, and for Left–Right for the Progress party – did not converge, so those estimated standard errors are approximate.

discounting factor d for the Norwegian election of 1989 is 0.47, suggesting significant discounting of party positions – that is, that voters anticipate that on average, the implemented policies of potential governing coalitions would be about half as extreme as those advocated by individual parties, relative to the center of the policy scales. Accordingly, we would expect that voters – in their attempt to compensate for the moderating effect of coalition government – would prefer parties whose positions were about twice as extreme as those of the voters themselves, relative to the status quo.

Parameter estimates for the unified discounting model for the 1989 Norwegian election are given in Table 6.3A (column 3); projected vote shares are given in Table 6.3B (row 4). The difference in log-likelihood between the unified and unified discounting models is 43.2, well beyond the .001 level of significance.

The unique equilibrium locations of the parties that we compute for the unified discounting model are reported in Table 6.6.[9] Figure 6.3 displays this

---

[9] We tested the uniqueness of this equilibrium as we did for the unified model, by using 100 starting configurations. All runs led to the same equilibrium.

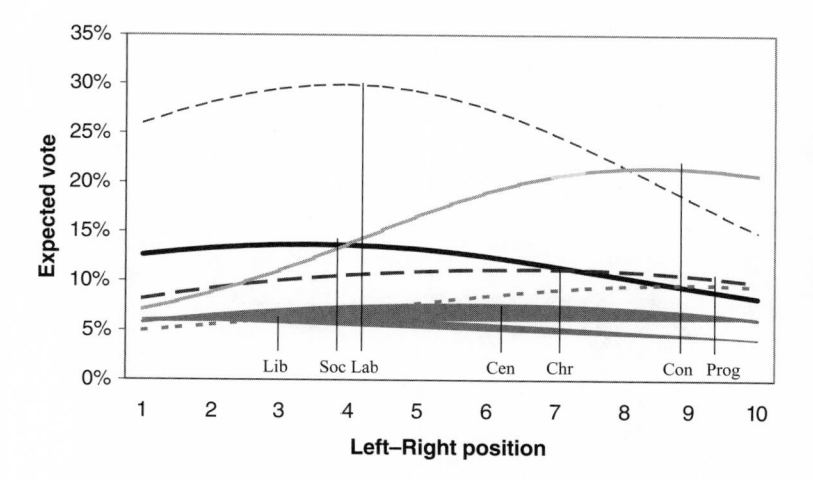

Figure 6.3. Parties' expected votes with rival parties at their equilibrium Left–Right positions, under the unified discounting model: Norway, 1989.

Note: The figure presents each party's expected vote as a function of its Left–Right position, with the rival parties fixed at their (vote-maximizing) Left–Right equilibrium positions (and with each party fixed at its equilibrium position along the additional policy dimensions included in the unified discounting specification). The labels "Lab," "Lib," "Soc," "Cen," "Chr," "Pr," and "Con" represent the equilibrium positions for the Labor, Liberal, Socialist, Center, Christian People's, Progress, and Conservative Parties, respectively. These parties' equilibrium positions were computed using the algorithm presented in Appendix 4.1, based on the unified discounting vote model parameters reported in Table 6.3A, column 3.

equilibrium configuration along the Left–Right dimension and also displays the parties' expected votes as a function of their ideologies, when the rival parties locate at their equilibrium positions. As expected, the parties' equilibrium positions for the unified discounting model are substantially more dispersed than those predicted by the unified model without discounting. With discounting, the Left–Right equilibrium location of the Liberal Party is the most leftist of the seven parties, while the location of the Conservative Party is well to the right at 8.45, nearly as extreme as the equilibrium position of the Progress Party. As expected, the Center party has the lowest value on agricultural policy (1.47); the Christian People's Party has the lowest value

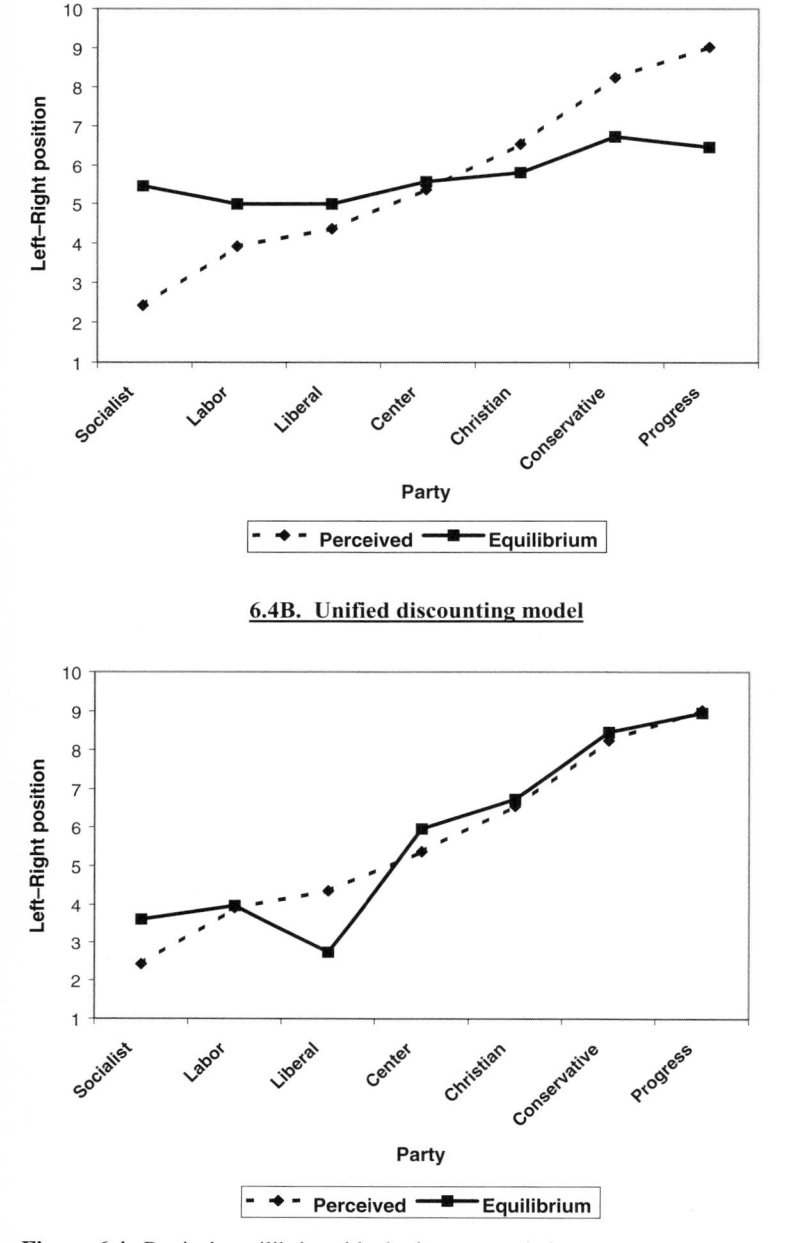

6.4A. Unified model

6.4B. Unified discounting model

Figure 6.4. Parties' equilibrium ideologies versus their actual (perceived) ideologies, for alternative voting models: Norway, 1989.

on alcohol policy (2.48); and the Progress Party has the highest value on immigration (slightly off the scale at 10.20).

Figure 6.4, which plots the parties' mean perceived Left–Right positions (Table 6.2) and their equilibrium Left–Right positions (Tables 6.5 and 6.6) on the same axis, shows that in conjunction with the assumption of vote-maximizing parties, the unified discounting model (Figure 6.4B) explains the parties' positioning quite well. Unlike the unified model without discounting (Figure 6.4A), the unified model with discounting yields equilibrium strategies that are within 0.6 units of the mean perceived party position for all but the Socialist and Liberal Parties (see Table 6.7). The correlation between actual (mean perceived) party positions and the equilibrium positions for the unified discounting model is 0.94. We are not too concerned by the discrepancy between the equilibrium and perceived locations of the Liberal Party – the smallest of the seven parties – particularly because of its splitting and realigning before the 1989 election, which may have left voters confused as to its true location (see Aardal 1990; Urwin 1997). The discrepancy of 1.2 units for the Socialist Party is less easy to explain, but at least the equilibrium location is much closer to its perceived position than is the case for the unified (nondiscounting) model.[10]

Figures 6.5A and 6.5B relate mass–elite linkages by plotting for each party the equilibrium position and the mean position of its supporters (i.e., the mean self-placements of the respondents who reported voting for the party in the 1985 election) on the same axis (see also Table 6.7). Although the correlation between the mean positions of supporters and the parties' equilibrium positions is greater for the unified discounting model (0.92) than for the unified model (0.84), the mean absolute deviation is greater for the discounting model. Note, however, that under the discounting model the parties' equilibrium positions are generally more extreme than the positions of their supporters – a relationship which denotes faithful representation, since these supporters prefer that their parties advocate

---

[10] The unified discounting model was run again using party-specific parameters as the discounting factor. Standard errors were higher, so the results were somewhat inconclusive, but the three centrist parties (Center, Christian, and Liberal) showed the least discounting, while Labor and the Socialists showed the greatest. One possible explanation for the Socialist Party's rather extreme position is that Norwegian voters discount this party's policy influence to an unusual extent, because the Socialists typically support the Labor Party from outside the governing coalition. This suggests that leftist voters might prefer that the Socialists adopt a rather extreme leftist position in order to shift expected government policy outputs under a Labor government.

Table 6.7. *Comparison of party equilibria with actual party positions and mean partisan positions: 1989 Norwegian Storting election*

Party	Actual Party Position	Mean Position of Supporters[a]	Equilibrium Positions	
			Unified Model	Unified Discounting Model
Socialist	2.42	3.44	5.46	3.62
Labor	3.92	4.32	4.99	3.98
Liberal	4.36	4.79	4.99	2.73
Center	5.36	5.99	5.57	5.95
Christian	6.54	6.09	5.80	6.73
Conservative	8.23	7.23	6.73	8.45
Progress	9.02	7.32	6.46	8.95
Correlation with actual party positions			.86	.94
Average deviation from actual party positions			1.39	.57
Correlation with mean positions of supporters			.84	.92
Average deviation from mean positions of supporters			.71	.87

[a] The parties' supporters are defined as the set of respondents who reported voting for the party in the previous (1985) election.

relatively extreme positions that are likely to be moderated by any prospective coalition.

6.6. Coalition-Seeking Motivations

So far, we have assumed that each party seeks to maximize its own vote share, independently of the other parties. Yet maximizing one's own vote share (or seat share) is by no means the only plausible electoral goal of a Norwegian party. Because of the frequent need to form coalitions in order to govern, and given the fixed coalition blocs in Norwegian politics, it is plausible that a member of either of the respective blocs may focus on how its policies affect the likelihood that the coalition of which it is a member will become the governing coalition. This objective depends not only on the electoral strength of the party in question but also on the aggregate vote obtained by the bloc (socialist or bourgeois) to which it belongs. This implies that in contrast to vote-seeking parties, coalition-seeking parties may be willing to trade off their own electoral support in exchange for electoral gains by the other member(s) of the coalition bloc. We will base our model on this simple idea, although there are many alternative spatial models of coalition

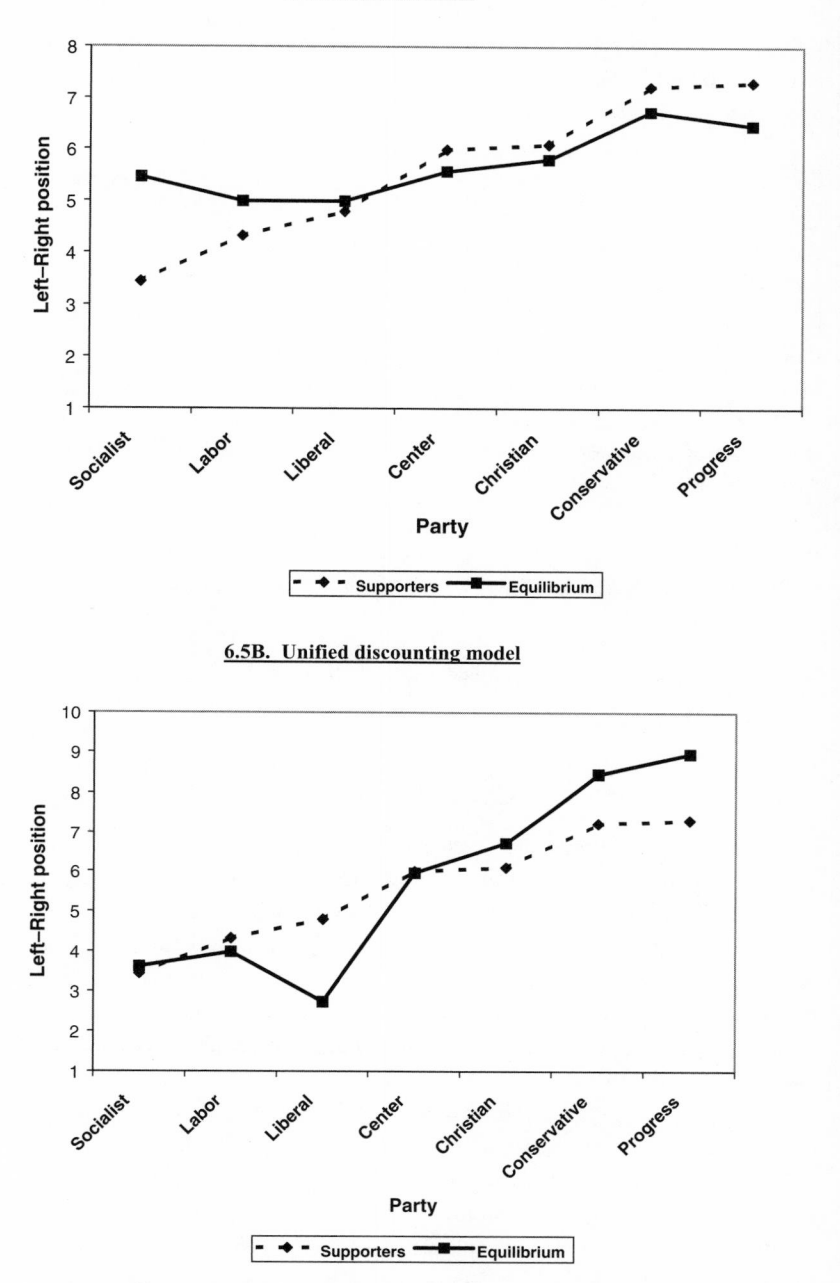

6.5A. Unified model

6.5B. Unified discounting model

Figure 6.5. Parties' equilibrium ideologies versus the mean positions of their supporters, for alternative voting models: Norway, 1989.

formation that we might apply (see, e.g., Axelrod 1970; Laver and Shepsle 1996; Schofield 1996; Schofield et al. 1998).[11]

An alternative, voter-centric development that is particularly appropriate for PR systems is that of Kedar (2002), who determines voter strategies that are at least in part outcome oriented – that is, that attempt to optimize the policy position of the outcome (such as the compromise policy of a governing coalition). In Appendix 6.1, we outline the Kedar approach and determine corresponding equilibrium strategies of the parties in response to outcome-oriented behavior by voters. Our results for the 1989 Norwegian election indicate that strategies at equilibrium would be about twice as dispersed under the Kedar model as under a traditional model.

We now develop our model for parties concerned not only about their own vote share but about that of their coalition as well. Under our scenario, for instance, the utilities U(Lab) and U(Soc) that Norwegian Labor and Socialist Party elites attached to an electoral outcome could be written as the weighted sum of each party's expected popular vote and the expected vote of its traditional coalition partner:

$$U(Lab) = EV(Lab) + \alpha EV(Soc)$$
$$U(Soc) = \alpha EV(Lab) + EV(Soc).$$

A similar calculus plausibly applies to the party elites of the Center, Christian People's, and Conservative Parties, who comprise the bourgeois coalition:

$$U(Cen) = EV(Cen) + \alpha EV(Chr) + \alpha EV(Con)$$
$$U(Chr) = \alpha EV(Cen) + EV(Chr) + \alpha EV(Con)$$
$$U(Con) = \alpha EV(Cen) + \alpha EV(Chr) + EV(Con),$$

where the coalition weighting parameter α represents the importance that the party attaches to the expected votes of its coalition partner(s) vis-à-vis its own votes. When $\alpha = 0$, the party is purely vote seeking; when $\alpha = 1$, it is willing to trade off its own expected votes against those of its

---

[11] Schofield and his coauthors (1998) argue (in the context of the Netherlands and Germany) that a party faces a policy trade-off when moving from its preferred position to its vote-maximizing position. The party may thereby obtain more seats and hence more strength in coalition bargaining, but the compromise policy necessary for coalition agreement may be too great a price to pay. Note that Schofield's approach rests on the policy-seeking motivations of the parties. Our analysis of coalition considerations, on the other hand, assumes that a party is concerned with whether a fixed coalition of which it is a member is the winning coalition – that is, we are concerned (in this chapter) with office-seeking motivations.

coalition partners on a one-to-one basis. We will refer to such a party as purely coalition-seeking. Values of α between zero and one indicate that a party weights both its own votes and those of its coalition partners, but that its own votes weigh more heavily in its utility calculus.[12] We label such parties partially coalition-seeking.

Intuitively, we might expect that most parties would fall into the partially coalition-seeking category. If an election outcome between two competing coalitions is expected to be close – as was the case in Norway in 1989 – a rational party is likely to be more concerned with maximizing the total vote of its coalition, so that α may be near 1.0. If, on the other hand, the winning coalition is not in doubt, parties – especially smaller members of the expected winning coalition – may be most interested in augmenting their own vote shares in order to increase their leverage during coalition negotiations. For such parties, α would be near zero.

Note that the Liberals and Progress, who were not potential members of either traditional bloc in 1989, are excluded from coalition calculations. Although the Liberals had during earlier periods been part of the left-wing coalition, the party had failed to win seats in the 1985 Storting election (and would fail again in 1989). Hence, it seems plausible that neither the Liberals themselves nor rival parties' elites viewed them as germane to coalition calculations. The case of Progress is more interesting, because the bourgeois coalition could have plausibly improved its prospects by broadening its parliamentary base to include Progress. However, not only was Progress's stand on immigration unacceptable to the other parties, but a report by Valen (1990) suggests that Progress was also far away from the Center and the Christian People's Parties along two other traditional cleavages: the moral–religious divide and the rural–urban dimension. This suggests that Progress would have remained an unacceptable coalition partner no matter what Left–Right position it presented.

In summary, in the context of Norway – a party system that features stable party positions as well as two stable opposing coalition blocs – we are led to commonsense definitions of vote-seeking and coalition-seeking parties. Vote-seeking parties will promote the policies that they believe will maximize their own electoral support, while coalition-seeking parties will present policies that maximize the collective appeal of their coalition bloc.

---

[12] If, for example, $\alpha = 0.5$, the focal party is willing to trade one vote for itself in exchange for two for a coalition partner.

Table 6.8. *Party equilibria on the Left–Right scale for partially coalition-seeking motivations: 1989 Norwegian Storting election*

	Mean Perceived Position	Mixing Parameter		
		$\alpha = 0$	$\alpha = 0.5$	$\alpha = 0.75$
Socialist	2.42	3.62	3.36	3.26
Labor	3.92	3.98	4.58	4.89
Liberal	4.36	2.73	2.33	2.17
Center	5.36	5.95	5.78	5.66
Christian	6.54	6.73	6.67	6.66
Conservative	8.23	8.45	8.20	8.02
Progress	9.02	8.95	9.04	9.11

Note: The mixing parameter α represents the extent of coalition-seeking motivations; $\alpha = 0$ represents pure vote-seeking, whereas $\alpha = 1$ would mean that a party values support for coalition partners on a par with support for itself.

Using the unified discounting model specified in section 6.5, Nash equilibrium locations were obtained under the assumption that parties are partially coalition seeking, and these are presented in Table 6.8. For simplicity, we limit our discussion to the Left–Right dimension, the most salient dimension in Norwegian politics. Columns 3 and 4 present the results for $\alpha = 0.5$ and 0.75, respectively; column 2 provides, for comparison, the equilibrium values for purely vote-seeking parties ($\alpha = 0$), while column 1 gives the mean positions of the parties as perceived by the survey respondents.

Remarkably, we note that the partially coalition-seeking equilibria are quite similar to the equilibrium configuration obtained for vote-maximizing parties and – for most parties – not greatly different from the parties' perceived positions.[13] Thus, even if the parties were free to move anywhere (and thereby risk rejection by their coalition partners), in the long run they appear to have little electoral incentive to do so.[14] These results suggest that the goals of coalition seeking and vote seeking may lead to similar party behavior.

---

[13] It is interesting to note that if the analyst permits only one party to move while fixing the other parties at their perceived positions, coalition-seeking parties would have optimal strategies that are somewhat bizarre – for example, Labor could move to the center or to the right of center while the Socialists remain on the left (or vice versa) in an effort to allow the socialist coalition to "cover all bases." Neither such movement limited to a single party nor the strategies it would imply appear realistic.

[14] For parties that are completely coalition seeking – an unlikely situation – no Nash equilibrium appears to exist.

6.7. Conclusion

In this chapter, we have provided evidence that in an electoral setting quite different from a French presidential election – namely, a Norwegian parliamentary election conducted under PR – a unified model incorporating party identification and sociodemographic variables leads nevertheless to a unique dispersed equilibrium configuration of party positions. These positions are generally correlated with the actual (perceived) positions of the parties, but the degree of dispersion is well short of that actually observed. However, the need for parties to enter coalition governments suggests that voters have reason to discount parties' positions in the sense that implemented governmental policies are likely to be more moderate than those advocated by the noncentrist parties. The equilibrium configuration of party positions predicted by the unified discounting model not only correlates well with actual party positions but also reflects the actual degree of dispersion. Finally, modifying the unified discounting model to account for the coalition-seeking motivations of Norwegian parties has little effect on their strategies at equilibrium. This result suggests that – insofar as this finding can be generalized – party elites need not balance conflicting objectives when devising their policy strategies. Within reason, for the 1989 Norwegian Storting election, whether party elites sought votes for their own party or for a prospective coalition, the unified discounting model accurately predicts parties' optimal strategies at equilibrium.

CHAPTER 7

The Threat of Abstention

Candidate Strategies and Policy Representation in U.S. Presidential Elections

7.1. Introduction

The unified theory of voting that we have studied in the multicandidate elections of France, Britain, and Norway – a theory that does not consider turnout effects – does not imply divergence of party strategies in two-party elections, such as those typical of presidential elections in the United States (see Chapter 4, section 4.3).[1] Indeed, Erikson and Romero (1990) have shown that for the unified voting model, a convergent equilibrium is likely to exist in which the two candidates locate at the *weighted mean* of the voter distribution, with each voter's policy preferences weighted according to the elasticity or marginality of her vote choice probability.[2]

How can we explain the persistent tendency – observed empirically – for the two main American parties to adopt positions that, although they may not be far apart by European standards, are nevertheless distinctly different? To this end, we include in the unified model not only the voter's choice of candidate or party, but also the voter's decision whether to vote at all. The high rate of abstention in the United States, relative to that of most European countries, is well documented (Lijphart 1997; Dalton 2002: Chapter 6).

---

[1] Expressed in the technical notation introduced in Chapter 4, if there are two candidates ($K = 2$), then $c_k = 0$ for each candidate k by Theorem 4.1, so that in turn the two quantities $s_k(0)$ are identical. Thus, although the theorem does not imply convergence of the Nash equilibrium strategies $s_k(a)$, it suggests this, and we know of no example in which divergence occurs in this setting.

[2] Erikson and Romero's result holds when voters employ a quadratic utility function with respect to policy distance. They demonstrate that the weighted mean is only guaranteed to be a local equilibrium; however, their empirical applications to the 1988 U.S. presidential election (to be discussed later) suggest that this location can be expected to be a global equilibrium in real-world elections.

Therefore, if abstention can affect party strategies, we might expect the effect to be particularly pronounced in the American context. We consider two possible motivations for abstention: (a) alienation, in which no candidate's utility reaches the voter's threshold for voting, and (b) indifference, in which the voter finds insufficient difference between the candidates to motivate casting a ballot. We label the resulting specification the *unified turnout model*. Later, in Chapter 9, we will explore policy strategies in Britain under the unified turnout model. The British political system resembles the American context in that Britain features a "two and a half" party system – with the large Labour and Conservative Parties competing against each other and also against the smaller Liberal Democratic party – and in that British elections have featured high abstention rates in recent years, by European standards.

We present illustrative arguments that, when we incorporate the turnout decision into the unified model, incentives to diverge occur in two-candidate elections, provided that some voters are prepared to abstain due to alienation – that is, in the event they find neither candidate sufficiently attractive to cast a ballot. The strategic logic that drives this result is that because of voters' non-policy-related motivations, the candidates cannot alter most voters' candidate preferences via policy appeals, but they can affect voters' turnout decisions. When abstention is due to alienation, each candidate is motivated to appeal to his own voting constituency. This occurs because he can affect his supporters' turnout decisions but has little effect on the turnout decisions of the rival party's supporters, since the latter depend primarily on these citizens' evaluations of the rival candidate. Thus, the unified turnout model that we now develop highlights the *joint* effects that voters' nonpolicy motivations and abstention due to alienation bring to bear on candidate strategies in two-party elections. In these situations, our model accounts for the fact that Democratic candidates typically present leftist policies, while Republicans locate on the right. Furthermore, in the more general situation where candidates pursue multiple objectives, the office-seeking strategies motivated by abstention due to alienation are usually compatible with alternative goals, including policy seeking, deterring entry by third candidates, and winning primary elections.

By contrast, we find that abstention resulting from indifference does not similarly motivate policy divergence by office-seeking candidates, a conclusion consistent with results reported by Erikson and Romero (1990: 1120–21). This is because when abstention is due to indifference, each candidate has incentives to appeal to the rival candidate's constituency as well as to his own supporters, since in this case candidates can influence the rival supporters' turnout decisions by diminishing these supporters' utility differentials between the candidates.

The illustrative arguments we present in this chapter support the conclusions just outlined. However, even though our examples are purposely simplified, the strategic logic that underlies our arguments is not always easy to follow. This is because our unified turnout specification contains enough "moving parts" – including citizens' policy-based candidate evaluations, their non-policy-based candidate evaluations, and their tendencies to abstain due to alienation and/or indifference – that the electoral effects of candidates' policy positioning are difficult to parse out, even in simple illustrative scenarios. For readers who prefer nontechnical intuitions, the following paragraph presents a highly stylized illustrative example (with no recourse to the mathematical notation we rely on in our subsequent arguments), which highlights how the combination of citizens' nonpolicy motivations and abstention due to alienation can motivate candidate divergence.

Suppose that a Democratic candidate D and a Republican candidate R compete for the support of an electorate consisting entirely of two voting blocs: a left-wing bloc whose members identify so strongly with the Democratic party that all of them prefer D to R, regardless of the candidates' policy positions; and a right-wing bloc whose members similarly prefer R to D, regardless of candidate positioning. Suppose further that members of both blocs are prone to abstain due to alienation – specifically, that they turn out to vote *only* if their preferred candidate presents policies they find congenial (in this example, we ignore abstention resulting from indifference).

In this scenario, the Democratic candidate D can influence the behavior of the members of the left-wing, Democratic voting bloc, since these partisans will turn out to vote for him only if he presents a sufficiently attractive policy. However, D cannot influence the behavior of the members of the right-wing, Republican bloc because they prefer R to D regardless of the candidates' positions, and their turnout decisions depend entirely on whether they find R's position sufficiently attractive. Therefore, D has electoral motivation to appeal to his leftist, Democratic constituency; and similarly, R has incentives to appeal to his right-wing, Republican, constituency; so the optimal strategies of D and R are not identical. Later, we will show that the logic of this highly stylized election scenario carries over to more realistic examples in which the partisan distributions overlap, partisan loyalties are not so strong that partisans always prefer their party's candidate, and citizens may abstain due to indifference as well as alienation.

Our results have implications not only for candidates' policy strategies but also for political representation. The effects of turnout and voters' non-policy-related motivations on candidates' strategies enhance representation in two ways: namely, candidates are motivated to present divergent policies that offer voters a genuine choice, *and* candidates have incentives to advocate policies that reflect the beliefs of their traditional voting constituencies. The latter result is consistent with the empirical finding of Bishin (2000) that congressional representatives' roll call votes are more responsive to shifts in the policy preferences of their party's partisans than they are to policy shifts of independents or of the rival party's partisans.

7.2. Incorporating the Turnout Decision into the Unified Voting Model

7.2.1. Abstention due to Alienation

Abstention resulting from alienation – which occurs when the voter decides that no candidate is sufficiently attractive to merit his support – has been extensively explored in spatial models of elections, in which the likelihood of abstention is assumed to increase with the policy distance between the voter and the nearest candidate (see Downs 1957: 118–120; Riker and Ordeshook 1973; Enelow and Hinich 1984; Hinich and Munger 1994). In addition, empirical studies by Riker and Ordeshook (1968), Brody and Page (1973), Hinich (1978), Thurner and Eymann (2000), and Gershtenson and Plane (1999) conclude that alienation accounts for significant levels of abstention in national elections.

In order to model voters' tendencies to abstain due to alienation, we postulate that each voter i has an *alienation threshold*, denoted by $T_i(A)$, where A refers to alienation. We interpret this to mean that if abstention is solely due to alienation, then the voter votes for his preferred candidate if his utility for that candidate exceeds his alienation threshold $T_i(A)$; otherwise, he abstains.

Lacy and Burden (1999; see also Burden and Lacy 1999; Adams and Merrill 2003a) develop a unified specification for the turnout and voting decision consistent with this definition. In their analyses of the 1968, 1980, 1992, and 1996 presidential elections, Lacy and Burden specify that the alienation threshold $T_i(A)$ may vary across individuals as a function of their personal characteristics, such as age, education, and race, as well as a function of their attitudes along such dimensions as system support and political efficacy. Following Burden and Lacy, we specify that voter i's abstention threshold due to alienation is given by

$$T_i(A) = \sum_l b_{Al} t_{il} + X_i = \mathbf{b}_A \mathbf{t}_i + X_i, \tag{7.1}$$

where $\mathbf{t}_i$ is a vector of the voter's characteristics t_{il}; $\mathbf{b}_A$ is a vector of parameters b_{Al} to be estimated; and the X_i are independent, random perturbation terms.[3] As before, the subscript l refers to the lth nonpolicy variable. Note that the term $\mathbf{b}_A \mathbf{t}_i$ represents the measured components of i's alienation threshold.

7.2.2. Abstention due to Indifference

A second motivation for abstention is that the voter does not have a strong preference between the candidates. In this case, he abstains *due to indifference* because the time and effort required to go to the polling booth (minus any benefits he gains from fulfilling his civic duty) outweigh his instrumental benefit from voting (see Riker and Ordeshook 1968). Abstention due to indifference has been incorporated into spatial models of candidate competition (see Riker and Ordeshook 1973; Enelow and Hinich 1984; Hinich and Munger 1994). It has also been explored in empirical studies of voter turnout that conclude that indifference does indeed motivate abstention (see Riker and Ordeshook 1968; Brody and Page 1973; Hinich 1978; but also see Weisberg and Grofman 1981 for a different conclusion).

Formally, let $T_i(I)$ represent voter i's *indifference threshold*, which is the minimum utility differential between the candidates such that the voter prefers voting to abstaining. In a two-candidate contest, the voter votes for his preferred candidate if the difference between his utilities for the two candidates exceeds his indifference threshold $T_i(I)$.[4] Indifference thresholds are assumed to be non-negative, since a negative indifference threshold implies

---

[3] As for previous models, our random-effect model is conditional logit (see Chapter 2), in which the random perturbation term follows a type 2 extreme-value distribution.

[4] Note that we are using the term "indifference" in a different sense than it is typically used, because in our terminology voters may abstain due to indifference even if their utility differentials are nonzero, as long as these differentials fall below a certain threshold.

that the voter may choose to vote for a candidate even though he prefers the rival candidate.

Sanders (1998, 2001; see also Erikson and Romero 1990: 1120–21) develops a unified specification of the turnout and vote choice consistent with this definition. Our specification follows Sanders's in that, as the subscript i indicates, indifference thresholds may vary across individuals as a function of their personal characteristics and their perceptions of the competitiveness of the election. For instance, certain groups of citizens may feel a particularly strong sense of civic obligation to vote; while the perceived costs and benefits of voting may also vary with citizens' sociodemographic characteristics, their political efficacy, and their beliefs about the likelihood of casting a decisive vote. Indeed, Sanders's (1998) study of turnout in the 1988 and 1992 presidential elections concludes that voters' indifference thresholds decrease with age, income, a sense of high political efficacy, and the expectation of a close election. Accordingly, we model the voter i's indifference threshold as:

$$T_i(I) = \exp\left[\sum_l b_{Il}t_{il}\right] = \exp[\mathbf{b}_I\mathbf{t}_i], \qquad (7.2)$$

where $\mathbf{t}_i$ is a vector of the voter's characteristics t_{il}, and $\mathbf{b}_I$ is a vector of parameters b_{Il} to be estimated.[5] The subscript l refers to the lth nonpolicy variable. We express the indifference threshold $T_i(I)$ as an exponential function of voters' personal characteristics in order to constrain it to be positive, because a negative threshold for indifference makes no sense.

7.2.3. A Unified Indifference-Alienation Model

We incorporate abstention resulting from indifference and alienation into a single model, the *unified indifference-alienation model* (which we label the *unified turnout model* for simplicity). This model is developed in detail in Adams, Dow, and Merrill (2001) and Adams and Merrill (2003a). Under this model, voter i votes for his preferred candidate if his utility for that candidate exceeds his alienation threshold $T_i(A)$ and the difference between his utilities for the candidates exceeds his indifference threshold $T_i(I)$. As

---

[5] We introduce no random term in equation 7.2 for mathematical tractability. This is also the approach used by Sanders (1998, 2001).

we have seen in Chapter 2, equation 2.6, the voter's utility for candidate k is given by

$$U_i(k) = V_i(k) + X_{ik} = -\sum_j a_j(x_{ij} - s_{kj})^2 + \mathbf{b}_k \mathbf{t}_{ik} + X_{ik}. \quad (7.3)$$

Previous empirical studies have generally concluded that both indifference and alienation contribute to abstention in presidential elections (see Riker and Ordeshook 1968; Brody and Page 1973; Hinich 1978; Guttman, Hilger, and Shacmurove 1994; Adams, Dow, and Merrill 2001; but also see Weisberg and Grofman 1981). In particular, the Adams–Dow–Merrill study – the only study we are aware of that distinguishes between alienation and indifference in the context of a unified turnout model – concludes that both motivations contributed significantly to abstention in the 1980, 1984, and 1988 presidential elections, with alienation depressing turnout to a somewhat greater extent than indifference. In the next section, we show that the distinction between alienation and indifference is important, because these motivations provide candidates with contrasting strategic incentives.[6]

7.3. Candidate Strategies under the Unified Turnout Model: Illustrative Arguments

As noted earlier, although spatial modelers have extensively explored the strategic implications of voter turnout, these models typically assume that candidates' positions are the only measured influence on the vote choice (see, e.g., Davis, Hinich, and Ordeshook 1970; Hinich and Ordeshook 1970; Enelow and Hinich 1984; Anderson and Glomm 1992). These studies conclude that for most realistic election scenarios, turnout effects do not alter

---

[6] Although models that combine alienation and indifference are common in spatial modeling (see Hinich, Ledyard, and Ordeshook 1972; Enelow and Hinich 1984; Anderson and Glomm 1992), spatial modelers typically focus on *policy-based* alienation and indifference, so that, for instance, an election featuring a center-left and a center-right candidate may trigger alienation among extreme ideologues while prompting indifference among centrist voters. By contrast, because our unified turnout model specifies that citizens' candidate evaluations are moved by nonpolicy as well as policy factors, there is no necessary connection between respondents' policy beliefs and their abstention motivations. For instance, an extreme left-wing citizen may abstain due to indifference, not alienation, if his policy preference for the Democratic candidate is offset by his preference for the Republican candidate on character grounds. Indeed, the empirical analyses we report in this chapter uncover only a weak connection between respondents' policy beliefs and their tendency to abstain due to alienation versus abstaining due to indifference.

the basic logic of the Downsian model that office-seeking candidates have incentives to present similar, centrist positions. Here we present illustrative arguments that when candidates account simultaneously for turnout effects *and* for voters' non-policy-related motivations, abstention resulting from alienation tends to draw candidates away from the center, in the direction of their partisan constituencies.

For these illustrations, we analyze a simplified electoral context that permits us to isolate the ways in which voters' nonpolicy motivations and their turnout decisions interact. Our illustrations assume deterministic voting and a linear utility function (i.e., the spatial component of utility declines linearly with distance between voter and candidate)[7] and consider only liberal–conservative ideology, one nonpolicy variable (partisanship), and abstention due to alienation or indifference. Specifically, in equation 7.3 let the policy salience parameter $a = 1$. To specify partisanship, let $t_i = 1$ if the voter identifies with the candidate's party and zero otherwise, and let b be the associated parameter for the salience of partisanship. We set the alienation and indifference parameters in equations 7.1 and 7.2 to the constants T_A and T_I for all voters. Thus the alienation-indifference (IA) model in our illustration becomes

$$U_i(k) = V_i(k) = -|x_i - s_k| + bt_{ik}. \qquad (7.4)$$

For convenience, we will use the terminology of American elections, referring to the candidate positions as D and R, suggestive of the nominees of the Democratic and Republican parties, respectively. Thus for Democratic partisans, $U_i(D) = b - |x_i - D|$ and $U_i(R) = -|x_i - R|$, whereas for Republican partisans, $U_i(D) = -|x_i - D|$ and $U_i(R) = b - |x_i - R|$, where x_i represents the voter's left-right position, and b represents partisans' utilities for their party's candidate due to partisan loyalty.

We assume a voter distribution composed entirely of two partisan constituencies: a Democratic constituency with density function f_D and a Republican distribution with density function f_R. For purposes of the illustration, we further assume that f_D and f_R are each symmetrically distributed (for example, normal), that each distribution extends to plus and minus infinity, and that each density function declines monotonically as one

---

[7] We assume linear policy losses, as this simplifies the mathematical exposition that accompanies our illustrative arguments. However, the strategic logic of these arguments would be quite similar if we employed the quadratic loss function.

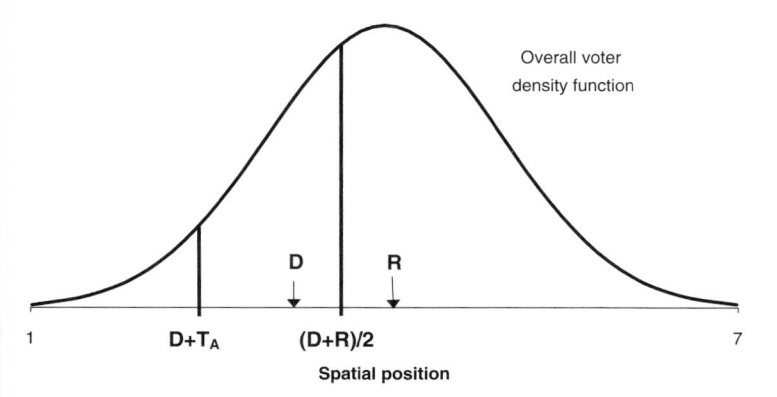

Figure 7.1. Policy-only turnout model.
Note: As the Democratic candidate D moves to the right, with the Republican candidate R fixed at the overall vote median, the former picks up more voters from the Republican, near $(D + R)/2$, than she loses to abstention, near $D + T_A$. Hence the Democratic candidate has an incentive to move toward the Republican candidate, resulting in equilibrium at the center.

moves away from the positions of the median (mean) Democrat μ_D and the median (mean) Republican μ_R. We also assume that f_D and f_R are identical except for location, with $\mu_D < \mu_R$ – that is, that Republicans are on average more conservative than Democrats. The overall voter distribution $f = \frac{f_D + f_R}{2}$, pictured in Figure 7.1, is also assumed to decline monotonically as one moves away from $\mu = \frac{\mu_D + \mu_R}{2}$, the position of the median voter. The NES data analyses reported later suggest that this illustrative example roughly approximates the actual distribution of American voters' policy and partisan inclinations.

The policy-only turnout model: The candidates stay at the center. Initially we consider a policy-only version of the unified turnout model in which partisanship does not affect utility (i.e., $b = 0$). Specifically, we consider the case in which the Republican is positioned at the location of the median voter (i.e., $R = \mu$), and the Democrat is positioned at D, to the left of μ.

First, consider the strategic dynamics relating to abstention due to alienation. As the Democratic candidate moves in the positive direction (to the right), he draws support away from the Republican candidate in the region near the midpoint between the two candidates' positions, that is, near

$c_{DR} = (D + R)/2$. In fact, if the Democrat moves a distance ε, the midpoint c_{DR} moves a distance $\varepsilon/2$ (see Figure 7.1). Because each vote picked up by the Democrat is the loss of a vote for the Republican, the change in the margin for the Democrat relative to the Republican is

$$2(\varepsilon/2)f[(D + R)/2] = \varepsilon \times f[(D + R)/2]. \tag{7.5}$$

Thus the rate of change of the margin for the Democrat over the Republican is given[8] by $f[(D + R)/2]$.

At the same time, the Democrat loses votes to abstention due to alienation near the point where $T_A = U(D)$, that is, near $D + T_A$ (see Figure 7.1). Specifically, when the Democrat moves a distance ε to the right of D, the point $D + T_A$ moves by the same amount and in the same direction. Thus the Democrat loses votes to abstention at the rate of $f(D + T_A)$. If $D - T_A$ is to the left of $(D + R)/2$, the Democrat also gains votes from abstention at the rate of $f(D + T_A)$. [If $D - T_A$ is to the right of the midpoint, $U(R) > U(D)$ near $D - T_A$, so that a voter there would vote Republican in any event.]

We conclude that the overall rate of gain for the Democratic candidate when moving to the right is

$$f[(D + R)/2] - f(D + T_A) \tag{7.6}$$

plus a possible additional positive term, $f(D - T_A)$. It follows that if the voter density f is greater near $(D + R)/2$ than near $D + T_A$ (as in our example), any movement of the Democratic candidate toward the position of the Republican candidate will result in a net gain relative to the vote share of the Republican. We conclude that the Democrat has an electoral incentive to converge to the position of the Republican.

The unified turnout model: Abstention resulting from alienation motivates the candidates to reflect their partisan constituencies' policy preferences. Next, we incorporate party ID, obtaining a *unified turnout model.* Specifically, we now assume that $b > 0$ – that is, that partisans are biased in favor of their party's candidate. To our knowledge, the only previous spatial analysis of this model is by Erikson and Romero (1990: 1120–21), who conclude that when voters abstain entirely due to indifference, the candidates will converge to identical positions. However, in Appendix 7.1 we

---

[8] Expressing the relationship in equation 7.5 in terms of derivatives, we obtain $\frac{\partial c_{DR}}{\partial D} = \frac{1}{2}$, so that the rate of change of the Democrat's margin is $2\frac{\partial c_{DR}}{\partial D} f[(D + R)/2] = f[(D + R)/2]$.

demonstrate the following lemma, which implies that the introduction of abstention due to alienation changes this conclusion:

Lemma 7.1. Assume the conditions on the voter distribution detailed for our illustrative example. Then, given $b > T_A$, $b > T_I$, and $b < \infty$ (i.e., not all voters abstain due to alienation, and partisans' biases are sufficiently strong that they do not abstain due to indifference when the candidates take identical positions), under the unified turnout model any possible equilibrium configuration must find the Democratic candidate taking a position strictly to the left, and the Republican candidate taking a position strictly to the right, of the median voter position μ.

Lemma 7.1 implies that under the unified turnout model, the candidates have strategic incentives to diverge from the center, in the direction of their partisan constituencies' policy preferences. What drives this result? While the strategic dynamics of candidate competition under the unified turnout model are complex, here we focus on a specific scenario that captures the central intuition about why abstention due to alienation – but not indifference – motivates candidate divergence. This is the case where D locates to the left of $R = \mu$, but the policy distance between D and R is less than b, as in Figure 7.2. As long as this condition holds, all voters prefer their party's nominee to the rival candidate due to partisan loyalties.

First, consider the strategic dynamics relating to abstention due to alienation. (For simplicity, we defer incorporation of abstention due to indifference until later.) Marginal shifts in D's position do not affect Republican partisans' behavior, because such shifts alter neither these partisans' preference for the Republican candidate over the Democrat, nor their calculus about whether they evaluate the Republican candidate positively enough to refrain from abstaining due to alienation. However, marginal rightward shifts in the Democratic candidate's position *do* affect Democratic partisans' turnout decisions, in that such shifts prompt additional Democrats located to the left of D to abstain due to alienation and additional Democrats located to the right of D to turn out to vote Democratic. The overall rate of change in D's vote margin vis-à-vis R is

$$-f_D(D - [b - T_A)]) + f_D(D + [b - T_A]). \tag{7.7}$$

Because the Democratic partisan distribution is centered to the left of the overall voter distribution, the Democratic candidate's vote margin will decline if he converges to the Republican candidate's position. This is illustrated

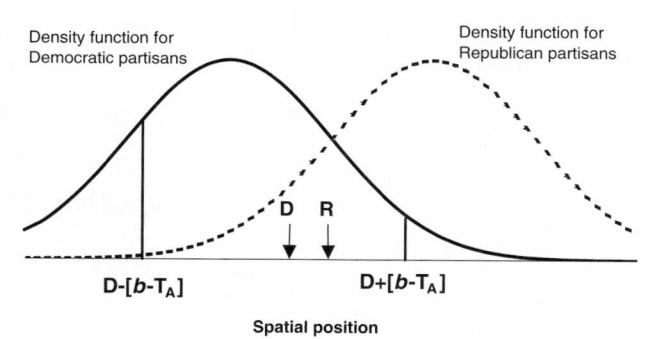

Density function for Democratic partisans

Density function for Republican partisans

D R

$D-[b-T_A]$ $D+[b-T_A]$

Spatial position

Figure 7.2. Unified turnout model.
Note: If the distance between the Democratic candidate D and the Republican candidate R is less than the partisan-salience parameter b, the Democratic candidate cannot pick up votes from the Republican candidate, and only Democratic partisans' turnout decisions are affected. Because these voters are concentrated on the left, as D moves to the right (with R fixed at the overall voter median), the Democratic candidate gains fewer votes from abstention near $D + [b - T_A]$ than she loses to abstention near $D - [b - T_A]$. Hence the Democratic candidate has an incentive to move left, away from the center.

in Figure 7.2, which shows that so long as D is located in the policy interval $[\mu_D, \mu]$, D loses support by shifting toward the center – that is, D has a strategic incentive to diverge from the position of the median voter, in the direction of his partisan constituency.

The central intuition is that due to voters' partisan loyalties, in this scenario the candidates cannot affect voters' preferences between the candidates, but the candidates can affect voters' turnout decisions. And *when abstention is due to alienation, each candidate is motivated to appeal to his own partisan constituency, since he can affect his supporters' turnout decisions but not the turnout decisions of the rival party's supporters, as the latter depend solely on these supporters' evaluations of the rival candidate.*

This strategic intuition depends on three factors: that voters are prepared to abstain due to alienation; that voters display partisan loyalties in addition to policy motivations; and that these partisan loyalties correlate with voters' policy positions. In Chapter 8, we show empirically that all three conditions were satisfied in the 1980, 1984, 1988, 1996, and 2000 U.S. presidential elections.

Finally, we incorporate abstention resulting from indifference. Consider first the case in which the distance between D and R exceeds $(b - T_I)$, where, as before, T_I is the indifference threshold. Now rightward shifts by the Democratic candidate gain additional votes from Democratic partisans located between D and R near the position $[(D + R)/2 + (b - T_I)/2]$ and from Republican partisans located between D and R near the position $[(D + R)/2 - (b - T_I)/2]$. Both of these groups switch from abstaining due to indifference to voting for D.[9] Hence the introduction of abstention due to indifference provides added incentives for candidate convergence, compared to the alienation-only model. Appendix 7.2 presents additional analysis of the candidates' support functions.

If, however, D and R are sufficiently close that $[b - T_I]$ exceeds the distance between D and R, then no voters abstain due to indifference.[10] In this case, the strategic logic of candidate competition is identical to the logic of the alienation-only model explored earlier, so that the candidates again have strategic incentives to diverge from the center in the direction of their partisan constituencies' policy preferences.

We conclude that situations where abstention due to indifference affects candidates' calculations – that is, situations where the distance between D and R exceeds $(b - T_I)$ – provide additional strategic incentives for the Democratic candidate to shift toward the Republican. The central argument is that, in this case, indifferent voters are located between the two candidates' positions, so that appealing to such voters necessarily motivates convergence. But Lemma 7.1 suggests that in the presence of abstention due to alienation, this motivation only goes so far. As the Democrat approaches the Republican at the median voter position, she stands to lose more of her partisans to abstention due to alienation on the left, where they are concentrated, than on the right, where they are few.

Figure 7.3 illustrates the unique equilibrium that exists for our hypothetical example, given plausible values for the unified turnout model parameters: $b = 2$, $T_A = -0.5$, and $T_I = 0.5$. We assume that each group of partisans is normally distributed, with common standard deviation $= 1$ and with a mean at 3 for Democratic partisans and a mean of 5 for Republican partisans. The

---

[9] In addition, D's vote margin vis-à-vis R improves further because any Democratic partisans located between D and R near the position $[(D + R)/2 + (b + T_I)/2]$ switch from voting for R to abstaining, as do any Republican partisans located near the position $[(D + R)/2 - (b + T_I)/2]$.

[10] To see this, note that in our illustrative example each voter i's utility differential between the candidates exceeds her indifference threshold provided that $|b - (|R - x_i|) - (|D - x_i|)| > T_I$, and that this condition is satisfied for all voters when $b - T_I > |R - D|$.

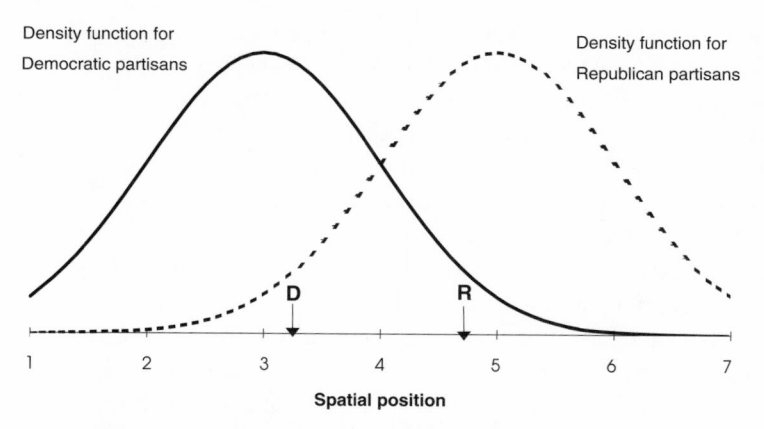

Figure 7.3. Equilibrium under the unified turnout model.
Note: For plausible parameter values in the unified turnout model ($b = 2$, $T_A = -0.5$, and $T_I = 0.5$), an equilibrium occurs in which the Democratic candidate D and the Republican candidate R hold positions that are at a substantial distance from the center.

equilibrium occurs at approximately the values $D = 3.25$ and R $= 4.75$ – that is, at distinct values for the Democratic and Republican candidates.

7.4. Conclusion

We have developed this illustration at length in order to convey the strategic logic of candidate competition under the unified turnout model. Our illustration suggests that the policy-only turnout model motivates office-seeking candidates to converge to identical policy positions, but that the unified turnout model – which incorporates voters' partisan loyalties – motivates candidate divergence. Furthermore, this policy divergence is driven by abstention due to alienation rather than by indifference, since it is the combination of voters' alienation and their partisan biases that motivates candidates to appeal to their own partisan constituencies, as these candidates can affect their own supporters' turnout decisions but not the turnout decisions of the rival candidate's supporters.

However, our illustrative scenarios in which the candidates take divergent positions that reflect their voting constituencies' beliefs do not prove that this is a *general* strategic incentive. Moreover, our simplified examples omit many features of real-world electorates that candidates may consider important. These include the presence of independent voters in the electorate;

additional measured voting influences arising from group loyalties; unmeasured voter motivations that render voters' decisions probabilistic from the candidates' perspectives; and multiple policy dimensions. In Chapter 8, we investigate the logic of candidate competition in a historical context (five American presidential elections from 1980 to 2000), which permits us to explore each of these complicating factors.

Candidate Strategies with Voter Abstention in U.S. Presidential Elections

1980, 1984, 1988, 1996, and 2000

8.1. Introduction

In this chapter, we analyze candidate strategies for the U.S. presidential elections of 1980, 1984, 1988, 1996, and 2000 under the unified turnout model developed in Chapter 7.[1] In exploring these elections we (1) focus on the divergence between the candidates' optimal strategies and how differing degrees of policy divergence between Democratic and Republican partisans affect the degree of divergence of optimal strategies, and (2) extend our analysis to encompass a fully unified turnout model in which voters discount the candidates' policy positions – a possibility that is empirically supported by Lacy and Paolino's (1998) analysis of voting in U.S. presidential elections.

Consistent with the theoretical analyses presented in Chapter 7, we find that for every presidential election we examine, the major party candidates had electoral incentives to present divergent policies when voters chose according to the unified turnout model. We also conclude that the degree of candidate divergence at equilibrium increases with the amount of divergence between the Democratic and Republican partisans. Finally, we find that policy discounting by voters would give the candidates additional incentives to diverge in the policy space, but not to diverge as much as the preferred positions of their partisan constituencies or the actual (perceived) positions of the candidates. We conclude that voters' turnout decisions are important

---

[1] We do not analyze the 1992 presidential election, as it featured three competitive candidates (Perot, Clinton, and Bush Sr.), and it is unclear how to model the effects of indifference on voters' turnout decisions in such multicandidate elections (see Sanders 1998; cf. Brody and Grofman 1982).

for candidate strategies, an effect office-seeking candidates should take into account.

8.2. Hypotheses on Voting Behavior and Candidate Strategies under the Unified Turnout Model

We begin with two hypotheses about candidate strategies that we will test using data from the five American election studies. Each hypothesis applies to candidates' margin-maximizing policy positions for an empirically estimated turnout model. Our first hypothesis tests our central theoretical argument:

H1: For a *unified turnout model*, the Democratic candidate's optimal positions diverge significantly from the Republican candidate's optima along the policy scales.

Specifically, our arguments from Section 7.3 suggest Democratic candidates' computed policy optima will be more liberal than those of the Republican candidate, since the elements of the Democratic party's voting constituency typically take more liberal positions than does the Republican constituency.

Note that the logic underlying Hypothesis 1 implies that the candidates' incentives to adopt divergent policies can vary across policy domains. On issues where Democratic and Republican partisans disagree sharply – such as traditional left–right economic issues – the candidates' incentives to reflect their voting constituencies' beliefs may prompt them to present distinctly divergent policies. By contrast, issue domains that do not sharply divide Democratic from Republican partisans (such as certain kinds of foreign policy debates) should not similarly motivate office-seeking candidates to present divergent positions. This suggests a second hypothesis, one that we can explore using the multiple policy scales included in the American National Election Studies:

H2: For a *unified turnout model*, the greater the degree of divergence between Democratic and Republican partisans' self-placements along a given policy dimension, the greater the divergence between the candidates' optimal positions along that dimension.

To the extent that Hypothesis 2 is supported, it will in turn support our argument that candidate policy divergence is driven by the divergent views held by the Democratic and Republican parties' voting constituencies.

8.3. Candidate Competition in the 1988 American Presidential Election

8.3.1. A Unified Turnout Model of the 1988 Presidential Vote

The 1988 election, on which we focus first, is particularly appropriate for our purposes, since it is the most recent U.S. presidential election for which the American National Election Study (ANES) provides validated voting data. The availability of validated voting is important, because respondents' over-reporting of turnout in unvalidated studies is a serious problem in analyzing the effects of abstention (Burden 2000b).[2]

In order to test our first hypothesis, we estimated the parameters of a unified turnout specification for the 1988 ANES respondents. This specification is based on equations 7.1–7.3, which we reproduce here:

$$U_i(k) = V_i(k) + X_{ik} = -\sum_j a_j(x_{ij} - s_{kj})^2 + \mathbf{b}_k \mathbf{t}_{ik} + X_{ik} \quad (8.1)$$

$$T_i(A) = \mathbf{B}_A \mathbf{t}'_i + \varepsilon_{ik} \tag{8.2}$$

$$T_i(I) = \exp\left[\mathbf{B}_I \mathbf{t}''_i\right], \tag{8.3}$$

where the X_{ik} and ε_{ik} are random disturbance terms that represent unmeasured sources of the voter's utilities. As in Chapter 7, $U_i(k)$ represents the voter i's utility for candidate k, while $T_i(A)$ and $T_i(I)$ represent i's alienation and indifference thresholds, respectively. We use a conditional logit model of voter choice, as we have done in previous chapters.

With respect to policy voting, we employed the seven-point ideology and policy scales included in the 1988 ANES: liberal–conservative ideology, domestic spending, health insurance, government aid to minorities/blacks, guaranteed jobs, dealing with Russia, women's role, and defense spending. Table 8.1 reports, for each dimension, the respondents' mean self-placements (column 1) and their placements of the Democratic candidate Dukakis and the Republican candidate Bush Sr. (columns 5–6). Also given are the mean placements for Democratic partisans (col. 2) and for Republican partisans (col. 3), as well as the policy distance between these two groups (col. 4). For each of these dimensions, we assumed that respondents' candidate utilities

---

[2] For instance, in the 1996 and 2000 ANES, respondents' reported turnout rates were near 75 percent, far higher than the actual turnout rates in these elections (see Table 8.5). By contrast, the validated turnout rate in the 1988 ANES is near 50 percent, which is close to the actual participation level for that election.

Table 8.1. *Respondent self-placements and candidate placements, 1988 ANES (N = 1,389)*

	Mean Respondent Self-placements				Mean Respondent Candidate Placements	
	All Respondents	Democratic Partisans[a]	Republican Partisans[a]	Partisan Divergence[b]	Dukakis	Bush
	(1)	(2)	(3)	(4)	(5)	(6)
Ideology	4.37	3.81	4.94	1.13	3.24	5.11
Domestic spending	3.93	3.40	4.49	1.09	2.90	4.45
Defense spending	3.89	3.44	4.36	0.92	3.30	5.28
Health insurance	3.95	3.37	4.58	1.21	3.10	5.05
Aid to minorities	4.57	4.10	4.95	0.85	3.30	4.83
Government jobs	4.51	3.93	5.08	1.15	3.38	5.05
Dealing with Russia	3.73	3.58	3.88	0.30	3.40	4.09
Women's role	2.50	2.40	2.62	0.22	2.86	3.70

[a] Democratic and Republican partisans are defined to include "leaners," so that Democratic partisans are those respondents coded 0–2 on the party identification variable, and Republican partisans are coded 4–6 on this variable.

[b] Partisan divergence is defined as the policy distance separating the mean self-placements of the Democratic respondents (column 2) and the mean self-placements of Republicans (column 3).

decreased with the squared[3] distance between the voter's preferred position x_{ij} and the candidate k's position s_{kj} along the jth dimension (see Chapter 2, section 2.3).

We model citizens' utilities for the candidates as a function of *party iden-tification, ideological distance* to each candidate, *policy distance* to each candidate, respondent assessment of *candidate character, race,* and *retro-spective evaluations of the national economy.* We model citizens' alienation and indifference thresholds as functions of *race, education, political efficacy, previous vote,* and (for indifference) *perceived election closeness.* Each of these variables has been identified as important in prior research on candidate choice and voter turnout (see, e.g., Markus and Converse 1979; Wolfinger and Rosenstone 1980; Alvarez and Nagler 1995; Sanders 1998; Lacy and Burden 1999). Our coding rules are given in Appendix 8.1, along with the complete model specification.

We estimated the model described in the preceding paragraph, based upon the subsample of 1,389 respondents included in the 1988 ANES who could self-place on the liberal–conservative dimension. In calculating the policy distance variables, for simplicity we took the candidates' positions as the mean respondent candidate placement along each dimension (see section 2.5).

Table 8.2 reports the parameter estimates and the standard errors for this *unified turnout model,* applied to the 1988 ANES. (Note that the table reports parameter estimates for additional election years, which will be discussed later). As expected, the coefficients relating to partisanship, ideological dis-tance, policy distances, and candidate character in column 1 are statistically significant at the .01 level and show the expected signs. With respect to respondents' turnout decisions, the coefficients reported in columns 2–3 suggest that blacks abstain disproportionately as a result of alienation, that high levels of political efficacy reduce the likelihood that voters abstain due to indifference, and that respondents who reported voting in the previous election are less likely to abstain in the current election than are those who abstained previously.

We use the coefficients in Table 8.2 to predict the probabilities that each respondent voted for the Democratic candidate, voted Republican, or

---

[3] We also analyzed a policy specification in which candidate utilities decreased with the absolute distance between respondents and candidates (the assumption we used in our illustrative arguments in Chapter 7). This analysis yielded substantive conclusions identical to those we report here.

Table 8.2. *Conditional logit equations for the unified turnout model: 1980, 1984, 1988, 1996, and 2000 presidential elections*

	Independent Variables	Candidate Parameters (1)	Indifference Threshold (2)	Alienation Threshold (3)
1980	Intercept (Rep.)	−.093 (.164)	1.88** (.67)	1.76** (.28)
N = 998	Ideology	.026 (.025)		
	Policy	.099** (.031)		
	Party identification	.65** (.11)		
	Candidate character	2.21** (.20)		
	Retrospective national economy (Dem.)	−.11 (.14)		
	Retrosp. econ. (Rep.)	−.25 (.15)		
	Black (Dem.)	2.88* (1.14)	−2.62 (11.27)	2.94* (1.23)
	Political efficacy		−.74 (.91)	−1.85 (1.05)
	Voted in 1976		−1.15** (.24)	−1.05* (.50)
	Education		.10 (.08)	.00 (.10)
	Close election		−.23 (.17)	
	Log-likelihood	−735.20		
1984	Intercept (Rep.)	.271** (.083)	1.05** (.18)	1.48** (.39)
N = 1,553	Ideology	.033 (.025)		
	Policy	.135** (.026)		
	Party identification	.93** (.12)		
	Candidate character	1.47** (.17)		
	Retrosp. econ. (Dem.)	−.17 (.09)		
	Retrosp. econ. (Rep.)	.13 (.10)		
	Black (Dem.)	.09 (.38)	−.31 (.45)	.70 (.51)
	Political efficacy		−3.28** (.94)	1.21* (.46)
	Voted in 1980		NA	NA
	Education		−.06 (.03)	−.32** (.05)
	Close election		.13 (.12)	
	Log-likelihood	−1183.90		
1988	Intercept (Rep.)	.127 (.093)	1.97** (.23)	1.19* (.52)
N = 1,389	Ideology	.062** (.020)		
	Policy	.155** (.033)		
	Party identification	1.12** (.11)		
	Candidate character	1.27** (.20)		
	Retrosp. econ. (Dem.)	−.36** (.11)		
	Retrosp. econ. (Rep.)	−.23* (.11)		
	Black (Dem.)	1.11* (.56)	−.09 (.21)	1.91** (.59)
	Political efficacy		−2.89** (.65)	.91 (.52)
	Voted in 1984		−1.65** (.24)	−1.17** (.31)
	Education		.01 (.05)	−.07 (.06)
	Close election		−.15 (.15)	
	Log-likelihood	−929.38		

	Independent Variables	Candidate Parameters (1)	Indifference Threshold (2)	Alienation Threshold (3)
1996	Intercept (Rep.)	−.570** (.123)	3.16* (1.44)	2.72** (.47)
N = 1,329	Ideology	.073** (.022)		
	Policy	.146** (.035)		
	Party identification	1.00** (.139)		
	Candidate character	2.84** (.229)		
	Retrosp. econ. (Dem.)	.212 (.128)		
	Retrosp. econ. (Rep.)	−.247 (.131)		
	Black (Dem.)	2.72* (1.082)	.71 (.50)	2.69* (1.00)
	Political efficacy		−2.52 (1.68)	−.08 (.49)
	Voted in 1992		−2.50* (1.16)	−2.80** (.22)
	Education		−.61 (.55)	−.23** (.07)
	Close election		−.23 (.41)	
	Log-likelihood	−685.91		
2000	Intercept (Rep.)	.201** (.096)	2.04** (.28)	2.95** (.76)
N = 1,328	Ideology	.150** (.056)		
	Policy	.219** (.068)		
	Party identification	1.02** (.108)		
	Candidate character	2.76** (.238)		
	Retrosp. econ. (Dem.)	−.25 (.18)		
	Retrosp. econ. (Rep.)	−.33 (.18)		
	Black (Dem.)	1.25** (.428)	.16 (.30)	.64 (.80)
	Political efficacy		−.28 (.46)	−5.71* (2.54)
	Voted in 1996		−1.24** (.20)	−2.73** (.42)
	Education		−.29** (.09)	−.32** (.05)
	Close election		−.38** (.18)	
	Log-likelihood	−697.37		

Note: The voting specifications used to estimate these parameters are given by equations A8.1–A8.4 in Appendix 8.1. The parameters for ideological distance, policy distance, party identification, and candidate character are constrained to have equal values with respect to respondents' utilities for the Democratic and Republican candidates. One asterisk signifies statistical significance at the .05 level; two asterisks signify statistical significance at the .01 level. Standard errors are in parentheses.

abstained.[4] Using the mean values of these probabilities as the expected outcomes, Table 8.3 reports predictions for the abstention rate and the candidates' vote percentages among ANES survey respondents for the unified turnout model (row 2). These closely match the ANES respondents' actual aggregate behavior (row 1).[5]

[4] The conditional logit choice probabilities associated with voting for Dukakis and Bush are given in Appendix 8.1.
[5] We also estimated that approximately 19 percent of the 1988 ANES respondents abstained due to alienation, 14 percent abstained due to indifference, and 18 percent abstained due

Table 8.3. *Projected candidate votes and abstention rates for the unified turnout model versus the actual ANES vote and abstention distributions, for the 1980, 1984, 1988, 1996, and 2000 presidential elections*

	Democratic Candidate's Vote	Republican Candidate's Vote	Abstention Rate
1980 ANES distribution	.236	.286	.478
Unified turnout model	.231	.269	.498
1984 ANES distribution	.225	.317	.458
Unified turnout model	.229	.313	.457
1988 ANES distribution	.231	.262	.507
Unified turnout model	.233	.261	.505
1996 ANES distribution	.429	.321	.250
Unified turnout model	.430	.321	.249
2000 ANES distribution	.398	.376	.226
Unified turnout model	.398	.375	.227

Note: The projected votes and abstention rate are calculated using the parameter estimates for the unified turnout model reported in Table 8.2.

8.3.2. Candidate Positioning and Electoral Outcomes under the Unified Turnout Model

We now evaluate Hypotheses 1 and 2, that under the unified turnout model Bush and Dukakis have electoral incentives to present divergent policy positions, and that these incentives increase with the degree of divergence between Democratic and Republican partisans' policy preferences. For this exercise, we performed an equilibrium analysis. The Nash equilibrium positions for ideology and each of the seven policy issues are reported in Table 8.4, in columns 1–2.[6] Bootstrap standard errors for these positions

to both alienation and indifference (the details of these calculations are reported in Adams, Dow, and Merrill 2001). The fact that both types of abstention were important suggests that candidates should take account of both motivations when devising their election strategies.

[6] In order to locate this equilibrium configuration, we employed the algorithm described in Appendix 4.1. The equilibrium we compute is such that no candidate can improve his expected vote margin over the other candidate (defined as the candidate's expected vote minus his opponent's expected vote) by moving along one issue dimension at a time. We performed alternative simulations in which the candidates maximized their expected votes rather than their expected vote margins. Vote-maximizing motivations generated equilibrium configurations that were similar to, but more dispersed than, the margin-maximizing equilibria reported here.

Table 8.4. *Candidate optima for the unified turnout model for the 1988 ANES*

Policy Dimension	Dukakis (1)	Bush (2)	Policy Divergence[a] (3)
Ideology	4.30 (.07)	4.57 (.08)	.27* (.14)
Domestic spending	3.90 (.06)	4.15 (.06)	.25* (.12)
Defense spending	3.78 (.06)	4.02 (.05)	.23* (.11)
Health insurance	3.91 (.08)	4.19 (.08)	.28* (.14)
Aid to minorities	4.46 (.06)	4.73 (.05)	.26** (.10)
Government jobs	4.52 (.07)	4.80 (.06)	.29* (.13)
Dealing with Russia	3.61 (.03)	3.71 (.03)	.10* (.06)
Women's role	2.40 (.04)	2.48 (.02)	.08* (.04)

[a] Policy divergence represents the distance between the candidates' equilibrium positions reported in columns 1–2. One asterisk indicates that the divergence is significantly greater than zero at the .05 level; two asterisks indicate significance at the .01 level.

Note: The candidates' policy optima at equilibrium were estimated using the parameters reported for the unified turnout model in Table 8.2 and the equilibrium algorithm described in Appendix 4.1. This equilibrium is such that no candidate can increase his expected margin (i.e., his expected plurality) over his opponent by moving along one issue dimension at a time. Parametric bootstrap standard errors are given in parentheses.

are given in parentheses. Figure 8.1 displays this equilibrium configuration along the liberal–conservative dimension, and also displays the candidates' expected votes as a function of their ideologies, with the rival candidate located at his equilibrium position.

Three important conclusions emerge from this analysis. The first is that *Dukakis's optimal positions are distinct from, and more liberal than, Bush's optimal positions along all of the policy and ideology dimensions.*[7] This supports Hypothesis 1, that in spatial competition under the unified turnout model, candidates have electoral incentives to present divergent positions that reflect the beliefs of their partisan constituencies.

Second, *the degree of divergence between the candidates' optima along the policy dimensions in the ANES increases with the degree of divergence between the Democratic and Republican partisans' self-placements on these dimensions* (see Table 8.1). This supports Hypothesis 2. The largest area of

[7] In the parametric bootstrap analysis, Dukakis's equilibrium position is significantly to the left of Bush's at the .05 level for the ideology dimension and for all seven policy dimensions.

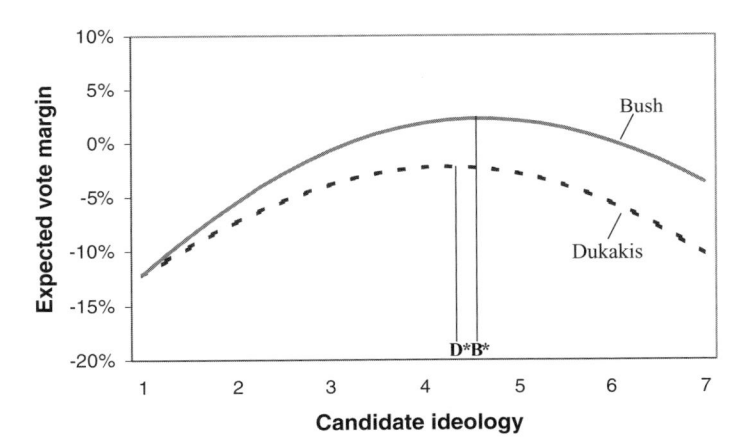

Figure 8.1. Equilibrium configuration for the presidential candidates in the 1988 U.S. presidential election, for the unified turnout model.
Note: The figure presents the expected vote margin for each candidate vis-à-vis his opponent as a function of his liberal–conservative position, with the rival candidate fixed at his (margin-maximizing) equilibrium ideology (and with each candidate fixed at his equilibrim position along the additional policy dimensions included in the unified model). A candidate's expected vote margin represents the difference between the proportion of ANES respondents expected to vote for the candidate and the proportion expected to vote for his opponent. The labels "B*" and "D*" represent the equilibrium positions for Bush and Dukakis, respectively. These positions were computed using the equilibrium algorithm and were based on the estimated parameters for the unified turnout model reported in Table 8.2.

policy disagreement between the parties' partisans is on the national health insurance dimension, where the mean Democratic partisan's self-placement is 3.37 and mean Republican's self-placement is 4.58 (see Table 8.1, column 4); the largest spread between the candidates' computed policy optima is also on the health insurance dimension (see Table 8.5, column 3). Furthermore, the two dimensions for which Democratic and Republican partisans' mean self-placements are similar – dealing with Russia and women's role – are also the two dimensions for which the candidates' computed optima are virtually identical. Overall, the correlation between the degree of partisan policy dispersion along the policy dimensions and the dispersion of the candidates' equilibrium positions is 0.97.

We emphasize that it is the *combination* of voters' non-policy-related motivations and abstention resulting from alienation that motivates candidate divergence. In a two-candidate model, neither abstention due to alienation alone nor nonpolicy motivations alone motivate policy divergence. In particular, as suggested by the illustrative arguments in Chapter 7, a unified turnout model with non-policy-related motivations but in which abstention is motivated solely by indifference leads to convergence along the policy scales. Analyses that illustrate these conclusions (for the 1988 ANES) are given in Appendix 8.2.

Finally, note that although the two candidates' optima diverge under the unified turnout model, they are still rather centrist and rather similar to each other. The most extreme optimum is Bush's optimum position on government jobs programs (4.80), which is only 0.29 policy units to the right of Dukakis's optimal position (4.52); furthermore, the candidates' optima are separated by less than 0.3 policy units along each policy dimension. Thus under the unified turnout model, we find that the candidates' optimal positions are correlated with, but less extreme than, the positions of their partisan constituencies; furthermore, these optimal positions are more moderate than the candidates' actual (perceived) positions.

8.4. Unified Turnout Models for the 1980, 1984, 1988, 1996, and 2000 U.S. Presidential Elections

Table 8.5 presents results for the 1980, 1984, 1988, 1996, and 2000 U.S. presidential elections, including voter turnout figures. Columns 1–2 report the Democratic and Republican candidates' shares of the two-candidate vote, and column 3 reports the turnout rate. Column 4 reports the ANES respondents' reported turnout rates. For 1980, 1984, and 1988, these turnout rates are based on validated vote data, while for 1996 and 2000 the turnout data are not validated; as expected, the reported turnout rates for 1996 and 2000 greatly exceed actual turnout in these elections. Column 5 reports the ANES respondents' mean ideological self-placements for each election; columns 6–7 report the respondents' mean placements of the Democratic and Republican candidates.[8] As expected, columns 6–7 show that respondents consistently placed the Democratic candidate to the left and

---

[8] For each election, the ANES respondents included in the calculations presented in Table 8.5, columns 4–7, are all those who could self-place on the liberal–conservative scale and who were coded as voting for one of the major party candidates or abstaining. Because the 2000 ANES ideological scale ran from 1 to 5 – instead of from 1 to 7, as in the other election years – we recalibrated respondents' ideological self-placements and candidate placements for 2000 so that they would be comparable to the placements for 1980, 1984, 1988, and 1996.

Table 8.5. *Candidate ideologies, voter ideologies, and presidential election results for 1980, 1984, 1988, 1996, and 2000*

	Actual Election Results			ANES Respondents' Turnout Rates, Ideological Self-placements and Candidate Placements[a]			
	Democratic Candidate[b]	Republican Candidate[b]	Voter Turnout	Respondent Reported Turnout[c]	Mean Respondent Position	Democratic Candidate's Position[d]	Republican Candidate's Position[d]
	(1)	(2)	(3)	(4)	(5)	(6)	(7)
1980	44.7%	55.3%	52.6%	52.2%	4.31	3.74	5.21
1984	40.8%	59.2%	53.1%	54.2%	4.23	3.45	4.96
1988	46.1%	53.9%	50.1%	49.3%	4.37	3.24	5.11
1996	54.7%	45.3%	49.0%	77.4%	4.36	3.15	5.15
2000	50.3%	49.7%	51.0%	75.0%	4.24	3.29	4.91

[a] The computations on ANES respondents' ideological placements comprise all respondents who could self-place on the liberal–conservative scale and who reported voting for one of the major candidates or abstaining in the election.

[b] Proportions of the popular vote for the Democratic and Republican candidates are percentages of the major party vote.

[c] For 1980, 1984, and 1988, the ANES respondents' reported turnout rates are based on validated voting data; for 1996 and 2000, the turnout data are not validated.

[d] The Democratic and Republican candidates' ideological positions represent the mean placements of these candidates by the ANES respondents.

the Republican candidate to the right of the midpoint of the 1–7 liberal–conservative scale. Furthermore, in each election the mean respondent self-placement falls between the candidates' (mean perceived) positions.

For each election year, parameter estimates and standard errors for the unified turnout specification introduced in Chapter 7 (see equations A8.1–A8.4 in Appendix 8.1) are presented in Table 8.2. However, as mentioned earlier, the analyses for 1980, 1984, and 1988 are based on *validated* voting data, while for 1996 and 2000 – years for which respondents' turnout reports were not validated in the ANES – the coding of respondents' turnout decisions was based entirely on their self-reports. Because self-reports of turnout are significantly inflated, our results for these latter two elections are only suggestive.

For each election, the coefficients for party identification, ideological and policy distance, and candidate character in column 1 show the expected signs, while the coefficients reported in columns 2–3 suggest that higher levels of political efficacy and voting in the previous election are associated with increased probabilities of voting in the current election. These results are consistent with those we reported in section 8.3 with respect to the 1988 presidential election.

We use the coefficients in Table 8.2 to predict the probabilities that each respondent voted for the Democratic candidate, voted Republican, or abstained.[9] Using the mean values as the expected outcomes, Table 8.3 reports predictions for the abstention rate and the candidates' vote percentages among ANES survey respondents for each election year. These closely match the ANES respondents' actual aggregate behavior.[10]

8.5. Candidate Equilibrium under the Unified Turnout Model

We now evaluate for the additional four elections the two hypotheses presented in section 8.2: namely, that under the unified turnout model, the Democratic and Republican candidates have electoral incentives to present divergent policy positions, and that this incentive increases with the degree of divergence between Democratic and Republican partisans' policy

---

[9] The probability functions for individual respondents' vote and turnout probabilities are given in Appendix 8.1.

[10] We also estimated that alienation and indifference both contributed significantly to voter abstention in each of the 1980, 1984, 1988, 1996, and 2000 elections (the details of these calculations are reported in Adams, Dow, and Merrill 2001).

preferences. For simplicity, we restricted the equilibrium analysis to candidate positioning on the liberal–conservative ideological scale; that is, the candidates were fixed at their actual (perceived) positions along the policy dimensions included in the empirical voting specifications, but could vary their ideological positioning.[11]

The Nash equilibrium positions in each presidential election are reported in columns 4–5 of Table 8.6. Column 6 reports the degree of policy divergence at equilibrium.

Three important conclusions emerge from this analysis, each of which supports the central results on candidate competition in the 1988 U.S. presidential election presented in section 8.3. The first is that *in each election, the Democratic candidate's equilibrium position is distinct from, and more liberal than, the Republican's equilibrium position.* This supports the first hypothesis developed in section 8.2, that in spatial competition under the unified turnout model, candidates have electoral incentives to present divergent positions that reflect the beliefs of their partisan constituencies.

Second, in comparing equilibrium configurations across elections, *the degree of divergence between the candidates' equilibrium positions increases with the degree of divergence between the Democratic and Republican partisans' ideological self-placements.* This is evident from the results presented in Table 8.6. As reported in column 3, the degree of partisan divergence was greatest in 1996, when the mean self-placements of Democratic and Republican partisans differed by 1.45 units along the 1–7 ideology scale, and was smallest in 2000 (only 1.06 units). Likewise, the degree of candidate divergence at equilibrium (reported in column 5) was greatest in 1996 (.41 units) and smallest in 2000 (.09 units). Although the correlation between partisan and equilibrium divergence is not significant, these observations are suggestive of the second hypothesis presented in section 8.2, that in spatial competition under the unified turnout model, candidate divergence increases with the degree of partisan divergence.

Finally, note that although the candidates' equilibrium positions diverge under the unified turnout model in each presidential election, these optima are still rather centrist and rather similar to each other. Every optimal candidate ideology is within .31 units of the mean respondent ideology along the

---

[11] The candidates' one-step optima (see Chapter 3, section 3.4) are very similar to their equilibrium policies, so that consideration of one-step optima supports substantive conclusions identical to those reported here.

Table 8.6. *Partisan divergence and candidate divergence at equilibrium (ideology dimension) for the unified turnout model: 1980, 1984, 1988, 1996, and 2000 ANES*

	Mean Respondent Self-placements			Candidates' Equilibrium Positions		
	Democratic Partisans[a] (1)	Republican Partisans[a] (2)	Partisan Divergence[b] (3)	Democratic Candidate (4)	Republican Candidate (5)	Candidate Divergence at Equilibrium[c] (6)
1980	3.82	4.98	1.16	4.16	4.42	.26
1984	3.68	4.85	1.17	4.04	4.38	.34
1988	3.81	4.94	1.13	4.22	4.62	.40
1996	3.73	5.18	1.45	4.26	4.67	.41
2000[d]	3.91	4.97	1.06	4.18	4.27	.09

[a] Democratic and Republican partisans are defined to include "leaners," so that Democratic partisans are those respondents coded 0–2 on the party identification variable, and Republican partisans are coded 4–6 on this variable.

[b] Partisan divergence is defined as the policy distance separating the mean self-placements of the Republican respondents (column 2) and the mean self-placements of Republicans (column 3).

[c] Candidate divergence at equilibrium represents the distance between the Democratic and Republican candidates' equilibrium positions along the liberal–conservative scale. For simplicity, the equilibria in this table are such that no candidate can increase his expected margin over his opponent by moving only along the liberal–conservative dimension, with the candidates fixed at their actual (perceived) positions along the policy dimensions. For this reason, the equilibrium reported for 1988 is slightly different from that given for the liberal–conservative dimension in Table 8.4. Parametric bootstrap standard errors were not computed but should be of the same order of magnitude as those given in Table 8.4.

[d] For the 2000 election, the candidates' equilibrium positions were recalibrated from the 1–5 scale used in the 2000 ANES to the 1–7 scale used in prior ANES studies.

1–7 liberal–conservative scale, and the most divergent equilibrium – that for the 1996 election – finds Dole located just .41 units to the right of Clinton's position. Thus under the unified turnout model, we find that the candidates' optimal positions are correlated with, but less extreme than, the positions of their partisan constituencies; furthermore, these optimal positions are more moderate than the candidates' actual (perceived) positions.

8.6. The Unified Turnout Model with Policy Discounting

As discussed in section 2.4, a major impetus for the study of policy discounting is the work of Lacy and Paolino (1998), who argue that due to the separation of powers between the executive and the legislature, U.S. voters may recognize that presidential candidates face obstacles to implementing their announced policy agendas. In a study of voting in the 1996 presidential election, the authors report empirical results suggesting that voters discounted Clinton's and Dole's policy proposals by about 30 percent – that is, that voters' projections of government policy under either candidate were shifted toward the center by a factor of approximately 0.3, compared to the candidates' actual (perceived) positions.[12]

Because it was not feasible for us to estimate directly the degree of policy discounting that voters engaged in across the 1980, 1984, 1988, 1996, and 2000 U.S presidential elections,[13] we reestimated the parameters of the unified turnout specification given by equations 8.1–8.3, using the assumption that in each election respondents discounted the candidates' policy positions by 30 percent relative to the midpoints of the policy scales (i.e., we set $d = 0.3$). The parameter estimates for the *unified turnout model with discounting* for 1988 are reported in Table 8.7A. (Because our substantive conclusions were similar across the 1980, 1984, and 1988 elections, here we

---

[12] Lacy and Paolino (1998: Table 1) report that respondents' mean liberal–conservative placements of Clinton and Dole were 3.14 and 5.15, respectively, so that the perceived policy distance between the candidates' proposals was 2.01 policy units. With respect to respondents' beliefs about government policy, the authors report that the respondents' mean placements were 3.53 for a Clinton administration and 4.97 for a Dole administration, so that the perceived policy distance between the candidates' administrations was 1.44 units. The ratio between these two sets of policy distances, 1.44 versus 2.01, suggests a discounting rate of approximately 30 percent.

[13] This is because in two-candidate elections, the discounting parameter d is confounded with candidate-specific intercepts. For detailed discussions of the methodological problems involved in estimating the discounting parameter in two-candidate elections, see Appendix 7.1 in Merrill and Grofman (1999) as well as Adams, Bishin, and Dow (2004).

Table 8.7. *Conditional logit equations and candidate equilibria for the unified discounting model, 1988 U.S. presidential election* (N = 1,389)

8.7A. *Parameter estimates*

Independent Variables	Candidate Parameters (1)	Indifference Threshold (2)	Alienation Threshold (3)
Intercept (Rep.)	.121 (.091)	1.96** (.22)	1.09* (.55)
Ideology	.083** (.028)		
Policy	.151** (.034)		
Party identification	1.11** (.11)		
Candidate character	1.29** (.20)		
Retrospective national economy (Dem.)	−.36** (.12)		
Retrosp. econ. (Rep.)	−.24* (.12)		
Black (Dem.)	1.08* (.55)	−.09 (.21)	1.92** (.58)
Political efficacy		−2.77** (.66)	1.00 (.52)
Voted in 1984		−1.60** (.23)	−1.16** (.33)
Education		.01 (.05)	−.07 (.06)
Close election		−.15 (.15)	
Log-likelihood	−929.11		

8.7B. *Margin-maximizing equilibrium configuration*

Policy Dimension	Dukakis (1)	Bush (2)	Policy Divergence[a] (3)
Ideology	4.44 (.10)	4.82 (.12)	.38* (.20)
Domestic spending	3.87 (.09)	4.21 (.09)	.34* (.17)
Defense spending	3.70 (.09)	4.02 (.07)	.32* (.15)
Health insurance	3.88 (.11)	4.27 (.12)	.39* (.21)
Aid to minorities	4.67 (.09)	5.04 (.07)	.37** (.15)
Government jobs	4.75 (.10)	5.15 (.09)	.40* (.18)
Dealing with Russia	3.45 (.05)	3.59 (.05)	.14* (.09)
Women's role	1.71 (.05)	1.83 (.02)	.12* (.06)

[a] Policy divergence represents the distance between the candidates' equilibrium positions reported in columns 1–2. One asterisk indicates that the divergence is significantly greater than zero at the .05 level; two asterisks indicate significance at the .01 level. Bootstrap standard errors are given in parentheses.

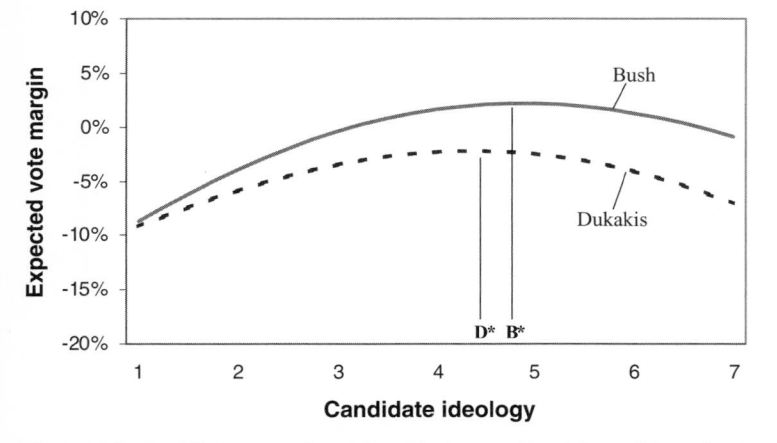

Figure 8.2. Equilibrium configuration for the presidential candidates in the 1988 U.S. presidential election, for the unified turnout model with policy discounting.
Note: The figure presents the expected vote margin for each candidate vis-à-vis his opponent as a function of his liberal–conservative position, with the rival candidate fixed at his (margin-maximizing) equilibrium ideology (and with each candidate fixed at his equilibrium position along the additional policy dimensions included in the unified model). A candidate's expected vote margin represents the difference between the proportion of ANES respondents expected to vote for the candidate and the proportion expected to vote for his opponent. The labels "B*" and "D*" represent the equilibrium positions for Bush and Dukakis, respectively. These positions were computed using the equilibrium algorithm and were based on the estimated parameters for the unified turnout model with discounting reported in Table 8.7A.

report results only for 1988.) Note that these parameter estimates are similar to those we computed for the unified turnout model without discounting (see Table 8.2). However, as expected, the computed equilibrium in margin-maximizing candidates' positions for the unified turnout model with discounting, reported in Table 8.7B, is distinctly more dispersed than the equilibrium configuration for the model without discounting (reported earlier in Table 8.5). In fact, the undiscounted equilibria are about 30 percent less dispersed, just what we would expect.[14] Figure 8.2 displays this equilibrium configuration along the liberal–conservative dimension, and also displays

---

[14] The locations of the equilibrium pairs for the discounting model are somewhat skewed because of our choice of the midpoints of the scales to define the status quo point. The *dispersion* between the candidates at equilibrium is, however, independent of the location of the status quo.

the candidates' expected votes as a function of their ideologies, with the rival candidate located at his equilibrium position.

Finally, note that while policy discounting motivates candidates to take more dispersed positions, the candidates' equilibrium positions for the unified turnout model with discounting are nonetheless distinctly more centrist than their actual (perceived) positions, and are also more centrist than the mean positions of the candidates' partisan constituencies.

In toto, our empirical applications suggest that the unified turnout model for margin-maximizing candidates – with or without discounting – provides some insights into candidate strategies and mass–elite policy linkages in the 1980, 1984, 1988, 1996, and 2000 U.S. presidential elections. Our approach illuminates the empirical observation that the Democratic and Republican candidates' positions were shaded in the directions of their partisans' policy beliefs. However, our approach cannot explain the *magnitude* of candidate divergence that we observed in these historical elections.

8.7. Discussion

In the years since the publication of Anthony Downs's *An Economic Theory of Democracy*, spatial modelers have proposed numerous explanations for why the contestants in two-candidate races fail to converge to the similar, centrist policies that Downs's theory predicts. To our knowledge, however, none of these explanations imply that both candidates actually maximize their plurality in the general election by presenting divergent policy images. That is the argument we present here. By combining two observations supported by extensive behavioral research – that voters are influenced by considerations such as race, class, and partisanship that are not entirely tied to the candidates' positions in the current campaign, *and* that voters are prepared to abstain if neither competitor is sufficiently attractive – we have shown how *vote-seeking candidates are rewarded for presenting divergent policies that reflect the beliefs of voters who are biased toward them for nonpolicy reasons.*

We have supported our illustrative arguments presented in Chapter 7 with applications to ANES data that suggest that in five presidential elections, both the Democratic and the Republican candidates had electoral motivation to appeal on policy grounds to their partisan constituencies. However, we find that this motivation does not extend to alternative voting specifications that omit nonpolicy variables, nor to specifications that incorporate nonpolicy variables but omit abstention due to alienation (see Appendix 8.2). Hence we see our central contribution as highlighting the *joint* influence of voters' nonpolicy motivations and turnout effects in two-candidate elections.

In addition, appeals that balance the tug of partisan constituencies with that of the median voter appear to be successful not only in winning elections, but also in the sense that more citizens turn out to vote when the two candidates offer distinct, but not extreme, policies. Abstention due to alienation should also be high for convergent positions, but it should drop off as the candidates recede from the center, finally rising again as they reach extreme positions. Thus turnout should be highest in the intermediate situation in which candidates take center-left and center-right positions. Normatively, high turnout means that more citizens have the satisfaction of direct participation in democracy.

Finally, our results suggest that many of the alternative candidate motivations that spatial modelers have explored – including policy seeking, winning primary elections, deterring entry by third candidates, and mobilizing party activists – are more compatible with pursuing general election support than the convergent strategies of traditional spatial models might suggest. Each of these alternative goals tends to draw candidates away from the center, and thus – in the view of traditional spatial modelers – candidates must trade off these objectives against their desire to maximize support in the general election by employing a centrist strategy. The noncentrist vote-maximizing strategies of our models suggest a different conclusion, and one that would be welcomed by many politicians. By shifting away from the center in the direction of their partisan constituencies, candidates can simultaneously advance *all* of the diverse objectives that plausibly motivate them to contest two-candidate elections. In particular, they can enhance their vote plurality in the general election!

CHAPTER 9

Policy Competition in Britain

The 1997 General Election

9.1. Introduction

The British political system is a parliamentary democracy in which three major political parties contest elections: Labour, the Conservatives, and a smaller, centrist party, the Liberal Democrats.[1] Labour is traditionally viewed as the major leftist party in British politics, one that emphasizes income redistribution, higher taxes, and expanded social services. The Conservatives, the major right-wing British party, have since the mid-1970s (when Margaret Thatcher was elevated to the party leadership) emphasized free markets, opposition to higher taxes, and personal responsibility. Labour and the Conservatives have dominated postwar general elections, finishing one–two (though in different orders) in vote share in every election since 1945. Furthermore, while neither party has captured a majority of the popular vote in any postwar election, the operation of Britain's plurality voting system generally awards a "seat bonus" to the largest party, so that the party that wins a plurality of the popular vote normally commands a parliamentary majority in the House of Commons.[2] As a result, Britain is classified as a strongly "majoritarian" political system (see Lijphart 1984, 1999), which typically features a single-party majority government that faces few obstacles to implementing its policy agenda.

---

[1] The Liberal Democrats represent the union of two parties, the Liberals and the Social Democrats, which formally merged in 1988.

[2] Either Labour or the Conservatives have captured a parliamentary majority in fifteen of the sixteen postwar elections. We note that in the 1951 general election, the Conservatives captured a parliamentary majority while Labour won a popular vote plurality.

152

Table 9.1. *British general election results, 1997*

	Popular vote (%)	Seats
Labour	43.2	419
Conservatives	30.7	165
Liberal Democrats	16.8	46
Other[a]	9.3	28

[a] The category "Other" includes the Scottish and Welsh national parties and the Plaid Cimru.
Note: Voter turnout = 71.4%.

The May 1, 1997, British general election was historic in that the Labour Party, which had been out of power for eighteen years, won a landslide victory, with a 12.5 percent vote plurality over the incumbent Conservatives and a stunning 419 of 658 parliamentary seats (see Table 9.1). Labour's 419 seats represented its largest total ever, as did its 179-seat parliamentary majority. By contrast, the Conservatives' 30.7 percent vote share was their lowest since 1832, and their 165 seats represented their worst showing since 1906. Meanwhile, the Liberal Democrats, with 16.8 percent of the popular vote, won 46 seats, more than any party other than Labour or the Conservatives had won since 1929. Also noteworthy was that voter turnout was only 71.4 percent, a postwar low, which suggests that the parties plausibly accounted for variable turnout in crafting their election strategies.

We shall assess the major parties' vote-seeking strategies in the 1997 British general election for three of the probabilistic voting models introduced in earlier chapters: a *policy-only model*, in which policy distance is the only measured influence on voters' decisions; a *unified model*, which incorporates measured non-policy-related voter motivations; and a *unified turnout model*, which incorporates the voting decision *and* the turnout decision into a single model.[3] Consistent with our results for the United States, we find that the optimal policy strategies of vote-seeking parties are quite centrist under the policy-only voting model and the unified model, both of which

---

[3] We do not explore policy discounting in British elections because, given the single-party majorities that typically govern Britain, British voters may reasonably conclude that the winning party will fully implement its policy agenda. Empirical work by Kedar (2002) supports the hypothesis that British voters do not significantly discount the parties' abilities to implement their announced policies.

specify that parties cannot influence voters' turnout decisions. However, we find that consideration of voters' turnout decisions – which are integrated into the unified turnout model – provides motivation for British party elites to diverge from the center, in the direction of their partisan constituencies.

9.2. Ideology and Policy Issues in the 1997 General Election

Our data comes from the 1997 British general election cross-section survey (BGES), in which 3,615 respondents were asked to place themselves and each of the major parties on numerous 0–10 scales, including Left–Right ideology and several policy dimensions.[4] We focus initially on the subset of 1,790 respondents who reported voting for one of the three major parties and who could place themselves on the Left–Right scale. Later, in our turnout model, we consider the expanded set of 2,371 respondents that also included those individuals who reported abstaining and who could place themselves on the Left–Right scale.[5]

Figure 9.1 presents the distribution of the BGES respondents' ideological (Left–Right) self-placements, the mean respondent self-placement, and the mean placement that respondents ascribed to each of the major political parties. Note first that the mean respondent self-placement was centrist at 5.02, and, furthermore, that these self-placements are heavily concentrated near the center of the 0–10 scale, with over 50 percent of respondents self-placing at 4, 5, and 6. With respect to the parties' positions, the respondents' perceived the Labour Party (on average) at the center-left position 3.97, the Liberal Democrats near the center at 4.69, and the Conservatives on the right at 7.16, perceptions that correspond well with experts' placements of the parties' positions as reported in a 1993 survey by Huber and Inglehart.[6]

In addition to ideology, the 1997 BGES contained questions on several policy dimensions that were salient in the general election. These included a *taxes versus spending scale*, which ran from 0 ("Government should put

---

[4] In the 1997 BGES, the Left–Right scale ran from 0 to 10, while the various policy scales (described below) ran from 1 to 11. We have recalibrated the latter scales to run from 0 to 10.

[5] In addition, in arriving at the data sets of 1,790 and 2,371 respondents, we randomly eliminated a number of Scottish respondents, so that the proportion of Scottish respondents in the remaining data sets matched the proportion of Scottish citizens in the electorate. This was done because these respondents were substantially overrepresented in the 1997 BGES.

[6] The experts' mean party placements, as reported by Huber and Inglehart (1995: 53), were 3.77 for Labour, 4.73 for the Liberal Democrats, and 7.47 for the Conservatives (with these expert placements, which were along a 1–10 scale in the Huber–Inglehart survey, recalibrated to the 0–10 scale used in the BGES).

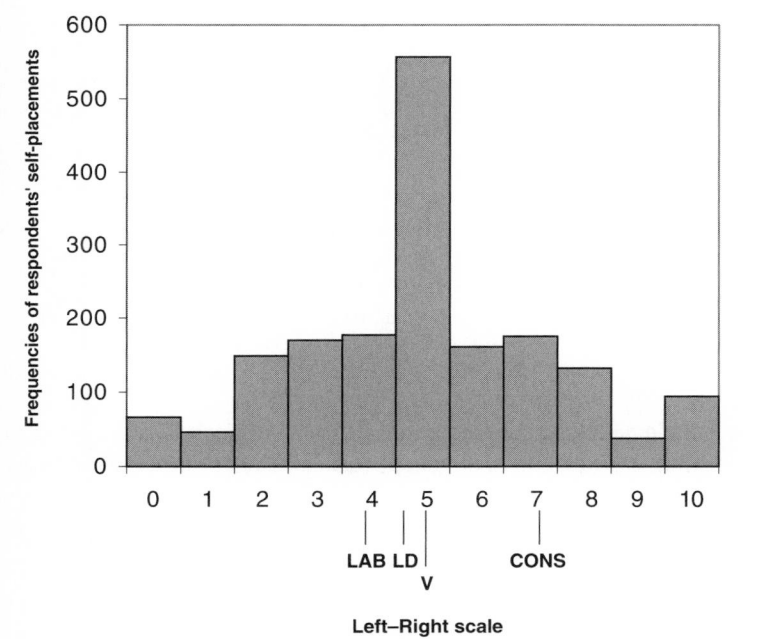

Figure 9.1. Distribution of respondents' ideological self-placements, and their mean party placements, 1997 British general election.
Note: The distribution of respondents' Left–Right self-placements is given for the 1,790 respondents in the 1997 British General Election Study who were used in the voting analyses reported in Table 9.3A (columns 1–2). The positions pictured for the three political parties (LAB, LD, CONS) represent the mean placements ascribed to these parties by the respondents, while "V" represents the mean respondent self-placement.

up taxes a lot and spend much more on health and social services") to 10 ("Government should cut taxes a lot and spend much less on health and social services"), and an *income redistribution scale* running from 0 ("Government should make much greater efforts to make peoples' incomes more equal") to 10 ("Government should be much less concerned with how equal peoples' incomes are"). Both dimensions tap long-standing economic debates that have divided Labour from the Conservatives, especially since the mid-1970s.[7] The survey also included a *European Union scale* running from 0

---

[7] From the late 1940s through the early 1970s – a period labeled the "Postwar Settlement" by scholars of British politics (see Kavanaugh 2000) – both Labour and the Conservatives largely

Table 9.2. *Parties' ideological and policy positions as perceived by the British electorate, 1997*

	Left–Right	Taxes/Spending	Income Redistribution	European Union
Mean voter position	5.05	2.58	3.32	5.41
Labour	3.97	2.59	2.48	3.73
Liberal Democrats	4.69	2.79	3.57	3.91
Conservatives	7.16	5.94	7.22	5.46

Note: Each of the ideological and policy scales runs from 0 to 10. The positions of the Labour, Liberal Democratic, and Conservative Parties represent the mean position ascribed to these parties by the survey respondents. N = 1,790.

("Britain should do all it can to unite fully with the European Union") to 10 ("Britain should do all it can to protect its independence from the European Union"). Policy debates over Britain's role in Europe grew increasingly salient throughout the 1990s, with the Conservatives typically adopting a cautious attitude toward European integration compared to the attitudes of Social Democrats and Labourites (see Kavanaugh 2000).[8]

Table 9.2 shows the respondents' mean positions, as well as their mean party placements, for the subsample of 1,790 respondents that we analyze. On each dimension, the Labour Party is perceived as taking a leftist position; the Conservatives are placed on the right (on average); while the Liberal Democrats are placed at center-left locations that are similar to, but more moderate than, Labour.

9.3. Party Competition under the Policy-only Model

Table 9.3A, column 1 presents parameter estimates for a policy-only voting specification, with voters' party utilities specified as a function of their

endorsed an expansion of social programs (which had the effect of redistributing income) and high rates of taxation. This period of policy consensus ended with the selection of Margaret Thatcher as Conservative Party leader in 1975, after which the Conservatives shifted sharply toward the right, advocating large tax cuts combined with cuts in social services.

[8] The 1997 BGES included several additional policy scales relating to trade-offs between unemployment and inflation, nationalization of industry, and women's role in the workplace. However, in our empirical analyses of the 1997 vote (described in section 9.3), the policy distances between respondents' self-placements along these dimensions and the mean respondent party placements did not show statistically significant effects, so these dimensions were dropped from the analyses.

Table 9.3A. *Logit equations predicting the vote, 1997 British general election*

	Policy-only Model	Unified Model	Unified Turnout Model
Policy parameters			
Left–Right	**.098**	**.073**	**.042**
	(.006)	(.008)	(.005)
Taxes	**.024**	**.019**	**.011**
	(.005)	(.006)	(.004)
Income redistribution	**.027**	**.016**	**.014**
	(.002)	(.003)	(.003)
European Union	**.046**	**.037**	**.012**
	(.006)	(.008)	(.003)
Previous vote	–	**1.79**	**1.77**
		(.081)	(.072)
Sociodemographic variables			
Union (Labour)	–	**.17**	**.01**
		(.12)	(.07)
Union (Liberal Democrats)	–	**.26**	**.08**
		(.12)	(.08)
Economy (Labour)	–	**−.99**	**−.34**
		(.10)	(.06)
Economy (Lib. Dems.)		**−.66**	**−.06**
		(.10)	(.07)
Education (Lib. Dems.)		**.12**	**.12**
		(.04)	(.03)
Wales (Labour)		**1.36**	**.42**
		(.51)	(.26)
Wales (Lib. Dems.)		**1.03**	**.16**
		(.54)	(.36)
Scotland (Labour)		**.49**	**−.06**
		(.20)	(.14)
Intercepts			
Labour	**.02**	**.74**	**.48**
	(.09)	(.15)	(.10)
Liberal Democrats	**−.95**	**.25**	**−.09**
	(.09)	(.15)	(.11)
Abstention threshold			
Intercept			**1.00**
			(.13)
Voted in 1992			**−1.03**
			(.13)
Log-likelihood	−1410.4	−971.5	−2229.3
	(N = 1,790)	(N = 1,790)	(N = 2,371)

Table 9.3B. *Projected votes for full-turnout models*

	Labour	Liberal Democrats	Conservatives
Sample vote	.496	.187	.317
Policy-only model	.495	.186	.319
Unified model	.496	.187	.318

Note: For these computations, the parties were placed at their actual (mean perceived) positions.

Table 9.3C. *Projected votes for the unified turnout model*

	Labour	Liberal Democrats	Conservatives	Abstain
Sample vote	.375	.141	.240	.245
Unified turnout model	.374	.141	.240	.245

Note: For these computations, the parties were placed at their actual (mean perceived) positions.

(squared) distances from each party along the ideology and policy scales included in the BGES.[9] Consistent with previous empirical studies of British voting behavior, the Left–Right scale emerges as the most salient dimension of party evaluation (see Butler and Stokes 1969; Bartle 1998). Table 9.3B reports the respondents' expected aggregate votes for this policy-only model (row 2), with parties at their actual (mean perceived) positions, along with the distribution of the respondents' actual reported vote shares.[10]

Table 9.4A reports one of several possible equilibria that we located for the policy-only voting model, which finds the two major parties located at nearly identical positions along each of the four policy and ideological dimensions, but with the Liberal Democratic Party located somewhat to the left. A second equilibrium configuration is approximately the mirror image of the first; a third equilibrium finds all parties at identical positions on each

---

[9] In order to better project the vote shares of the parties, we have added intercepts to the models. Because we do not try to estimate the parameters of a discounting model for Britain (see note 3), the introduction of intercepts does not lead to unidentified models, as would be the case if we had introduced intercepts in the discounting models for France and Norway.

[10] See Chapter 2 (equations 2.4 and 2.5) for the calculation of probabilities that a voter votes for each party and the expected vote share for each party. Note that in these and all subsequent calculations, parties' votes are expressed as percentages of the three-party vote, thereby eliminating from consideration the smaller parties that contested the election.

Table 9.4. *Party equilibria for alternative voting models, 1997 British general election*

Table 9.4A. *The policy-only model*

	Left–Right	Taxes	Income Redistribution	European Integration
Labour	5.10	2.59	3.35	5.48
Liberal Democrats	4.40	2.35	2.87	4.37
Conservatives	5.11	2.60	3.36	5.49

Table 9.4B. *The unified model*

	Left–Right	Taxes	Income Redistribution	European Integration
Labour	**4.97**	**2.59**	**3.26**	**5.31**
	(.07)	(.04)	(.09)	(.06)
Liberal Democrats	**4.77**	**2.60**	**3.33**	**5.00**
	(.08)	(.04)	(.08)	(.12)
Conservatives	**5.56**	**2.83**	**3.88**	**5.92**
	(.08)	(.03)	(.07)	(.06)

Table 9.4C. *The unified turnout model*

	Left–Right	Taxes	Income Redistribution	European Integration
Labour	**4.71**	**2.46**	**2.93**	**5.27**
	(.06)	(.04)	(.08)	(.05)
Liberal Democrats	**4.92**	**2.68**	**3.41**	**5.26**
	(.04)	(.03)	(.07)	(.05)
Conservatives	**5.76**	**2.95**	**4.04**	**6.11**
	(.04)	(.03)	(.04)	(.04)

Note: The equilibrium configurations for these alternative voting models were computed using the algorithm described in Appendix 4.1, based on the parameter values reported in Table 9.3A. Bootstrap standard errors of these equilibrium estimates are given in parentheses.

dimension.[11] This is consistent with the theoretical arguments advanced in Chapters 3 and 4. Of course, the computed equilibria bear no resemblance to

---

[11] Investigation of numerous random starting points suggests that only the three equilibrium configurations described here are possible. The exact Left–Right locations of (L, LD, C) for these configurations are (5.10, 4.39, 5.11), (5.00, 5.73, 4.99), and (5.05, 5.05, 5.05). The sufficient condition for uniqueness of the equilibrium specified in Appendix 4.1 is not clearly satisfied (the Jacobian norm is approximately 1.0).

the actual configuration of parties in the 1997 British general election, nor do these equilibria illuminate the policy linkages between the parties and their supporters. We conclude that the policy-only voting model, in conjunction with the assumption of vote-maximizing parties, does not illuminate the parties' policy strategies in the 1997 British general election.[12]

9.4. Party Competition under the Unified Model

Next, we explored the parties' policy strategies under a unified model that incorporated – in addition to policy distances – voter-specific attributes not directly tied to the candidates' policies in the current campaign. Using the specification introduced in Chapter 2 (see equation 2.5), we estimated the effects of respondents' perceptions of national and personal economic conditions, the respondent's geographic region, and sociodemographic characteristics relating to sex, age, income, home ownership, union membership, and education, variables that have a long history of inclusion in prior analyses of British voting behavior (see Rose and McAllister 1990; Bartle 1998; Alvarez, Nagler, and Bowler 2000). Also included was the respondent's previous vote – coded 1 if the respondent reported voting for the party in the previous election and zero otherwise – which we used as a surrogate for the respondent's partisanship,[13] and intercept terms for the parties. In order to simplify the subsequent simulations on party movement, parameter estimates for nonpolicy variables that were not statistically different from zero in the initial analysis were set to zero, and the remaining parameters were recalculated on this basis.

Table 9.3A, column 2 displays the resulting parameter estimates for this *unified model*. Note that the estimated parameter for previous vote, 1.76, is quite similar to the parameters we estimated for partisanship in the candidate-centered presidential elections for France and the United States (see Tables 5.3A and 8.2 in Chapters 5 and 8). This suggests that the respondent's report of her previous vote may be a good surrogate for partisanship. Of the

---

[12] Were these Nash equilibria politically plausible, they could be considered as alternative party configurations that might be adopted, with the choice made by historical chance, as suggested by Schofield (2003; see also Schofield and Sened 2003).

[13] We used previous vote, rather than current party identification, because British elections revolve largely around the parties' national images rather than the qualities of the local parliamentary candidates, so that respondents may view current party identification and current vote intention as equivalent (see Rose and McAllister 1990: 155–6). The recalled vote variable, which represents an action taken at a point separated by over four years from the vote choice, is more likely to be independent of current vote intention.

additional variables examined, only retrospective evaluations of the national economy, education, union membership, and region were estimated to have statistically significant impacts.[14] Specifically, our estimates suggest that voters penalized the incumbent Conservative Party when they perceived unfavorable economic conditions, that highly educated voters tended to support the Liberal Democrats, that union membership motivated positive evaluations of both Labour and the Liberal Democrats, and that Scottish and Welsh voters supported Labour (with Welsh voters also favoring the Liberal Democrats over the Conservatives). These estimates accord well with results reported in previous empirical analyses of British elections (Bartle 1998; Alvarez, Nagler, and Bowler 2000).

In addition, note that the party intercept is large and positive for Labour, indicating that there are unmeasured sources of voters' party evaluations that benefited Labour relative to the Conservatives and the Liberal Democrats; furthermore, the intercept for the Liberal Democrats is small and positive, indicating that this party benefited from modest unmeasured advantages relative to the Conservatives. These systematic unmeasured influences plausibly stem in part from respondents' evaluations of the Labour Party leader, Tony Blair – who was evaluated positively by a majority of respondents – vis-à-vis the Conservative leader, John Major, who received predominantly negative evaluations.[15] Table 9.3B reports the parties' expected aggregate vote shares for the unified model under the assumption that parties are located at their actual (mean perceived) positions. These projected vote shares closely match the distribution of the respondents' actual votes in the survey sample.

Table 9.4B reports the unique policy equilibrium that we located when applying the equilibrium algorithm (Appendix 4.1) to the unified model. This equilibrium finds the parties presenting dispersed positions along each policy scale, with Labour and the Liberal Democrats consistently shaded

---

[14] The general standard of living variable runs from − 2 (national economic conditions are much worse) to 2 (national economic conditions are much better). The education variable runs from − 3 to 3. The union membership variable runs from − 1 (respondent is not a union member) to 1 (respondent is a union member). The variables for Wales and Scotland are dummy variables that take on the value 1 if the respondent resides in the region and zero otherwise.

[15] We did not incorporate respondents' party leader evaluations into the unified specification, as such evaluations are plausibly endogenous to the model. However, a factor that supports our analysis is that during the period 1992–97, the Conservative Party was plagued by a series of setbacks relating to perceptions of economic mismanagement, government sleaze, and party divisions, which were viewed as reflecting poorly on the party in general and on John Major in particular (see Denver 1998).

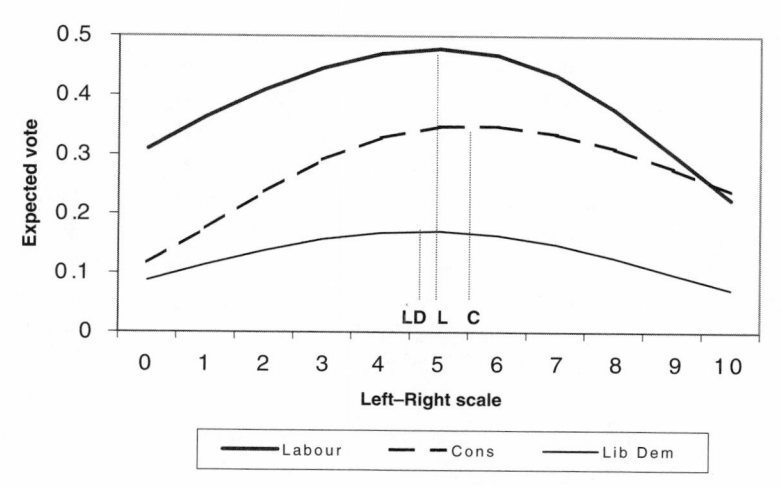

Figure 9.2. Parties' expected votes with rival parties at their equilibrium Left–Right positions, as computed for the unified model.

Note: The figure presents the expected vote for each party as a function of its Left–Right position, with the rival parties fixed at their (vote-maximizing) equilibrium Left–Right positions (and with each party fixed at its equilibrium position along the additional policy dimensions included in the unified model). The labels "L," "LD," and "C" represent the equilibrium positions for the Labour, Liberal Democratic, and Conservative parties, respectively. These positions were computed using the equilibrium algorithm and were based on the estimated parameters for the unified model reported in Table 9.3A, column 2.

slightly to the left of the mean voter position and the Conservatives slightly to the right.[16] Note, however, that the degree of policy dispersion for this three-party equilibrium is quite modest, with the parties located within 0.7 policy units of each other along each 0–10 scale – less dispersion than we found in our equilibrium analyses of the five-candidate French presidential election and the seven-party Norwegian Storting election (see Tables 5.4B and 6.5 in Chapters 5 and 6). This greater centrism of the British equilibrium, compared with France and Norway, is consistent with our theoretical analyses from Chapter 4, which suggest that policy dispersion increases with the number of parties. Figure 9.2 displays the parties' equilibrium configuration along the Left–Right scale, the dimension that emerged as the most salient in our

---

[16] The projected vote shares (L = .482, LD = .177, C = .341), assuming that the parties are located at their equilibrium positions, suggest that the Conservative Party could have benefited modestly by moving from its actual location to its equilibrium (optimal) position.

9.3A. Parties' equilibrium positions versus their actual (perceived) positions

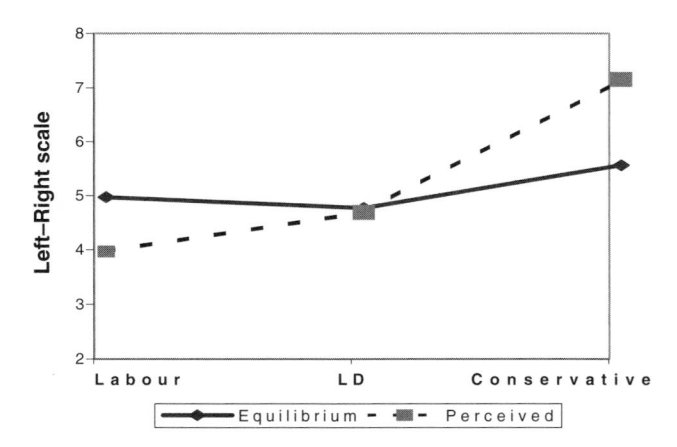

9.3B. Party equilibrium versus the mean positions of their partisan constituencies

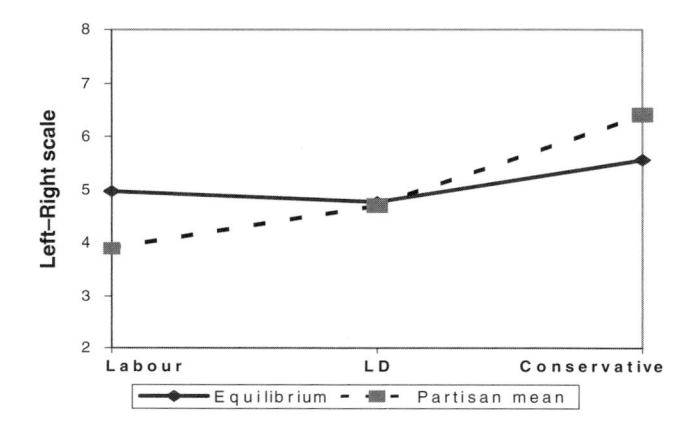

Figure 9.3. The linkages between the parties' equilibrium ideologies, their observed ideological positions, and their partisan constituencies' preferred positions, for the unified model.

analysis. The figure displays each party's expected vote as a function of its Left–Right position, with the rival parties fixed at their equilibrium positions on the Left–Right scale (and with each party fixed at its equilibrium positions on the three remaining policy scales).

Figure 9.3 presents evidence on the extent to which the computed vote-seeking equilibrium for the unified model illuminates the parties' observed policy strategies and mass–elite linkages in the 1997 election. Figure 9.3A plots each party's equilibrium ideological position against its actual (perceived) position. While the parties' equilibrium positions correlate with their actual positions, the equilibrium positions for Labour and the Conservatives are far more centrist than their actual positions.

Figure 9.3B relates to mass–elite linkages by plotting each party's equilibrium ideology against the mean ideological self-placements of its supporters, defined as the respondents who reported voting for the party in the previous election. The figures show that the parties' equilibrium positions are similar to, but more moderate than, the mean positions of their supporters. Again, this is entirely consistent with the theoretical arguments presented in Chapters 3 and 4. Thus to the extent that the unified model captures voters' decision processes in the 1997 British general election, the parties had electoral incentives to present views that were distinctly more moderate than those of their partisan constituencies.

We conclude that while the unified model sheds some light on the parties' policy positioning, it cannot illuminate the *degree* of divergence that was observed in the 1997 British general election, nor can it illuminate the strength of the mass–elite policy linkages that we observed in this election.

9.5. Party Competition under a Unified Turnout Model: The Strategic Effects of Abstention due to Alienation

As noted earlier, voter turnout in the 1997 British general election was only 71.4 percent, a postwar low.[17] Given the arguments we advanced in Chapters 7 and 8 – that abstention resulting from alienation motivates vote-seeking politicians to diverge from the center in the direction of their partisan constituencies – the possibility of voter abstention plausibly influenced British party elites' policy strategies in 1997. In order to explore this possibility, we estimated the parameters of a *unified turnout model*, which combined

---

[17] In the 2001 British general election, the turnout rate fell below 60 percent.

voters' turnout decisions with their decisions about which party to support in the event they voted. This unified turnout specification was similar to the one we employed in Chapters 7 and 8 for the United States, *except* that in our British analyses we specified that abstention was due solely to alienation, not to indifference. This specification decision is motivated by the fact that conceptual difficulties arise in specifying indifference in multiparty elections.[18]

Table 9.3A presents parameter estimates for our unified turnout specification (column 3), which we estimated based on the set of 2,371 respondents who placed themselves on the ideology scale and who reported either voting for a major party or abstaining in 1997. The parameter estimates associated with the alienation threshold indicate that, ceteris paribus, respondents who reported voting in the 1992 election were significantly more likely to vote in 1997. Table 9.3C reports the parties' expected aggregate votes and the expected abstention rate for this unified turnout model, assuming that the parties were located at their actual (mean perceived) positions. These projections closely match the distribution of the respondents' behavior reported in the sample.

Table 9.4C reports the unique policy equilibrium that we located when applying the equilibrium algorithm to the unified turnout model.[19] Consistent with the theoretical and empirical results reported in Chapters 7 and 8, this equilibrium for the turnout-based voting model finds the parties presenting

[18] Indifference is difficult to specify in multiparty elections, because respondents may be indifferent between certain pairs of parties but not others (where we define indifference to mean that the respondent's utility differential between two parties falls below her indifference threshold). In such situations, it is unclear how indifference affects voter turnout (see Sanders 1998: Appendix 1). Furthermore, in the 1997 British general election, supporters of Labour and the Conservatives may have discounted comparisons with the Liberal Democrats, reasoning that the latter had no realistic chance of winning. Given these considerations, we did not feel confident that we could develop a specification for voter indifference that realistically captured respondents' turnout decisions in the 1997 British general election.

[19] In the unified turnout model, as in the case of the unified model discussed earlier, projected vote shares (L = .364, LD = .135, C = .268) – assuming that the parties are located at their equilibrium positions – suggest that the Conservative Party could have benefited modestly by moving from its actual location to its equilibrium (optimal) position. In applying the equilibrium algorithm, we assumed that each party maximized its expected *number* of votes, rather than its expected *proportion* of the three-party vote. In practice, we have found that in elections with variable voter turnout, it is difficult to modify the algorithm to encompass proportion-maximizing motivations. However, we computed the proportion-maximizing equilibrium using a brute force approach in which we successively shifted each party to its proportion-maximizing position, with these shifts continuing until no party could increase its expected vote proportion. We found that this equilibrium was quite similar to the vote-maximizing equilibrium.

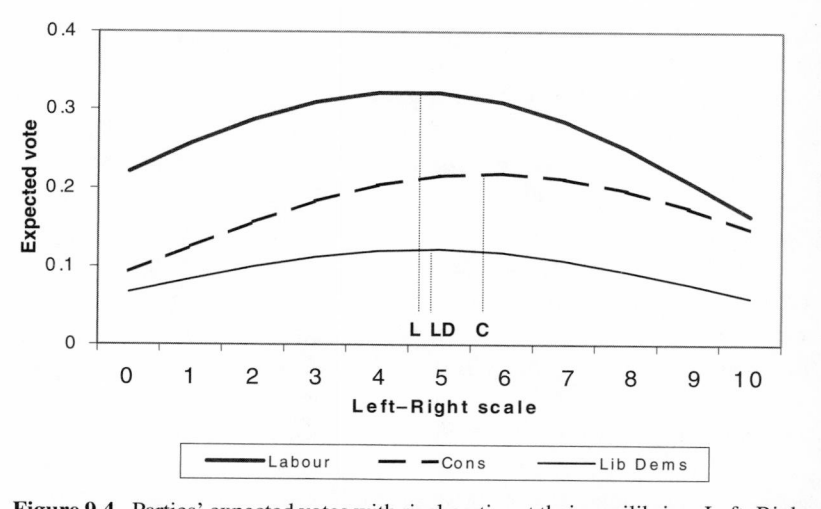

Figure 9.4. Parties' expected votes with rival parties at their equilibrium Left–Right positions, as computed for the unified turnout model.

Note: The figure presents the expected vote for each party as a function of its Left–Right position, with the rival parties fixed at their (vote-maximizing) equilibrium Left–Right positions (and with each party fixed at its equilibrium position along the additional policy dimensions included in the unified model). The labels "L," "LD," and "C" represent the parties' equilibrium positions. These positions were computed using the equilibrium algorithm and were based on the estimated parameters for the unified turnout model reported in Table 9.3A, column 3.

more dispersed positions than those we computed for the unified model. The Labour Party's equilibrium ideology, 4.71, is to the left of their equilibrium position for the unified model (4.97), which does not include abstention; the Conservatives' equilibrium position, 5.76, is to the right of their optimum position for the unified model (5.56). The parties' equilibrium positions along the three remaining policy dimensions show similar patterns. Thus we find that consideration of voters' turnout decisions provides an added electoral incentive for party elites to diverge from the center of the voter distribution, in the direction of their partisan constituencies. Note, however, that the degree of policy dispersion for the unified turnout model remains modest, with the parties located within 1.2 units of each other along each 0–10 policy scale. Figure 9.4 displays the parties' equilibrium configuration along the Left–Right scale, for the unified turnout model.

Figure 9.5 presents evidence on the extent to which the computed equilibrium for the unified turnout model illuminates the parties' observed

9.5A. Parties' equilibrium positions versus their actual (perceived) positions

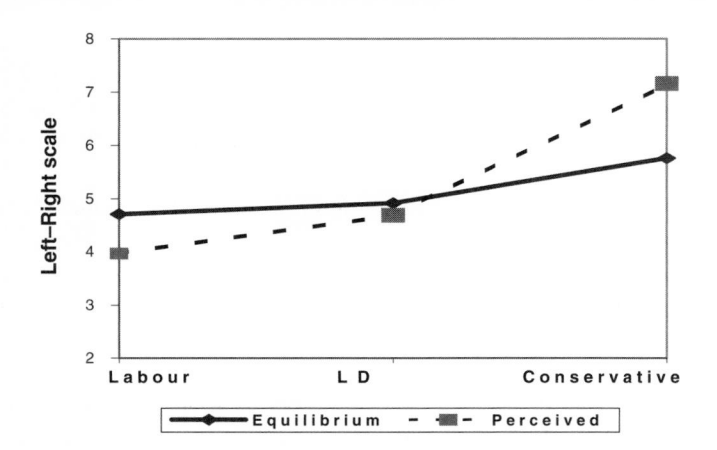

9.5B. Party equilibrium versus the mean positions of their partisan constituencies

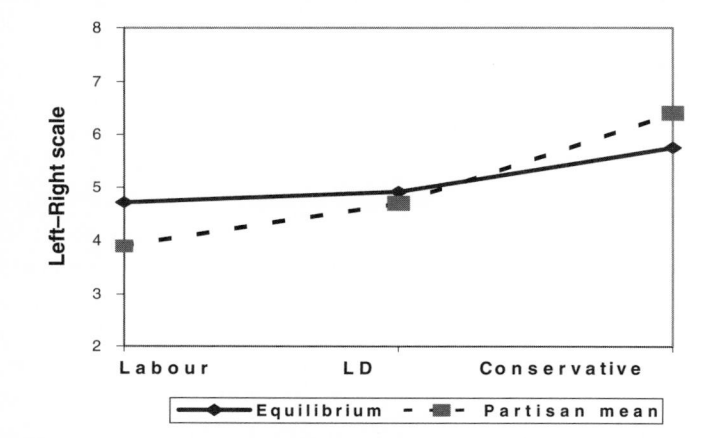

Figure 9.5. Linkages between the parties' equilibrium ideologies, their observed ideological positions, and their partisan constituencies' preferred positions, for the unified turnout model.

policy strategies and mass–elite linkages in the 1997 election. Figure 9.5A, which plots each party's equilibrium Left–Right position against its actual (perceived) position, shows that the parties' equilibrium positions are similar to, but more moderate than, their actual positions. However, Figure 9.5B, which plots each party's equilibrium position against the mean position of its supporters given abstention, displays a tighter fit than does the corresponding figure without abstention.

Why do the British parties have electoral incentives to faithfully reflect their supporters' policy beliefs when citizens choose according to the unified turnout model? The reason is that the possibility of abstention due to alienation gives party elites additional incentives to appeal to their supporters, so as to ensure that these supporters are sufficiently motivated to turn out to vote. By contrast, the possibility of voter alienation renders policy appeals to rival parties' supporters even more problematic, because even if a party siphons off support from these citizens, they may not find the new party sufficiently attractive to motivate them to turn out.

We conclude that the unified turnout model sheds some light on the parties' policy positioning, for while it cannot illuminate the *degree* of policy divergence that was observed in the 1997 British general election, it does illuminate the strength of the mass–elite policy linkages that we observed in this election.

9.6. Conclusion

In this chapter, we have explored the major British parties' policy strategies in the 1997 general election, using successively more complex models of voter choice: a policy-only voting model, a unified model that incorporates voters' non-policy-related motivations, and a unified turnout model that incorporates nonpolicy motivations *and* voters' turnout decisions. Consistent with our results from earlier chapters, we find that the policy-only model motivates major party convergence to the center of the voter distribution, while the unified models motivate policy divergence. The parties' equilibrium positions for the unified model (without abstention) correlate strongly with their actual (perceived) positions, but the degree of dispersion at equilibrium is far short of what we actually observe. Incorporating the turnout decision – as we do in the unified turnout model – increases the degree of policy dispersion at equilibrium, yet this dispersion still falls short of that which we actually observe. However, when parties take account of voters' nonpolicy motivations and the possibility of abstention due to alienation, their vote-maximizing positions reflect to some extent the mean policy preferences of their supporters – the linkage that underlies the responsible party model of representation.

Although the degree of divergence that our model implies for a single British election is modest, consideration of the dynamics of successive elections may help to explain the policy distance that is observed between the two major parties. In a careful study of British elections over half a century (1945–97), Nagel (2001) finds that the Liberal Democratic (LD) party mediates major party divergence in Britain in two ways. As the LD vote increases, leaving centrist voters less accessible, Labour and Conservative positions move to the extremes in the next election (an outcome that Nagel labels the "occupied-center" effect). Conversely, as the major parties disperse, LD reaps the benefits of alienated centrist voters and gains in vote share (the "vacated-center" effect). Empirically, Nagel shows that these effects depend primarily on the position of the Conservatives, rather than of Labour, as the Conservatives and LD compete over policy for middle-class voters.

The occupied-center and vacated-center effects tend to feed on each other, as LD strength is followed (in the next election) by major party divergence, which in turn permits an even greater increase in LD strength and hence more major party divergence, and so on. Hence we should expect relatively long periods of major party divergence (and expansion of LD strength), as occurred in Britain between 1959 and 1983. Nagel suggests that the organizational leadership of Jo Grimond of the Liberal Party started this period of expansion.[20] Ironically, when the Liberal Democrats improve their vote share, the policy implemented by the victorious major party is likely to be less centrist than it would be without the presence of the centrist LD party – providing a difficult quandary for the Liberal Democrats.

---

[20] Nagel equates the Liberal and later Liberal Democratic Parties in his analysis.

CHAPTER 10

The Consequences of Voter Projection

Assimilation and Contrast Effects

10.1. Introduction

In the standard Downsian model, voters are assumed to choose parties based on the extent of ideological proximity between the voter's own position and that of the party. Yet voters may misestimate the policy platforms of candidates or parties, either out of ignorance or in a fashion that reflects systematic bias. For example, some voters may subjectively position parties that they favor closer to the voter's own preferred policy location than do voters as a whole.[1]

Insights taken from the psychological literature on persuasion (Sherif and Hovland 1961; Parducci and Marshall 1962) distinguish between two different types of bias/projection effects: assimilation and contrast. *Assimilation* effects refer to shortening the perceived ideological distance between oneself and parties (or candidates) whom one favors; *contrast* effects refer to exaggerating the distance between oneself and parties (or candidates) whom one does not support.

The importance of assimilation and contrast to our study of optimal party locations and equilibrium configurations is that perceptions of where the parties are located can alter the effects of party positioning on voters' decision calculus. If, for example, Republican voters in the United States perceive the Democratic candidate to be significantly more liberal than do other voters

---

[1] See, e.g., Page (1976), Markus and Converse (1979), Page and Jones (1979), Granberg and Brent (1980), van der Eijk and Niemöller (1983), Conover and Feldman (1986), Granberg (1987), Hoch (1987), Granberg and Holmberg (1988), Granberg and Brown (1992), Listhaug, Macdonald, and Rabinowitz (1994), Husted, Kenny, and Morton (1995), Gerber and Green (1999); cf. Merrill and Grofman (1999). The material is this chapter is taken from Merrill, Grofman, and Adams (2001).

(and we present evidence that this is the case), they will be even less likely to vote for the Democrat (and less likely to abstain due to indifference) than might be predicted by our models, which use mean placement by all voters to specify party position.[2]

Therefore, assimilation and contrast have the effect of intensifying the centrifugal effect of party ID on party strategies. Because of assimilation, a party's partisans are likely to overrate their party, and because of contrast, they tend to underrate opposition parties. This effect accentuates the value accruing to a party from an appeal to its own partisans when the party moves from the center toward the partisan mean. Because, however, the projection that leads to this over- or underevaluation is endogenous with voter preference, we will not attempt to go beyond a qualitative statement about the centrifugal effects of projection. We turn instead to an empirical evaluation of the existence and degree of assimilation and contrast in the four countries that we analyze in this book.

10.2. Data Analysis

10.2.1. Data Resources

We analyze the same elections that were studied in Chapters 5–9.[3] Recall that the 1988 French Presidential Election Study employed a seven-point Left–Right scale (with 7 representing far right). The full data set of 1,013 was restricted to the 677 respondents who voted for one of the five major candidates (see Chapter 5) and who could, in addition, place both themselves and all five major candidates on the Left–Right scale.

Respondents in the 1989 Norwegian study placed themselves and each of the seven major parties on a ten-point Left–Right scale, with 1 representing far left and 10 representing far right (see Chapter 6). Recall that these parties, arranged in their conventional order from left to right, are Socialist, Labor, Liberal, Center, Christian People's, Conservative, and Progress. The Norwegian data set was restricted to those respondents who reported voting for one of these seven major parties and who were able to place themselves on the Left–Right scale. The number in this subset who could place each

---

[2] Use of idiosyncratic, rather than mean, placements in the 1988 American National Election Study, however, generated only slight differences in the equilibrium locations of the candidates.

[3] In France, we focus only on the first ballot of the runoff election; in the United States, we ignore the Electoral College aspects.

party on the same scale varied slightly, from 1,866 (for the Liberal Party) to 1,935 (for the Conservative Party).[4]

For U.S. presidential elections (see Chapters 7 and 8), we focus on the two major party candidates and the elections of 1984 (N = 1,330), 1988 (N = 835), and 1992 (N = 1,066), but we also include Perot in 1992. The data sets – from the American National Election Studies – were restricted to those respondents who reported voting for either the Democrat or the Republican (or Perot in 1992) and who placed both themselves and the major candidates on the seven-point liberal–conservative scale (with 1 representing *extremely liberal* and 7 representing *extremely conservative*).

In the 1997 British election (see Chapter 9), we consider three major parties (Labour, Liberal Democratic, and Conservative). The data set consisted of the 1,562 respondents who voted for one of these three parties and who could place themselves and each of the three parties on a 0–10 Left–Right scale.

10.2.2. Hypotheses about Assimilation and Contrast Effects

Hypothesis 1: Supporters of a party assimilate that party's ideological location to their own ideological self-placement.

Hypothesis 2: Nonsupporters of a party distance the location they assign to that party from their own ideological self-placement.

For each party in France, Norway, the United States, and Britain for which we present data, we will test Hypotheses 1 and 2 by dividing voters into two groups, supporters and nonsupporters of that party. We plot the median[5]

---

[4] The total number of respondents in the survey was 2,196. Separate specifications of the data set for each party were used in Norway in order to avoid the substantial reduction in the size of the data set that occurs when only respondents who placed all parties are included.

[5] Median placements are computed in the standard manner for discrete data – i.e., as if values at, say, 3 were uniformly distributed between 2.5 and 3.5, etc. Because of the Downsian emphasis on the importance of the median voter and the resistance of the median to the influence of outliers, we have preferred to present the data for medians rather than for means. For most parties, the distribution of party placements is fairly symmetrical (so the means and medians are similar), but for some extreme parties (notably the Norwegian Progress Party and the French National Front) the distribution is quite skewed, so that the median is a better indicator of a typical placement than the mean because the latter is heavily influenced by a few respondents who provide aberrant placements. Use of the median also ameliorates the problem of some respondents in the United States who appear to have reversed the meanings of the words liberal and conservative. Their highly atypical (and incorrect) liberal–conservative placements have less effect on a median than on a mean. Nevertheless, a test run (for the 1984

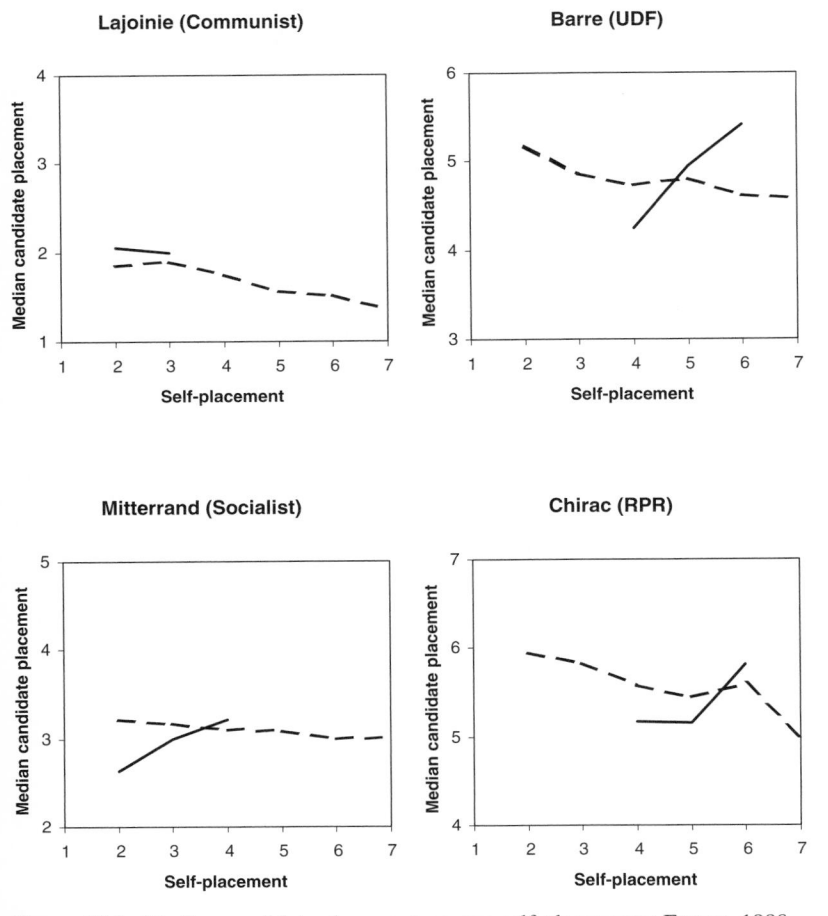

Figure 10.1. Median candidate placements versus self-placements: France, 1988. *Note:* Solid lines = supporters of the focal candidate; dashed lines = nonsupporters of the focal candidate. Cells with fewer than ten respondents are not represented on the plots.

placement of that party against the voter self-placement for supporters and nonsupporters as separate lines on the same graph. If Hypothesis 1 is correct, then for each party being examined, the line for party supporters should be

U.S. election) was done using means; the results were almost identical to those presented in Table 10.1, which is based on medians, except that the slopes were slightly less steep. Merrill, Grofman, and Adams (2001) investigate the effect of omitting those respondents who appear to reverse the scale.

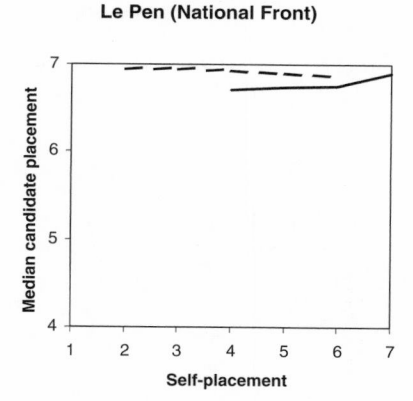

Figure 10.1 (*continued*)

upward sloping; that is, the more conservative the supporter, the more conservative will be the median position assigned to that party (an assimilation
effect). If Hypothesis 2 is correct, then for each party being examined, the
line for party nonsupporters should be *downward* sloping; that is, the more
conservative the nonsupporter, the more liberal will be the position assigned
to that party by that nonsupporter (a contrast effect). These plots are presented for France (1988) in Figure 10.1, for Norway (1989) in Figure 10.2,
for the United States (1984, 1988, 1992) in Figure 10.3, and for Britain
(1997) in Figure 10.4.

As can be seen graphically, both Hypothesis 1 and Hypothesis 2 are
supported for nearly all of the parties. In order to test these hypotheses statistically for each party, we regress median party placement for that party
against voter self-placement, separately for supporters and nonsupporters.
The slopes for each party and category of voters (supporters and nonsupporters) are presented in Table 10.1. For each party's supporters, we test the
hypothesis that the slope of the regression line is positive; for nonsupporters, we test the hypothesis that the slope of the regression line is negative.[6]

---

[6] Granberg (1987) presents similar plots and tests correlation coefficients for the 1984 U.S.
election and for two parties in the 1982 Swedish election, using mean rather than median
placements, and finds evidence of both assimilation and contrast. We also regressed individual placements (as opposed to median or mean placements), obtaining results similar
in toto to those based on medians, although with some differences in slopes for individual
parties.

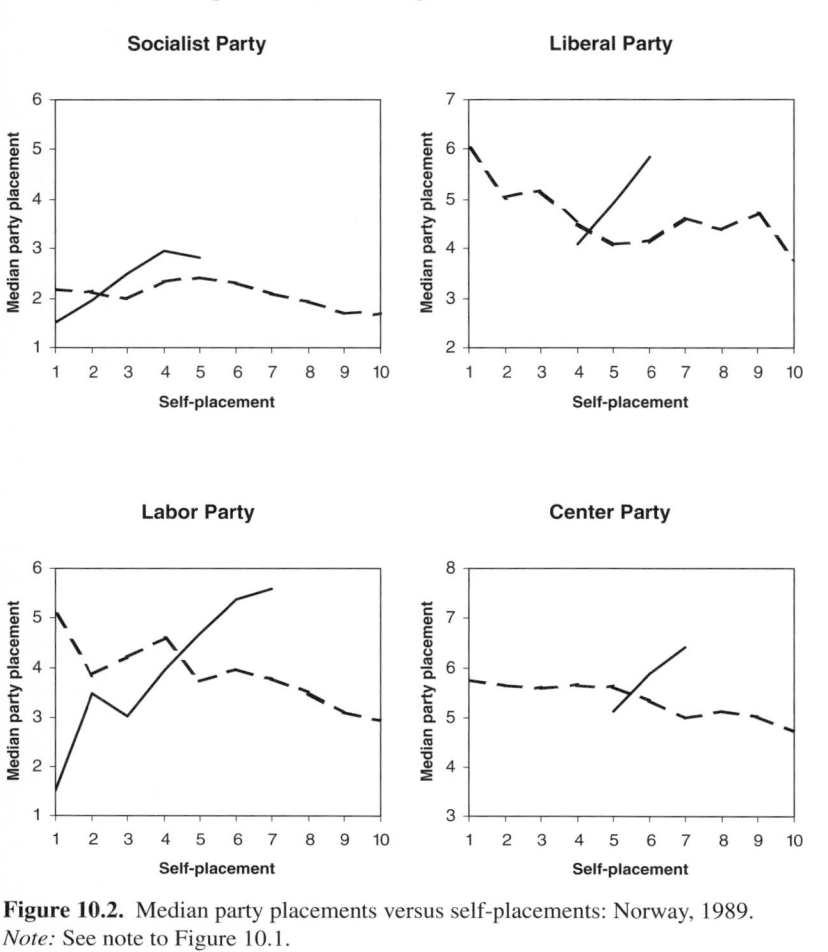

Figure 10.2. Median party placements versus self-placements: Norway, 1989. *Note:* See note to Figure 10.1.

The *p*-values for the respective one-tailed tests of the slopes are given in Table 10.1.[7]

The slopes are in the expected direction for each party and category of voters, except for supporters of Lajoinie (the candidate of the French Communist Party, for whom the plot has only two points and whose

---

[7] Although the ten-point scale for Norway and the eleven-point scale for Britain are broader than the 1–7 scales for France and the United States, for each country the independent and dependent variables have the same scale, so that the slopes are comparable across countries.

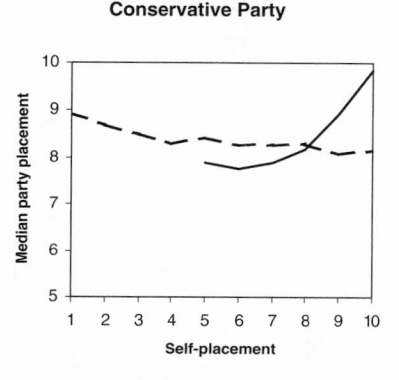

Figure 10.2 (*continued*)

medians are substantially equal), and for nonsupporters of the British Liberal Democratic Party (for whom the plot is essentially flat). The directions of all other slopes are significant at the 0.05 level, with the exception of those for the supporters of Chirac, Le Pen, and Bush in 1988, and two of these slopes are close to significance. Most of the slopes for supporters fall between 0.3 and 0.6.[8] For the European parties and candidates, these slopes are substantially steeper than those for nonsupporters (which are typically -0.1 or -0.2). This finding is in agreement with that of Granberg (1987) for

---

[8] The steepness of the slopes for the three centrist parties in Norway (Liberal, Center, and Christian People's) may be an artifact of the very small number of data points plotted due to the small size of these parties.

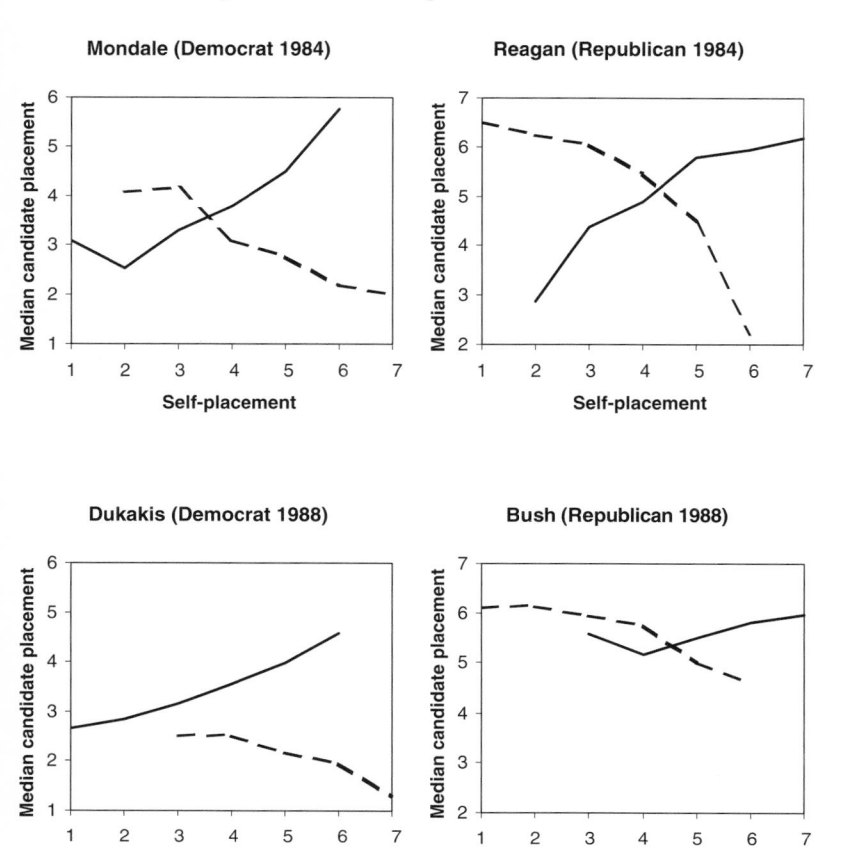

Figure 10.3. Median candidate placements versus self-placements: United States, 1984, 1988, and 1992.
Note: See note to Figure 10.1.

Swedish elections. The average magnitudes of the slopes for nonsupporters differ significantly among the four countries ($p = 0.01$); they are close to significantly different for supporters ($p = 0.09$). For nonsupporters, the magnitude is greatest for the United States; for supporters, it is greatest for Norway and Britain.

Slopes for nonsupporters of the American candidates, however, are generally as great (in absolute value) as those for supporters; that is, we find contrast and assimilation of comparable strength for the elections of 1984, 1988,

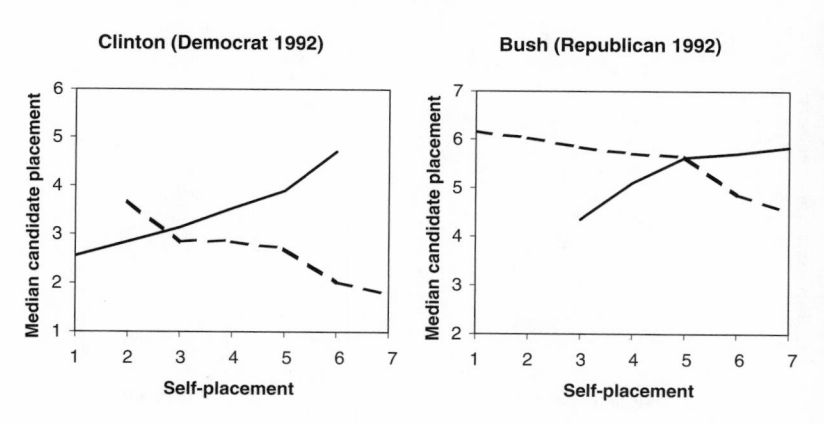

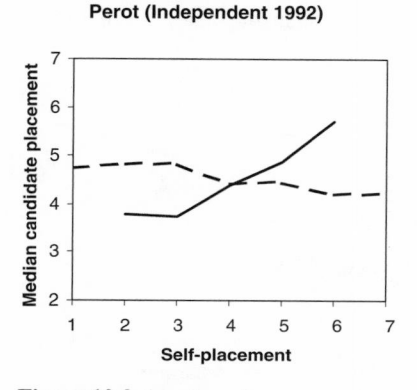

Figure 10.3 (*continued*)

and 1992. This latter result contrasts with those of Granberg and Jenks (1977) and Granberg, Harris, and King (1981), who found assimilation stronger than contrast for the 1972 and 1976 U.S. elections. Our results are, however, in agreement with that of Granberg (1987: Table 4) for the one U.S. election (1984) that was analyzed both by Granberg and by ourselves. Granberg reports a correlation between candidate and self-placement that is about the same (in absolute value) for nonsupporters (– 0.40) and for supporters (0.46); that is, he finds that contrast and assimilation are comparable for this election. We consistently find assimilation and contrast to be of comparable strength for the major party candidates in U.S. elections since 1984, suggesting that findings of stronger effects for assimilation than

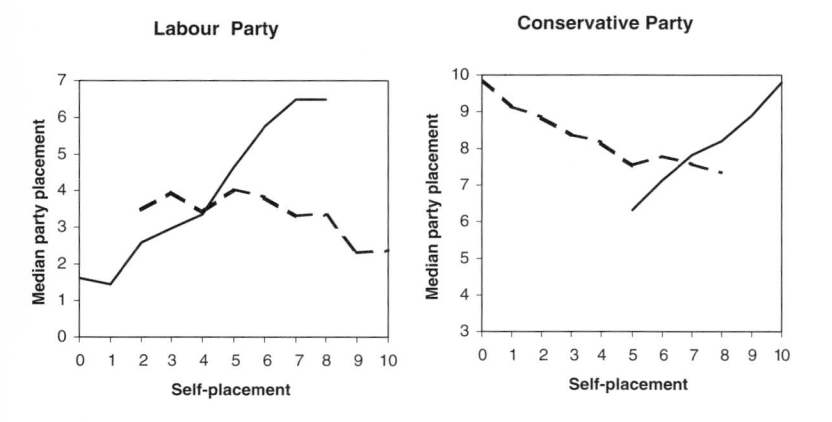

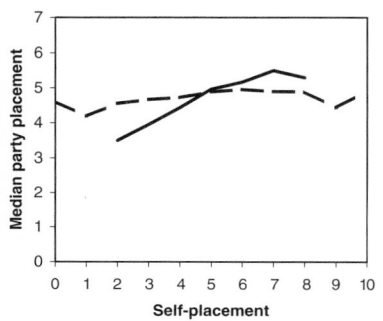

Figure 10.4. Median candidate placements versus self-placements: Britain, 1997. *Note:* See note to Figure 10.1.

for contrast in the 1970s cannot be generalized to more recent American politics.

Our next hypothesis is suggested by our expectation that the perception that a party or candidate is ideologically extreme would be more pronounced among nonsupporters than among supporters.

Hypothesis 3: For each party or candidate, the median placement by non-supporters is more extreme than that of supporters.

Table 10.2 presents the median placement for each party or candidate, stratified by supporters and nonsupporters of that party. For all but five

Table 10.1. *Estimated slopes and significance levels for median party placement, stratified by party and by supporters/nonsupporters*

Country	Party or Candidate	Supporters		Nonsupporters	
		Slope	p-value	Slope	p-value
France 1988	Lajoinie (Communist)	−0.05	–	−0.1	.001
	Mitterrand (Socialist)	0.3	.04	−0.05	<.001
	Barre (UDF)	0.6	.04	−0.1	.007
	Chirac (RPR)	0.3	.18	−0.2	.008
	Le Pen (National Front)	0.1	.06	−0.02	.01
Norway 1989	Socialist	0.4	.01	−0.1	.03
	Labor	0.6	<.001	−0.2	<.001
	Liberal	0.9	.01	−0.2	.01
	Center	0.6	.03	−0.1	<.001
	Christian People's	0.6	.003	−0.1	.004
	Conservative	0.4	.01	−0.1	<.001
	Progress	0.3	.005	−0.1	.04
United States 1984	Mondale (Democrat)	0.6	.005	−0.5	<.001
	Reagan (Republican)	0.6	.002	−0.8	.007
United States 1988	Dukakis (Democrat)	0.4	<.001	−0.3	.01
	Bush (Republican)	0.1	.08	−0.3	.004
United States 1992	Clinton (Democrat)	0.4	<.001	−0.5	.002
	Perot (Independent)	0.5	.005	−0.1	.002
	Bush (Republican)	0.4	.01	−0.3	.001
Britain 1997	Labour	0.8	<.001	−0.2	.01
	Liberal Democratic	0.3	<.001	0.04	.96
	Conservative	0.7	<.001	−0.3	<.001

of the twenty-two parties or candidates, the median for nonsupporters is more extreme (i.e., further from the center of the scale) than the median for supporters.[9] Three of the exceptions are Mitterrand and the Labour and Liberal Democratic Parties in Britain, for none of whom does the difference between medians exceed 0.09. The other two are the Norwegian Center Party and the American Independent candidate Perot, both of whose centrist positions make relative extremity largely meaningless. The mean difference between medians for supporters and nonsupporters is 0.16 for France, 0.08 for Britain, 0.25 for Norway, and 0.18 for Republican candidates in the United States. After adjustment for the differing scales, these values are substantially the same, with slightly lower values for Britain.

---

[9] A one-tailed, paired t-test of the hypothesis that supporter medians are more extreme is significant at the 0.002 level (for this test, the scales were adjusted to be of equal width).

Table 10.2. *Comparing the median in locating a party ideologically between its supporters and nonsupporters*

Country	Party or Candidate	Median		
		Supporters	Nonsupporters	Difference
France 1988	Lajoinie (Communist)	1.99	1.73	0.26
	Mitterrand (Socialist)	3.00	3.08	−0.08
	Barre (UDF)	4.74	4.84	0.10
	Chirac (RPR)	5.38	5.73	0.35
	Le Pen (National Front)	6.75	6.92	0.17
Norway 1989	Socialist	2.51	2.15	0.36
	Labor	4.07	3.82	0.25
	Liberal	5.17	4.53	0.64
	Center	5.74	5.34	−0.40
	Christian People's	6.55	6.63	0.08
	Conservative	8.15	8.36	0.21
	Progress	9.10	9.69	0.59
United States 1984	Mondale (Democrat)	3.58	2.80	0.78
	Reagan (Republican)	5.64	5.81	0.17
United States 1988	Dukakis (Democrat)	3.36	2.12	1.24
	Bush (Republican)	5.63	5.80	0.17
United States 1992	Clinton (Democrat)	3.22	2.48	0.74
	Perot (Independent)	4.57	4.47	−0.10
	Bush (Republican)	5.58	5.77	0.19
Britain 1997	Labour	3.70	3.61	−0.09
	Liberal Democratic	4.85	4.80	−0.05
	Conservative	7.77	8.14	0.37

The difference in medians for the Democratic candidates in the United States, however, averages 0.92 (0.78 for Mondale in 1984, 1.24 for Dukakis in 1988, and 0.74 for Clinton in 1992) and is strikingly higher than the differences for other candidates or parties. That is to say, supporters of the Republican candidate view the Democratic candidate in the United States as far more liberal than do those who vote for the Democrat (or those who voted for Perot in 1992). This effect occurs consistently across American presidential elections.[10]

[10] Granberg (1987) notes this same effect in the 1984 U.S. election. Lacy and Paolino (1998) find an even greater difference between the mean placement of Clinton in 1996 by Democrats (3.66) and by Republicans (2.41). By contrast, Democratic and Republican partisans gave similar mean placements to Dole (5.24 and 5.41, respectively). The *difference* given in Table 10.2 is the extremity of the median placement by nonsupporters minus the extremity

10.3. Discussion

Establishing the extent of projection is important, because if such effects are present, the power of spatial models to predict voting may be overestimated. In testing such models, if the locations of parties are biased due to either assimilation or contrast, assessment of the proximity of the parties to a median voter position (or to other game-theoretic solution sets, such as the core or the yolk) may be compromised. If different groups of voters (e.g., supporters and nonsupporters of a party) perceive the party to be in different places, the traditional concept of a single spatial location for each party or candidate is called into question. Our findings suggest that the latter is particularly important in U.S. presidential elections because of an unusually strong contrast effect with regard to nonsupporters of Democratic candidates.

We have tested three hypotheses about the relationship between party support and the perception of party locations and about the dispersion of perceptions of party locations. All have generally been confirmed over four countries. We find that there is both an assimilation and a contrast effect in that party supporters tend to view the party they support as closer to themselves than do voters as a whole, while opponents tend to view disliked parties as further away from themselves. As a consequence, we get an extremism effect such that (generally speaking) parties on the right and left are seen as less ideologically extreme by their supporters than they are by other voters.

Merrill, Grofman, and Adams (2001) address two methodological issues, each of which involves random variations in subjective placements whose effects might be confounded with those of assimilation or contrast. First, voters may perceive a common scale but perceive differently the location of a party; that is, their sincere placements of a party may be subject to random variation due to incomplete information. Second, voters may perceive the scale itself differently – for example, anchoring it at different points.

In both cases, we find that random variation can lead to the same relationships between party placement and self-placement that we have observed for assimilation, but that this is not so likely to lead to the patterns observed from contrast. In fact, random variation of the anchor point of the scale leads to an effect opposite to that of contrast. Thus the two random-variation

of the corresponding placement by supporters. Extremity is measured relative to the center of the scale. Thus, for example, on a 1–7 scale, if a party is placed at 3.0 by supporters but at 2.0 by nonsupporters, the difference would be 1.0.

effects tend to accentuate the apparent effects of assimilation while partially neutralizing the apparent effects of contrast. Thus, the real effects of contrast may be larger, and those of assimilation smaller, than is apparent from the plots in Figures 10.1–10.4 and from Table 10.1. In turn, this may explain why the magnitudes of the assimilation effects we observe in our empirical study appear larger than the observed contrast effects. Because the effects of assimilation can easily be confounded with those of random variation, we must be very careful in interpreting apparent evidence of assimilation. The effects of contrast, however, are much less likely to be confounded in this manner, so that observation of a negative slope for nonsupporters of a party is more convincing evidence of contrast than a positive slope for supporters is evidence of assimilation.

CHAPTER 11

Policy-Seeking Motivations of Parties in Two-Party Elections

Theory

11.1. Introduction

In previous chapters, we have seen that both the effects of nonpolicy predispositions of voters and the threat of abstention can motivate policy divergence by candidates. In addition, such divergence may be engendered by the potential entry of third parties, the influence of party activists, or – in America – by the polarizing effects of primary elections, and the degree of divergence may be augmented by voter discounting of party positions.

While the approaches already described have generated substantial study, perhaps the most widely cited motivation for policy divergence is that the competing candidates or party leaders have policy motivations – that is, that politicians seek office in order to implement desired policies, rather than proposing policies in order to win office. As Donald Wittman (1990: 66) has argued, this motivation fits comfortably within the spatial modeling framework, since it is strange to think that voters' decisions are moved by policy concerns (a key spatial modeling assumption) but that politicians do not similarly care about policies, except as a means of winning office. And indeed, empirical studies of elite decision making conclude that politicians at times attach considerable weight to pursuing policy objectives (see Fiorina 1974; Muller and Strom 1999). In this and the following chapters, we investigate the effects of parties' policy preferences on their positioning in two-party contests.

In the years since Wittman's (1973, 1977, 1983) seminal articles, spatial modelers have elaborated many approaches to theorizing about policy-motivated politicians' strategic choices (Cox 1984; Calvert 1985; Chappell and Keech 1986; Mitchell 1987; Brams and Merrill 1991; Londregan

184

and Romer 1993; Kollman, Miller, and Page 1992; Groseclose 2001; Roemer 2001). These studies emphasize two factors that plausibly motivate policy-seeking politicians in two-party elections to propose divergent policy platforms.

The first factor is uncertainty over the election outcome. When party elites cannot predict the election outcome with certainty based on the policy declarations of candidates/parties, they face a trade-off between their utility for their policy, on the one hand, and an increase in the probability of winning and thus being able to implement their policy, on the other (see Wittman 1977, 1983; Calvert 1985).

The second factor that motivates divergence arises in situations where one candidate enjoys an electoral advantage that is not tied to her policy positions in the current election (see Wittman 1983; Feld and Grofman 1991; Londregan and Romer 1993; Groseclose 2001; Schofield 2003). Such a *valence* advantage – which applies across the board to all voters – may be due to incumbency during favorable economic conditions, superior name recognition, charisma, competency, or other factors. We might expect a valence advantage to give the advantaged candidate the leeway to propose noncentrist policies that reflect her sincere beliefs, since her non-policy-related advantage may compensate for any electoral losses sustained due to noncentrist positioning.

It is reasonable to expect that parties will typically have a mixture of policy-seeking and office-seeking motivations, and that this mix will vary among parties. Parties that seek office as a first priority will – as we have seen – tend to choose moderate (although not necessarily centrist) policies in an attempt to maximize votes. If successful, they will grow large. On the other hand, parties that put policy before office may locate in positions that are not vote-maximizing and may remain small. Such parties – often under pressure from activists with strong views – typically fill the policy vacuums in the wings of the policy spectrum that office-seeking parties avoid. Under plurality, these parties have little hope of winning (unless they are geographically based), so vote maximization may be a low priority for them, although occasionally the lure of someday winning office by gaining a plurality may motivate a small party to emphasize vote share. Under PR on the other hand, increases in vote share may lead to greater impact in coalition bargaining and may be critical in achieving institutional thresholds for seat allotment. Thus under PR, small parties may place a higher value on vote share than they might under plurality.

We pursue two approaches – one theoretical and one empirical. Theoretically, we develop a model to determine the equilibrium strategies of parties in a two-party election in which each party has policy-seeking goals, and in which voters are motivated by a combination of policies and valence-related considerations. These models will be used to assess the likely effects of model parameters on the location of candidates at equilibrium – parameters such as the size of the valence advantage, the degree of uncertainty about the valence advantage, the distance between the candidates' true policy preferences, and the location of the voter distribution. Comparisons to the related analyses of Londregan and Romer (1993) and Groseclose (2001) will be made.

While the theoretical literature on policy-seeking candidates is extensive, empirical applications of the policy-seeking perspective are less developed. To our knowledge, there exists no empirical study that explores whether policy-seeking goals can motivate the degree of policy divergence that we actually observe in real-world, two-candidate elections.[1] That is what we explore here. Specifically, we investigate whether the strategic effects of candidates' valence advantages, coupled with the complicating factor of election uncertainty, can explain the substantial policy divergence between candidates that was observed in two of the elections studied earlier in this book: the 1988 French and U.S. presidential elections.

Our empirical analysis in Chapter 12 leads us to the following conclusion: that the candidates in the second round of the 1988 French presidential election and the 1988 American presidential election, and the major parties in the 1997 British election, would have policy motivations to propose positions that were divergent and more sharply so than predicted by the effects of abstention dealt with in Chapters 7–9. In particular, the winning candidates

---

[1] Studies by Wittman (1983), Londregan and Romer (1993), and Groseclose (2001) test how candidates' policies shift in response to changes in the uncertainty surrounding the election and/or in the magnitude of one candidate's non-policy-related electoral advantage. However, these studies do not estimate the magnitude of policy divergence between candidates that should be expected in real-world elections. One of our objectives here is to establish that the order of magnitude of divergence between candidates in real-world elections is comparable to what is predicted by the models. It should be emphasized that because of the many factors that no reasonable model can incorporate, theoretical models cannot be expected to predict the exact positions of real candidates. In addition, we note that studies by Martin and Quinn (2000) and Schofield and colleagues (1998) employ spatial models to compute policy-seeking politicians' optimal strategies in real-world elections in multiparty parliamentary democracies, but they do not similarly assess the degree of divergence in the two-candidate contests that concern us here.

enjoyed significant valence-related electoral advantages, and therefore had both the leeway and the motivation to propose distinctly noncentrist policies.[2] We also present reasons why our results for the French, U.S., and British contests are likely to generalize to other real-world elections.

11.2. Spatial Models with Full Information: How Valence Advantages Motivate Divergence between Policy-Seeking Candidates

The assumption driving policy-seeking models is that the preelection policy proposals of candidates who are policy-motivated constrain their ability to implement policy if they win office, so that, ceteris paribus, candidates prefer to propose policies that reflect their sincere preferences. In particular, policy-seeking candidates evaluate election outcomes not according to which candidate wins office, but according to their evaluations of the winning candidate's policies. Thus in a two-candidate election involving a purely policy-seeking Democratic candidate, D, who proposes the policy d, and a Republican, R, who proposes the policy r, D's utility $U_D(d, r)$ for the election outcome is

$$U_D(d, r) = \begin{cases} D\text{'s utility for the policy proposal } d \text{ if } D \text{ is elected,} \\ D\text{'s utility for the policy proposal } r \text{ if } R \text{ is elected.} \end{cases}$$

(11.1)

R has a comparable utility function.[3]

While policy-seeking models represent a fundamental departure from Downs's office-seeking perspective, policy motivations alone do not necessarily motivate candidate divergence. In particular, in the most basic spatial modeling scenario in which voters are purely policy-motivated and candidates are fully informed about voters' policy beliefs, policy-seeking

---

[2] Note that this result contrasts with that for *vote-maximizing*, valence-advantaged candidates, whose best strategies are near the center (see Appendix 3.1).

[3] For convenience, we use the terms "Democrat" and "Republican" to refer to the leftist and rightist candidates, respectively. In some circumstances, candidates may prefer to win while proposing policies that do not correspond to their sincere preferences. For instance, in U.S. presidential elections a candidate who holds slightly liberal (conservative) beliefs might prefer to win while proposing a very liberal (conservative) platform, since Congress will likely moderate her proposals – that is, candidates may employ the same policy discounting metric that we explored in empirical voting analyses in earlier chapters. Here we shall refer to the candidate's sincere policy preferences as those policies she would prefer to have proposed in the event she wins office.

candidates will converge to identical policies – the same result predicted for office-seeking candidates (see Calvert 1985). To see this, consider an election in which candidate D's proposed policy is more liberal than the position of the median voter. R can then propose a policy that is closer to, but more conservative than, the median voter, thereby winning the election and obtaining his proposed policy as the implemented outcome. In order to avert this outcome, candidate D has an incentive to move in toward the median voter. It follows that the only stable policy configuration is the one where both candidates adopt the median voter's position.[4]

Incorporating candidates' valence advantages into the spatial model offers a possible solution to the puzzle that arises because, empirically, candidates do not converge. Recall that a *valence* advantage is one that applies equally for all voters. Suppose, for example, that candidate D enjoys a valence advantage such that he wins election *unless* R's policy proposal is more than y policy units closer to the median voter's position than is D's proposal. In this case, D is guaranteed to win so long as she locates within y units of the median voter, and she therefore has the leeway to diverge from the median position, in the direction of her preferred policy. Provided that D's sincere policy preference is more than y units to the left of the median position, a (deterministic) equilibrium occurs with the candidates separated by y policy units, with R proposing policy at the median position and D proposing a winning platform y units to the left.

11.3. A Policy-Seeking Model with Incomplete Information, Part 1: The Effects of Uncertainty about the Impact of Valence Issues

For our theoretical model, we suppose that there are two parties, which we will refer to as the Democratic and Republican Parties, and that there is a single policy issue, for example, Left–Right. The preferred policy positions of the Democratic candidate, D, and the Republican candidate, R, are also denoted by D and R, respectively; and, as before, their declared policy positions in the campaign are denoted by d and r. We assume that voters have quadratic policy losses. In order to simplify presentation of our results, we

---

[4] Matters are somewhat different when both candidates' sincere preferences lie to the left (right) of the median voter. In this case, the candidates converge to whichever candidate's preferred position is closer to the position of the median voter.

set the location of the median voter M to $m = 0$; thus in our analysis we calibrate the candidates' equilibrium positions relative to the position of the median voter.

Assume that voters' comparative evaluations of the candidates depend on their evaluations of the candidates' positions, plus a valence component V that is identical across voters. V is composed of *measured valence characteristics*, v, plus unmeasured characteristics represented by a random variable, X, which the candidates do not know with certainty at the time they choose their strategies.[5] Thus

$$V = v + X.$$

We take V to represent the difference between the Democrat's and the Republican's valence evaluations, and we label v, the measured valence characteristics, as candidate D's *expected valence advantage* (note that v takes on a negative value if R's known valence-related attributes are superior to D's attributes). Finally, assume that X, the unknown component of voters' valence evaluations (of the Democrat relative to the Republican), is selected at random from a normal distribution with a mean of zero and standard deviation σ_V, and that X takes on an identical value across voters. Thus

$$V \sim N(v, \sigma_V^2).$$

We label σ_V the *degree of valence-related uncertainty*. Thus the median voter M's utility differential for D versus R is:

$$M\text{'s utility differential} = (m - r)^2 - (m - d)^2 + V$$
$$= (r^2 - d^2) + v + X$$

because $m = 0$ and $V = v + X$.

Our model of voting behavior is similar to the one presented by Londregan and Romer (1993), which posits that voters' decisions are motivated by a combination of policy concerns and their valence-related evaluations of the candidates' abilities to provide constituent service. Crucially, our model

---

[5] Measured valence-related characteristics include observable variables such as incumbency and the candidates' comparative levels of name recognition. While the impact of these variables cannot be known with certainty in advance of the election, their expected impacts may be denoted by v, while the unmeasured impact of these measured candidate characteristics contributes to the random component X. Also contributing to X are additional factors that cannot be known in advance of the election, such as how skillfully each candidate will campaign, and the possible impact upon the campaign of "exogenous shocks" arising from government scandals, international or domestic crises, and so on.

follows the Londregan–Romer model in that we assume that from the candidates' perspectives, the uncertainty over the election outcome revolves entirely around voters' valence considerations – that is, the candidates know the voter distribution with certainty but are unsure about voters' comparative evaluations of the candidates' non-policy-related attributes.[6] This is not the only reasonable way to model election-related uncertainty, and later we will also explore an alternative formulation, developed by Groseclose (2001), in which candidate uncertainty revolves around the voter distribution. We shall see that the source of election uncertainty has crucial implications for policy-seeking candidates' strategies.

11.3.1. Policy-Seeking Equilibrium Strategies with $v = 0$

Given the assumptions in our model, the Democratic candidate D wins the election if and only if the median voter votes for D.[7] Furthermore, it is easily seen that the probability $P_M(D)$ that the median voter M votes for D is $P_M(D) = \Phi[(r^2 - d^2 + v)/\sigma_V]$, where Φ denotes the standard cumulative normal distribution.[8] It follows that the probability that D will be elected, denoted by $F(d, r)$, is given by

$$F(d, r) = \Phi[(r^2 - d^2 + v)/\sigma_V]. \tag{11.2}$$

For simplicity, we assume that either candidate, if she wins, will implement the policy on which she ran and that this is the policy location that is perceived by the voters during the campaign. If the candidates are interested only in policy, the utility of the outcome to the Democratic candidate, $U_D(d, r)$, based on quadratic loss, is the sum of her utilities for the two candidates' policy positions, weighted by the probabilities that each candidate will win, that is,

$$U_D(d, r) = -(d - D)^2 F(d, r) - (r - D)^2 [1 - F(d, r)], \tag{11.3A}$$

and the utility for the Republican candidate, $U_R(d, r)$, is given by

$$U_R(d, r) = -(d - R)^2 F(d, r) - (r - R)^2 [1 - F(d, r)]. \tag{11.3B}$$

---

[6] In the Londregan–Romer formulation, this uncertainty relates to voters' evaluations of the candidates' abilities to perform constituent service.

[7] For any realization of X, if D wins the median voter, D also wins all the voters to her side of the median, and hence a majority.

[8] Note that the probability that the median voter votes for the Democratic candidate is $P[r^2 - d^2 + v + X > 0] = P[X > -r^2 + d^2 - v] = \Phi[(r^2 - d^2 + v)/\sigma_V]$.

First we present a result when there is no expected valence advantage, that is, when $v = 0$:

Theorem 11.1. If the measured component v of the valence $= 0$, if the candidates' preferred positions D and R are symmetric about the median of the voter distribution, and if an equilibrium exists with $d = -r$, then the divergence between strategies is given by

$$r - d = \frac{-\sqrt{\pi/2}\sigma_V + \sqrt{(\pi/2)\sigma_V^2 + 2\sqrt{2\pi}\sigma_V(R - D)^2}}{2(R - D)} \qquad (11.4)$$

Proof. See Appendix 11.1.

An obvious question arises: How much candidate divergence could we expect at equilibrium for this model, given realistic values of the model parameters? The answer depends on the value of the valence-related uncertainty parameter σ_V. While it is difficult to determine realistic values given the highly stylized nature of our election model, arguments based on empirical research about the accuracy of preelection polls suggest that when the candidates are placed at realistic positions along the 1–7 ideology scale used in the American National Election Study (ANES), σ_V plausibly lies in the range of 0.5 to 1.0 for U.S. presidential elections. These arguments are presented in Appendix 11.2. Thus given the value $\sigma_V = 1.0$, if the preferred locations of the Democratic and Republican candidates are $D = 2$ and $R = 6$ (where we assume the median voter is at 4.0), then by substituting in equation 11.4, we find that the separation between the strategies of the two candidates at equilibrium is given by

$$(r - d) = 2r = 0.98,$$

so that, on the 1–7 scale, we have $d = 3.51$ and $r = 4.49$. Thus, the model motivates significant divergence between policy-seeking candidates, given a realistic value for σ_V.

11.3.2. Effects of a Valence Advantage

If the valence advantage v is not zero, we cannot solve the equilibrium equations 11.3 analytically for utility-maximizing values of d and r, but we can determine their values numerically for specific values of the parameters. Table 11.1A and Figure 11.1A present equilibrium positions for which

Table 11.1. *Policy-seeking equilibrium strategies under the valence-related uncertainty model*

11.1A. *Equilibria as a function of valence-related bias and valence-related uncertainty*

Valence Bias v	$\sigma_V = 0.5$			$\sigma_V = 1.0$		
	d	r	$r - d$	d	r	$r - d$
0.0	3.64	4.36	.72	3.51	4.49	.98
1.0	3.27	4.15	.88	3.27	4.31	1.04
2.0	2.90	4.08	1.18	3.01	4.20	1.19

11.1B. *Equilibria for a mixed policy-seeking and office-seeking model, with valence bias $v = 1.0$*

Mixing Parameter λ	$\sigma_V = 0.5$			$\sigma_V = 1.0$		
	d	r	$r - d$	d	r	$r - d$
0.0	3.27	4.15	.88	3.27	4.31	1.04
0.5	3.32	4.12	.81	3.33	4.27	.94
0.9	3.50	4.04	.54	3.59	4.12	.53
0.95	3.61	4.02	.42	3.73	4.06	.34
1.00	4.00	4.00	.00	4.00	4.00	.00

Note: The candidates' preferred positions are set at $D = 2$ and $R = 6$. The mixing parameter λ equals 0 for pure policy-seeking motivations, and λ equals 1 for pure office-seeking motivations.

candidate preferences are $D = 2.0$ and $R = 6.0$ (on the 1–7 scale), v is in a range from 0 to 2, and (in the table) σ_V ranges from 0.5 to 1.0; a rationale for choosing these ranges of values as realistic is given in Appendix 11.2.[9] Equilibria for candidate preferences at, say, $D = 3.0$ and $R = 5.0$ (not shown) are similar but slightly less divergent, as are equilibria for linear instead of quadratic voter utilities.

Note that the divergence between the optimal positions of the Democrat and the Republican increase moderately as both the valence-characteristic

---

[9] Equilibria for values $v = -1$ and -2 (representing a Republican valence advantage) are mirror images of those presented in Table 11.1.

11.1A Equilibria as a function of valence-related bias *v*

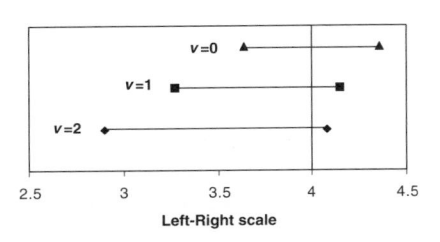

11.1B Equilibria for a mixed policy-seeking and office-seeking model (valence bias *v* = 1.0;
λ is the mixing parameter)

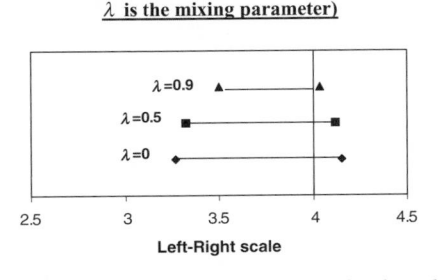

Figure 11.1. Policy-seeking equilibrium strategies under the valence-related uncertainty model.
Note: For each value of the valence bias v or of the mixing parameter λ, the end points of the line segment represent the locations of the Democratic and Republican candidates at equilibrium. $\lambda = 0$ specifies a pure policy-seeking model. The valence-related uncertainty σ_V is set at 0.5, and the candidates' preferred positions are $D = 2$ and $R = 6$. The vertical line indicates the location of the median voter.

parameter v and the valence-related uncertainty parameter σ_V increase. Furthermore, d and r shift to the left – in the direction of D's preferred position – when the Democrat is advantaged, and to the right when the Republican has the valence advantage. Thus a candidate with a valence advantage not only has leeway, but also has motivation to move closer to his preferred policy position. This is consistent with Wittman's (1990) conclusion that an advantaged candidate is willing to trade off a part of his non-policy-related electoral advantage in favor of the likelihood of being elected on a platform that closely resembles his sincere policy preferences.

11.3.3. Mixtures of Policy-Seeking and Office-Seeking Motivations

Equilibria for candidates whose motivations are a *mixture* of policy seeking and office seeking are generally similar to those based on policy seeking alone. The effect of mixing these two motivations appears to be nonlinear in the mixing parameter, with policy-seeking motivations having a greater effect on equilibrium positions. Following Groseclose (2001), we may define a utility function that mixes office seeking and policy seeking for the Democrat as

$$U_D(d, r) = \lambda F(d, r) - (1 - \lambda)(d - D)^2 F(d, r)$$
$$- (1 - \lambda)(r - D)^2 [1 - F(d, r)], \tag{11.5}$$

where the mixing parameter λ varies between 0 (pure policy seeking) and 1 (pure office seeking). A similar function is defined for the Republican. Policy-seeking utility under this definition tends to have a larger magnitude and to vary more than office-seeking utility [because of the size of the terms $(d - D)^2$ and $(r - D)^2$], so that it is difficult to interpret the meaning of λ. However, the following illustrations provide intuitions about the substantive interpretation of this parameter. If $\lambda = 0.5$, then each candidate prefers to hold office (i.e., to win the election) while implementing policies that diverge by up to one policy unit from his ideal point, compared to being out of office (i.e., losing the election) while his preferred policies are implemented by his opponent. If $\lambda = 0.8$, each candidate prefers to implement policies located up to two policy units away from his ideal point, in preference to watching his opponent implement his ideal policies from out of office; if $\lambda = 0.9$, the candidates are willing to implement policies up to three units away from their ideal points, compared to any possible out-of-office scenario.[10]

As indicated in Table 11.1B and Figure 11.1B, for $D = 2$ and $R = 6$, for $v = 1.0$, $\sigma_V = 0.5$, and $\lambda = 0.5$, the equilibrium is (3.32, 4.12), which is very close to the equilibrium for pure policy seeking (3.27, 4.15). Even for

---

[10] In general, when $\lambda = k^2/(1 - k^2)$, a candidate equates the outcome of winning and implementing policy k units from his preferred policy position with the outcome of having his preferred policy implemented by his opponent.

$\lambda = 0.9$, the equilibrium is (3.50, 4.04), which suggests that policy-seeking motivations dominate in determining the locations of equilibria. Similar results are obtained for $\sigma_V = 1.0$ (see Table 11.1B). Thus for realistic model parameters, as long as policy seeking makes a substantial contribution to candidate motivations, the candidates should diverge significantly in the policy space, and the valence-advantaged candidate should locate further from the median than the disadvantaged candidate.

As suggested earlier (section 11.1), the motivations of small parties may often be more heavily weighted toward policy seeking than those of larger parties. This tendency may help to explain why the observed policy positions of small parties – such as the French Communist and National Front and the Norwegian Socialist and Progress Parties – are often more extreme than those of larger ones, despite the theoretical arguments presented in Chapter 4 that *vote-maximizing* optima of small parties are less extreme than those of their larger counterparts.

11.4. A Policy-Seeking Model with Incomplete Information, Part 2: The Effects of Uncertainty about the Voter Distribution

In contrast to the Londregan–Romer assumption that candidate uncertainty revolves around the effects of valence-related factors, Groseclose (2001) posits that candidates are certain about the effects of valence issues – that is, that $\sigma_V = 0$ and $V = v$, according to the notation introduced in the preceding section – but are uncertain of the location of the median voter. We represent this uncertainty by specifying the location of the median voter M as $(m + \varepsilon)$, where m represents the measured component of the median voter's position – which we set to zero without loss of generality – and ε represents the unmeasured component of this position. We assume that ε is selected at random from a normal distribution with a mean of zero and standard deviation σ_m, which we label the *degree of policy-related uncertainty*. Under the Groseclose model, the probability that the Democratic candidate will win is

$$\bar{F}(d, r) = \Phi \left\{ \left[\frac{d + r}{2} + \frac{v}{2(r - d)} \right] \bigg/ \sigma_m \right\} \qquad (11.6)$$

Table 11.2. *Policy-seeking equilibrium strategies under the Groseclose model*

Valence Bias v	$\sigma_m = 0.25$			$\sigma_m = 0.50$			$\sigma_m = 1.00$		
	d	r	$r - d$	d	r	$r - d$	d	r	$r - d$
Quadratic utility									
0.0	3.73	4.23	.54	3.52	4.48	.96	3.23	4.77	1.54
1.0	3.33	4.44	1.11	3.41	4.68	1.27	3.30	4.95	1.64
2.0	3.00	4.50	1.50	3.19	4.79	1.60	3.27	5.11	1.84
Linear utility									
0.0	3.73	4.23	.54	3.52	4.48	.96	3.23	4.77	1.54
1.0	3.10	4.10	1.00	3.12	4.12	1.00	2.89	4.41	1.52
2.0	2.50	4.50	2.00	2.27	4.27	2.00	2.41	4.41	2.00

Note: Equilibria are given as a function of valence bias, policy-related uncertainty, and utility function, with candidates' preferred positions set at $D = 2$ and $R = 6$.

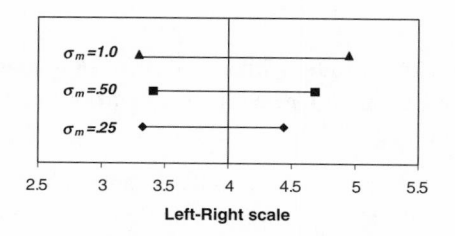

Figure 11.2. Policy-seeking equilibrium strategies under the Groseclose model. *Note*: Equilibria are given as a function of policy-related uncertainty σ_m, with valence bias set at $v = 1.0$ and candidates' preferred positions set at $D = 2$ and $R = 6$. Voter utility is quadratic.

(assuming that voters have quadratic policy utilities).[11] This differs significantly from the formula in equation 11.2, which obtains when the candidate uncertainty revolves around valence issues. Equilibria computed

[11] Under the Groseclose model, $P[D \text{ wins}] = P[\text{cut-point} > \text{median voter}] = P[\frac{d+r}{2} + \frac{v}{2(r-d)} > \varepsilon] = \Phi[\frac{d+r}{2} + \frac{v}{2(r-d)}/\sigma_m]$. This contrasts with the corresponding probability for the valence-uncertainty model, for which $P[D \text{ wins}] = P[\text{cut-point} > \text{median voter}] = P[\frac{d+r}{2} + \frac{v+X}{2(r-d)} > 0] = P[(d+r)(r-d) + v + X > 0] = \Phi[(r^2 - d^2 + v)/\sigma_V]$. Note that the probability that D wins under the Groseclose model is far more sensitive to the value of $(r - d)$ – because this term appears in a denominator in the argument of Φ – than is the corresponding probability under the valence-uncertainty model.

using Groseclose's assumptions are given in Table 11.2 and Figure 11.2, for varying degrees of policy-related uncertainty σ_m, and (in the table) for varying values of the valence parameter v.[12] Note that in this model, σ_m represents the standard deviation of uncertainty about the location of the voter distribution, a parameter that is not directly comparable to the valence-related uncertainty parameters in the model from section 11.3.

The equilibria in Table 11.2 modestly support Groseclose's remarkable and counterintuitive conclusion that a valence disadvantage may induce a policy-seeking candidate to move *toward* her preferred policy position.[13] This is the opposite of the effect we obtained for the valence-uncertainty model presented in the preceding section. As Groseclose argues, this surprising result revolves around the fact that when uncertainty centers on the voter distribution, then the degree to which this introduces uncertainty about the election outcome increases with the policy distance between the candidates. To see this, note that if the candidates present identical positions in the Groseclose model, then they experience no uncertainty over the election outcome, since, with all voters indifferent between the candidates' policy positions, the valence-advantaged candidate is certain to win. By contrast, if the candidates diverge, then the election outcome is uncertain, since it depends on the (unknown) location of the median voter. This consideration motivates what Groseclose (2001: 870) labels the "Extremist Underdog" result – that valence-disadvantaged candidates may have motivation to diverge from their opponent's position, thereby accentuating the policy divergence between the candidates and increasing uncertainty over the election outcome.[14]

---

[12] Our equilibrium values for the Groseclose model are slightly more divergent than those presented in Groseclose (2001: Table 2) because we set $D = 2$ and $R = 6$, whereas Groseclose uses $D = 3$ and $R = 5$. Using Groseclose's exact parameters, we obtain results identical to those in his Table 2.

[13] Groseclose also demonstrates the possibility of a related effect, which he labels the "Moderating Front-Runner" result (2001: 871): that valence-advantaged candidates have strategic incentives to converge toward their opponent's position in order to reduce policy-related uncertainty surrounding the election outcome. However, this effect occurs only for specified values of the model parameters and does not show up in Table 11.2. Groseclose provides an example of a valence-advantaged Democrat, a candidate who is 75 percent office-seeking and 25 percent policy-seeking, moving to the right of center. As he points out, a *purely* office-seeking but valence-advantaged Democrat might try to mimic the Republican's position on the grounds that the election would then turn on his valence advantage alone (see also Appendix 3.1).

[14] As Groseclose points out (2001: 872), his paradoxical findings do not occur for linear (as opposed to quadratic) utility, or in general if the valence advantage translates into a constant

Groseclose presents equilibria for values of v up to 1.0, which strikes us as low for presidential elections. As we argue in Appendix 11.2, it appears more plausible that v varies from 0 up to 2 or 3. On the other hand, the value of 0.5 that Groseclose uses for σ_m appears to be high, at least to the extent that σ_m represents presidential candidates' uncertainty over the electorate's ideological orientation. This value suggests that the candidates' uncertainty about the location of the center of the voter distribution is typically one-half unit on the 1–7 scale, far higher than, for example, the standard deviation of the median-voter ideological locations in the ANES studies for 1980–96, which is only 0.14 (see Merrill and Grofman 1999: Table 9.1).[15] The standard deviation of the mean Left–Right self-placement in the Eurobarometer Surveys for France for the twenty-two-year period from 1976 to 1997 (adjusted to a 1–7 scale) is 0.106, a value that is even smaller than that for the United States (see Adams et al. forthcoming: Table 1).

Accurate estimation of the empirical range of σ_m is important, because the Groseclose effect – namely, the Extremist Underdog result – is noticeable for high values of σ_m such as 1.0, but disappears or reverses for smaller values of σ_m. For example, if $\sigma_m = 0.25$ (see Table 11.2), the equilibrium strategy of

---

probability advantage (as in Wittman 1983). If linear – instead of quadratic – utility is used for voter evaluation, the Groseclose formula for the probability that the Democrat wins is

$$\tilde{F}(d, r) = \Phi \left\{ \left[\frac{d+r}{2} + \frac{v}{2} \right] \middle/ \sigma_m \right\} if\ v \leq (r - d),$$

and 1 otherwise. We observe that the cut-point for determining who wins is extremely sensitive to $(r - d)$ in the quadratic-utility version of Groseclose's model [note the term $1/(r - d)$ in equation 11.6], but not in the linear-utility version. Although Groseclose argues in favor of using the quadratic utility, this very sensitivity may be an argument against it. At the very least, the sensitivity of the Groseclose model to the type of utility makes the conclusions from his model presented in his Table 2 problematic.

[15] The variation reported in Merrill and Grofman for the location of the median voter is over a sixteen-year period. As any one election approaches, one would expect the uncertainty to be even less. We note, however, that candidate uncertainty is plausibly much greater in situations where policy competition is over new or evolving issues, as opposed to long-standing ideological debates. This consideration appears to be particularly relevant to congressional elections – which Groseclose explicitly references in his paper, and which sometimes revolve around emerging local issues (Fenno 1978), or which alternatively may turn on voters' beliefs about national policy debates that are only loosely tied to general Left–Right orientations. To the extent that many 1994 congressional elections revolved around voters' assessments of the Clinton administration's health care proposals, for example, or to the extent that the 2002 congressional elections turned on public evaluations of the Bush administration's Homeland Security agenda, congressional candidates may have experienced substantial uncertainty about the outcome of these elections. In these situations, σ_m plausibly takes on larger values, of the magnitude that Groseclose investigates.

the valence-disadvantaged candidate is closer to the center than is that of the valence-advantaged candidate, just as in our model. As the underdog recedes from her opponent, her expected vote share drops further and further below 50 percent. Only a large variance in the vote share is capable of overcoming this deficit and offering an increased (but still small) probability of winning.

We conclude that, although dramatic Extremist Underdog effects may occur for less common values of the parameters v and σ_m, uncertainty about the location of the voter distribution will not necessarily bring the valence-advantaged candidate nearer to the center than the disadvantaged candidate, at least in the presidential elections that concern us here (see note 15). On the other hand, uncertainty about the extent of the valence effect will draw advantaged candidates distinctly *further* from the center. No doubt both types of uncertainty occur in reality. Equilibria assuming both types of uncertainty are given in Table 11.3. For the reasons given earlier, we would judge the valence-related effect to be more likely to dominate in presidential elections, and we therefore expect the advantaged candidate to locate further from the center than the disadvantaged one unless the policy-related uncertainty is very high.

11.5. Conclusion

We have seen in this chapter that policy-seeking motivations may motivate candidates in two-party elections to present divergent policy positions, particularly in the face of election uncertainty or a valence imbalance between the candidates. In fact, uncertainty about the valence effects – even if there is no expected advantage for either candidate – implies divergence for policy-seeking candidates, although the degree of divergence is magnified by a valence imbalance. Furthermore, given valence uncertainty, a valence-advantaged candidate has motivation to assume a policy position closer to her preferred position than does a disadvantaged candidate.

As long as election uncertainty does not vary greatly with the distance between candidates, valence-advantaged candidates are able to adopt strategies more to their liking, while disadvantaged candidates must move toward the center in order to counteract their non-policy-related handicap. If, on the other hand, uncertainty is based not on valence but on the location of the voter distribution, so that uncertainty in vote share increases sharply with the distance between candidates, the tables are turned, and it is the valence-disadvantaged candidate who assumes a strategy near his preference, while

Table 11.3. *Equilibria for policy and valence-related uncertainty including both office-seeking and policy-seeking motivations*

Mixing Parameter λ	$\sigma_m = 0.25$			$\sigma_m = 0.50$			$\sigma_m = 1.00$		
	d	r	$r - d$	d	r	$r - d$	d	r	$r - d$
0.0	3.34	4.35	1.01	3.39	4.63	1.24	3.29	4.94	1.65
0.5	3.39	4.33	.94	3.46	4.62	1.16	3.38	4.92	1.54
0.9	3.60	4.25	.65	3.78	4.66	.88	3.95	5.02	1.07

Note: The valence bias is set at $v = 1.0$, the valence-related uncertainty is set at $\sigma_V = 0.5$, and the candidates' preferred positions are set at $D = 2$ and $R = 6$. The mixing parameter λ varies between 0 for pure policy-seeking motivations and 1 for pure office-seeking motivations.

the advantaged candidate must move toward the center. An increase in uncertainty with policy distance sufficient to produce this effect, however, would appear to stretch the limits of empirical likelihood in presidential elections. Furthermore, insofar as uncertainty depends primarily on non-policy factors – on public perception of candidate character, charisma, and leadership, or on world events – that uncertainty is largely independent of candidate spatial separation. In this case, valence-advantaged candidates are also advantaged in the sense that their equilibrium strategies are likely to be closer to their preferences than those of their opponents.

In the next chapter, we explore empirically these expectations for the effects of policy-seeking motivations in the presence of valence bias, valence uncertainty, or uncertainty about the voter distribution. The elections we analyze for this purpose are the U.S. presidential election of 1988, the second round of the French presidential election of 1988, and, more briefly, the 1997 British general election.

CHAPTER 12

Policy-Seeking Motivations
of Parties in Two-Party Elections

Empirical Analysis

12.1. Introduction

While the theoretical results presented in Chapter 11 are suggestive, they rest upon simplified voting models that omit several factors that influence real-world voters' decisions. These include influences that vary across voters, such as party identification and sociodemographic characteristics, as well as voter-specific random disturbance terms that render voters' choices probabilistic from the candidates' perspectives. In this regard, simulations based upon election survey data offer a possible bridge between our theoretical results and empirical applications. Here we explore policy-seeking candidates' strategies, using survey data from the two-candidate 1988 American presidential election and from the second round of the 1988 French presidential election, which was also a two-candidate contest. We also report applications to the 1997 British general election, which featured a three-party contest.

The 1988 U.S. and French presidential elections provide an appropriate testing ground for spatial models of policy-seeking candidates, since the presidents of both countries have broad constitutional powers to influence government policy (see Pierce 1995; Safran 1998). As in our theoretical analyses, we first explore these issues using the assumption that the candidates had full information. Then, in the next section, we extend our analysis to incomplete information scenarios, and we explore candidate strategies when uncertainty centers on the electoral effects of valence issues and, alternatively, when uncertainty revolves around positional issues.

12.1.1. The Contexts of the 1988 American and French
Presidential Elections

Both the 1988 U.S. presidential election and the second round of the 1988 French presidential election pitted a candidate from a traditionally right-wing party against an opponent from a traditionally left-wing party. In the United States, the contest was between the Republican George Bush – the incumbent vice president serving under the conservative President Ronald Reagan – and the Democrat Michael Dukakis, governor of the traditionally liberal state of Massachusetts. The decisive ballot in the 1988 French presidential election pitted the Socialist Francois Mitterrand, the incumbent president, against Jacques Chirac, the incumbent prime minister *and* the leader of the right-wing Gaullist party.[1] Both elections ended in victory for the incumbent party's nominee, with Vice President Bush defeating Dukakis by a 54 percent to 46 percent popular vote margin, and President Mitterrand winning reelection over Chirac by the same 54–46 percent margin.

We analyze the subsamples of 935 ANES respondents and 744 FPES respondents who reported voting for one of the major candidates and who could place themselves on the 1–7 ideological scales.[2] Figure 12.1 displays the distributions of these respondents' self-placements as well as their mean candidate placements, for the FPES respondents (Figure 12.1A) and for the ANES respondents (Figure 12.1B). The American and French publics appear to be centrist (on average), with ANES respondents averaging a self-placement of 4.41 and the FPES respondents reporting a mean self-placement of 3.96, along the 1–7 scales. Furthermore, respondents perceived significant amounts of ideological dispersion between the candidates, in that the Democrat Dukakis and the Socialist Mitterrand were perceived (on average)

---

[1] French presidential elections involve two rounds of voting, with the two top finishers in round one advancing to the decisive second ballot, where the winner is chosen by direct popular vote. Chapter 5 presents analyses of candidate strategies in the first round of the 1988 French presidential election (see also Adams and Merrill 2000).

[2] For France, the 744 FPES respondents represent a subsample of the 862 respondents who reported voting in round two and who could place themselves on the ideology dimension, randomly selected so that their reported votes reproduce Mitterrand's 54–46 percent vote margin over Chirac in round two. For this purpose, 77.2 percent of the self-claimed Mitterrand voters were retained in the sample. We focus on this subsample because in the overall FPES sample, the respondents reported voting for Mitterrand over Chirac in much greater proportions than did the actual French electorate, which could lead to incorrect inferences about the French electorate's political beliefs in 1988.

12.1A. 1988 French Presidential Election Study

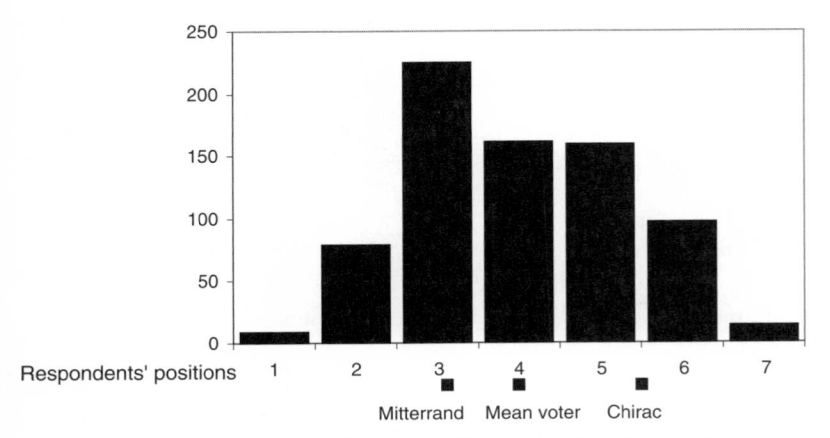

Mean candidate and voter placements

12.1B. 1988 American National Election Study

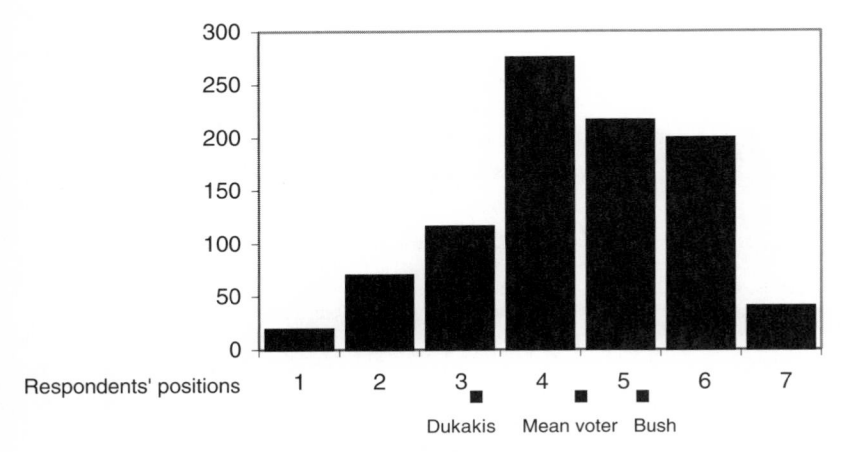

Mean candidate and voter placements

Figure 12.1. Distributions of respondents' ideological self-placements and candidate placements, 1988 French and American presidential elections.

at the leftist positions 3.10 and 3.09, respectively, while the Republican Bush and the Gaullist Chirac were placed at the right-of-center positions 5.23 and 5.55.

We specify random utility frameworks (conditional logit) in which voters' candidate utilities are a function of ideological distance, economic perceptions, sociodemographic characteristics, party identification, and a random component, and in which voters support the candidate who offers the highest utility.[3] The ideology variables are negatives of quadratic distances between the respondents' self-placements and the mean perceived candidate ideology; the economic variables are measures of respondents' retrospective evaluations of their personal finances and of national economic conditions; the sociodemographic variables include race, income, and class in the United States, and income, religion, and class in France. The party identification variables are dummy variables for Democratic and Republican Party identification in the United States, and for identification with a left-wing party (Socialist or Communist) versus a right-wing party (UDF or RPR) in France.[4] Table 12.1A presents the parameter estimates for the 1988 American presidential election and the 1988 French presidential election. Table 12.1B shows that the projected aggregate vote for each model closely matches the sample vote.

12.2. Equilibrium Strategies under Electoral Certainty

We first address the question: Under the assumption of full information, could the losing candidates have overcome their electoral deficits by changing their ideological positions in the 1988 elections? In order to address

---

[3] In contrast to our analyses of American and British election survey data reported in Chapters 7–9, here we do not incorporate the turnout decision into our empirical specifications, nor do we incorporate multiple policy dimensions. This is due to our desire to explore policy-seeking candidates' strategies using empirical voting specifications that approximate those used in the theoretical analyses presented in Chapter 11, which build on the work of Groseclose (2001) and Londregan and Romer (1993). We have also analyzed U.S. presidential candidates' policy-seeking strategies when voters choose according to the unified turnout specification introduced in Chapter 7 (which incorporates turnout effects and multiple policy dimensions), and we find that policy-seeking candidates' computed equilibrium locations under this model display similar patterns to those we report elsewhere in this chapter.

[4] Our decision to specify the French party identification variable in terms of leftist party identification versus right-wing party identification is motivated by the fact that French politics is largely structured around competition between a left-wing Communist–Socialist coalition and a right-wing UDF–Gaullist coalition (see Pierce 1995; Safran 1998; Adams and Merrill 2000).

Table 12.1A. *Conditional logit equations for voting in the 1988 U.S. presidential election and the 1988 French presidential election*

	1988 U.S. Presidential Election	
Intercept	0.64*	(.30)
Democrat	2.13**	(.34)
Republican	1.20**	(.35)
Ideology	.13**	(.02)
Retrospective national economy	.43**	(.12)
Retrospective family finances	.23*	(.11)
Black	−2.01**	(.56)
Income	.13	(.11)
Class	−.04	(.11)
Log-likelihood	−307.9	
		(N = 935)
	1988 French Presidential Election, Second Round	
Intercept	.19	(.19)
Leftist party identification	3.01**	(.31)
Right-wing party identification	2.60**	(.31)
Ideology	.21**	(.03)
Retrospective national economy	.39*	(.20)
Retrospective family finances	.06	(.16)
Income	.23	(.19)
Religion	.21	(.12)
Class	.69**	(.20)
Log-likelihood	−132.9	
		(N = 744)

Note: A single asterisk denotes significance at the .05 level. Two asterisks indicate significance at the .01 level. Standard errors are in parentheses.

this issue, we computed the expected vote for the losing candidate in each election (Dukakis in the United States, Chirac in France) as we moved him across the ideology dimension, while holding the position of the winning candidate unchanged. In order to capture the full-information context, we assumed that the candidates believed that their actual votes on election day would exactly equal their expected vote. Substantively, this implies that the candidates employed the strong assumptions that the estimated voting model parameters reported in Table 12.1 were precisely accurate (i.e., that the standard errors associated with these estimates were all zero), that the

Table 12.1B. *Projected votes for the 1988 U.S. presidential election and the 1988 French presidential election*

	1988 U.S. Presidential Election	
	Bush Vote	Dukakis Vote
ANES distribution	54.4%	45.6%
Projected vote	54.9%	45.1%
	1988 French Presidential Election, Second Round	
	Mitterrand Vote	Chirac Vote
FPES distribution	54.0%	46.0%
Projected vote	54.1%	45.9%

Note: The projected votes are computed by averaging the projected voting probabilities across all respondents, using the probability functions given in Chapter 11. For each election, these projected probabilities are computed using the parameters reported in Table 12.1A.

distribution of the survey respondents' ideological self-placements and their personal characteristics exactly mirrored those of the voting population, *and* that the candidates' election day votes would exactly match their expected votes.[5] We placed no restrictions on candidate positioning.[6]

We compute that Chirac – by shifting unilaterally from his perceived position at 5.55 to his computed vote-maximizing position (4.02) along the 1–7 Left–Right scale – could have gained only about 2 percent of the vote. Dukakis would have increased his expected vote by about 1.5 percent, had he shifted from his perceived liberal–conservative position (3.10) to his computed vote-maximizing position at 4.42, while Bush remained fixed at his perceived position. Such modest gains would not have overcome the losing candidates' electoral deficits. Hence we conclude that *under conditions of full information, the candidates Chirac and Dukakis would have lost the popular vote no matter what ideologies they had presented.* This conclusion

---

[5] We further simplified the American electoral context by assuming that the winner of the popular vote would be elected.

[6] Because our conclusions hold given the assumption of costless policy mobility, these results certainly extend to more realistic scenarios in which voters penalize candidates for changing their policy platforms.

is particularly striking given that the winning candidates Bush and Mitterrand presented distinctly noncentrist ideologies.

Our second question is: Under conditions of full information, how much "policy leeway" did Bush and Mitterrand enjoy due to non-policy-related election advantages? That is, what was the range of ideologies these candidates could present such that their expected votes would exceed 50 percent, no matter what position their opponent presented?

The set of Mitterrand's positions that would win over 50 percent of the expected vote versus any Chirac strategy – which we label Mitterrand's *dominance zone* – consists of all ideologies located in the interval [2.69, 5.13]; Bush's dominance zone is the interval [3.48, 5.56]. The large size of these zones suggests that *under conditions of full information, Mitterrand and Bush had the leeway to present a wide range of distinctly noncentrist ideologies.*

Next we ask: Under conditions of full information, what were the plausible equilibrium configurations for policy-seeking candidates in the 1988 presidential elections? While we cannot know with certainty, it seems plausible that Bush held beliefs that roughly corresponded to the designation "conservative," at 6 on the 1–7 ANES ideology scale, while the Socialist Mitterrand held beliefs that roughly matched the designation "leftist," at 2 on the 1–7 FPES ideology scale. Given these assumptions about the winning candidates' policy preferences, the policy-seeking equilibrium for the 1988 French election locates Mitterrand at 2.69 and Chirac at 3.93. The candidates diverge by 1.24 units, with Mitterrand located at a distinctly leftist position and Chirac near the mean. For the 1988 U.S. election, the equilibrium locates Bush at 5.56 and Dukakis at 4.51. The American candidates diverge by 1.15 units along the 1–7 scale, with Bush clearly on the right and Dukakis near the voter mean.

In both cases, the advantaged candidate's equilibrium position is the ideology in his dominance zone that is closest to his sincere preference, while the losing candidate's equilibrium position is the location that maximizes this candidate's support, given the winning candidate's position.[7] We conclude that given reasonable assumptions about the candidates' sincere policy

---

[7] In fact, it is easily seen that the U.S. equilibrium configuration obtains, provided that Bush's sincere preference lies anywhere to the right of 5.56 – the conservative boundary of his win set – and, similarly, that the French equilibrium obtains for all scenarios in which Mitterrand's sincere preference lies to the left of 2.69. If an advantaged candidate's sincere ideological preference lies inside his dominance zone, then his equilibrium strategy is to announce this

preferences and under full information, *the valence advantages that Mitterrand and Bush enjoyed in the 1988 presidential elections permitted equilibrium strategies for both that shaded strongly in the direction of their respective preferred policies, while the optimal strategies of the disadvantaged candidates fell near the voter means, far from their preferred policies.*

12.3. Modeling Election Uncertainty over Valence Issues in Empirical Applications

While the results reported in section 12.1 are suggestive, the complete certainty about the election outcome that we ascribed to the candidates obviously misrepresents the informational environments that obtained during the preelection period. Here we explore extensions along the lines of the Londregan–Romer and Groseclose models discussed in Chapter 11; that is, we incorporate candidate uncertainty over valence issues and over the voter distribution. We show that while consideration of these factors greatly complicates exact computations of the candidates' equilibrium positions, there are simplifying assumptions available that provide quite accurate approximations of these positions. When we employ these approximations, the candidate equilibria we obtain consistently support the theoretical results on candidate strategies presented in sections 11.3 and 11.4.

In section 11.3, we explored a model inspired by Londregan and Romer (1993) in which policy-seeking candidates had complete information about all aspects of voting behavior *except* for the impact of valence issues. Given the simple model setup that we used in section 11.3, the candidates' perceived election probabilities could be represented by the closed-form equation 11.2, which was a function of the candidates' positions (relative to the median voter), the measured component v of the candidate-specific intercept that captures voters' valence-related motivations, and the uncertainty parameter σ_V associated with this intercept. Note that these election probabilities did not depend on the specifics of the voter distribution, nor upon the distribution across voters of voter-specific motivations such as party ID and sociodemographic characteristics (since these were omitted from the model).

Here we again explore candidate strategies when uncertainty centers entirely on the candidate-specific intercept (which models the expected valence

sincere preference, and in this case an equilibrium obtains regardless of the disadvantaged candidate's strategy.

advantage), but now we assume that voters choose according to the unified voting models that we estimated for France and the United States. Specifically, we carry over the assumptions from section 12.1 – that the distributions of the French and American respondents' ideologies and their personal characteristics exactly match those of the voting population, and that with the exception of the candidate-specific intercept, the estimated voting model parameters reported in Table 12.1A exactly match the true model parameters. However, here we assume that the candidates were unsure of the value of the candidate-specific intercept, and that, as in the Londregan–Romer model, they represented this intercept as a normally distributed random variable centered on its estimated value (as reported in Table 12.1A), but with a standard error σ_V. In real-world elections, this uncertainty plausibly arises because at the time the candidates select their policy positions, they cannot accurately project the subsequent course of the campaign or how these campaign-related effects will influence voters' decisions. A partial list of factors that could affect voters' valence-related evaluations – and that the candidates cannot know with certainty at the time they announce their policies – includes the skill with which each candidate will campaign, the amount of money each campaign will ultimately raise, and the effects of "exogenous shocks" arising from such events as campaign-related scandals and international or domestic crises.

While it is a simplification to represent the candidates' preelection uncertainty entirely in terms of a single parameter σ_V associated with the candidate-specific intercept, note that introducing this uncertainty greatly complicates analyses of candidates' strategies. The reason is that given the unified voting specifications we estimate, we cannot represent the candidates' probabilities of winning strictly in terms of the median voter's vote probabilities – the approach we used for the simplified election model presented in section 11.3. Instead, here we must account for the distributions of the respondents' non-policy-related characteristics and their ideologies, for how the uncertainty associated with the candidate-specific intercept term affects each respondent's vote probability, and – most challenging of all – for how the joint distribution of the respondents' vote probabilities translates into an overall election probability for each candidate. This is a daunting task. We can simplify it, however, by using the following approximation, one that applies to the candidates' expected votes given the estimated voting model parameters (as reported for the 1988 French and U.S. presidential elections in Table 12.1A): namely, that *when election uncertainty revolves entirely around the normally distributed candidate intercept (and this standard deviation is not unduly large), the probability distribution associated with the candidates' expected votes will also be approximately normal, and the standard deviation of this distribution will not vary significantly with the candidates' ideological positions.*[8] Substantively, this implies that we can approximate each candidate F's vote share $V(F)$ as

$$V(F) = EV(F) + \varepsilon, \qquad (12.1)$$

where $EV(F)$ is F's expected vote, which is a function of the candidates' policy positions, and ε is a normally distributed random variable centered on zero with a fixed standard deviation σ_ε. Henceforward, we employ this parameter σ_ε as our measure of valence-related election uncertainty in the vote share. Given the approximation in equation 12.1, we can approximate candidate F's probability of receiving over 50 percent of the two-candidate vote (and thus his probability of winning election) as

$$P(F) = \Phi[(EV(F) - 0.5)/\sigma_\varepsilon]. \qquad (12.2)$$

Suppose, for example, that Chirac represents his expected vote via the approximation formula 12.1, and that he perceives the degree of election uncertainty as $\sigma_\varepsilon = .04$, a value consistent with empirical studies on the accuracy of preelection polling (see Appendix 11.2). Figure 12.2A shows Chirac's expected vote as a function of his ideological position, with Mitterrand fixed at his perceived position (3.09) along the 1–7 Left–Right scale. We also display the 95 percent confidence interval for Chirac's election day vote, based on equation 12.1, and his probability of winning the election as given by the approximation formula 12.2. The 95 percent confidence interval for Chirac's election day vote extends about two standard deviations on either side of his expected vote, so that Chirac perceives a probability of .95 that his election day vote will fall within approximately $(2 \times .04) = .08$ of

---

[8] Our computations suggest that these approximations hold reasonably well for realistic variations in candidate positioning. The reason this is the case is that, for realistic values of the candidate-specific intercept: (1) increases (decreases) in the intercept increase (decrease) the candidates' expected votes at a roughly linear rate, and (2) the rate of change in the candidates' expected votes (as a function of the intercept) does not depend significantly on the policy distance between the candidates. The computations that support this conclusion are presented on our website: http://course.wilkes.edu/Merrill. The website also reports computations of the U.S. and French candidates' policy-seeking equilibria based on more complex approximation formulas, and shows that these equilibria are quite similar to the ones we obtain using the simple approximations given in equations 12.1 and 12.2.

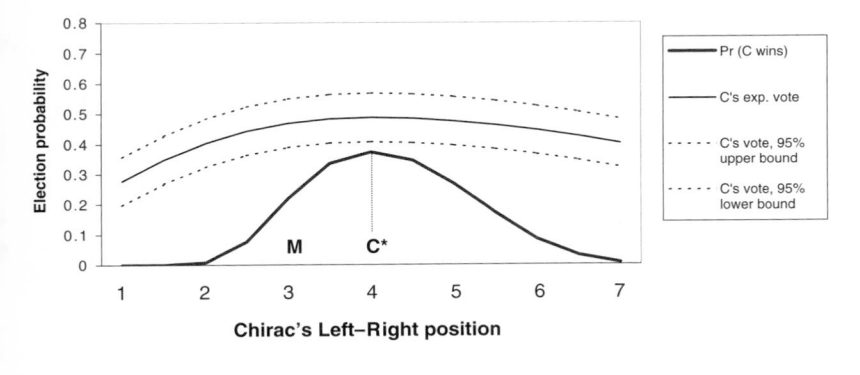

Figure 12.2. Chirac's beliefs about his election prospects, when election uncertainty is over valence issues: illustrative examples for the second round of the 1988 French presidential election.

Note: In these examples, the degree of election uncertainty is set to $\sigma_\varepsilon = .04$. C* is the position that maximizes Chirac's subjective probability of being elected, while C** maximizes Chirac's expected policy utility. Mitterrand is fixed at his actual (perceived) position, denoted by M. For the policy utility calculations, we assume that Chirac has quadratic policy losses and that his preferred Left–Right position is 6 on the 1–7 scale.

his expected vote. Note that while Chirac's expected vote declines slowly as he shifts away from his computed vote-maximizing position (3.92), his perceived probability of winning declines sharply, and in fact approaches zero, for extreme left-wing or right-wing positioning.

Figure 12.2B displays Chirac's expected policy utility (the right vertical axis) as a function of his ideological position, for the scenario where Chirac's sincere preference is 6.0 along the 1–7 Left–Right scale and where he has quadratic policy losses (for this example, Mitterrand is again located at his actual position 3.09, and the degree of election uncertainty is set at $\sigma_\varepsilon = .04$).[9] Chirac's approximate probability of winning the election is shown on the left vertical axis. Note that Chirac's expected policy utility peaks on the center-right (at $C^* = 4.58$), at a location between his vote-maximizing position (3.92) and his sincere ideological preference (6.0). Chirac's expected policy utility peaks to the right of his vote-maximizing position because – up to a point – his enhanced policy utility from winning election on a rightist platform compensates for the diminished probability of election that this right-wing positioning entails, compared to centrist positioning. However, Chirac has incentives to present a platform that is more moderate than his sincere right-wing beliefs, since proposing these right-wing policies would reduce his election probability to less than .10. In general, it can be shown that when policy-seeking candidates employ the approximation formulas 12.1 and 12.2, they will always choose a position that lies between their vote-maximizing position and their sincere policy preference.

12.4. Candidate Equilibria under Valence-Related Election Uncertainty

Our primary interest concerned the candidates' *Nash equilibrium locations* – that is, the positions to which policy-seeking candidates should jointly gravitate in order to maximize their expected utilities. In our simulations under our valence-uncertainty model, we computed a policy-seeking Nash equilibrium for every election scenario that we investigated for both France and the United States.[10]

---

[9] Chirac's policy utility function is $U(C) = [- P(C)(x_C - x_C^*)^2 - P(M)(x_M - x_C^*)^2]$, where $P(C)$ and $P(M)$ represent Chirac's election probability and Mitterrand's election probability, respectively; $x_M = 3.09$ and x_C represent the candidates' ideological positions; and $x_C^* = 6.00$ is Chirac's sincere ideological preference.

[10] We located equilibrium configurations using a brute force approach, in which we successively relocated candidates to their optimal positions until neither candidate could improve

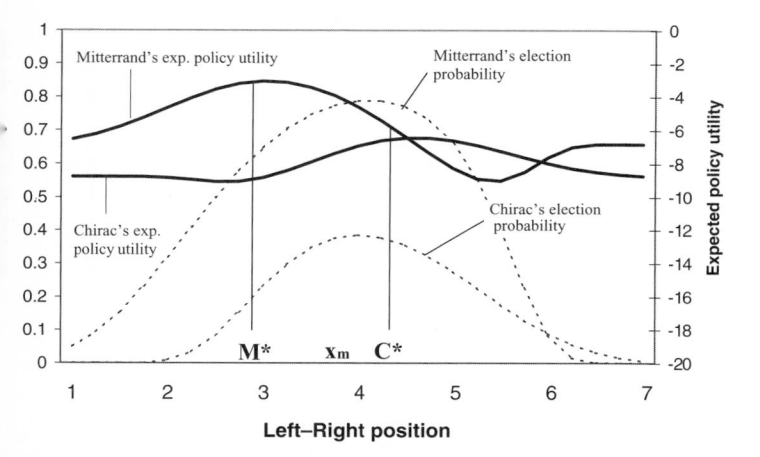

Figure 12.3. Candidates' policy-seeking equilibrium for the valence-uncertainty model, with $\sigma_\varepsilon = .04$: second round of the 1988 French presidential election.
Note: The policy-seeking equilibrium was calculated using the assumption that the candidates had quadratic losses and that their sincere ideological preferences were 2 for Mitterrand and 6 for Chirac. M* and C* represent Mitterrand's and Chirac's equilibrium positions, respectively, while x_m represents the mean voter position. Expected probabilities and expected policy utilities were computed assuming that the opposing candidate was at his equilibrium position.

12.4.1. Equilibria in the 1988 French Presidential Election under Valence-Related Uncertainty

Figure 12.3 illustrates the equilibrium configuration that we located in the 1988 French presidential election, for a valence-uncertainty model in which the candidates were assumed to have quadratic policy losses; their preferred Left–Right locations were set at 2.00 for Mitterrand and 6.00 for Chirac; the candidates employed the approximation formulas 12.1 and 12.2; and the degree of election uncertainty was set at $\sigma_\varepsilon = .04$. This configuration displays substantial dispersion between the candidates, with Mitterrand located at 3.04 and Chirac at 4.61 – a gap of 1.57 units along the 1–7 Left–Right scale. The mean voter position, 3.96, is also pictured. The vertical axis

his expected policy utility by shifting his position, given the policy location of his opponent. For these computations, we restricted candidates' strategies to the set of 701 possible locations {1.00, 1.01, ... , 6.00}. Simulations in which we varied the candidates' initial policy locations invariably converged to identical equilibrium configurations, which suggests that the equilibria we located were unique.

displays the candidates' perceived probabilities of winning the election (the leftmost axis) and their expected policy utilities (the rightmost axis) as a function of their location, with the rival candidate fixed at his equilibrium position.

At equilibrium, Mitterrand – the candidate who benefits from non-policy-related election advantages – takes a distinctly leftist position relative to the mean voter location, while the disadvantaged Chirac locates closer to the voter mean. This configuration is consistent with the theoretical result on policy-seeking candidates presented in section 11.3 (and developed earlier by Wittman [1990]), that under a policy-invariant model of election uncertainty, an increase in a candidate's non-policy-related advantage shifts his equilibrium position away from the center while shifting his opponent's position toward the center.[11]

Note that the candidates' policy-seeking strategies contrast sharply with their office-seeking strategies, which would motivate both candidates to converge to vote-maximizing positions at the center of the voter distribution, consistent with the theoretical results of Chapter 4.[12] This supports the commonsense intuition that in real-world elections, the distinction between office-seeking and policy-seeking objectives can motivate sharply different candidate strategies.

Table 12.2 reports equilibrium configurations for varying degrees of election uncertainty, ranging from $\sigma_\varepsilon = .01$ to $\sigma_\varepsilon = .10$ (a range that encompasses the varying degrees of accuracy reported in election forecasting studies), and for two alternative assumptions about the candidates' sincere policy preferences, one in which the candidates were assumed to have modestly divergent preferences (3.00 for Mitterrand and 5.00 for Chirac), and another in which they had sharply divergent preferences (2.00 for Mitterrand and 6.00 for Chirac). The candidates' actual (perceived) positions in this historical election are also reported.

Several interesting results emerge from this table. First, note that consistent with Wittman's (1983, 1990) theoretical results, the equilibrium position of the advantaged candidate, Mitterrand, is consistently less centrist than Chirac's. Second, Mitterrand's computed equilibrium positions are similar to

---

[11] We note that Wittman's model differs from ours in that in Wittman's formulation, the candidate's non-policy-related advantage (which Wittman labels bias) translates into a constant increase in the candidate's probability of winning.

[12] The candidates' vote-maximizing equilibrium finds the candidates converging to identical locations at 4.02 along the 1–7 Left–Right scale.

Table 12.2. *Candidate equilibria in the 1988 French presidential election, for the valence-uncertainty model of elections[a]*

Candidates' Policy Preferences[b]	Degree of Election Uncertainty (1)	Mitterrand's Equilibrium Position (2)	Chirac's Equilibrium Position (3)	Policy Dispersion[c] (4)	Probability That Mitterrand Is Elected[d] (5)
$x_M = 2, x_C = 6$	$\sigma_\varepsilon = .01$	3.05	4.16	1.11	.89
$x_M = 2, x_C = 6$	$\sigma_\varepsilon = .02$	3.10	4.35	1.25	.77
$x_M = 2, x_C = 6$	$\sigma_\varepsilon = .04$	3.04	4.61	1.57	.66
$x_M = 2, x_C = 6$	$\sigma_\varepsilon = .10$	2.83	5.02	2.19	.57
$x_M = 3, x_C = 5$	$\sigma_\varepsilon = .01$	3.19	4.15	0.96	.94
$x_M = 3, x_C = 5$	$\sigma_\varepsilon = .02$	3.28	4.31	1.03	.83
$x_M = 3, x_C = 5$	$\sigma_\varepsilon = .04$	3.30	4.51	1.21	.70
$x_M = 3, x_C = 5$	$\sigma_\varepsilon = .10$	3.23	4.74	1.51	.59
Candidates' actual positions:		3.09	5.55	2.46	

[a] Candidates are assumed to have quadratic losses with respect to policies.
[b] x_M and x_C represent the preferred policies of Mitterrand and Chirac, respectively.
[c] Policy dispersion represents the policy distance between Mitterrand's equilibrium position and Chirac's equilibrium position.
[d] The probability that Mitterrand is elected is the likelihood that Mitterrand's vote exceeds 50 percent, when the candidates locate at their equilibrium positions.

his actual location (3.09), which suggests that our policy-seeking perspective accounts well for Mitterrand's positioning. Third, note that as the candidates' perceived election uncertainty increases, so does the degree of policy dispersion at equilibrium. The intuition underlying this result is that as uncertainty increases, the candidates' perceived election probabilities become less responsive to shifts in their ideological positioning, so that the candidates believe they have more leeway to propose noncentrist policies that reflect their sincere preferences.

Under this valence-related model of election uncertainty, policy-seeking candidates are motivated to present significantly divergent policies for all possible election scenarios. The candidates' equilibrium positions diverge by more than 0.95 policy units along the 1–7 scale for every scenario that we investigated, and for those scenarios that strike us as the most realistic – those for which the candidates' sincere preferences were set at 2.0 for Mitterrand and 6.0 for Chirac and the degree of election uncertainty was set near $\sigma_\varepsilon = .04$ (the value suggested by Campbell's 1996 analysis of pre-election polls) – these equilibrium positions diverge by more than 1.4 units.

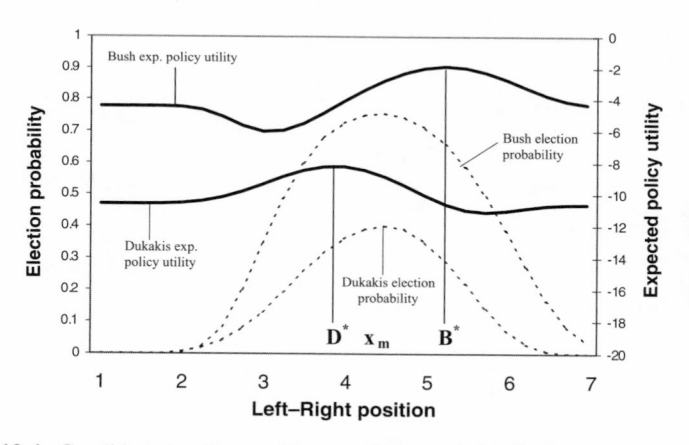

Figure 12.4. Candidates' policy-seeking equilibrium for valence-related election uncertainty, with $\sigma_\varepsilon = .04$; 1988 U.S. presidential election.
Note: The policy-seeking equilibrium was calculated using the assumption that the candidates had quadratic losses and that their sincere ideological preferences were 2 for Dukakis and 6 for Bush. D* and B* denote Dukakis's and Bush's equilibrium positions, respectively; x_m is the voter mean. Expected probabilities and expected policy utilities were computed assuming that the opposing candidate was at his equilibrium position.

We therefore conclude that *under the valence-related model of election uncertainty, policy-seeking goals would have motivated significant divergence between the candidates in the 1988 French presidential election.*

12.4.2. Equilibria in the 1988 U.S. Presidential Election under Valence-Related Uncertainty

Figure 12.4 displays the equilibrium configuration for policy-seeking candidates in the 1988 U.S. presidential election, under the assumptions that the candidates represented their election probabilities using the approximation formulas 12.1 and 12.2, that their preferred ideological locations were set at 2.0 for Dukakis and 6.0 for Bush, that they had quadratic policy loss functions, and that they perceived the degree of election uncertainty as $\sigma_\varepsilon = .04$. As was the case for France, this configuration displays substantial dispersion between the candidates' equilibrium positions, with Dukakis located at 3.89 and Bush at 5.26 – a gap of 1.37 units along the 1–7 liberal-conservative scale. Also consistent with the French analysis (and with our earlier theoretical results) is our finding that Bush, who benefits from non-policy-related

Table 12.3. *Candidate equilibria in the 1988 U.S. presidential election, for the valence-related model of election uncertainty*[a]

Candidates' Policy Preferences[b]	Degree of Election Uncertainty (1)	Dukakis's Equilibrium Position (2)	Bush's Equilibrium Position (3)	Policy Dispersion[c] (4)	Probability That Bush Is Elected[d] (5)
$x_D = 2, x_B = 6$	$\sigma_\varepsilon = .01$	4.32	5.24	0.92	.87
$x_D = 2, x_B = 6$	$\sigma_\varepsilon = .02$	4.14	5.22	1.08	.75
$x_D = 2, x_B = 6$	$\sigma_\varepsilon = .04$	3.89	5.26	1.37	.66
$x_D = 2, x_B = 6$	$\sigma_\varepsilon = .10$	3.45	5.39	1.94	.59
$x_D = 3, x_B = 5$	$\sigma_\varepsilon = .01$	4.31	4.96	0.65	.96
$x_D = 3, x_B = 5$	$\sigma_\varepsilon = .02$	4.12	4.91	0.79	.84
$x_D = 3, x_B = 5$	$\sigma_\varepsilon = .04$	3.87	4.89	1.02	.73
$x_D = 3, x_B = 5$	$\sigma_\varepsilon = .10$	3.52	4.90	1.38	.63
Candidates' actual positions:		3.10	5.23	2.13	

[a] Candidates are assumed to have quadratic losses with respect to policies.
[b] x_D and x_B represent the policy preferences of Dukakis and Bush, respectively.
[c] Policy dispersion represents the policy distance between Bush's equilibrium position and Dukakis's equilibrium position.
[d] The probability that Bush is elected is the likelihood that Bush's vote exceeds 50 percent, when the candidates locate at their equilibrium positions.

election advantages, takes a distinctly noncentrist policy-seeking position (5.26) relative to the mean voter location (4.41), while the disadvantaged Dukakis locates at 3.89, nearer to the voter mean.

Table 12.3 reports equilibrium results for alternative sets of assumptions about the candidates' preferred ideologies and the degree of election uncertainty. These equilibrium results display patterns that are in all important respects similar to those we reached with respect to the 1988 French presidential election.

The candidates' office-seeking equilibrium configuration, on the other hand, involves identical centrist positions at 4.39.[13] This result, which mirrors our findings for France, underscores the fact that for the full-turnout voting model we employ here, office-seeking goals motivate policy convergence, while policy-seeking goals motivate significant divergence. We conclude that under our model of valence-related election uncertainty,

[13] The candidates' office-seeking optima are quite similar to the ones located by Erikson and Romero (1990: Table 2) in their analysis of vote-maximizing candidate strategies in the 1988 U.S. presidential election.

policy-seeking candidates in France and the United States would be motivated to present significantly divergent ideologies, skewed in the direction of the valence-advantaged candidate.

12.4.3. Applications of the Valence-Related Uncertainty Model to the 1997 British General Election

To this point, our empirical applications suggest that the assumption of policy-seeking motivations, coupled with valence-related uncertainty, can illuminate candidate strategies in two-candidate elections in France and the United States. Here we report empirical applications to the 1997 British general election.

Recall from Chapter 9 that British postwar politics has featured three major parties – the Liberal Democrats, Labour, and the Conservatives – and that one of the latter two parties typically wins a parliamentary majority, giving it a near-monopoly of political power and allowing it to implement its policy vision. Thus it seems reasonable to posit that Labour and Conservative Party elites believe that postelection government policies in Britain will reflect the preelection promises of whichever party wins a parliamentary majority. By contrast, preelection polls suggested that in the run-up to the 1997 British general election, the Liberal Democratic party had no realistic chance to win a majority.

Accordingly, we explored policy-seeking competition between the Labour and Conservative Parties in the 1997 British general election, under the valence-related model of uncertainty. For these exercises, we fixed the Liberal Democrats at their actual (perceived) policy positions, and we assumed that the Labour and Conservative Party elites' utilities for the election outcome depended entirely on their utilities for the winning party's policy positions. We further assumed that the Labour and Conservative Party elites assessed the Liberal Democrats' likelihood of winning a parliamentary majority as zero, and that these elites equated their own party's probability of winning a parliamentary majority with the probability that their party would win a plurality of the popular vote, vis-à-vis its main rival.[14] Finally, we

[14] In fourteen of sixteen British postwar elections, the party winning a vote plurality has won a parliamentary majority. Furthermore, in one of the two postwar elections that did not follow this pattern (the February 1974 election, in which no party won a parliamentary majority), the government called for a new election just eight months later.

assumed that party elites represented their vote party's vote margin vis-à-vis its main competitor as a function of their party's expected vote margin plus a randomly distributed variable. Thus we posit that Labour Party elites represented their election day margin over the Conservatives, M(L), as

$$M(L) = EV(L) - EV(C) + \varepsilon = EM(L) + \varepsilon, \tag{12.3}$$

where $EM(L) = [EV(L) - EV(C)]$ is Labour's expected vote margin, which is a function of the parties' policy positions, and ε is once again a normally distributed random variable centered on zero with a fixed standard deviation σ_ε, which we employ as our measure of valence-related election uncertainty in the vote margin.[15] We posit that Conservative elites employed a comparable representation of the probability distribution of their party's vote margin vis-à-vis Labour.

Given the approximation in equation 12.3, we can represent Labour's perceived probability of winning a vote plurality vis-à-vis the Conservatives – and thus of winning a parliamentary majority – as

$$P(L) = \Phi[[EV(L) - EV(C)]/\sigma_\varepsilon] = \Phi[EM(L)/\sigma_\varepsilon], \tag{12.4}$$

with the Conservatives' perceived election probability given as $[1 - P(L)]$.

Using the election probability function given in equation 12.4, we computed policy-seeking equilibrium configurations for the Labour and Conservative Parties for the 1997 British general election, for varying values of the uncertainty parameter σ_ε. For these exercises, we estimated the parameters of a one-dimensional unified voting model that was identical to the model explored in Chapter 9 (see Table 9.3A, column 2), *except* that here we incorporated a single-policy distance variable – namely, the distance between the respondent and the parties along the Left–Right dimension. The parameter estimates for this model are reported in Table 12.4A, while Table 12.4B shows that the parties' expected votes under this model precisely match the actual distribution of reported votes among the 1790 BGES survey respondents used in our analysis.

---

[15] Note that the specification in equation 12.3 differs from the one for two-party elections given earlier in equation 12.1, in that here the random variable is associated with the party's vote *margin* vis-à-vis its opponent, rather than with its vote share. This distinction is necessary because in three-party elections, unlike the two-party context, the extent to which a party's vote differs from its expected vote does not allow one to infer the extent to which each of the other parties' votes diverges from its expected vote.

Table 12.4. *Conditional logit equations for voting in the 1997 British general election* (N = 1,790)

12.4A. *Estimated vote model parameters*

Intercept (Labour)	0.96**	(.12)
Intercept (LD)	0.47**	(.13)
Ideology	.083**	(.007)
Voted for party in 1992	1.87**	(.08)
Retrospective national economy (Labour)	−1.09**	(.09)
Retrospective national economy (LD)	−1.74**	(.10)
Union member (Labour)	.18	(.11)
Union member (LD)	.28*	(.11)
Education (LD)	.11**	(.04)
Resident of Wales (Labour)	1.19*	(.48)
Resident of Wales (LD)	0.86	(.52)
Resident of Scotland (Labour)	.57*	(.20)
Log-likelihood	−1002.70	

12.4B. *Projected party votes*

	Labour Vote	Liberal Democratic Vote	Conservative Vote
BGES distribution	49.6%	18.7%	31.7%
Projected vote	49.6%	18.7%	31.7%

Note: The parameters in Table 12.4A refer to the effect of each independent variable on the respondent's utility for Labour or for the Liberal Democrats, relative to his or her utility for the Conservatives. The parameters for ideological distance and for voting for the party in the previous election apply to all parties. One asterisk indicates statistical significance at the .05 level. Two asterisks indicate significance at the .01 level. Standard errors are in parentheses. The projected votes reported in Table 12.4B are computed by averaging the projected voting probabilities across all respondents, using the probability functions given in Chapter 9. For each election, these projected probabilities are computed using the parameters reported in Table 12.4A.

Figure 12.5 illustrates the equilibrium configuration that we located in the 1997 British general election, for a valence-uncertainty model in which the parties' preferred Left–Right locations were set at 2.00 for Labour and 8.00 for the Conservatives; the parties employed the approximation formulas 12.3 and 12.4; and the degree of election uncertainty associated with the Labour–Conservative vote margin was set at $\sigma_\varepsilon = .08$.[16] As in the policy-seeking

[16] Note that because the election uncertainty parameter for Britain is associated with the vote *margin* between Labour and the Conservatives, the specification $\sigma_\varepsilon = .08$ for Britain is

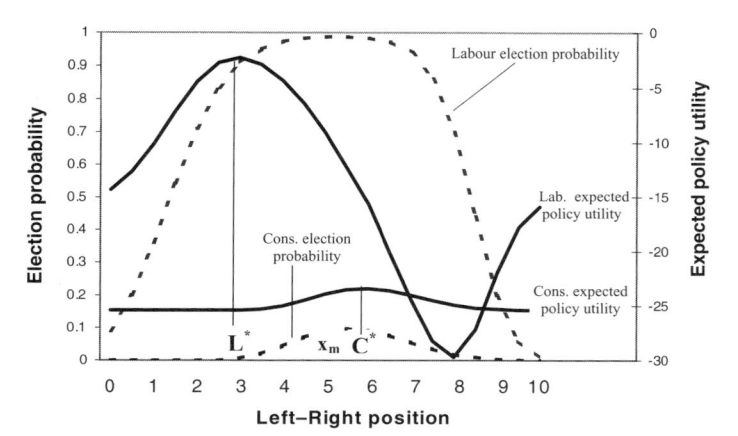

Figure 12.5. Parties' policy-seeking equilibrium for valence-related election uncertainty, with $\sigma_\varepsilon = .08$: 1997 British general election.
Note: The policy-seeking equilibrium was calculated using the assumption that the parties had quadratic losses and that their sincere ideological preferences were 2 for Labour and 8 for the Conservatives. For these calculations, the Liberal Democrats were assumed to be located at 4.69, their actual (perceived) position. L* and C* denote the policy-seeking equilibrium positions for Labour and the Conservatives, respectively; x_m is the voter mean. Expected election probabilities and expected policy utilities were computed assuming that the rival party was located at its equilibrium position.

simulations for France and the United States, this configuration displays substantial dispersion between the parties, with Labour located at 2.96 and the Conservatives at 5.91, a gap of nearly three units along the 0–10 scale. Also consistent with our applications to France and the United States, we find that the Labour Party – which, as discussed in Chapter 9, enjoyed a large non-policy-related electoral advantage – has a policy-seeking equilibrium position that is far less centrist than the disadvantaged Conservatives' policy-seeking optimum, relative to the mean voter position ($x_m = 5.05$). Table 12.5, which reports equilibrium configurations for varying degrees of valence-related election uncertainty and for varying assumptions about the parties' sincere policy preferences, shows that these results generalize to other plausible election scenarios. We conclude that our central conclusions on two-party elections with policy-seeking politicians and valence-related uncertainty generalize to the three-party British general election of 1997.

roughly equivalent to the specification $\sigma_\varepsilon = .04$ for France and the United States, where σ_ε represents the uncertainty associated with a candidate's vote.

Table 12.5. *Party equilibria in the 1997 British general election, for the valence-related model of election uncertainty[a]*

Parties' Policy Preferences[b]	Degree of Election Uncertainty[c] (1)	Labour's Equilibrium Position (2)	Conservatives' Equilibrium Position (3)	Policy Dispersion[d] (4)	Probability That Labour Is Elected[e] (5)
$x_L = 1, x_C = 9$	$\sigma_\varepsilon = .02$	2.04	5.50	3.46	.988
$x_L = 1, x_C = 9$	$\sigma_\varepsilon = .04$	2.41	5.63	3.22	.96
$x_L = 1, x_C = 9$	$\sigma_\varepsilon = .08$	2.77	5.94	3.17	.88
$x_L = 1, x_C = 9$	$\sigma_\varepsilon = .20$	2.90	6.67	3.77	.72
$x_L = 2, x_C = 8$	$\sigma_\varepsilon = .02$	2.19	5.50	3.31	.997
$x_L = 2, x_C = 8$	$\sigma_\varepsilon = .04$	2.56	5.62	3.06	.98
$x_L = 2, x_C = 8$	$\sigma_\varepsilon = .08$	2.96	5.91	2.95	.91
$x_L = 2, x_C = 8$	$\sigma_\varepsilon = .20$	3.14	6.55	3.41	.73
Parties' actual postions:		3.97	7.16	3.19	

[a] Parties are assumed to have quadratic losses with respect to policies.

[b] x_L and x_C represent the policy preferences of the Labour and Conservative Parties, respectively.

[c] The degree of election uncertainty represents the uncertainty that party elites associate with Labour's election day vote margin vis-à-vis the Conservatives.

[d] Policy dispersion represents the policy distance between Labour's equilibrium position and the Conservatives' equilibrium position.

[e] The probability Labour is elected is the likelihood that the Labour vote exceeds the Conservative vote, when the parties locate at their equilibrium positions.

12.5. Equilibria under Policy-Related Uncertainty: Application to France

In section 11.4, we explored a model developed by Groseclose (2001) in which the candidates' uncertainty revolved around the voter distribution, and we saw that this policy-related uncertainty could motivate different types of candidate strategies than does valence-related uncertainty. Following Groseclose (2001), we posit that the candidates were certain about all aspects of the election *except* for the location parameter (median) of the voter distribution, which is assumed to be a normally distributed random variable with a standard error σ_m. We then compute policy-seeking candidates' optimal positions, using the assumption that the candidates employed the following approximation: that *when election uncertainty revolves entirely around the voters' positions, and this uncertainty is represented by a normally distributed random variable, the probability distribution associated with the candidates' expected votes is also approximately normal*, and *the standard deviation of this distribution is approximately proportional to the policy distance between the candidates*.[17] This implies that each candidate F can again approximate his vote share as in equation 12.1 – that is, $V(F) = EV(F) + \varepsilon$ – but that the random error term ε now has a variable standard deviation proportional to the policy distance between the candidates.

As noted in Chapter 11, ANES data suggest that σ_m (the standard deviation of the median-voter location) is on the order of .14 on the seven-point liberal–conservative scale, while Eurobarometer data suggest that the corresponding value for France (also on a seven-point scale) is on the order of 0.11. These values are much lower than .50, the quantity used by Groseclose for σ_m. Simulation suggests that uncertainty about the location of the voter distribution (σ_m) consistently translates into uncertainty about vote shares (denoted by σ_u), given approximately by

$$\sigma_u = .03\sigma_m |x_C - x_M|. \tag{12.5}$$

For $\sigma_m = .14$ – the value suggested by recent American presidential elections – equation 12.5 implies that $\sigma_u = .0042|x_C - x_M|$, where x_C and x_M represent the positions of the candidates. Because uncertainty about voters' policy preferences involves issues not captured by the ideology scale as well as misjudgments about the salience of issues, the election uncertainty parameter σ_u may be somewhat larger than indicated in equation 12.5. Accordingly, we computed equilibrium configurations for values of σ_u ranging as high as $\sigma_u = .03|x_C - x_M|$, more than seven times the magnitude of policy-related uncertainty suggested by the ANES data and our simulations, and nearly ten times as high as that suggested by the French data.

Table 12.6 and Figure 12.6 report equilibrium configurations for policy-seeking candidates in the 1988 French presidential election, under varying assumptions about the candidates' preferred ideological locations and about the degree of policy-related election uncertainty. These configurations were computed under the assumption that the candidates represented their election probabilities using the approximation formulas 12.1 and 12.2. As was the case for the valence-uncertainty model, the equilibrium configurations display substantial dispersion between the candidates, with Mitterrand located at least 1.4 policy units to the left of Chirac in all cases.

---

[17] The computations that support this conclusion are presented on our website: <http://course.wilkes.edu/Merrill>.

Table 12.6. *Candidate equilibria in the 1988 French presidential election, for the policy-related uncertainty model of elections[a]*

Candidates' Policy Preferences[b]	Degree of Election Uncertainty (1)	Mitterrand's Equilibrium Position (2)	Chirac's Equilibrium Position (3)	Policy Dispersion[c] (4)	Probability That Mitterrand Is Elected[d] (5)
$x_M = 2, x_C = 6$	$\sigma_u = .005\,|x_C - x_M|$	3.00	4.41	1.41	.96
$x_M = 2, x_C = 6$	$\sigma_u = .010\,|x_C - x_M|$	3.18	4.74	1.56	.92
$x_M = 2, x_C = 6$	$\sigma_u = .020\,|x_C - x_M|$	3.36	5.20	1.84	.84
$x_M = 2, x_C = 6$	$\sigma_u = .030\,|x_C - x_M|$	3.37	5.41	2.04	.75
$x_M = 3, x_C = 5$	$\sigma_u = .005\,|x_C - x_M|$	3.12	4.52	1.40	.99
$x_M = 3, x_C = 5$	$\sigma_u = .010\,|x_C - x_M|$	3.35	4.83	1.48	.97
$x_M = 3, x_C = 5$	$\sigma_u = .020\,|x_C - x_M|$	3.57	5.05	1.48	.89
$x_M = 3, x_C = 5$	$\sigma_u = .030\,|x_C - x_M|$	3.63	5.07	1.44	.81
Candidates' actual positions:		3.09	5.55	2.46	

[a] Candidates are assumed to have quadratic losses with respect to policies.
[b] x_M and x_C represent the preferred policies of Mitterrand and Chirac, respectively.
[c] Policy dispersion represents the policy distance between Mitterrand's equilibrium position and Chirac's equilibrium position.
[d] The probability that Mitterrand is elected is the likelihood that Mitterrand's vote exceeds 50 percent, when the candidates locate at their equilibrium positions.

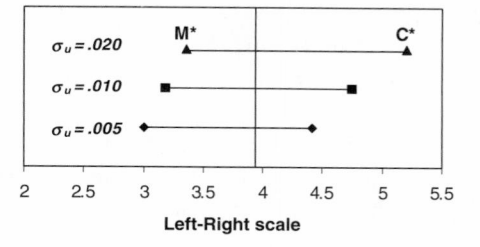

Figure 12.6. Policy-seeking equilibria under the Groseclose model for the second round of the 1988 French presidential election.
Note: For each value of the policy-uncertainty parameter σ_u, the endpoints of the line segment represent the locations of Mitterrand (M*) and Chirac (C*) at equilibrium. The vertical line indicates the mean location of the voter distribution.

The equilibrium configurations display interesting patterns when we compare the distance between the valence-advantaged Mitterrand and the mean voter position (3.96) to the corresponding distance for the disadvantaged Chirac. When the degree of election uncertainty is set at

$\sigma_u = .005 \, | \, x_C - x_M |$, which is near the value suggested by our analysis of the data, Mitterrand takes a more extreme position than Chirac. This is the same pattern we obtained for the valence-related uncertainty model. However, if the degree of election uncertainty is set at $\sigma_u = 0.02 \, | \, x_C - x_M |$ or $\sigma_u = 0.03 \, | \, x_C - x_M |$ – that is, four to six times higher than the value suggested by the data – then Chirac's equilibrium position is more extreme than Mitterrand's position – the "Extremist Underdog" result reported by Groseclose. We obtained similar results (not shown) for Bush and Dukakis in the 1988 U.S. presidential election, and for the Labour and Conservative Parties in the 1997 British general election. Thus, for national elections in Western democracies for which we can expect uncertainty about the voter distribution to be low (on the order of that found in U.S. presidential elections), election uncertainty will probably fall below the threshold needed for the Groseclose Extremist Underdog effect to be realized. In local contests or in elections in less developed countries, higher levels of uncertainty – and the Extremist Underdog effect – are more likely. In any event, policy-seeking goals consistently motivate candidates to present sharply divergent policies.

12.6. Discussion

Since the publication of Wittman's (1973, 1983) seminal articles, the possibility that policy-seeking motivations can explain the divergent policies that real-world candidates present has attracted widespread attention. Can policy motivations explain, theoretically and empirically, the *nature* and *degree* of policy divergence that we observe in historical elections? These are the questions we have addressed in this chapter, both theoretically and in the context of the 1988 U.S. and French presidential elections and the 1997 British parliamentary election.

For these elections, our calculations suggest that as long as election uncertainty does not vary greatly with the distance between candidates, valence-advantaged candidates are able to adopt strategies much to their liking, while disadvantaged candidates must move toward the center in order to counteract their non-policy-related handicap. If, on the other hand, uncertainty is based not on valence, but on the location of the voter distribution, so that uncertainty in vote share increases sharply with distance between candidates, theory suggests the possibility that the tables would be turned and the valence-disadvantaged candidate would assume a strategy near his preference, while the advantaged candidate would move toward the center. An increase in uncertainty with distance sufficient to produce this effect, however, would appear to stretch the limits of empirical likelihood. For the French and U.S. elections studied, we find that even in the face of uncertainty about the location of voters, the valence-advantaged candidate assumes a position at equilibrium nearer his preference than does the valence-disadvantaged candidate.

We realize that understanding candidates' policy-seeking strategies in real-world elections is a challenging task. In particular, it is difficult to know what type of subjective uncertainty the candidates experienced, how the candidates incorporated this uncertainty into their strategic calculations, or what the candidates' sincere ideological preferences actually were. However, using alternative assumptions about the candidates' ideological preferences and how they represented election uncertainty, we conclude that the French and American presidential candidates in 1988 and the two major British parties in 1997 would have policy motivation to propose sharply divergent positions, with the valence-advantaged candidates/parties able to assume positions closer to their respective preferences. Overall, the equilibrium strategies we compute for these two elections match our theoretical expectations. The empirical approach that we have developed can easily be extended to alternative scenarios, including competition over multiple policy dimensions, elections in which candidates have mixtures of office-seeking and policy-seeking motivations, and different sets of historical elections.

CHAPTER 13

Concluding Remarks

13.1. Introduction

Our central goal has been to integrate the spatial model of elections, which posits that policy considerations are the dominant influence on voter choice, with the behavioral model, in which voters are moved by a mixture of non-policy as well as policy issues. We believe that by merging the behavioral perspective and the spatial modeling paradigm associated with rational choice theory, we can provide insights into parties' election strategies that neither approach provides by itself. We label our behavioral–rational choice hybrid the *unified theory of party competition.*

We have used our unified theory to explain – both theoretically and empirically – parties' and presidential candidates' election strategies in several Western democracies. Theoretically, we have presented a systematic account of how the strategic incentives of vote-seeking parties vary with a multitude of factors, including the size and extremity of partisan constituencies, the number of parties, the dispersion of voters' policy preferences, the electoral salience of policies, the degree to which voters discount the parties' policy promises, and the extent to which voter abstention is motivated by alienation. We have also presented an algorithm – one that can be applied to election survey data – that can quickly locate equilibrium policy configurations for vote- or margin-maximizing parties, and that can be used to evaluate whether any computed equilibrium configuration is unique.

Empirically, we have applied the unified model of party competition in an effort to account for the observed policy positions of parties and presidential candidates in four diverse democracies: France, Norway, Britain, and the United States. Specifically, we have estimated the parameters for alternative voting models using election survey data from these four countries. These models include a *policy-only model* in which policy distance is the only measured component, and a *unified model* that incorporates the full diversity of measured influences on the vote, including partisanship, retrospective economic evaluations, and sociodemographic characteristics, in addition to policy distance. We have also extended this unified model to incorporate added motivations that appear relevant to subsets of the countries we examine: a *unified discounting model* that incorporates voter discounting of the parties' policy promises, which may arise due to divided government in France and the United States or due to the policy compromises entailed in Norwegian coalition governments, and a *unified turnout model* that incorporates abstention resulting from alienation, which appears relevant to U.S. and British elections that feature relatively low voter turnout.

Our empirical applications suggest that in France and Norway, the unified discounting model, in conjunction with the assumption of vote-maximizing politicians, illuminates the observed distribution of the parties' policy positions, at least for all parties that had a realistic chance of winning office. In the context of U.S. and British elections, our empirical applications suggest that when voters choose according to the unified turnout model, politicians' vote-maximizing policies should be similar to, but more centrist than, the British and U.S. parties' observed positions – that is, in the United States and Britain, our unified approach explains the *direction* but not the *extremity* of party/candidate positioning, relative to the center of the voter distribution.[1] By contrast, we find that in all of the countries we examine, an electorate choosing according to the policy-only model would motivate vote-seeking parties to converge to similar, centrist policy positions that do not reflect the parties' observed behavior. The distribution of party positions that we actually observe is one that we may characterize as "spaced-out politics," that is, one in which the parties locate in distinct areas of the issue space.

We believe that our study makes seven major contributions to scholarship on spatial modeling, political behavior, and political representation.

First, we have shown that a spatial model with vote-seeking politicians, which incorporates a diverse set of factors that influence voters, can account well for the observed configurations of party positions in real-world elections. This suggests that a unified model of spatial competition (one that

---

[1] Recall that our empirical applications to U.S. presidential elections also incorporate voter discounting of the candidates' positions.

incorporates insights from behavioral voting research) is a valuable tool for understanding party strategies.

Second, our theoretical results and empirical applications suggest that each of the three voting influences we have highlighted – voters' measured non-policy-related motivations, voter discounting of politicians' policy promises, and abstention resulting from alienation – are important for understanding party strategies. Measured nonpolicy motivations – particularly, party ID and sociodemographic characteristics that correlate with voters' policy preferences – are important because parties have electoral incentives to appeal on policy grounds to voters who are biased toward them, in part for nonpolicy reasons. Voter discounting and abstention due to alienation are important because these factors accentuate parties' incentives to appeal to their partisan constituencies. Thus we can view voters' measured nonpolicy motivations as determining the *policy direction* (i.e., left or right) in which vote-seeking parties will shift relative to the mean voter position, while policy discounting and abstention from alienation influence the degree of *policy extremity* of vote-seeking parties, relative to the mean voter position.[2] Thus it is important to employ a "fully" unified theory – one that accounts for measured nonpolicy motivations *and* turnout effects *and* the possibility of policy discounting – when analyzing party strategies in real-world elections.

Our third, theoretical contribution is to show that a unique equilibrium in vote-maximizing policy strategies almost always exists in the unified model of party competition, given the vote model parameters and the distribution of voters' policy preferences that we estimate from survey data from real-world elections. This demonstrates that it is feasible to incorporate the behavioralists' complex voting specifications into the spatial modeling paradigm, while still deriving point predictions about parties' policy strategies that can then be compared to their actual behavior. By contrast, we find that when voters choose according to the policy-only model of spatial research, multiple equilibria typically exist, as might be expected from theoretical analysis (see Schofield, Sened, and Nixon 1998; Schofield and Sened 2003). This suggests that application of the policy-only model – which omits the measured nonpolicy-related factors that behavioralists find important – makes the prediction of party strategies extremely difficult. Paradoxically, then, application

---

[2] Of course, as discussed earlier, policy extremity depends on additional factors, including the size and extremity of the party's voting constituency, the proportion of independent voters, and the number of parties.

of our unified and more complex model of party competition may actually simplify predictions and explanations of party strategies in real-world elections.

Fourth, we extend our analyses beyond party response to voter behavior by allowing party positioning also to be a consequence of policy-seeking motivations. For two-party elections, if there is uncertainty about the valence advantage of candidates, we find that policy-seeking motivations imply substantial divergence of party positions and that these locations are skewed in the direction of the valence-advantaged party. By contrast, Groseclose's (2001) model is based on uncertainty about the location of the voter distribution. For model parameters in the expected range for national elections in developed democracies, however, we find that optimal locations in the Groseclose model are similarly skewed in the direction of the valence-advantaged party. This finding contrasts with Groseclose's conclusion of a skew in the opposite direction. We show that his conclusion holds only for substantially higher levels of uncertainty about the voter distribution than we find in our data. (Extension of our model to multiparty competition is, however, left for further research.)

Fifth, our theoretical and empirical results have important implications for mass–elite policy linkages. Not only do the standard models of party competition lead to results that are at variance with observed empirical evidence, these models also give rise to deeply troubling normative implications that cast doubt on the possibility of genuine citizen influence on public policy. Overall, the spatial modeling literature suggests that vote-seeking parties will present similar positions that provide neither a diversity of policy choices nor the possibility of representing each of several different policy constituencies. The behavioralist approach suggests that policies will affect voter choice only in a limited way, because most voters' choices will be heavily determined by non-policy-related considerations.

Neither school of research supports the expectation of strong mass–elite policy linkages. If voters are purely policy-oriented, as pure spatial modeling assumes, then we should expect that all the parties' policies will be similar, so that voters are not afforded the option of choosing between truly distinct policy visions. If voters are not strongly influenced by policy differences between the parties – at least in the short run, as behavioral researchers suggest – then it would appear that there is little reason to expect election outcomes to reflect shifts in public opinion. Indeed, parties' policies may not represent even their supporters' beliefs, since (proposed) policy platforms are not the primary basis of these supporters' party preferences. By contrast, our finding that parties gain votes by presenting policies that appeal (at least approximately) to their partisan constituencies suggests that parties are motivated to reflect the views of their supporters.

Our sixth, related finding is that candidate support curves are typically concave – that is, they drop off only slightly at points near a party's vote-maximizing optimum but much more steeply further from that optimum. This permits parties/candidates some latitude in deviating from their optimum positions without great loss of support, suggesting that parties – particularly those with valence advantages – can afford to move out beyond their vote-maximizing optima if, for example, they desire to do so for policy-seeking reasons. Typically, this positions them closer to the mean of their supporters. On the other hand, at least for plurality-based elections, parties far from their optimum values (and typically far from the center) have little chance of winning.

These results support the responsible party model of political representation (see Sartori 1968; Dalton 1985; Powell 1989, 2000), which emphasizes at a dyadic level (Weissberg 1978) the link between parties' policy proposals and their supporters' policy beliefs.[3] Because our model, under empirically plausible assumptions, gives rise to the expectation of distinctive party positions that reflect the preferences of their identifiers, our work, unlike the Downsian and behavioral models, generates an expectation of normatively desirable outcomes.

Seventh, our results highlight the fact that several long-standing controversies in behavioral research have crucial implications for parties' policy strategies, and thus that behavioral researchers' debates are important for spatial modeling. Three of the central strategic variables we have emphasized are partisan loyalties, abstention resulting from alienation, and voter discounting of party policies; and, as we have described repeatedly, behavioralists disagree sharply over the extent to which each of these factors actually influences voters in real-world elections. While we find that our

---

[3] By contrast, the *majoritarian* model of representation emphasizes the degree of concordance between the policies proposed by the victorious party or candidate in a national election (or by the governing coalition in a parliamentary democracy) and the central policy tendency, such as the median, of the *entire* electorate. Thus, the majoritarian model emphasizes a *collective* notion of representation (Weissberg 1978). Investigating the nature of the policies pursued by governing coalitions and their degree of congruence with the views of the median voter is beyond the scope of the present volume. For important work along these lines, see Huber and Powell (1994), Powell (2000), and Budge and McDonald (2003).

conclusions on party strategies are not sensitive to the exact strength of voters' partisan loyalties,[4] we find that vote-seeking parties' strategies – in particular, their incentives to present noncentrist policies – may vary substantially depending on the degree of policy discounting and abstention from alienation in the electorate. Our analyses suggest that these empirical questions, which have long preoccupied behavioral researchers, may be equally important for spatial modelers.

13.2. Evaluating the Unified Model: Does It Satisfactorily Explain Party Behavior?

As we bring this book to a close, two questions arise: Does our finding that the unified model roughly *predicts* parties' strategies in real-world elections imply that we have *explained* these parties' strategies? To the extent that the answer to this question is yes, is ours the preferred explanation for party strategies; that is, are there alternative approaches that can explain parties' observed behavior with equal or greater accuracy and with equal or greater parsimony?

Turning to the first of these questions, we recognize that descriptive accuracy is not proof that we have correctly identified the causal mechanisms responsible for the observed behavior. Yet we believe that the fact that the unified model generates reasonably accurate predictions of party strategies in France, Norway, Britain, and the United States suggests that our approach is indeed capturing critical causal variables. In particular, we are unaware of any alternative approach that generates similarly accurate point predictions of parties' policy strategies across such a variety of party systems. Moreover, as we have observed at various points in this book, specific predictions about party strategies derived from our model are supported by the findings reported in empirical studies of party and candidate behavior by many other scholars. For instance, Kenny and Lotfinia's (forthcoming) study on the relationship between American presidential candidates' policy positioning and election outcomes reaches conclusions that support our argument that in American elections, candidates maximize support by presenting policies that are similar to, but more moderate than, the preferences of their

---

[4] That is, we find that our substantive conclusions about party optima do not vary significantly even if the salience of party identification is much less than our empirical analyses suggest. On this point, see Chapter 4, section 4.5, and also note 7 to Chapter 6.

partisan constituencies. Similarly, Alvarez, Nagler, and Willette's (2000) study of party positioning and voting behavior in four Western European democracies reports results that support another prediction derived from our unified model: that parties contesting multiparty elections are motivated to present more extreme policies when voters attach greater importance to policy issues. Finally, Adams and colleagues' (forthcoming) empirical study of party positioning in eight Western European democracies supports our prediction that parties' policy dispersion increases with the dispersion of the voter distribution.

In toto, we believe that the weight of the evidence suggests that the unified model of party competition significantly advances our understanding of parties' policy strategies. The unified model generates reasonably accurate predictions of party strategies in four Western democracies, and independent empirical studies support several of the comparative statics predictions derived from the model. Furthermore, we have successfully predicted these empirical patterns while using a quite general version of the unified model of party competition, one that avoids the introduction of country-specific institutional factors such as electoral laws and campaign dynamics.[5]

The second question we posed at the beginning of this section – Does our unified model constitute the preferred explanation for party strategies? – is difficult to answer. In favor of our model are its scope and parsimony, as well as the evidence we have presented about its broad applicability to democratic nations that differ greatly in their institutional rules. In particular, while there are numerous empirical single-country studies of patterns of party competition, few offer a general model, and many incorporate country-specific factors that would make it hard to generalize their approach to other situations, such as party primaries. On the other hand, while game-theoretic models of the sort reviewed by Shepsle (1991) have a comparable generality and often an even greater simplicity, such models fail the empirical test. By and large, they simply do not predict the pattern of "spaced-out competition" observed in real-world party systems.

However, there has been some game-theory-inspired work on the nature of multiparty competition that is more closely linked to empirical evidence

---

[5] Grofman (in press) discusses more than a dozen factors that have been claimed to affect the degree of party divergence in systems involving primarily or exclusively two-party competition.

(e.g., Cox 1997). Of particular relevance – and the only real body of work that is comparable to our own in terms of the wide range of cases to which it has been applied – is that of Norman Schofield and his colleagues.[6] While Schofield has made use of a variety of different models, several of which we have discussed earlier, here we will emphasize his recent work on resource contributions by party activists. In a series of important papers, Schofield and his coauthors (Miller and Schofield 2003; Schofield 2003) present theoretical and empirical analyses of party competition in situations where parties influence activists' resource contributions (money, campaign activity, etc.) via their policy positions (see also Cameron and Enelow 1992; Ingberman 1992; Baron 1994; Moon [in press]). Given that party activists typically hold more extreme preferences than does the general population, Schofield's analyses suggest that endogenizing activists' resource contributions exerts a centrifugal incentive that pushes vote-seeking parties to present more extreme policies than they would otherwise advocate. In this regard, we note that Schofield's "party activist" argument and the argument we have developed based on the unified model have similar implications – that parties have electoral motivations to present policies that appeal to their partisan constituencies. Indeed, given that parties' partisan constituencies and their activist constituencies overlap, Schofield's resource contribution model provides parties with what we regard as important additional motivations to shift in the direction of the partisan constituencies. We find Schofield's approach a very promising one, and we hope in future work to incorporate some of his ideas into our unified theory.

13.3. Directions for Future Research

As suggested earlier, while we believe that our unified model of party competition represents a significant contribution to studies of party strategies and political representation, we make no claim that we have incorporated all of the critical variables. Indeed, we believe that a strength of our unified approach is that it can be extended to incorporate numerous additional factors, such as the role of party activists, that may be important for understanding party strategies. Some additional promising extensions that could

---

[6] To some extent the authors' previous books (Merrill and Grofman 1999; Adams 2001b) represent attempts to explain many of the same empirical patterns we have explored here. Given that the present book builds on this earlier research, we view our unified model of party competition as superseding the approaches developed in these earlier books.

offer sufficient additional explanatory power to justify their inclusion in the unified model include the following:

Motivations of Small Parties

While the results just summarized constitute a strong body of evidence consistent with our unified model of party competition, we do wish to acknowledge one empirical anomaly. While our unified approach predicts that small vote-seeking parties should present more moderate positions than large parties, we actually observe that small parties – such as the French Communists and National Front, as well as the Norwegian Progress and Socialist Parties – take more extreme positions than do the larger parties in these countries. Following Muller and Strom (1999; see also Owen and Grofman 1984), we speculate that this is due to differences in party motivations. Parties that seek to win or to dominate a governing coalition have an incentive to maximize their vote share and, if they are successful, they will be large. As we have seen, such large, dominant parties typically maximize votes by locating at intermediate positions between the overall voter mean and the mean location of their supporters, and such positions are therefore generally moderate.[7] Moderate positioning by major parties, however, leaves more extreme voters less adequately represented, and other parties may seek to fill this representation gap. Such parties can expect to receive relatively small vote shares. With no chance of dominance and, in many instances, little chance of becoming policy-relevant members of a governing coalition, such parties may pursue expressive motivations by articulating extreme policies.

In presidential elections, parties such as the French Communist and National Front parties and the Green Party in the United States provide expressive outlets for their supporters and forums for alternative ideas. In PR systems, parties such as the Norwegian Socialist and the German Green Party not only provide these expressive outlets, but also have the opportunity to pull coalition policy in their direction. Alternatively, some smaller parties, such as the Norwegian Center and Christian People's Parties, may be centrist

---

[7] If the major parties are sufficiently polarized spatially, as in Britain, there may be room for a smaller centrist party such as the Social Democrats (see Nagel 2001). Such a party in Britain may find it difficult to become a major party because of traditional party allegiance to the major players and for institutional reasons such as first-past-the-post voting, which makes it difficult for a small party to gain seats.

on traditional Left–Right scales that capture primarily economic concerns. These parties, nevertheless, constitute expressive vehicles for views outside the mainstream on peripheral issues (agricultural policy for the Center Party, alcohol policy for the Christian People's Party). Such considerations suggest that a modified version of the unified model of party competition, one that incorporates alternative motivations for different parties, might better explain the policies presented by small, extremist parties. As noted in Chapter 6, Norman Schofield has suggested that motivations based on policy preferences and coalition bargaining may lead small, extremist parties to maintain extreme stands in order to pull a prospective coalition in their direction.[8]

Party Strategies and Electoral Laws

We have focused primarily on how parties' policies influence their vote shares, while barely considering the strategic impact of the electoral laws that translate votes into seats. Yet it is well-known that electoral laws influence several variables that we have identified as important for party strategies, including, perhaps most importantly, the number of parties (Duverger 1954; Taagepera and Shugart 1989; Cox 1997) as well as the likelihood that a party obtains a parliamentary majority or becomes a member of the governing coalition (Laver and Shepsle 1996; Lijphart 1999). However, it remains to be seen whether, after we have controlled for the number of political parties, there are substantial further independent effects of electoral laws (see Dow 2001). In the cases considered in this volume, which include both PR and plurality systems, we have demonstrated – when we take the number of parties as fixed – that our model is capable of predicting party strategies across this range of electoral institutions without the need to use electoral laws as an independent variable. Also, for the real-world party systems we have examined, the optimal party locations identified by our algorithm do not appear to depend significantly upon whether parties are operating as vote-share maximizers or as plurality maximizers. If we are right in our

---

[8] Just as this book was going to press, we became aware of additional results advanced by Schofield and Sened (2003), which provide an alternative explanation for the empirical observation that small parties frequently take distinctly noncentrist policy positions: namely, that such positioning may in fact be *vote-maximizing* for parties that are disadvantaged on valence issues (see also Hug 1995; Adams 1999b). The intuition underlying this result is that parties that suffer from valence-related disadvantages need to differentiate their policies from those of their valence-advantaged competitors.

conjecture that the principal effect of electoral systems on the nature of party competition is an indirect one, mediated primarily by the number of political parties induced by the electoral rules, this finding would have important implications for the study of constitutional design.

The Geographic Distribution of Party Support

Political geography is one of the most neglected areas of study within political science.[9] But in the study of party competition, it would seem obvious that geographic factors could and should play an important role. For example, we would not expect to see the same patterns of cross-party political competition if most supporters of a given party were concentrated in a handful of districts, as compared to being nearly uniformly distributed across districts. In particular, it seems plausible to believe that geographically concentrated parties would have stronger links to their party supporters and would be less likely to take positions that move away from those supporters' preferences, since success in other districts would be unlikely. Looking to see how issues of geographic distribution of party support might affect the degree of party convergence/divergence seems a natural direction for future work.

Heterogeneity in Models of Voter Choice

Our theoretical and empirical analyses rely on a homogeneity assumption, that all voters employ identical decision rules and that all parties have identical motivations. This simplification ignores the possibility that voters differ in the importance they attach to issues (see Converse and Pierce 1986; Rivers 1988; Zaller 1992); in particular, it runs counter to evidence of the existence of issue publics (Converse 1964, 1970), that is, groups of voters who care intensely about a particular policy area. The existence of issue publics and single-issue voters may have important implications for party divergence, especially if such voters refuse to support any party that deviates from their preferred position. Likewise, as noted earlier, parties may vary in their motivations. Some value attainment of office over policy, while others seek policy

---

[9] While there has been something of a renaissance in the study of political geography within the discipline of geography (for a review, see Grofman 1982), this renaissance has for the most part not extended to political science. For example, in the study of American electoral politics, sometimes the only reference to political geography during much of the early period of national election studies was the investigation of whether or not "the South is different."

above everything else. The implications of this heterogeneity may help to explain why some parties locate in positions that maximize votes and grow large, while others – in order to faithfully reflect the policy preferences of their activists – locate on the spatial periphery and remain small.

The Implications of Voter Uncertainty

While we have incorporated uncertainty over election outcomes into our study of policy-seeking candidates (see Chapters 11 and 12), we have not accounted for the effects of voter uncertainty about parties' policy positions, nor for the fact that political information is unequally distributed across the electorate (see Zaller 1992; Alvarez 1997). In particular, it appears plausible that parties' policy shifts increase the level of voter uncertainty, so that risk-averse voters may penalize parties that drastically shift their policies (but see Stokes 1999). Such uncertainty effects may deter parties from drastically changing their positions, thereby "freezing" the configuration of party policies and contributing to the stability of the party system.

The topics summarized here by no means exhaust the list of possible extensions to our unified model of party competition. Additional extensions include: incorporating the possibility of entry and exit from the party system (Palfrey 1984); allowing parties the strategic option of introducing new dimensions of policy debate, or of suppressing existing policy debates (Riker 1986); exploring the implications of politicians' expressive motivations with regard to their policy proposals (Roemer 2001); considering the strategic implications of party primaries for American candidates (Coleman 1971; Aranson and Ordeshook 1972; Glazer, Grofman, and Owen 1998; Burden 2000a; Grofman and Brunell 2001; Ezrow 2003); and, more broadly, evaluating the implications of party primaries versus the wide range of other types of candidate selection mechanisms used throughout the world. Such extensions promise to further enhance our understanding of parties' policy strategies.

A more general consideration than simply adding variables to the unified model is the need to extend that model to allow for a consideration of party dynamics. In this context, ideas about realignment and the introduction of new issue dimensions, factors effecting the birth or death of political parties, the impact of changes in the location of the status quo, the differences in perceived incentives in subsequent elections for parties that lose and for those that win, and the nature of political persuasion may all be relevant.

Here we will focus on just one such topic: accounting for the reciprocal relationships between parties' policy programs, voters' policy preferences, and party identification.

In common with virtually all previous simulation studies on the electoral effects of party policies in real-world elections (Alvarez and Nagler 1995, 1998b; Schofield et al. 1998; Schofield, Sened, and Nixon 1998; Alvarez, Nagler, and Bowler 2000), our analyses invoke the assumption that voters' policy preferences and partisan loyalties are *exogenous* – that is, that these factors are not influenced by the parties' policy positions. However, there is extensive empirical evidence that party policies, voters' policy beliefs, and voter partisanship exert reciprocal influences on each other (see Jackson 1975; Page and Jones 1979; Gerber and Jackson 1993; Fleury and Lewis-Beck 1993).[10] Accounting for such reciprocal influences may alter our conclusions about parties' vote-seeking and policy-seeking strategies. For instance, charismatic politicians who can persuade voters to shift their policy beliefs, or who can mislead voters about their true intentions, may have the leeway to propose extreme policy alternatives at minimal electoral cost. Furthermore, to the extent that voters' partisan loyalties and their policy preferences shift in response to the parties' policies, parties' proposals in the current election will alter the electoral landscape of future elections. To our knowledge, Jackson's (1997) simulation of the dynamics of U.S. parties' policy positioning is the only study to account for such reciprocal effects. We hope to explore such ideas in future research.

13.4. Final Remarks

Our discussion of potential extensions of our research should not obscure the fact that our unified model of party competition represents a significant advance in applied spatial modeling and, we believe, in our understanding of the nature of party competition in the world's democracies. By merging the behavioral perspective on voters (initially associated with the University of Michigan) and the rational choice perspective on parties (initially associated with the University of Rochester), we have explored the ways in which vote-seeking and policy-seeking parties' strategic incentives vary with a

---

[10] We note that such studies reach conflicting conclusions about the strength and direction of these reciprocal relationships, which is one reason why we have not incorporated such effects into our simulations.

multitude of factors. Some of these factors – such as the size and extremity of the parties' partisan constituencies, the proportion of independent voters, and voter discounting of the parties' policy promises – are important to behavioral researchers but have not been systematically considered in prior spatial modeling research. Other factors, including the number of parties, the electoral salience of policies relative to unmeasured voter motivations, and the extent to which voter abstention is motivated by alienation, have been explored in previous spatial modeling research, but we have shown that the strategic effects of these variables can be quite different when we look at their effects in the context of a more fully specified model that includes behavioral variables relating to partisanship and policy discounting.

Downs's fundamental insight was that political competition revolves around the linkages between parties' programs, voters' policy preferences, and voter choices. Our contention is that voter choices are moved by their policy preferences *and* by a set of additional variables that are at most indirectly related to the parties' policy platforms in the current election. The key insight of this book is that accounting for this full set of factors that influence voters enhances our understanding of the ways in which parties respond to voters' policy preferences. Our theoretical analyses demonstrate that the unified model of party competition can generate the types of equilibrium analyses that are important to spatial modelers. Our empirical applications to Britain, France, Norway, and the United States show that our unified model can illuminate party policy strategies in a variety of real-world elections. Thus it is our hope that the work in this volume will prove of importance to all students of party behavior, and to all those who are interested in the study of political representation and its implications for democratic theory.

Literature Review

Work Linking Behavioral Research to Spatial Modeling

The three key elements of the unified theory offered in this book reflect a synthesis of previous work by the present authors, singly and in combination.

The *discounting model*, in which voters discount the claims of policy change offered by candidates or parties, was first proposed in Grofman (1985), but the idea lay dormant until Merrill (Merrill and Grofman 1997, 1999) showed its connection to a model that incorporates both proximity motivations and directional motivations (in the sense of Rabinowitz and Macdonald 1989). We note that this model is also related to important theoretical and empirical work on divided government by Alesina and Rosenthal (1995), Lacy and Paolino (1998, 2001), Burden and Kimball (2002), and Lewis-Beck and Nadeau (2004).

The potential role of *party loyalty* as a centrifugal force in spatial models of party competition was identified by Adams (1998, 2001a,b; see also Adams and Merrill 1999a,b). These models generally give rise to moderate divergence of party strategies in multiparty contests with probabilistic voting, and to substantial policy divergence when voting is deterministic. Adams and Merrill also consider a mixed proximity–directional model, which resembles a discounting model, and which implies optimal strategies that fit very well with the actual (mean perceived) strategies of the parties. Using the same model, Adams and Merrill (2000) obtain similar conclusions for the competitive candidates in the 1988 French presidential election. Drawing on Adams' work, Merrill and Grofman (1999: Chapter 10) report the divergence of optimal vote-maximizing strategies in Norway for spatial models that incorporate partisanship.

Adams and Merrill (2003a; see also Adams 2001b: Chapter 7) use the idea of *abstention through alienation* in conjunction with probabilistic voting and nonpolicy factors to show how the threat of abstention due to alienation can draw the candidates' optimal strategies away from the center. This phenomenon is particularly notable in a two-candidate race in which, without abstention, convergence of strategies would be expected. Extreme leftist and/or rightist citizens are alienated because of their policy distance from both candidates; the threat of their potential abstention implies divergence of strategies. Thus, while at first blush it might appear that those who abstain from voting cannot influence policies, if the citizens who abstain – or at least a significant fraction of them – do so in response to proposed party policies, the threat of their abstention may have an important effect on those policies.

Of course, the ideas we have identified do not come out of nowhere. The linkages between behavioral research and spatial modeling have been recognized at least since the 1960s, when Donald Stokes (1963) argued that spatial models needed to account for the non-policy-related aspects of voter decision making identified by behavioralists. Beginning in the 1980s, spatial modelers increasingly heeded this call as they incorporated into the spatial model such factors as unmeasured candidate characteristics (Enelow and Hinich 1981, 1984; Coughlin 1992) and measured nonpolicy influences arising from incumbency and candidate charisma (Hinich and Pollard 1981; Enelow and Hinich 1982; Feld and Grofman 1991; Macdonald and Rabinowitz 1998; Adams 1999b; Berger, Munger, and Potthoff 2000; Groseclose 2001; Schofield 2003).

While we owe an intellectual debt to all these studies (as well as to many others that we discuss later in this volume), there are three particular sets of studies that have shaped our approach to analyzing candidate strategies and political representation that we wish to call attention to here.

The first of these is Erikson and Romero's (1990) groundbreaking analysis of candidate strategies in the 1988 U.S. presidential election, which explores vote-seeking candidates' policy strategies in situations where voters have multiple factors affecting their choices. The Erikson–Romero study is, to our knowledge, the first to estimate the electoral effects of policy shifts by candidates in an historical election, as well as the first to provide theoretical analyses of vote-seeking candidates' strategies when voters choose according to the behavioral model of the vote. Thus Erikson and Romero were the first to employ something very like the unified perspective on behavioral voting research and spatial competition that informs this book.

The second set of studies is that of Norman Schofield and his coauthors (Schofield et al. 1998; Schofield, Sened, and Nixon 1998; Schofield 2003;

Schofield and Sened 2003; see also Laver and Schofield 1990; Martin and Quinn 2000), which explores parties' policy strategies in historical elections in Britain, Israel, the Netherlands, and Germany. Like Erikson and Romero, Schofield and his coauthors employ the behavioralist's multivariate voting model to compute the electoral effects of parties' policy shifts (although Schofield explicitly excludes some non-policy-related motivations that we include in our empirical analyses). However, these authors extend the Erikson–Romero approach in three ways: first, by moving from the U.S. two-party system to the Israeli, Dutch, and German multiparty systems; second, by exploring how considerations of postelection coalition negotiations affect parties' policy strategies in these parliamentary democracies; and third, by exploring how parties' policy-seeking motivations may affect election strategies. Our treatment of these topics has been largely motivated by the Schofield studies.

The third set of studies are those of Alvarez, Nagler, and their coauthors (Alvarez and Nagler 1995, 1998b; Alvarez, Nagler, and Bowler 2000; Alvarez, Nagler, and Willette 2000), which explore the relative impacts of policy voting and economic conditions on election outcomes. Alvarez and Nagler employ a methodology similar to those of Erikson and Romero and of Schofield, in that they estimate the parameters of behavioral voting specifications from election survey data and then compute the electoral effects of hypothesized changes in the candidates'/parties policy declarations. However, unlike the spatial modeling studies listed here, Alvarez and Nagler are not primarily concerned with determining vote-seeking or policy-seeking parties' optimal positions, but instead with estimating how the overall impact of policy voting in elections compares to the impact of economic voting. Thus the authors consider the questions: Could the losing candidates/parties in these historical elections have won by shifting their policies? Could the identities of the winning candidates/parties have been altered by realistic shifts in voters' perceptions of economic conditions? Our approach to studying mass–elite policy linkages is strongly influenced by Alvarez and Nagler's methodology.

Alvarez, Nagler, and their coauthors apply the methodology described here to survey data from historical elections in order to assess the relative impacts of policy factors and nonpolicy factors, such as the state of the economy, on election outcomes. Alvarez, Nagler, and Bowler (2000) and Alvarez, Nagler, and Willette (2000) conclude from an examination of five historical elections (one in Britain, two in Canada, and two in the United

States) that the effects of plausible changes in the economy on party vote share were greater than the potential effects of policy factors in three of the elections, but that the potential effects of the economy had less effect than policy in the other two. Furthermore, they found that although changing the economy in the 1993 Canadian election would not have reversed the result, such a reversal would have occurred in the 1988 Canadian election and in the 1996 U.S. election. In the latter election, however, Alvarez and Nagler (1998b) found that moving Clinton to his optimum policy position on all issues studied would have improved his vote share substantially (by about five percentage points); Dole could similarly have increased his vote share by an extra two to three percentage points. These authors found, moreover, that the parties typically presented policies that diverged sharply from the median (and mean) voter's position along the policy dimensions. In toto, the Alvarez and Nagler results establish that both policy and nonpolicy factors significantly affected candidates' vote shares in varying degrees in different elections.

To date, work along lines similar in important ways to what is offered in this volume has been extended outward from the United States to encompass elections in Canada, Britain, Germany, Norway, the Netherlands, and Israel.[1]

One last set of authors whom we wish to acknowledge are those who have studied the relationship between turnout and party location. Abstention either due to alienation – that is, nonvoting by citizens whose utility for all candidates drops below some threshold – or due to indifference among the alternatives has been separately modeled by Lacy and Burden (1999) and Sanders (1998, 2001), along lines initially suggested by Garvey (1966).[2]

---

[1] For analyses of elections in Canada, see Alvarez, Nagler, and Willette (2000) and Dow (2001); in Britain, see Alvarez, Nagler, and Bowler (2000); in Germany, see Schofield et al. (1998); in Norway, see Adams and Merrill (1999a,b); in the Netherlands, see Schofield et al. and Dow (2001); and in Israel, see Dow (2001), Schofield, Sened, and Nixon (1998); Schofield and Sened (2003).

[2] Weisberg and Grofman (1981) is an early, almost purely descriptive study of the prevalence of different motivations for abstention using American National Election Study data.

Alternative Statistical Models
of Voter Choice

An apparent limitation of the conditional logit (CL) model is that it assumes that the error terms X_{ik} are independent not only among voters but also among candidates. However, such independence – often referred to as independence of irrelevant alternatives – need not be the case. In a contest among two liberals and one conservative, for example, the two liberals are likely to compete against each other for unmeasured, nonpolicy evaluations (represented by the X_{ik} terms), whereas their competition with the conservative may be more on ideological grounds, represented instead by the $V_i(k)$ terms. As a result, if we specify the two liberals by the subscripts 1 and 2 and the conservative by the subscript 3, we may expect the perturbation terms X_{i1} and X_{i2} to be negatively correlated (because higher nonpolicy evaluations of one liberal are likely to come at the expense of the other). On the other hand, neither of these two terms may be significantly correlated with X_{i3} (because relative evaluation of liberals versus conservatives is more likely to be based on policy). In particular, the ratio between the support of the two liberals is little affected by the presence of the conservative (or an additional liberal) in the race, whereas the ratio between the support of one of the liberals and the support of the conservative would be strongly affected by the entry of an additional candidate.

An alternative model that permits limited correlation structures of the type suggested here is the *generalized extreme value* (GEV) model. Under this model, the candidate set may be partitioned into subsets within each of which there may be nonzero correlations, but correlations between perturbation terms in different subsets are constrained to zero. As in the example just given, if the set of candidates consists of a subset of liberals and a subset of conservatives, there may be correlation within each of these ideological groups but not across groups. In our empirical analysis of French data (see Chapter 5, section 5.4), we compare results for the GEV and CL models. Our experience indicates that the differences between both the parameter estimates and the equilibrium strategies for these two models are modest.

A second alternative for estimating model parameters is *multinomial probit* (MNP), which in principle permits correlated error terms between all pairs of candidate terms. In order to identify the models, however, some of these terms must be constrained, so that here too the correlation structure is limited. Although inclusion of such a more complete correlation structure potentially alters the results, identification of this structure is quite fragile (Keane 1992). Adams and Merrill (2000: n. 12) report empirical evidence that the equilibrium configuration of party strategies need not be sensitive to the choice of model. Dow and Endersby (2004) compare MNP and CL both theoretically and via Monte Carlo studies. They conclude that the two methods yield comparable substantive results and that because of the complexity and instability inherent in MNP, it may not be cost effective for the small gain achieved in specificity. They find that when no entry or exit of candidates is considered, the independence-of-irrelevant-alternatives assumption inherent in CL is not as restrictive as it might appear.

Controversies in Voting Research

The Electoral Impact of Party Identification

Behavioral researchers disagree sharply about how voters decide. These debates can be traced to various factors, including measurement problems inherent in survey research and the reciprocal relationships among the various independent variables that affect the vote choice. Here we focus on the impact of party identification on the vote. In subsequent chapters, we will show the relation of this issue to our analyses of party strategies. Behaviorists are similarly divided about the interrelationships among voting behavior, considerations arising from economic conditions, group attachments rooted in class and religion, and retrospective evaluations of incumbent performance.[1]

The impact of party identification on voting behavior is a central feature of the "Michigan model" of voting (Campbell et al. 1960), in which the vote choice is conceptualized as the outcome of long-term forces – such as group loyalties and citizens' basic value orientations and partisan predispositions – and short-term factors, including candidate images, campaign issues, and

---

[1] There are numerous other controversies in the empirical voting literature. A partial list of additional behavioral voting controversies would include: the question of whether there is heterogeneity in the voting population with respect to the model of electoral choice – that is, the extent to which different blocs of voters employ differing decision rules to evaluate candidates (see Rivers 1988; Glasgow 2001); the question of whether economic voting revolves primarily around evaluations of personal economic circumstances or evaluations of the national economy (Kinder and Kiewiet 1981; Lewis-Beck 1988); and the types of information that voters employ to arrive at performance-based evaluations of the party elites' competence and integrity in order to estimate the candidates' policy positions (Brady and Sniderman 1985; Zaller 1992; Alvarez 1997). Finally, an additional controversy, which we examine in detail in Chapter 7, concerns the factors that affect citizens' decisions about whether to turn out to vote (see Wolfinger and Rosenstone 1980; Piven and Cloward 1988; Sanders 1998).

economic conditions. According to this model, partisanship represents a long-term, affective, psychological identification with one's preferred party that is nonetheless distinct from voting preference, so that voters may vote for a candidate of one party while expressing loyalty to another party. Because the Michigan model posits that partisanship is an *affective* orientation – one that typically grows out of early socialization experiences – it does not necessarily represent some cognitive or "rational" decision process (see Jennings and Niemi 1981; Jennings and Markus 1984). Indeed, voters need not even be aware that partisanship affects their vote choices.

Although the development of the concept of party identification represents one of the most significant findings of public opinion research, both the nature of partisanship and its impact on the vote have been the subject of extensive debate. While the Michigan model stresses the affective character of partisanship, other behavioral researchers argue that partisanship has both affective *and* cognitive components, so that voters may develop loyalties to a party based in part on agreement with the party's long-term policy agenda or on approval of the party's performance in office. Thus Fiorina (1981), in his influential study of voting, conceptualizes party identification as a "running tally" of all of the voter's past experiences, including socialization experiences and evaluations of the party's previous policy performance.

Although Fiorina's conception appears reasonable, it introduces inevitable complications into attempts to estimate the relative influence on the vote of policies versus party identification. This is because this conception of partisanship implies not only that policies and partisanship both influence the vote, but also that each influences the other – that is, partisan identification is in part determined by ideology, and conversely, voters may come to support an ideology or a set of policies in part because it fits with their partisan identity. Attempts to disentangle these two influences on the vote choice using simultaneous equation models involve constraints that are difficult to justify, so that, unsurprisingly, empirical studies that estimate such models from election survey data reach conflicting conclusions about the electoral impact of partisanship (see Markus and Converse 1979; Page and Jones 1979; Converse and Pierce 1993; Fleury and Lewis-Beck 1993).

Complicating this situation are problems that arise from survey research. For instance, questions intended to elicit party allegiance may blur the line between ongoing partisan identity and vote intention in a current election. Thus voters' designations of a party identity may be colored by how they intend to vote in that election, compromising the usefulness of this designation as an explanatory factor in the vote choice. This problem is particularly acute outside the United States, because foreign elections tend to revolve around parties, not candidates.[2] Therefore, non-American respondents may not see any difference between queries regarding their party identification and questions about their current vote intention; indeed, many studies on European voting behavior exclude partisanship as an explanatory variable for precisely this reason (see Rose and McAllister 1990: 155–6). Furthermore, this problem is exacerbated because empirical studies find that respondents' answers to survey questions about partisanship are strongly affected by question wording and question ordering (Converse and Pierce 1986; Heath and Pierce 1992; Dalton 2002).

Due to the problems just outlined, empirical studies reach sharply different conclusions about the electoral impact of partisanship, with some behaviorists arguing that partisanship exercises a preeminent influence on voting (Campbell et al. 1960; Converse and Pierce 1986, 1993; Endersby and Galatas 1997), others that voting is primarily determined by group attachments such as social class and religion (Baker, Dalton, and Hildebrandt 1981; Bartle 1998), others that ideology drives the vote (Fleury and Lewis-Beck 1993), and still others that the impact of partisanship varies with the institutional context (Lewis-Beck and Chlarson 2002).

Given that the results we develop in subsequent chapters largely revolve around how voters' partisan loyalties affect party strategies, these debates appear crucial to our theoretical and empirical arguments. However, we will show that our substantive conclusions obtain even if partisanship exerts a very modest influence on the vote – that is, our results on party strategies

---

[2] In Western democracies that employ some form of proportional representation, citizens may explicitly cast votes for a party rather than for a specific candidate. In addition, the high degree of party cohesion in parliaments outside the United States can motivate non-American voters to emphasize the candidates' party affiliations (Barnes 1977; Farah 1980; Converse and Pierce 1986). We note (Chapter 5) that in presidential elections in France, significant numbers of voters either claim no party allegiance or vote for a candidate of a different party from the one to which they claim allegiance. The same is true for presidential elections in the United States. Hence for presidential elections, the partisan information available from survey research may be sufficiently independent of vote intention to be useful. For parliamentary elections, as in Britain and Norway, we will suggest alternative sources of information concerning partisanship.

depend primarily on the *existence* of partisan loyalties, not on the *strength* of these loyalties (see especially section 4.5 and note 7 in Chapter 5). Given the nearly universal agreement among behavioralists that partisanship exerts some degree of influence on the vote, we feel confident that our emphasis on the strategic importance of party identification illuminates party strategies in real-world elections.

Relationship between the Unified Discounting Model and the Directional Model of Rabinowitz and Macdonald

One of the three major factors that we analyze as a determinant of party strategies for vote-maximizing parties is the effect of voter discounting of the claimed policy positions of the parties. We represent this factor in our unified discounting model through the discounting concept introduced by Grofman (1985). Voter utilities under discounting are mathematically similar to those under a combination of the directional model of Rabinowitz and Macdonald (1989) and the traditional proximity spatial model.

Under the directional model of Rabinowitz and Macdonald, voters do not conceive of policy choices as lying along a continuum that admits a variety of alternatives, but instead see policy debates revolving around dichotomous choices or directions, such as pro-life versus pro-choice positions on abortion rights, support versus opposition to gun control laws or to the death penalty, and so on. In directional voting theory, voters evaluate candidates positively when the two are on the same side of the issue but negatively when they are on opposing sides. Furthermore, the more intensely the candidate promotes his proposed policy direction – and the more intensely the voter feels about the policy debate – the more strongly this issue affects the voter's (positive or negative) candidate evaluation. On each issue, intensity is specified relative to a neutral point, which represents indifference on that issue. A voter's utility for a candidate's policy is specified as the product of the deviation of the voter's position from the neutral point N and the deviation of the candidate's position from N, that is,

$$V_i(k) = (x_i - N)(s_k - N).$$

Because these assumptions of the model place a premium on intense positions of candidates, candidates are motivated to take arbitrarily intense

251

positions. In order to alleviate this implication, Rabinowitz and Macdonald (1989) restrict candidates to a "region of acceptability."

Some behaviorists argue instead that voters employ a combination of proximity and directional criteria in decision making (see Iversen 1994a,b; Merrill and Grofman 1999; Adams and Merrill 1999a,b, 2000). Iversen, and Merrill and Grofman, argue that the proximity component may be interpreted as a voter-specific constraint on directional utility and thus may provide a more justifiable solution to the concern about acceptability than the "region of acceptability" imposed by Rabinowitz and Macdonald. In general, a *mixed proximity–directional* model may provide greater flexibility in describing voter utility. Such a model can be specified by the utility function that combines the utility functions for proximity and directional utility:

$$V_i(k) = 2(1 - \beta)(x_i - N)(s_k - N) - \beta(x_i - s_k)^2,$$

where β is a mixing parameter whose value is 1 for a pure proximity utility and 0 for a pure directional utility. There is, however, a conceptual difficulty with combining proximity and directional utilities based on the same scale (see Warwick 2004). In a proximity model, the scale measures extremity of position on an issue (or ideology) on which a continuum of positions is plausible; in the directional model, the scale reflects the intensity with which an agent maintains one pole of a dichotomous issue. Placement on a Left–Right or liberal–conservative scale might represent position (or extremity), whereas placement on an abortion scale might represent intensity of feeling.

We now indicate the relation between the voter utilities under Grofman's discounting model and those of a mixed proximity–directional model. Specifically, for each voter, these voter utilities are equivalent[1] if the status quo point of the discounting model is the same as the neutral point of the directional model and if the discounting factor d is (one minus) the mixing parameter of the proximity–directional model (Merrill and Grofman 1999: 48, n. 10). Because vote-maximizing strategies depend only on these utilities, our analysis of party competition under a discounting model is mathematically similar to what it would be under the corresponding mixed proximity–directional model. Similarly, an interpretation of discounting in anticipation of coalition governments due to Kedar (2002) will be seen to lead to utility

---

[1] Utilities are equivalent if one is a positive linear transformation of the other.

functions that also resemble those of Rabinowitz and Macdonald (see Appendix 6.1). In this book, we focus on the discounting concept because of its simplicity and because it avoids confounding position and intensity on the same scale. Specific justifications of the plausibility of discounting will be developed in the country-specific chapters.

Spatial Models That Incorporate Valence Dimensions of Candidate Evaluation

Until about fifteen years ago, spatial modelers focused almost exclusively on elections in which the candidates/parties competed over what Donald Stokes (1963) labeled "positional" dimensions of candidate evaluation – that is, dimensions along which voters (and candidates) could plausibly hold a range of preferred positions. Positional dimensions encompass policy debates relating to such issues as abortion (where voters may prefer pro-life or pro-choice positions), gun control, tax policy, the European Union, immigration policy, as well as overarching ideological dimensions where voters' preferences are typically arrayed along a Left–Right or liberal–conservative scale. A central feature of spatial models of position is that voters are assumed to display a *distribution* of preferred positions along the dimensions included in the model, and candidates compete by shifting their announced positions in an effort to attract support from policy-motivated voters.

In an influential early review of the spatial modeling literature, Stokes (1963) argued for the need to incorporate *valence* dimensions of candidate evaluation into spatial models of elections. In Stokes's formulation, valence dimensions were those along which all voters held identical positions (preferring more to less), such as reducing crime, increasing economic growth, or desiring candidates/party leaders who display valued personal characteristics such as integrity, competence, and charisma. The two critical aspects of valence dimensions of evaluation are first, that voters hold identical preferences along these dimensions but may perceive the candidates as being at different locations (i.e., candidates may be perceived as more or less honest, charismatic, or effective at reducing crime or managing the economy); second, that candidates may find it difficult or impossible to substantially alter their reputations along these dimensions (i.e., a candidate cannot easily

254

change his public image with respect to competence and integrity). Thus for the purposes of spatial modeling studies, candidates may be considered to be "anchored" at their locations along the valence dimensions, but to enjoy policy mobility with respect to positional issues. Stokes argued that "[i]t will not do to exclude valence issues from the discussion of party competition. The people's choice too often depends upon them. At least in American presidential elections of the past generation, it is remarkable how many valence issues have held the center of the stage" (1963: 37).

In recent years, spatial modelers have incorporated valence dimensions into their analyses of two-candidate elections, concluding that valence considerations can fundamentally alter the candidates' strategic incentives (see, e.g., Feld and Grofman 1991; Macdonald and Rabinowitz 1998; Ansolabehere and Snyder 2000; Berger, Munger, and Potthoff 2000).[1] The central insight is that valence-advantaged, vote-maximizing candidates can typically assure themselves of an electoral majority by presenting centrist positions along the positional dimensions included in the model.[2] This centrist positioning leaves the valence-disadvantaged candidate with no viable strategic options: if she converges to centrist positions near the advantaged candidate, then voters are nearly indifferent between the candidates on positional grounds and hence prefer the advantaged candidate on valence grounds. Conversely, if the disadvantaged candidate presents positions substantially diverging from those of her centrist opponent, then by definition these positions are noncentrist, and a majority of voters will prefer the valence-advantaged candidate on positional grounds – in addition to which, all voters prefer this candidate on valence grounds. Hence in two-candidate competition,

---

[1] We note that some of these cited studies do not explicitly invoke valence issues, but instead posit that candidates may hold an advantage deriving from such factors as greater voter certainty surrounding their policy positions compared to their opponent's positions (see, e.g., Berger, Munger, and Potthoff 2000), or that voters grant one of the competing candidates the "benefit of the doubt" (see Feld and Grofman 1991). However, these influences appear to be substantively equivalent to valence advantages. Additional studies by Wittman (1990), Londregan and Romer (1993), Groseclose (2001), and Roemer (2001) explore the impact of valence issues in models with policy-seeking candidates, a topic we consider in Chapters 11 and 12.

[2] We note that this result – namely, that the optimal strategy for the valence-advantaged candidate is nearer the center – assumes that the candidates are purely office-seeking – that is, that the advantaged candidate attaches equal utility to any set of positions that cannot be beaten, while the disadvantaged candidate is indifferent between any set of losing positions. If instead the candidates are policy-seeking, the equilibrium strategies are qualitatively different; in particular, the valence-advantaged candidate may be motivated to take a noncentrist stand, as we argue in Chapters 11 and 12.

valence-advantaged, vote-maximizing candidates have strategic incentives to locate near the center of the policy space, as this centrist positioning may guarantee their election – thus "solving" the prediction of majority-rule cycling that is central to the spatial modeling literature (see Schofield, 1978; McKelvey 1986).[3]

While there exist relatively few spatial analyses of multicandidate elections with valence issues, these studies suggest that the strategic incentives that characterize two-candidate competition – namely, that vote-maximizing, valence-advantaged candidates should locate near the center of the voter distribution while their opponents adopt noncentrist positions – extend to the multicandidate context. Hug (1995), in an analysis of a three-candidate election with purely policy-oriented, risk-averse voters who have varying degrees of uncertainty over the candidates' positions,[4] demonstrates that at equilibrium the candidate with the most clearly articulated position will locate near the center of the normally distributed voter distribution, with her two opponents nearer the wings. Adams (1999b), who analyzes a three-candidate election with a uniform voter distribution, probabilistic voting, and candidate-specific "popularity variables," similarly locates candidate equilibria in which the popular candidates locate nearer to the center of the positional dimension than do the unpopular candidates.

Finally, Schofield (2003, 2004) presents a general theoretical analysis of multiparty competition with probabilistic voting and valence issues, delineating the conditions for the existence of a unique positional equilibrium along with the conditions that support multiple "local equilibrium" configurations. His results suggest that when there are no voter-specific nonpolicy factors such as partisanship, multiple local equilibria may be the norm. Schofield and Sened's (2003) empirical application of the valence model to Israeli elections supports this conclusion. Although Lin, Enelow, and Dorussen (1999) showed that concavity of the vote-share functions implies that a unique,

---

[3] If the candidates are vote-maximizing, then an equilibrium is unlikely to exist in two-candidate elections with valence advantages and deterministic voting, because in this scenario the valence-advantaged candidate is motivated to converge to her opponent's positions – thereby winning 100 percent of the vote – while the disadvantaged candidate is motivated to diverge from her opponent's positions. However, in two-candidate models with probabilistic voting, an equilibrium in vote-maximizing positions will typically exist, with this equilibrium shaded in the direction of the disadvantaged candidate's supporters (Erikson and Romero 1990).

[4] While Hug does not explicitly invoke valence issues in his analysis, voters' degrees of uncertainty over the candidates' positions function as a valence dimension, in that the less uncertainty risk-averse voters experience with respect to a candidate's position along the positional dimension, the higher they rate the candidate.

centrist Nash equilibrium will occur, the policy-salience parameters must be quite small in order for the vote-share functions to be concave. If the latter is not the case – and if there are no voter-specific nonpolicy factors – nonconvergent equilibria may occur, or some parties may minimize rather than maximize votes when assuming a centrist position, so that such parties have an incentive to move to the periphery (see Schofield 2003, 2004). In this book, however, we incorporate voter-specific nonpolicy factors such as partisanship into our unified models, accounting for stability in the political system and typically finding a unique, but dispersed, Nash equilibrium.

Note that in all of the studies summarized here, candidates' valence characteristics are assumed to be identical across voters – that is, we assume that all voters have identical perceptions of the candidates' positions along the valence dimensions of evaluation. In terms of the behavioral voting model described in Chapter 2, this is equivalent to modeling valence advantages in terms of candidate-specific intercepts. Valence issues thus differ from nonpolicy-related motivations such as partisanship, class, education, religion, and race, which vary across voters and hence can motivate different voters to support different candidates.

Uniqueness Theorem and Algorithm for Computing Nash Equilibria

In this appendix, we present a uniqueness theorem for Nash equilibria and describe an algorithm (Merrill and Adams 2001) that successively updates optimal positions for all parties and that can very quickly calculate Nash equilibria (when such exist). Referred to as the *equilibrium algorithm*, this procedure is used for calculations for the various data sets throughout the book.[1]

Under the conditional logit model in a K-party election, according to equation 2.4, the probability that voter i chooses party k is given by

$$P_{ik}(\mathbf{s}, a) = \frac{\exp[V_i(s_k, a)]}{\sum\limits_{j=1}^{K} \exp[V_i(s_j, a)]}, \tag{A4.1}$$

where

$$V_i(s_k, a) = -a(x_i - s_k)^2 + \mathbf{B}_k \mathbf{t}_{ik}. \tag{A4.2}$$

Here a is the policy salience parameter; x_i represents the voter's ideal location; s_k is party k's strategic location; $\mathbf{s}$ is the vector of all parties' strategic locations; $\mathbf{t}_{ik}$ is a vector of voter i's individual nonpolicy characteristics; and $\mathbf{B}_k$ represents a vector of salience parameters for these characteristics. Our notation here indicates explicitly the dependence of P_{ik} and V_i on s_k and a.

At a Nash equilibrium, each party k cannot increase its vote share by changing strategy; that is, its vote share is at a maximum. The vote share of party k is given by the expected value

$$EV_k(\mathbf{s}, a) = \sum_i P_{ik}(\mathbf{s}, a).$$

---

[1] Typically, Nash equilibria for conditional logit models applied to national election studies can be computed in a fraction of a second using the algorithm.

Hence, at a Nash equilibrium, the partial derivative of $EV_k(s, a)$ with respect to s_k is zero for all k; that is, for all k

$$\frac{\partial EV_k(s, a)}{\partial s_k} = 0,$$

that is,

$$\frac{\partial EV_k(s, a)}{\partial s_k} = \sum_i \frac{\partial P_{ik}(s, a)}{\partial s_k} = \sum_i \frac{\partial P_{ik}(s, a)}{\partial V_i(s_k, a)} \frac{\partial V_i(s_k, a)}{\partial s_k}$$

$$= \sum_i P_{ik}(s, a)[1 - P_{ik}(s, a)](2a)(x_i - s_k) = 0.$$

$$\text{(A4.3)}$$

Solving for the last occurrence of s_k, we obtain:

$$s_k = \frac{\sum_i P_{ik}(s, a)[1 - P_{ik}(s, a)]x_i}{\sum_i P_{ik}(s, a)[1 - P_{ik}(s, a)]}. \tag{A4.4}$$

Define

$$g_k(s) = \frac{\sum_i P_{ik}(s, a)[1 - P_{ik}(s, a)]x_i}{\sum_i P_{ik}(s, a)[1 - P_{ik}(s, a)]} \tag{A4.5}$$

for each $k, k = 1, \ldots, K$. Let $\mathbf{I}$ be an interval including in its interior all voter positions – say, with an appropriate change of coordinates, $[-M, M]$. We obtain the following theorem:

Theorem A4.1: Uniqueness Theorem for Nash Equilibrium. If there exists a constant Q such that for all $s \in \mathbf{I}^K$,

$$\max_k \sum_j \left| \frac{\partial g_k(s)}{\partial s_j} \right| \leq Q < 1, \tag{A4.6}$$

then there exists a unique Nash equilibrium $s = (s_1, \ldots, s_K)$ of party strategies.

Proof. Note that each function g_k is a function of all $s_1, \ldots, s_K$. Because

$$|g_k(s)| = \left| \frac{\sum_i P_i(s, a)[1 - P_i(s, a)]x_i}{\sum_i P_i(s, a)[1 - P_i(s, a)]} \right| \leq \left| \frac{\sum_i P_i(s, a)[1 - P_i(s, a)]}{\sum_i P_i(s, a)[1 - P_i(s, a)]} \right| M = M,$$

together the functions $g_k, k = 1, \ldots, K$, define a vector-valued mapping $\mathbf{g}$ of $\mathbf{I}^K$ into $\mathbf{I}^K$. Condition A4.6 states that the supremum norm of the Jacobian matrix of this mapping is less than 1. Hence, we infer that $\mathbf{g} = (g_1, \ldots, g_K)$ is a contraction mapping on $\mathbf{I}^K$ whenever equation A4.6 holds for all $\mathbf{s}$ in $\mathbf{I}^K$. If this is the case, it follows (Ortega 1972: 152–4) that there is a unique fixed point $\mathbf{s}$ of $\mathbf{g}$ – that is, such that $g_k(\mathbf{s}) = s_k$ for $k = 1, \ldots, K$. Thus, this $\mathbf{s}$ is the unique solution to equations of the form A4.3, $k = 1, \ldots, K$. Because

$$\frac{\partial EV_k(\mathbf{s}, a)}{\partial s_k} = \sum_i P_i(s, a)[1 - P_i(s, a)](2a)(x_i - s_k),$$

by A4.3, we conclude that

$$\frac{\partial EV_k(\mathbf{s}, a)}{\partial s_k} \begin{cases} > 0 \; if \, s_k \leq -M \\ < 0 \; if \, s_k \geq M \end{cases}.$$

Thus $\mathbf{s}$ must be a maximum of EV_k for each k, because if not, EV_k would have more than one critical point. Hence, $\mathbf{s}$ is a Nash equilibrium. Because a Nash equilibrium is a fixed point, and the fixed point of $\mathbf{g}$ is unique on $\mathbf{I}^K$, the Nash equilibrium is unique. This completes the proof.[2]

These same arguments lead us to a procedure by which this Nash equilibrium can be computed. Although s_k appears implicitly on both sides of equation A4.4, we may use equation A4.4 as the basis of an iterative algorithm that determines a sequence of strategy sets that converge to a Nash equilibrium. Begin with a vector $\mathbf{s_0}$ of starting locations for the parties – for example, let each coordinate of $\mathbf{s_0}$ be 0. For each party k, define the kth coordinate of $\mathbf{s_1}$ as

$$g_k(\mathbf{s_0})$$

and in general define the kth coordinate of $\mathbf{s}_{m+1}$ as

$$g_k(\mathbf{s}_m). \tag{A4.7}$$

Theorem A4.2: Algorithm for Computing a Nash Equilibrium. If criterion A4.6 holds, then for starting values $\mathbf{s}_0 \in \mathbf{I}^K$, the values $g_k(\mathbf{s}_m)$ defined by equation A4.7 converge to solutions of equation A4.3 that together constitute a unique Nash equilibrium.

---

[2] We thank Jeremy Staum for helpful comments on the proof.

Proof. By the contraction mapping theorem, the sequence $\mathbf{g}(\mathbf{s}_m)$ converges to the unique fixed point $\mathbf{s}$ of $\mathbf{g}$, which defines solutions to equation A4.3 and constitutes the unique Nash equilibrium.

The precision of the last iterate obtained by the algorithm is known not to exceed $Q/(1 - Q)$ times the absolute difference between the last two iterates (Ortega 1972: 153). In practice, if Q is not near 1, one continues the iteration until the values do not change in at least the number of decimal places desired. Convergence can be speeded up considerably by use of the Aitken acceleration technique (Henrici 1964: Chapter 4). Implemented in Excel, the algorithm can determine equilibria to four significant digits for an election with several hundred voters and five candidates in a fraction of a second. By contrast, to obtain even three significant digits, a brute force search by an experienced user requires about ten minutes of user–computer interaction. An Excel spreadsheet implementing the algorithm is available on the website http://course.wilkes.edu/merrill.

Note that the uniqueness of the critical points – and hence the uniqueness of the Nash equilibrium – is independent of any algorithm (or its starting points) by which they may be computed. Because of the continuity of the iteration functions g_k, if the algorithm converges, it must converge to a solution of equation A4.3. Because condition A4.6 is motivated by mathematical considerations, we present empirical applications to election survey data, as well as Monte Carlo simulations, which suggest that equation A4.6 holds in many situations that are likely to occur in practice, and hence that the algorithm frequently converges and converges to a unique equilibrium configuration.

Adaptation of the Algorithm for Linear Utility

If quadratic utility is replaced by *linear* utility, given by $-|x_i - s_k|$, for each $k, k = 1, \ldots, K$, we may define $g_k(\mathbf{s}) = \tilde{s}_k$, where $\tilde{s}_k$ is the point such that

$$\sum_{x_i \leq \tilde{s}_k} w_{ik} \geq \frac{1}{2} \quad \text{and} \quad \sum_{x_i \geq \tilde{s}_k} w_{ik} \geq \frac{1}{2},$$

where

$$w_{ik} = \frac{P_{ik}(\mathbf{s}, a)[1 - P_{ik}(\mathbf{s}, a)]}{\sum_i P_{ik}(\mathbf{s}, a)[1 - P_{ik}(\mathbf{s}, a)]}.$$

The iteration function $g_k(\mathbf{s}) = \bar{s}_k$ converges to a unique Nash equilibrium provided that the functions g_k define a contraction mapping. Computer simulation and analysis of an historical election suggest that convergence often occurs, and that although multiple maxima may occur, the separation between maxima is far too small to be substantively significant.

Adaptation of the Algorithm for Alternative Motivations

In certain types of elections – particularly those involving candidates, not parties – some competitors may emphasize their expected vote margins relative to a particular opponent. For example, in the 1988 French presidential election, the two center-right candidates Barre and Chirac may plausibly have focused on maximizing their vote margins relative to each other, rather than on maximizing their expected vote shares.

The algorithm can easily be modified to accommodate margin-maximizing motivations, or a combination of vote and margin maximization. If party k is motivated to maximize its margin relative to party j, the terms $P_{ik}[1 - P_{ik}]$ are replaced by the terms $P_{ik}[1 - P_{ik}] + P_{ik}P_{ij}$ in the definition of $g_k(\mathbf{s})$.[3] Alternatively, if party k is motivated to maximize the total vote share of a coalition of parties consisting of a subset C of parties (including party k), then the terms $P_{ik}[1 - P_{ik}]$ are replaced by the terms $P_{ik}[1 - \sum_{j \in C} P_{ij}]$. With either of these changes, the uniqueness theorem and the algorithm hold as before.

---

[3] This follows by straightforward calculation because $\frac{\partial[P_{ik} - P_{ij}]}{\partial V_i(s_k, a)} = P_{ik}[1 - P_{ik}] - [-P_{ik}P_{ij}]$.

Proof of Theorem 4.1

Theorem 4.1. Assuming that the mean, μ_0, of the independent voters is the same as the overall mean, μ_V, the quantities $s_k(0)$ are given by

$$s_k(0) = \mu_V + c_k(\mu_k - \mu_V),$$

where the c_k are defined by

$$c_k = \frac{(K - 2)(e^b - 1)m_k}{(K - 2)(e^b - 1)m_k + (e^b + K - 2) + m_0 \left[(e^b + K - 1)^2 \left(\frac{K-1}{K^2}\right) - (e^b + K - 2)\right]}.$$

Proof. Without loss of generality, we set $\mu_V = 0$. Suppose that the partisans of the various parties have spatial locations that follow continuous distributions with means μ_k and probability density functions f_k. We fix a party k, $k = 1, \ldots, K$. Because $P_{ik}(\mathbf{s}, 0)$ is the same for all partisans of the same party, we may denote by $P_{kj} = P_{ik}(\mathbf{s}, 0)$ the probability that a voter i who is a partisan of party j votes for party k. Thus, if voter i is a partisan of party k:

$$P_{kk} = \frac{e^b}{e^b + K - 1}.$$

If, instead, voter i is a partisan of another party j, then

$$P_{kk} = \frac{1}{e^b + K - 1}.$$

Similarly, if voter i is an independent, then

$$P_{k0} = \frac{1}{K}.$$

Recall that we have assumed, without loss of generality, that $\sum_j m_j \mu_j = \mu_V = 0$. By assumption, $\mu_0 = 0$, so that $\sum_{j=0}^{K} m_j \mu_j = 0$. Because all terms other than x_i in the expression for s_{k0} are independent of the voter locations, asymptotically, we have:

$s_k(0)$

$$= \frac{P_{kk}[1 - P_{kk}]m_k \int_{-\infty}^{\infty} x f_k(x)dx + \sum_{j \neq k,0} P_{kj}[1 - P_{kj}]m_j \int_{-\infty}^{\infty} x f_j(x)dx + P_{k0}[1 - P_{k0}]m_0 \int_{-\infty}^{\infty} x f_0(x)dx}{P_{kk}[1 - P_{kk}]m_k + \sum_{j \neq k,0} P_{kj}[1 - P_{kj}]m_j + P_{k0}[1 - P_{k0}]m_0}$$

$$= \frac{P_{kk}[1 - P_{kk}]m_k \mu_k + \sum_{j \neq k,0} P_{kj}[1 - P_{kj}]m_j \mu_j + P_{k0}[1 - P_{k0}]m_0 \mu_0}{P_{kk}[1 - P_{kk}]m_k + \sum_{j \neq k,0} P_{kj}[1 - P_{kj}]m_j + P_{k0}[1 - P_{k0}]m_0}$$

$$= \frac{\frac{e^b(K-1)}{(e^b+K-1)^2} m_k \mu_k + \frac{e^b+(K-2)}{(e^b+K-1)^2} \sum_{j \neq k,0} m_j \mu_j + \frac{1}{K}\left(1 - \frac{1}{K}\right) m_0 \mu_0}{\frac{e^b(K-1)}{(e^b+K-1)^2} m_k + \frac{e^b+(K-2)}{(e^b+K-1)^2} \sum_{j \neq k,0} m_j + \frac{1}{K}\left(1 - \frac{1}{K}\right) m_0}$$

$$= \frac{e^b(K-1)m_k \mu_k + [e^b + (K-2)] \sum_{j \neq k,0} m_j \mu_j + 0}{e^b(K-1)m_k + [e^b + (K-2)] \sum_{j \neq k,0} m_j + [e^b + K - 1]^2 \left[\frac{K-1}{K^2}\right] m_0},$$

because we have assumed that μ_0, the mean of the distribution of independent ideal points, is zero. In turn, our expression is

$$= \frac{[e^b(K-1) - (e^b + K - 2)]m_k \mu_k + [e^b + (K-2)] \sum_{j \neq 0} m_j \mu_j}{[e^b(K-1) - (e^b + K - 2)]m_k + [e^b + (K-2)] \sum_{j \neq 0} m_j + (e^b + K - 1)^2 \left(\frac{K-1}{K^2}\right) m_0}$$

$$= \frac{(K-2)(e^b - 1)m_k \mu_k}{(K-2)(e^b - 1)m_k + (e^b + K - 2)(1 - m_0) + (e^b + K - 1)^2 \left(\frac{K-1}{K^2}\right) m_0}$$

$$= \frac{(K-2)(e^b - 1)m_k \mu_k}{(K-2)(e^b - 1)m_k + (e^b + K - 2) + m_0[(e^b + K - 1)^2 \left(\frac{K-1}{K^2}\right) - (e^b + K - 2)]}$$

$$= c_k \mu_k,$$

where

$$c_k = \frac{(K-2)(e^b - 1)m_k}{(K-2)\left(e^b - 1\right)m_k + \left(e^b + K - 2\right) + m_0\left[\left(e^b + K - 1\right)^2 \left(\frac{K-1}{K^2}\right) - \left(e^b + K - 2\right)\right]}.$$

This completes the proof.

Simulation Analysis and an Approximation Formula for Nash Equilibria

In order to investigate the relationship between the optimal strategies $s_k(a)$ and the quantities $s_k(0)$, we computed Nash equilibria for randomly generated election scenarios in which we varied the number of candidates K (between 3 and 7), the means μ_k of the partisan groups (each chosen randomly from a uniform distribution between -2.5 and 2.5), the policy salience coefficient a (from a uniform distribution between 0 and 0.20), the partisan salience coefficient b (from a uniform distribution between 1.0 and 3.0), and the proportions m_k of partisans falling into each party group as well as the proportion m_0 of independent voters.[1] Five hundred elections (100 each with three candidates, four candidates, ..., seven candidates) were simulated, with parameters chosen as described here, generating a total of 2,500 simulated candidates.[2]

---

[1] The proportion of nonpartisans, m_o, was generated from a uniform distribution between 0 and 0.5, which is roughly the observed range for the proportions of nonpartisans in a number of historical elections. The partisan proportions m_k were generated from a uniform distribution – normalized so that together with m_o they summed to 1 – and under the restriction that no candidate's party would have more than ten times the partisans of any other. The latter was done to eliminate minor parties that would be hard to compare to real parties, since national election surveys typically contain only a few data points on partisans of such parties. The standard deviation of the positions of the partisans of each party and for independent voters was chosen uniformly from 0.5 to 1.0, roughly the range of deviations suggested by survey data, as will be shown.

[2] Equilibria were found to exist for all 500 of the randomly generated election scenarios. This result contrasts with the situation for simple deterministic multicandidate models, where, in general, equilibria do not even exist (Eaton and Lipsey 1975). It is consistent, however, with equilibrium analyses of multiparty elections in Israel (Schofield, Sened, and Nixon 1998), Norway (Adams and Merrill 1999a,b), and France (Adams and Merrill 2000). Given that the voting parameters used in the simulations were chosen to reflect the range of estimates reported in empirical voting studies, these simulation results – in combination with the empirical

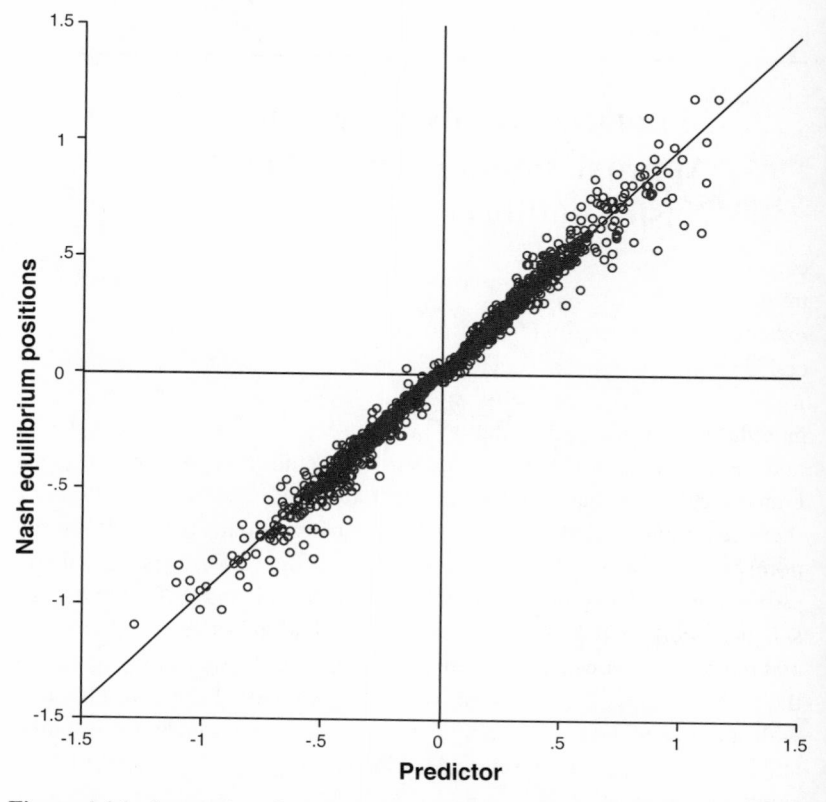

Figure A4.1. Scatterplot of exact Nash equilibrium positions versus approximate equilibrium positions predicted by equation A4.8.

By applying multiple regression to the simulation results, we estimated the following relationship:

$$s_k(a) \cong s_k(0) \pm 0.5a\sigma_V^2\sqrt{s_k(0)}\ln(K-1). \tag{A4.8}$$

The coefficient 0.5 is estimated from the multiple regression; the plus sign is used if μ_k is positive and the minus sign if it is negative. For fixed k, the configuration of equilibrium positions $s_k(a), k = 1, \ldots, K$, is an expansion of the configuration of the $s_k(0), k = 1, \ldots, K$; the degree of expansion depends primarily on policy salience. Figure A4.1 shows the relationship

studies cited earlier – strongly suggest that equilibria in vote-maximizing strategies will exist in real-world multicandidate elections.

between the exact equilibrium position obtained by the algorithm and the approximate predictor on the right-hand side of equation A4.8. The R-squared for this regression is 0.982; the mean absolute value of the error on a seven-point scale is 0.023; and 97 percent of the prediction errors are less than 0.1. That is, in most cases the formula given in equation A4.8 is a quite accurate approximation for $s_k(a)$.[3]

Thus, by the approximation equation A4.8, for a given value of a each candidate k's equilibrium position $s_k(a)$ becomes more extreme for more extreme values of $s_k(0)$.[4] *Hence the factors that cause $s_k(0)$ to become more/less extreme will exert similar effects for higher degrees of policy voting.*[5] In general, conclusions about the centrifugal (or centripetal) effects of the variables K, m_k, m_0, b, and μ_k, on $s_k(0)$ extend, at least approximately, to scenarios in which a significantly exceeds zero.

---

[3] The values of R-squared and prediction errors reported here were obtained by calibrating formula A4.8 from one simulated data set and then applying it to a fresh set of simulated data.

[4] This is because the second term on the right-hand side of equation A4.8 is $0.5a\sigma_V^2\sqrt{s_k(0)}\ln(K-1)$, and, by inspection, this term is invariably positive.

[5] One of the variables on the right-hand side of equation A4.8, K, affects the party's approximate equilibrium location $s_k(a)$ both through its effect on $s_k(0)$ and also through its inclusion in the second expression on the right-hand side of equation A4.8. Thus increases in K exercise centrifugal effects in two ways: by making $s_k(0)$ more extreme, and by increasing the value of $0.5a\sigma_V^2\sqrt{s_k(0)}\ln(K-1)$.

Derivations of Formulas Relating Electoral Factors to the Shrinkage Factor, c_k

4.4.1

The shrinkage factor, c_k, increases with m_k, the proportion of partisans of party k. To see this, it suffices to show that $1/c_k$ decreases as m_k increases. Because, by Theorem 4.1, $\frac{1}{c_k} = 1 + C\frac{(1-m_0)}{m_k} + D\frac{m_0}{m_k}$ where C and D are positive constants, it is clear that if m_0 is constant, then $1/c_k$ decreases as m_k increases. It can be shown that this relation continues to hold if m_0 decreases by no more than the increase in m_k.

4.4.2

If $m_0 = 0$, then c_k increases as b increases throughout the range of b. To see this, note that for $m_0 = 0$, $\frac{1}{c_k} = 1 + C\frac{[(e^b-1)+(K-1)]}{(e^b-1)}$, where C is a positive constant. The latter clearly decreases as b increases.

4.4.3

As the number of candidates K increases, c_k increases in value for any $b > 0$. To see this, it suffices to show that $1/c_k$ decreases as K increases. But

$$
\frac{1}{c_k} = 1 + \frac{1}{(e^b - 1)m_k} \left[\frac{(1 - m_0)e^b}{K - 2} + (1 - m_0) \right.
$$

$$
\left. + m_0 \frac{(e^b + K - 1)^2}{K^2} \frac{(K - 1)}{(K - 2)} \right].
$$

268

The first two terms in brackets decrease with K or are constant. The final term in brackets is of the form $m_0 \frac{(K+\varepsilon)^2}{K^2} \frac{(K-1)}{(K-2)}$, where $\varepsilon = e^b - 1 > 0$. But $\frac{K+\varepsilon}{K} = 1 + \frac{\varepsilon}{K}$ decreases as K increases, and so does $\frac{K-1}{K-2} = 1 + \frac{1}{K-2}$, which completes the argument.

Equilibria for Outcome-Oriented Motivations

The Kedar Model

In polities in which governments are formed by coalitions of parties or in which the government is frequently divided between an executive and a legislature of different parties, there is in general no single winning party or candidate. Rather, the outcome is a composite of the interests of several parties or their representatives. Accordingly, a rational voter may be expected to use his vote to try to achieve what that voter perceives as the best policy outcome rather than expressively voting for the most attractive party or candidate. Kedar (2002) develops a model that is intended to implement this objective. She notes, "In this model, voters reward parties not only for presenting a platform proximate to their own positions, but also for pulling policy outcomes in their direction" (2002: 2). Thus outcome-oriented behavior is menu-dependent. When policy is formed by compromise among multiple players, voters understand that their support for a single party will be diluted by other parties in the system. Hence they may have an incentive to "overpull" by voting for a party more extreme than their own policy position.

For example, suppose that four parties that are expected to form a governing coalition are of about equal strength and arranged from left to right in the following order: A, B, C, and D. The compromise policy is likely to be near the midpoint between parties B and C. A voter whose ideal point is near that of party B may prefer policy to the left of this midpoint and would thus like to move the coalition policy leftward. He may reason that a vote for party A (rather than party B) will help to strengthen the party that will pull the compromise furthest to the left. Thus, voting for party A helps to achieve the outcome the voter desires, although his preferred government policy outputs are closest to Party B's proposals.

Unlike Downsian motivations, outcome-oriented motivations encourage support for more extreme parties. Correspondingly, we might expect that Nash equilibria under the Kedar model might be more divergent than equilibria under a traditional Downsian model.

Specification of the Kedar Model

Kedar models policy outcome as an average of the policy positions of all parties in a parliament, $j = 1, \ldots, K$, weighted by their relative impacts, w_j, where $\sum_{j=1}^{K} w_j = 1$. Thus, if s_j denotes the policy position of party j, the policy outcome, P, is given by

$$P = \sum_{j=1}^{K} w_j s_j. \tag{A6.1}$$

A voter's utility for party j is the difference between the voter's utility for the policy outcome of a parliament including party j and the voter's utility for the same parliament without party j. If utility for a policy position is quadratic, the utility of a voter at location v for party j is thus:

$$U_j = -[(v - P)^2 - (v - P_{-j})^2], \tag{A6.2}$$

where P_{-j} denotes the policy outcome produced by a parliament of all parties except party j, as given by[1]

$$P_{-j} = \sum_{i \neq j} w_i s_i / (1 - w_j). \tag{A6.3}$$

---

[1] Adams and Merrill (2003b) show that the utility function specified in equation A6.2 is also given by

$$U_j = \frac{2w_j}{1 - w_j} [s_j - P] \left[v - \frac{P + P_{-j}}{2} \right].$$

This utility is mathematically similar to that defined by Rabinowitz and Macdonald (1989), except that in the Kedar model utility is also roughly proportional to w_j. It would appear, however, that a single voter would contribute about equally to any party rather than in proportion to the impact of w_j. A redefinition of the Kedar utility (as she suggests in her equation 7) leads to a more plausible interpretation. If the voter's utility for party j is the difference between her utility for the position in parliament *with her vote* and her utility for the position in parliament *without her vote* – a difference we denote by U_j' – Merrill and Adams (personal communication) obtain:

$$U_j' = \frac{2}{n - 1} (s_j - P)(v - P) - \left[\frac{1}{(n - 1)^2} (s_j - P)^2 \right],$$

where n is the number of voters, including the focal voter. This quantity is again related to the Rabinowitz–Macdonald utility, but this time without being proportional to the size of

Table A6.1. *Logit estimates for the Kedar and proximity models for Norway, 1989* (weights are proportional to vote shares) (N = 1,786)

	Proximity Model	Pure Kedar Model	Mixed Kedar–Proximity Model
Left–Right	**.111**	**.277**	**.248**
	(.007)	(.015)	(.017)
Party identification	**2.46**	**2.81**	**2.56**
	(.06)	(.06)	(.06)
Mixing parameter	(1.0)	(0.0)	**.362**
			(.038)
Log-likelihood	−1915.9	−1964.7	−1878.6

Party Strategies under the Kedar Model

We refer to P_{-j} as the *complementary* policy of party j. Note that from a voter's perspective, the ideal is to vote for a party whose position balances the complementary policy of that party, so that the overall weighted average is at the voter's ideal point.

Kedar further suggests that in practice, a voter's utility for a party is unlikely to be purely outcome-oriented, but rather represents both expressive and outcome-oriented motivations. Accordingly, utility may be a mixture of a proximity metric and the Kedar metric:

$$U_j = -\beta(v - s_j)^2 - (1 - \beta)[(v - P)^2 - (v - P_{-j})^2]. \quad (A6.4)$$

In order to compare the Kedar model and its implications with the traditional proximity model, we fit each using a one-dimensional, partisan-only conditional logit (CL) specification and compare the Nash equilibria among the pure Kedar, proximity, and mixed Kedar–proximity models.[2]

Table A6.1 provides the logit estimates for these probabilistic models, applied to the 1989 Norwegian parliamentary election (see section 6.2);

the party. The logic on which this formulation of the Kedar model is based appears more intuitive, and in fact provides a plausible interpretation or justification for the basic idea of the Rabinowitz–Macdonald utility function.

[2] Note that in a one-dimensional *deterministic* pure Kedar model, only the two parties whose complementary policies are the most extreme (one on the left and one on the right) receive any votes. This situation leads to instability rather than equilibrium, as parties jockey to achieve an extreme complementary policy. Instability may be reduced in a probabilistic model, especially if there is a proximity component.

Table A6.2. *Nash equilibria for the Kedar and proximity models for Norway, 1989* (weights are proportional to vote shares) (N = 1,786)

		Mixed Kedar–Proximity Model[a]		
	Proximity Model	Equilibrium	Vote (%)	P_{-j}
Socialist	**4.90**	**4.56**	9.8	5.67
Labor	**4.84**	**4.17**	30.5	6.30
Liberal	**5.43**	**5.52**	7.8	5.55
Center	**5.71**	**5.80**	9.0	5.54
Christian People's	**5.84**	**5.95**	9.7	5.51
Conservative	**6.56**	**7.23**	24.4	5.06
Progress	**6.16**	**6.73**	8.8	5.37

[a] Typically, there is no convergence for the pure Kedar model unless the party locations are constrained to the scale, in which case the equilibrium strategies are clumped at the end points of the scale. Clearly, the pure outcome-oriented model leads to unrealistically divergent strategies. Kedar introduces this model only as a component of a mixed model.

Table A6.2 presents the corresponding equilibrium configurations. No convergence to equilibrium occurs for the pure Kedar model, but equilibria are obtained for the mixed Kedar–proximity model, with mixing parameter β estimated from the CL specification.

In an effort to obtain weights for each party that represent at least a first approximation to the relative impact of the parties in coalition bargaining, we assume weights that are proportional to the vote shares received in the survey.[3] The mixing parameter for the mixed Kedar–proximity model is 0.362, suggesting that the Kedar component is more heavily weighted. The equilibrium configuration for the mixed model is almost twice as dispersed as that for the proximity model. Table A6.2 also presents the party vote shares at equilibrium, which are quite similar to the vote shares in the sample, and the complementary policies when the candidates are at equilibrium.

We note that under the mixed Kedar–proximity model, the equilibrium strategies for the smaller Socialist and Progress Parties were not more extreme than those for the center-left Labor and center-right Conservative Parties, although their actual (perceived) positions were more extreme. Simulation with only three candidates and artificial data helps to explain this

[3] These proportions are given in Table 6.3B.

result. In the simulation, two candidates – one representing a small party and the other a large party – were each placed at 3 on a 1–7 scale; a third candidate representing a large party was placed at 5. In a mixed model – even with a value of the mixing parameter β as low as 0.25 – the parties were only modestly dispersed at equilibrium, with the small leftist party slightly to the right of the larger leftist party.[4] Greater dispersion for larger parties is what we would expect under the proximity model (see Chapter 4); even a small dose of proximity appears to dominate positioning at equilibrium.

We conclude that outcome-oriented motivations may encourage voters to support more extreme parties, and correspondingly, that party configurations at equilibrium may be more dispersed than configurations under proximity motivations alone. Voter motivations alone, however, are insufficient to explain the frequently observed extreme positions advocated by small parties, particularly by ideologically based small parties.

---

[4] The equilibrium configuration for the pure Kedar model was $(-6.38, 4.29, 5.34)$, that for the mixed Kedar–proximity model with mixing parameter 0.25 was $(3.73, 3.64, 4.34)$.

Proof of Lemma 7.1

Lemma 7.1. Assume the conditions on the voter distribution detailed for our illustrative example. Then, under the unified turnout model, given $b > T_A$, $b > T_I$, and $b < \infty$, any possible equilibrium configuration (D, R) must satisfy $D < \mu < R$.

Proof. Note first that given the voter distribution assumed for our illustrative example, a candidate obtains as many votes as his opponent whenever he locates at a position symmetric to his opponent's position with respect to μ, the position of the median voter. This implies that both candidates must receive equal vote shares at equilibrium. Now suppose that $R < \mu$. Then if D pairs with R, each candidate receives support only from his own partisans and only from those in a common interval that is symmetric about the common point, $D = R < \mu$ (note that given $b > T_A$, $b > T_I$, and $b < \infty$, this interval must be of finite, nonzero length). Because this point is closer to the median Democratic voter than to the median Republican, this interval contains more Democrats than Republicans. Hence when $R < \mu$, the Democratic candidate can defeat the Republican, which violates the condition that any equilibrium configuration must find the candidates receiving equal vote shares.

Next consider the case where $R = \mu$. Now the Democratic candidate can defeat the Republican by locating at any point in the policy interval $[\mu_D, \mu]$ such that $b > (R - D)$. To see this, note that for such positioning the Democratic candidate receives support from Democrats located in the policy interval $[D - (b - T_A), D + (b - T_A)]$, while the Republican candidate is supported by Republicans located in the interval $[R - (b - T_A), R + (b - T_A)]$. (Here again the assumptions that $b > T_A$, $b > T_I$, and $b < \infty$

ensure that these intervals are of finite, nonzero length.) These policy intervals are of equal width, but the Democratic candidate's support interval is centered closer to the median Democratic partisan than the Republican candidate's support interval is to the median Republican partisan. This implies that the Democratic candidate has a positive vote margin vis-à-vis his opponent, which contradicts the condition for existence of equilibrium.

These arguments establish that $\mu < R$ for any possible equilibrium configuration. Analogous arguments show that equilibrium requires that $D < \mu$.

Derivations for the Unified Turnout Model

We assume that all voters are party identifiers, with f_D and f_R representing the densities of the two partisan groups, respectively. Under the unified turnout model, the transition points at which Democratic partisans switch from abstaining due to indifference to voting Democratic, or switch from voting Republican to abstaining, are given by

$$c_{DR} = \frac{D + R}{2} + \frac{b \pm T(I)}{2} \tag{A7.1}$$

as long as these points are between D and R (where b is the party ID salience parameter). The plus sign between the two main terms is replaced by a minus sign for Republican partisans. Focusing on Democratic partisans for the moment, the rates of movement of the transition points as D moves are given by $\frac{\partial c_{DR}}{\partial D} = \frac{1}{2}$. The points at which $T(A) = U(D)$ are given by $c_A = D \pm [b - T(A)]$ as long as $b > T(A)$ (otherwise, all voters abstain). It follows that $\frac{\partial c_A}{\partial D} = 1$. Thus, for Democratic partisans, the rate of change in the margin of the Democrat over the Republican as D moves is

$$\frac{1}{2}f_D\left(\frac{D+R}{2} + \frac{b - T(I)}{2}\right) + \frac{1}{2}f_D\left(\frac{D+R}{2} + \frac{b + T(I)}{2}\right)$$
$$-f_D(D - [b - T(A)]) + f_D(D + [b - T(A)]). \tag{A7.2}$$

Similarly, for Republican partisans, the rate of change in the margin for the Democrat as D moves is

$$\frac{1}{2}f_R\left(\frac{D+R}{2} + \frac{-b - T(I)}{2}\right) + \frac{1}{2}f_R\left(\frac{D+R}{2} + \frac{-b + T(I)}{2}\right)$$
$$-f_R(D - [b - T(A)]) + f_R(D + [b - T(A)]). \tag{A7.3}$$

Note that inclusion of the indifference threshold in the model (equations A7.2 and A7.3) replaces the densities evaluated at $\frac{D+R}{2} \pm \frac{b}{2}$ with averages of the densities at pairs of points on either side of these values, so that optimal values of D and R are only modestly affected.

Coding and Model Specifications

Party identification is scored at one if the respondent identified with the candidate's party and zero otherwise; ideological distance is the negative of the squared distance between the respondent's self-placement and the candidate's position along the liberal–conservative scale; policy distance is the negative of the mean squared distance between the respondent's self-placements and the candidate's positions along the policy scales; candidate character is calculated as the average score the respondent assigned to the candidate on attributes such as intelligence, honesty, and leadership ability; race is scored at one if the respondent was black and zero otherwise; retrospective evaluation of the economy is coded from -2 (much worse) to 2 (much better). Each variable was included in the specifications for both the Democratic and Republican candidates' utilities *except* for race, which was omitted from the Republican candidate's utility. This was necessary in order to identify the model, since, as discussed in section 8.3, race was also included in the specifications for respondents' indifference and alienation thresholds.

Education is coded on a seven-point scale ranging from less than high school education to post baccalaureate degree; political efficacy is calculated as the citizen's mean self-placement on the ANES political efficacy scales (recoded on a scale from zero to one representing low to high efficacy); previous vote is scored at one if the respondent reported having voted in the previous presidential election and zero otherwise; perceived election closeness is scored at one if the respondent believed the presidential election would be close and zero otherwise. Each variable was included in the specifications for both indifference and alienation except for election closeness, which was included only in the indifference specification. Our logic for this specification is that election closeness is a proxy for the respondent's perception of the likelihood of casting a decisive ballot, which is relevant to the instrumental decision to abstain as a result of indifference but not to the expressive decision to abstain due to alienation (see Adams, Dow, and Merrill 2001).

Equations A8.1–A8.4 display the specifications in the unified turnout model for the respondents' candidate utilities, their alienation thresholds, and their indifference thresholds. The D and B designators refer to Dukakis and Bush, respectively:

$$U_i(D) = b_1(\text{Party ID}) - b_2 \text{ (squared ideological distance}$$
$$\text{between } i \text{ and } D)$$
$$- b_3 \text{ (mean squared policy distance between } i \text{ and } D)$$
$$+ b_4 \text{ (}D \text{ character)}$$
$$+ b_5 \text{ (retrospective economy)} + b_6 \text{ (race)} + \varepsilon_{iD}$$
$$= V_i(D) + \varepsilon_{iD} \tag{A8.1}$$

$$U_i(B) = b_7 + b_1 \text{ (party ID)} - b_2 \text{ (squared ideological distance}$$
$$\text{between } i \text{ and } B)$$
$$- b_3 \text{ (mean squared policy distance between } i \text{ and } B)$$
$$+ b_4 \text{ (}B \text{ character)}$$
$$+ b_8 \text{ (retrospective economy)} + \varepsilon_{iB}$$
$$= V_i(B) + \varepsilon_{iB} \tag{A8.2}$$

$$T_i(A) = b_9 + b_{10} \text{ (race)} + b_{11} \text{ (efficacy)} + b_{12} \text{ (previous vote)}$$
$$+ b_{13} \text{ (education)} + \varepsilon_{iA}$$
$$= V_i(A) + \varepsilon_{iA} \tag{A8.3}$$

$$T_i(I) = \exp[b_{14} + b_{15} \text{ (race)} + b_{16} \text{ (efficacy)} + b_{17} \text{ (previous vote)}$$
$$+ b_{18} \text{ (education)} + b_{19} \text{ (perceived election closeness)]}$$
$$= V_i(I). \tag{A8.4}$$

Note that in these equations, we constrain the coefficients for partisanship, ideology, policies, and character (coefficients $b_1 - b_4$) to be equal. This imposes the assumption that these variables are equally salient with respect to respondents' evaluations of each candidate. Our data analysis confirms that this is a reasonable constraint.

Finally, the conditional logit choice probabilities $P_i(D)$ and $P_i(R)$ associated with voting for Dukakis and Bush, respectively, are given by:

$$P_i(D) = e^{V_i(D)} \Big/ \Big[e^{V_i(D)} + e^{V_i(R)+V_i(I)} + e^{V_i(A)} \Big] \tag{A8.5}$$

and

$$P_i(R) = e^{V_i(R)} \Big/ \Big[e^{V_i(D)+V_i(I)} + e^{V_i(R)} + e^{V_i(A)} \Big], \tag{A8.6}$$

where the specifications for $V_i(D)$, $V_i(R)$, $V_i(A)$, and $V_i(I)$ are given in equations A8.1–A8.4. The probability of abstention is $P_i(\text{abstain}) = [1 - P_i(D) - P_i(R)]$.

Alternative Turnout Models

Candidate Strategies for a Policy-only Turnout Model

Here we assess two alternative voting models concerning candidate strategies that place Hypotheses 1 and 2 (introduced in section 8.2) in perspective. Both the illustrative arguments from Chapter 7, section 7.3 and the results presented in prior spatial modeling studies (e.g., Riker and Ordeshook 1968; Hinich and Ordeshook 1970; Enelow and Hinich 1984; Erikson and Romero 1990; Anderson and Glomm 1992) suggest the following hypotheses for margin-maximizing candidates:

H3: For a *policy-only turnout model* – that is, one that omits measured nonpolicy variables – the two candidates' optimal policy positions converge along the policy scales.[1]

H4: For a *unified turnout model that omits abstention due to alienation* – that is, one in which abstention is specified as being motivated solely by indifference – the two candidates' optimal policy positions converge along the policy scales.

Hypotheses 3 and 4 are important because if they are supported, these results will bolster our central theoretical claim that while the *combination* of voters' non-policy-related motivations and abstention due to alienation

---

[1] We note that some earlier spatial modeling studies (see Downs 1957: Chapter 8; Ordeshook 1969) have demonstrated the possibility of nonconvergence when voter turnout is variable, provided that the voter distribution is not single-peaked. However, given that the distributions of respondents' self-placements along the policy scales included in the ANES are virtually always single-peaked, we should expect that Hypothesis 3 will hold in empirical applications to ANES data.

motivates candidate divergence (H1), neither alienation nor nonpolicy motivations alone motivates divergence (H3 – H4).

In contrast to the unified turnout model explored earlier, most spatial modeling studies omit measured nonpolicy variables. First, we evaluate Hypothesis 3, that such a voting model motivates candidates to present convergent policies – the standard result in the spatial modeling literature. In order to explore this hypothesis, we estimated the parameters of a *policy-only turnout model* for the 1988 ANES that included only respondents' policy evaluations as independent variables. The parameter estimates for this model are reported in Table A8.1. Note that the log-likelihood for this policy-only specification is significantly worse than the log-likelihood for the unified specification ($p < .001$), suggesting that in excluding nonpolicy variables, the policy-only turnout model loses significant explanatory power.

Table A8.2 presents projected candidate support and abstention rates for alternative models, with the candidates located at their actual (perceived) positions along the various policy dimensions. Table A8.3 reports the candidates' computed policy optima for the alternative turnout models, with parametric bootstrap standard errors in parentheses. As expected, for the policy-only turnout model, these results support Hypothesis 3, that the policy-only model motivates the candidates to present convergent policies in equilibrium.

Candidate Strategies for a Unified
Indifference-only Turnout Model

In their analysis of candidate strategies and the behavioral model of the vote, Erikson and Romero (1990: 1120–1) analyzed candidates' policy strategies in the 1988 presidential election for a unified turnout model where abstention was specified as being motivated solely by indifference. Here we evaluate Hypothesis 4, that such a model motivates candidates to present convergent policies – the conclusion suggested by our illustrative arguments and supported by Erikson and Romero's empirical results. In order to explore this hypothesis, we estimated the parameters of a *unified indifference-only turnout model* that was identical to the unified turnout specification estimated earlier, *except* that we omitted the alienation threshold (i.e., the specification comprised the candidate utility functions given earlier by equation 7.3 and the

Table A8.1. *Conditional logit equations for the 1988 vote, for alternative voting models* (N = 1,389)

Voting Model	Independent Variables	Candidate Utilities (1)		Indifference Threshold (2)		Alienation Threshold (3)	
Unified	Intercept (Bush)	.127	(.093)	1.97**	(.23)	1.19*	(.52)
Turnout	Ideology	.062**	(.020)				
Model	Policy	.155**	(.033)				
	Party identification	1.12**	(.11)				
	Candidate character	1.27**	(.20)				
	Retrospective national economy (Dukakis)	−.36**	(.11)				
	Retrosp. econ. (Bush)	−.23*	(.11)				
	Black (Dukakis)	1.11*	(.56)	−.09	(.21)	1.91**	(.59)
	Political efficacy			−2.89**	(.65)	.91	(.52)
	Voted in 1984			−1.65**	(.24)	−1.17**	(.31)
	Education			.01	(.05)	−.07	(.06)
	Close election			−.15	(.15)		
	Log-likelihood	−929.38					
Policy-only	Intercept (Bush)	.032	(.070)	−.35*	(.14)	−1.04**	(.14)
Turnout	Ideology	.142**	(.019)				
Model	Policy	.282**	(.026)				
	Log-likelihood	−1315.59					
Unified	Intercept (Bush)	.070	(.064)	1.59**	(.10)		
Indifference-	Ideology	.028*	(.013)				
only	Policy	.032	(.024)				
Turnout	Party identification	.96**	(.09)				
Model	Candidate character	1.11**	(.16)				
	Retrosp. econ. (Dukakis)	−.04	(.04)				
	Retrosp. econ. (Bush)	.04	(.04)				
	Black (Dukakis)	.37	(.26)	.23*	(.11)		
	Political efficacy			−.99**	(.14)		
	Voted in 1984			−.96**	(.06)		
	Education			−.02	(.02)		
	Close election			−.12	(.07)		
	Log-likelihood	−961.96					

Note: The voting specifications used to estimate these parameters are given by equations A8.4–A8.7 in Appendix 8.1. As noted in this appendix, the parameters for ideological distance, policy distance, party identification, and candidate character are constrained to have equal values with respect to respondents' utilities for Dukakis and Bush. One asterisk signifies statistical significance at the .05 level; two asterisks signify statistical significance at the .01 level. Standard errors are in parentheses.

Table A8.2. *Projected candidate support and abstention rates for alternative voting models for the 1988 ANES*

	Bush Vote	Dukakis Vote	Abstain
ANES distribution	.262	.231	.507
Unified turnout model	.261	.233	.505
Policy-only turnout model	.262	.230	.508
Unified indifference-only turnout model	.256	.234	.510

Note: The projected votes and abstention rate are computed by averaging the projected voting probabilities across all respondents, using the parameters reported in Table A8.1.

Table A8.3. *Candidate equilibria for alternative voting models*

Policy-only Turnout Model			
Policy Dimension	Dukakis	Bush	Policy Divergence[a]
Ideology	4.41 (.01)	4.41 (.01)	0
Domestic spending	3.96 (.01)	3.96 (.01)	0
Defense spending	3.90 (.003)	3.90 (.003)	0
Health insurance	4.01 (.01)	4.01 (.01)	0
Aid to minorities	4.63 (.01)	4.63 (.01)	0
Government jobs	4.62 (.01)	4.62 (.01)	0
Dealing with Russia	3.70 (.01)	3.70 (.01)	0
Women's role	2.41 (.01)	2.41 (.01)	0

Unified Indifference-only Turnout Model			
Policy Dimension	Dukakis	Bush	Policy Divergence[a]
Ideology	4.41 (.03)	4.41 (.02)	0
Domestic spending	3.97 (.03)	3.97 (.02)	0
Defense spending	3.90 (.02)	3.90 (.01)	0
Health insurance	4.01 (.03)	4.01 (.02)	0
Aid to minorities	4.58 (.01)	4.58 (.02)	0
Government jobs	4.62 (.03)	4.62 (.02)	0
Dealing with Russia	3.70 (.01)	3.70 (.01)	0
Women's role	2.49 (.01)	2.49 (.01)	0

[a] Policy divergence represents the distance between the candidates' equilibrium positions reported in columns 1–2.

Note: The candidates' policy optima were estimated using the parameters reported for the unified policy-only turnout model and the unified indifference-only turnout model in Table A8.1. These equilibrium positions were located using the equilibrium algorithm described in Appendix 4.1. This equilibrium is such that no candidate can increase his expected margin over his opponent by moving along one issue dimension at a time. Parametric bootstrap standard errors are given in parentheses.

indifference threshold given by equation 7.2 in Chapter 7). The parameter estimates for this model are given in Table A8.1.[2]

The candidates' computed policy optima for the unified indifference-only turnout model (reported in Table A8.3) support Hypothesis 4, that this model motivates the candidates to present convergent policies. The candidates' equilibrium positions are virtually identical to those obtained by Erikson and Romero (1990: see Table 2, column 8).

We conclude that while models that jointly incorporate nonpolicy variables and the possibility of abstention due to alienation motivate the candidates to present divergent policies shaded in the direction of their partisan constituencies, models that omit nonpolicy variables and models that omit abstention resulting from alienation do not. We find that the nonpolicy factors that influence voters – even if the candidates in the course of an election campaign cannot manipulate them – strongly affect the logic of candidates' spatial competition. Furthermore, the distinction between abstention resulting from alienation and abstention due to indifference is also crucial for understanding candidate strategies, since we find that alienation – but not indifference – motivates candidate divergence.

---

[2] The likelihood ratio test comparing the unified turnout model with and without the alienation component is significant at the .001 level.

Proof of Theorem 11.1

Theorem 11.1. If the measured component v of the valence $= 0$, if the candidates' preferred positions D and R are symmetric about the median of the voter distribution, and if an equilibrium exists with $d = -r$, then the divergence between strategies is given by

$$r - d = \frac{-\sqrt{\pi/2}\sigma_V + \sqrt{(\pi/2)\sigma_V^2 + 2\sqrt{2\pi}\sigma_V(R - D)^2}}{2(R - D)}.$$

Proof. If an equilibrium exists, we must have $\frac{\partial U_D}{\partial d} = \frac{\partial U_R}{\partial r} = 0$. We observe that

$$\frac{\partial F}{\partial d} = \phi\left[\frac{r^2 - d^2}{\sigma_V}\right]\frac{2r}{\sigma_V} = \phi(0)\frac{2r}{\sigma_V} = \frac{\partial F}{\partial r}, \tag{A11.1}$$

where ϕ denotes the standard normal density function (note that $d = -r$ by assumption). We denote the common value of $\frac{\partial F}{\partial d}$ and $\frac{\partial F}{\partial r}$ as $F'(d, r)$. It follows that

$$\frac{\partial U_D}{\partial d} - \frac{\partial U_R}{\partial r} = F'(d, r)[-(d - D)^2 + (r - D)^2 + (d - R)^2 - (r - R)^2]$$

$$-2F(d, r)[(d - D) + (r - R)] + 2(r - R)$$

$$= 0. \tag{A11.2}$$

For convenience, write $x_1 = (d - D)$ and $x_2 = (R - r)$. Under the assumptions of the theorem, $x_1 = x_2$. Setting their common value to x, equation (A11.2) yields:

$$\frac{\partial U_D}{\partial d} - \frac{\partial U_R}{\partial r} = F'(d, r)[4r(2x + 2r)] - 2x = 0. \tag{A11.3}$$

Noting that $(R - D) = 2x + 2r$, and solving for r, we obtain

$$
\begin{aligned}
r &= \frac{(R - D)}{2 + 4F'(d, r)(R - D)} \\
&= \frac{R - D}{2 + 4\phi[(r^2 - d^2)/\sigma_V]\frac{2r}{\sigma_V}(R - D)} \\
&= \frac{R - D}{2 + \frac{8r}{\sqrt{2\pi}\sigma_V}(R - D)}.
\end{aligned}
\tag{A11.4}
$$

The last equality follows because $d = -r$. Solving the resulting quadratic equation for r, we obtain

$$
r - d = \frac{-\sqrt{\pi/2}\sigma_V + \sqrt{(\pi/2)\sigma_V^2 + 2\sqrt{2\pi}\sigma_V(R - D)^2}}{2(R - D)}.
\tag{A11.5}
$$

Empirical Estimation of the Mean and Standard Deviation of Valence Effects

Order-of-Magnitude Estimates for v and σ_v

We obtain order-of-magnitude estimates for both v and σ_v from the typical margin of victory and the typical accuracy of national polls in American and French presidential elections. Let g be the probability density of the voter distribution. Initially, we focus on the expected value of $v + X$, which is v. Elementary algebra shows that this term, v, shifts the cut-point between supporters of D and of R by the quantity $v/[2(r - d)]$ and thus adds to D's vote share a proportion given by the integral of g over an interval of length $v/[2(r - d)]$.

We use the traditional 1–7 scales of the American National Election Study and French Presidential Election Study. Because the interval just described is typically near the middle of the scale where, empirically, values of g are on the order of 0.20, that integral is of the order of $0.20v/[2(r - d)]$. Typically, in American and French elections, d is near 3.0 and r is near 5.0 (or 6.0), and the vote share of the winner ranges from 50 percent to about 62 percent[1] – that is, a range of about twelve percentage points, or 0.12 when expressed as a proportion. Because variation in the winner's margin from election to election is due only in part to valence effects, this represents only an upper bound for the effect of valence characteristics on vote share. For this upper

---

[1] The single presidential election vote that falls outside this range is the 2002 French election, in which the incumbent Chirac received over 80 percent of the second-round vote. This election was exceptional in that it pitted a right-wing candidate (Chirac) against an extreme right-wing opponent (Le Pen). All other postwar presidential elections in France and the United States have matched a candidate from a traditionally leftist or center-left party against an opponent from a center-right or right-wing party.

bound for v, we have, very roughly, $0.12 = 0.20v/[2(5.0 - 3.0)]$, or $v \cong 2.4$. Thus values of v in the range from 0 to 2 or 3 appear to be plausible.

Next, as we will argue, polling inaccuracy is typically on the order of four percentage points – that is, the proportion 0.04. Solving for σ_V in $0.04 = 0.20\sigma_V/[2(5.0 - 3.0)]$ yields $\sigma_V \cong 0.8$. If, however, polling inaccuracy ranges from 0.02 to 0.08 (see below), σ_V might lie in the range from 0.4 to 1.6. Rounding off, we suggest a plausible range from 0.5 to 1.5.

Estimates of Polling Accuracy

Perhaps the most practical way to assess the uncertainty about election outcomes that is likely to affect campaign strategy is to compare polling results substantially before elections – say, at the beginning of September for American presidential elections (the traditional beginning of the campaign) – with the actual results of the elections. Academic studies of presidential election forecasting report conflicting findings on the degree to which elections can be accurately forecast in advance, with some studies suggesting that the presidential vote can usually be predicted to within about two percentage points (see Bartels and Zaller 2001) and others that forecast errors are typically on the order of four to eight percentage points (Campbell 1996).[2]

Given the wide range of error rates reported in these studies – and the further complicating factor that real-world candidates may base their forecasts on different data than do political scientists – we shall explore a wide range of values for election uncertainty in our empirical applications to the

---

[2] The standard deviation of the error of early September trial-heat polls for the twelve American presidential elections from 1948 to 1992 (by *error* we mean the difference between the poll results and the actual results) is 4.27 percentage points, as computed from the data in Campbell (1996: Table 3). For use in this chapter, we have rounded this to 4 percent, or 0.04 as a proportion. The corresponding measure of accuracy of Gallup polls in June is 8.55 percentage points (see Campbell 1996: Table 2). It is reasonable to believe that parties and candidates discount such early polls, realizing that better predictions of the division of the vote can be obtained by incorporating other variables, such as historical party allegiance. Thus it is difficult to believe that the uncertainty is as high as 8 or 9 percent as late as June of the election year. On the other hand, more accurate forecasts may be obtained by incorporating economic data in addition to early September trial-heat polls. Based on data in Campbell (1996: Table 6), the standard deviation of the accuracy of out-of-sample forecasts using a model involving economic data is only 1.68 percentage points. We believe that this is a low estimate for uncertainty from the perspective of the candidates, because there is little evidence that the candidates actually use such forecasts. Studies of election forecasting in French presidential elections are far less extensive than those for the United States, but they suggest that the uncertainty French presidential candidates experience is at least as great as that for U.S. candidates (see Charlot and Charlot 1997).

1988 U.S. and French presidential elections. To the extent that alternative assumptions about election uncertainty motivate similar candidate positioning, we shall have increased confidence in our substantive conclusions about policy-seeking candidates' strategies in real-world elections. Following Campbell (1996), we will use 0.04 as our base estimate of the degree of election uncertainty, but also present results from 0.02 to 0.08, in order to provide perspective.

References

Aardal, Bernt. 1990. "The Norwegian Parliamentary Election of 1989." *Electoral Studies* 9: 151–8.

Aardal, Bernt, and Henry Valen. 1997. "The Storting Elections of 1989 and 1993: Norwegian Politics in Perspective." In *Challenges to Political Parties: The Case of Norway*, edited by Kaare Strom and Lars Svasand. Ann Arbor: University of Michigan Press.

Adams, James. 1998. "Partisan Voting and Multiparty Spatial Competition: The Pressure for Responsible Parties." *Journal of Theoretical Politics* 10: 5–31.

Adams, James. 1999a. "Multicandidate Spatial Competition with Probabilistic Voting." *Public Choice* 99: 259–74.

Adams, James. 1999b. "Policy Divergence in Multiparty Probabilistic Spatial Voting." *Public Choice* 100: 103–22.

Adams, James. 2001a. "A Theory of Spatial Competition with Biased Voters: Party Policies Viewed Temporally and Comparatively." *British Journal of Political Science* 31: 121–58.

Adams, James. 2001b. *Party Competition and Responsible Party Government: A Theory of Spatial Competition Based upon Insights from Behavioral Voting Research.* Ann Arbor: University of Michigan Press.

Adams, James, Benjamin Bishin, and Jay Dow. 2004. "Representation in Congressional Campaigns: Evidence for Directional/Discounting Motivations in United States Senate Elections." *Journal of Politics* 66 (2): 348–73.

Adams, James, Michael Clark, Lawrence Ezrow, and Garrett Glasgow. Forthcoming. "Understanding Change and Stability in Party Ideologies: Do Parties Respond to Public Opinion or to Past Election Results?" *British Journal of Political Science.*

Adams, James, Jay Dow, and Samuel Merrill III. 2001. "The Political Consequences of Abstention Due to Alienation and Indifference: Applications to Presidential Elections." Paper presented at the annual meeting of the American Political Science Association, San Francisco, CA, August 30–September 2.

293

Adams, James, and Samuel Merrill III. 1998. "A Downsian Model of Candidate Competition in the 1988 French Presidential Election." Paper presented at the annual meeting of the Western Political Science Association, Los Angeles, CA, March 10–12.

Adams, James, and Samuel Merrill III. 1999a. "Party Policy Equilibria for Alternative Spatial Voting Models: An Application to the Norwegian Storting." *European Journal of Political Research* 36: 235–55.

Adams, James, and Samuel Merrill III. 1999b. "Modeling Party Strategies and Policy Representation in Multiparty Elections: Why Are Strategies So Extreme?" *American Journal of Political Science* 43: 765–91.

Adams, James, and Samuel Merrill III. 2000. "Spatial Models of Candidate Competition and the 1988 French Presidential Election: Are Presidential Candidates Vote-Maximizers?" *Journal of Politics* 62: 729–56.

Adams, James, and Samuel Merrill III. 2003a. "Voter Turnout and Candidate Strategies in American Elections." *Journal of Politics* 65: 161–89.

Adams, James, and Samuel Merrill III. 2003b. "Policy-Seeking Motivations When One Candidate Has a Valence Advantage: Strategic Implications and Emprical Applications to Presidential Elections." Paper presented at the annual meeting of the American Political Science Association, Philadelphia, PA, August 28–31.

Aldrich, John. 1983a. "A Downsian Spatial Model with Party Activism." *American Political Science Review* 77: 974–90.

Aldrich, John. 1983b. "A Spatial Model with Party Activists: Implications for Electoral Dynamics." *Public Choice* 41: 63–100.

Aldrich, John. 1995. *Why Parties? The Origins and Transformation of Party Politics in America.* Chicago: University of Chicago Press.

Alesina, Alberto, and Howard Rosenthal. 1995. *Partisan Politics, Divided Government, and the Economy.* New York: Cambridge University Press.

Alvarez, R. Michael. 1997. *Information and Elections.* Ann Arbor: University of Michigan Press.

Alvarez, R. Michael, and Jonathan Nagler. 1995. "Economics, Issues and the Perot Candidacy: Voter Choice in the 1992 Presidential Election." *American Journal of Political Science* 39: 714–44.

Alvarez, R. Michael, and Jonathan Nagler. 1998a. "When Politics and Models Collide: Estimating Models of Multiparty Elections." *American Journal of Political Science* 42: 55–96.

Alvarez, R. Michael, and Jonathan Nagler. 1998b. "Economics, Entitlements, and Social Issues: Voter Choice in the 1996 Presidential Election." *American Journal of Political Science* 42: 1349–63.

Alvarez, R. Michael, Jonathan Nagler, and Shaun Bowler. 2000. "Issues, Economics, and the Dynamics of Multiparty Elections: The 1987 British General Election." *American Political Science Review* 94: 131–49.

Alvarez, R. Michael, Jonathan Nagler, and Jennifer Willette. 2000. "Measuring the Relative Impact of Issues and the Economy in Democratic Elections." *Electoral Studies* 19: 237–53.

Anderson, Simon, and Gerhard Glomm. 1992. "Alienation, Indifference, and the Choice of Ideological Position." *Social Choice and Welfare* 9: 17–31.

Ansolabehere, Stephen, and James Snyder. 2000. "Valence Politics and Equilibrium in Spatial Elections Models." *Public Choice* 103: 327–36.

Aranson, Peter, and Peter C. Ordeshook. 1972. "Spatial Strategy for Sequential Elections." In *Probability Models of Collective Decision Making*, edited by R. Niemi and Herbert Weisberg. Columbus, OH: Merrill.

Austen-Smith, David. 1986. "Legislative Coalitions and Electoral Equilibrium." *Public Choice* 50: 18–210.

Austen-Smith, David, and Jeffery Banks. 1988. "Elections, Coalitions, and Legislative Outcomes." *American Political Science Review* 82: 405–22.

Axelrod, Robert. 1970. *Conflict of Interest*. Chicago: Markham.

Baker, Kendall, Russell Dalton, and Kai Hildebrandt. 1981. *Germany Transformed: Political Culture and the New Politics*. Cambridge, MA: Harvard University Press.

Barnes, Samuel. 1977. *Representation in Italy*. Chicago: University of Chicago Press.

Baron, David. 1994. "Electoral Competition with Informed and Uninformed Voters." *American Political Science Review* 88: 33–47.

Bartels, Larry, and John Zaller. 2001. "Presidential Vote Models: A Recount." *PS: Political Science and Politics* 34: 9–20.

Bartle, John. 1998. "Left–Right Position Matters, but Does Social Class? Causal Models of the 1992 British General Election." *British Journal of Political Science* 28: 501–29.

Berger, Mark, Michael Munger, and Richard Potthoff. 2000. "The Downsian Model Predicts Divergence." *Journal of Theoretical Politics* 12: 228–40.

Berinski, Adam, and Jeffrey Lewis. 2001. "Voting under Uncertainty: Estimating Voters' Risk Preferences." Paper presented at the annual meeting of the American Political Science Association, San Francisco, CA, August 30–September 2.

Bishin, Benjamin. 2000. "Constituency Influence in Congress: Does Subconstituency Matter?" *Legislative Studies Quarterly* 25: 389–415.

Brady, Henry, and Paul Sniderman. 1985. "Attitude Attribution: A Group Basis for Political Reasoning." *American Political Science Review* 79: 143–63.

Brams, Steven, and Samuel Merrill III. 1991. "Final-Offer Arbitration with a Bonus." *European Journal of Political Economy* 7: 79–92.

Brody, Richard A., and Bernard Grofman. 1982. "Stimulus Differentiation versus Stimulus Complexity as Factors Affecting Turnout in Two-Candidate and Multicandidate Races." *Political Behavior* 4: 83–92.

Brody, Richard A., and Benjamin Page. 1973. "Indifference, Alienation, and Rational Decisions: The Effects of Candidate Evaluations on Turnout and the Vote." *Public Choice* 15: 1–17.

Budge, Ian. 1994. "A New Theory of Party Competition: Uncertainty, Ideology, and Policy Equilibria Viewed Comparatively and Temporally." *British Journal of Political Science* 24: 443–67.

Budge, Ian, and Michael McDonald. 2003. "Elections, Parties, and Democracy: Conferring the Median Mandate." Unpublished manuscript.

Burden, Barry. 2000a. "The Polarizing Effects of Congressional Primaries." In *Congressional Primaries and the Politics of Representation*, edited by Peter Galderisi, Marni Ezra, and Michael Lyons. New York: Rowman and Littlefield.

Burden, Barry. 2000b. "Voter Turnout and the National Election Studies." *Political Analysis* 8: 389–98.

Burden, Barry, and David Kimball. 2002. *Why Americans Split Their Tickets: Campaigns, Competition, and Divided Government*. Ann Arbor: University of Michigan Press.

Burden, Barry, and Dean Lacy. 1999. "The Vote-Stealing and Turnout Effects of Third-Party Candidates in United States Presidential Elections, 1968–1996." Paper presented at the annual meeting of the American Political Science Association, Atlanta, GA, September 1–4.

Butler, David, and Donald Stokes. 1969. *Political Change in Britain*. New York: St. Martin's.

Callander, Steven. 2000. "Electoral Competition with Entry: Non-Centrist Equilibria and the Domain of Duverger's Law." Paper presented at the annual meeting of the Public Choice Society, Charleston, SC, March 10–12.

Callander, Steven, and Simon Wilkie. 2002. "Candidate Flexibility." Paper presented at the annual meeting of the Public Choice Society, San Diego, CA, March 16–18.

Calvert, Randall. 1985. "Robustness of the Multidimensional Voting Model: Candidates, Motivations, Uncertainty, and Convergence." *American Journal of Political Science* 29: 69–95.

Cameron, Charles, and James Enelow. 1992. "Asymmetric Policy Effects, Campaign Contributions, and the Spatial Theory of Elections." *Mathematical and Computer Modeling* 16: 117–32.

Campbell, Angus, Philip Converse, Warren Miller, and Donald Stokes. 1960. *The American Voter*. New York: Wiley.

Campbell, James. 1996. "Polls and Votes: The Trial-Heat Presidential Election Forecasting Model, Certainty, and Political Campaigns." *American Politics Quarterly* 24: 408–33.

Chapman, David. 1967. "Models of the Working of a Two-Party Electoral System – I." *Papers on Non-Market Decision-Making* 3: 19–38.

Chapman, David. 1968. "Models of the Working of a Two-Party Electoral System – II." *Public Choice* 5: 19–38.

Chappell, Henry W., and William R. Keech. 1986. "Policy Motivation and Party Differences in a Dynamic Spatial Model of Party Competition." *American Political Science Review* 80: 881–99.

Charlot, Jean, and Monica Charlot. 1997. "The Polls and the 1995 Election." In *French Presidentialism and the Election of 1995*, edited by John Gaffney and Lorna Mills. Aldershot, UK: Ashgate.

Coleman, James. 1971. "Internal Processes Governing Party Positions in Elections." *Public Choice* 11: 35–60.

Conover, Pamela Johnston, and Stanley Feldman. 1986. "The Role of Inference in the Perception of Political Candidates." In *Political Cognition*, edited by Richard R. Lau and David O. Sears. Hillsdale, NJ: Erlbaum.

Converse, Philip. 1964. "The Nature of Belief Systems in Mass Publics." In *Ideology and Discontent*, edited by David Apter. New York: Free Press.

Converse, Philip. 1970. "Attitudes and Nonattitudes: Continuation of a Dialogue." In *Quantitative Analysis of Social Problems*, edited by E. Tufte. Reading, MA: Addison-Wesley.

Converse, Philip, and Roy Pierce. 1986. *Political Representation in France*. Cambridge, MA: Harvard University Press.

Converse, Philip, and Roy Pierce. 1993. "Comment on Fleury and Lewis-Beck." *Journal of Politics* 55: 1110–17.

Coughlin, Peter J. 1992. *Probabilistic Voting Theory*. Cambridge: Cambridge University Press.

Cox, Gary. 1984. "An Expected-Utility Model of Electoral Competition." *Quality and Quantity* 18: 337–49.

Cox, Gary W. 1990. "Centripetal and Centrifugal Incentives in Electoral Systems." *American Journal of Political Science* 34: 903–35.

Cox, Gary W. 1997. *Making Votes Count*. Cambridge: Cambridge University Press.

Dalton, Russell. 1985. "Political Parties and Political Representation." *Comparative Political Studies* 17: 267–99.

Dalton, Russell. 2002. *Citizen Politics: Public Opinion and Political Parties in Advanced Industrial Societies*, 3rd ed. Chatham, NJ: Chatham House.

Davis, Otto, Melvin Hinich, and Peter Ordeshook. 1970. "An Expository Development of a Mathematical Model of the Electoral Process." *American Political Science Review* 64: 426–48.

de Palma, A., V. Ginsberg, M. Labbe, and J.-F. Thisse. 1989. "Competitive Location with Random Utilities." *Transportation Science* 23: 244–52.

de Palma, A., G. Hong, and J.-F. Thisse. 1990. "Equilibria in Multiparty Competition under Uncertainty." *Social Choice and Welfare* 7: 247–59.

Denver, David. 1998. "The Government That Could Do No Right." In *New Labour Triumphs: Britain at the Polls*, edited by Anthony King. Chatham, NJ: Chatham House.

Dow, Jay. 1999. "Voter Choice in the 1995 French Presidential Election." *Political Behavior* 21: 305–24.

Dow, Jay. 2001. "A Comparative Spatial Analysis of Majoritarian and Proportional Systems." *Electoral Studies* 9: 109–25.

Dow, Jay, and James Endersby. 2004. "A Comparison of Conditional Logit and Multinomial Probit Models in Multiparty Elections." *Electoral Studies* 23: 107–22.

Downs, Anthony. 1957. *An Economic Theory of Democracy*. New York: Harper and Row.

Duverger, Maurice. 1954. *Political Parties*. New York: Wiley.

Eaton, B. Curtis, and Richard G. Lipsey. 1975. "The Principle of Minimum Differentiation Reconsidered: Some New Developments in the Theory of Spatial Competition." *Review of Economic Studies* 42: 27–49.

Endersby, James, and Steven Galatas. 1997. "British Parties and Spatial Competition: Dimensions of Evaluation in the 1992 Election." Paper presented at the annual meeting of the Public Choice Society, San Francisco, CA, March 21–23.

Enelow, James, and Melvin Hinich. 1981. "A New Approach to Voter Uncertainty in the Downsian Spatial Model." *American Journal of Political Science* 25: 483–93.

Enelow, James, and Melvin Hinich. 1982. "Non-Spatial Candidate Characteristics and Electoral Competition." *Journal of Politics* 44: 115–30.

Enelow, James, and Melvin Hinich. 1984. *The Spatial Theory of Voting*. Cambridge: Cambridge University Press.

Erikson, Robert, and David Romero. 1990. "Candidate Equilibrium and the Behavioral Model of the Vote." *American Political Science Review* 84: 1103–26.

Ezrow, Lawrence. 2003. "Exploring Convergence." Unpublished manuscript.

Farah, Barbara. 1980. "Political Representation in West Germany." Ph.D. dissertation, University of Michigan.

Feld, Scott, and Bernard Grofman. 1991. "Voter Loyalty, Incumbency Advantage, and the Benefit of the Doubt." *Journal of Theoretical Politics* 3: 115–37.

Fenno, Richard. 1978. *Home Style*. Boston: Little, Brown.

Fiorina, Morris. 1973. *Congress: Keystone of the Washington Establishment*. New Haven, CT: Yale University Press.

Fiorina, Morris. 1974. *Representatives, Roll Calls, and Constituencies*. Lexington, MA: Lexington.

Fiorina, Morris. 1981. *Retrospective Voting in American National Elections*. New Haven, CT: Yale University Press.

Fiorina, Morris. 1994. "Divided Government in the American States: A By-Product of Legislative Professionalism?" *American Political Science Review* 88: 304–16.

Fiorina, Morris. 1996. *Divided Government*. New York: Macmillan.

Fleury, Christopher, and Michael Lewis-Beck. 1993. "Anchoring the French Voter: Ideology versus Party." *Journal of Politics* 55: 1100–9.

Frears, John. 1991. *Parties and Voters in France*. London: Hurst.

Garvey, Gerald. 1966. "The Theory of Party Equilibrium." *American Political Science Review* 60: 29–38.

Gerber, Alan, and Donald Green. 1999. "Misperceptions about Perceptual Bias." *Annual Review of Political Science* 2: 189–210.

Gerber, Elizabeth, and John Jackson. 1993. "Endogenous Preferences and the Study of Institutions." *American Political Science Review* 87: 639–56.

Gerber, Elizabeth, and Rebecca Morton. 1998. "Primary Elections Systems and Representation." *Journal of Law, Economics, and Organization* 14: 304–24.

Gershtenson, Joseph, and Dennis Plane. 1999. "The Effects of Candidate Ideological Location on Individual Propensity to Vote and Aggregate-Level Voter Turnout in United States Senate Elections." Paper presented at the annual meeting of the American Political Science Association, Atlanta, GA, September 1–4.

Glasgow, Garrett. 2001. "Mixed Logit Models for Multiparty Elections." *Political Analysis* 2: 116–36.

Glazer, Amihai, Bernard Grofman, and Guillermo Owen. 1998. "A Neo-Downsian Model of Group-Oriented Voting and Racial Backlash." *Public Choice* 97: 23–34.

Granberg, Donald. 1987. "A Contextual Effect in Political Perception and Self-Placement on an Ideology Scale: Comparative Analyses of Sweden and the United States." *Scandinavian Political Studies* 10: 39–60.

Granberg, Donald, and Edward Brent. 1980. "Perceptions and Issue Positions of Presidential Candidates." *American Scientist* 68: 617–85.

Granberg, Donald, and Thad A. Brown. 1992. "The Perception of Ideological Distance." *Western Political Quarterly* 45: 727–50.

Granberg, Donald, Wayne Harris, and Michael King. 1981. "Assimilation but Little Contrast in the 1976 United States Presidential Election." *Journal of Psychology* 108: 241–47.

Granberg, Donald, and Sören Holmberg. 1988. *The Political System Matters: Social Psychology and Voting Behavior in Sweden and the United States.* New York: Cambridge University Press.

Granberg, Donald, and Richard Jenks. 1977. "Assimilation and Contrast Effects in the 1972 Election." *Human Relations* 30: 623–40.

Grofman, Bernard. 1982. Book review: Political Geography. *American Political Science Review* 76(4): 883–5.

Grofman, Bernard. 1985. "The Neglected Role of the Status Quo in Models of Issue Voting." *Journal of Politics* 47: 230–7.

Grofman, Bernard. 2001. "Introduction: The Joy of Puzzle Solving." In *Political Science as Puzzle Solving*, edited by Bernard Grofman. Ann Arbor: University of Michigan Press.

Grofman, Bernard. In press. "Downs and Two-party Convergence." *Annual Review of Political Science.*

Grofman, Bernard, and Thomas Brunell. 2001. "Explaining the Ideological Differences between the Two United States Senators Elected from the Same State: An Institutional Effects Model." In *Congressional Primaries and the Politics of Representation*, edited by Peter Galderisi, Marni Ezra, and Michael Lyons. New York: Rowman and Littlefield.

Grofman, Bernard, William Koetzle, Michael McDonald, and Thomas Brunell. 2000. "A New Look at Ticket-Splitting for House and President: The Comparative Midpoints Model." *Journal of Politics* 62: 34–50.

Groseclose, Timothy. 2001. "A Model of Candidate Location When One Candidate Has a Valence Advantage." *American Journal of Political Science* 45: 862–86.

Guttman, Joel, Naftali Hilger, and Yochanen Shacmurove. 1994. "Voting as Investment and Voting as Consumption: New Evidence." *Kyklos* 47: 197–207.

Heath, Anthony, and Roy Pierce. 1992. "It Was Party Identification All Along: Question Order Effects on Reports of Party Identification in Britain." *Electoral Studies* 11: 93–105.

Henrici, Peter. 1964. *Elements of Numerical Analysis.* New York: Wiley.

Himmelweit, H. T., M. Jaeger, and J. Stockdale. 1978. "Memory for Past Vote: Implications of a Study of Bias in Recall." *British Journal of Political Science* 8: 365–76.

Hinich, Melvin. 1978. "Some Evidence on Non-Voting Models in the Spatial Theory of Electoral Competition." *Public Choice* 33: 83–102.

Hinich, Melvin, John Ledyard, and Peter Ordeshook. 1972. "Nonvoting and Existence of Equilibrium under Majority Rule." *Journal of Economic Theory* 4: 44–53.

Hinich, Melvin, and Michael Munger. 1994. *Ideology and the Theory of Political Choice.* Ann Arbor: University of Michigan Press.

Hinich, Melvin, and Peter Ordeshook. 1970. "Plurality Maximization vs. Vote Maximization: A Spatial Analysis with Variable Participation." *American Political Science Review* 64: 772–91.

Hinich, Melvin, and Walker Pollard. 1981. "A New Approach to the Spatial Theory of Electoral Competition." *American Journal of Political Science* 25: 323–41.

Hoch, Stephen J. 1987. "Perceived Consensus and Predictive Accuracy: The Pros and Cons of Projection." *Journal of Personality and Social Psychology* 53: 221–34.

Huber, John, and Ronald Inglehart. 1995. "Expert Interpretations of Party Space and Party Locations in 42 Societies." *Party Politics* 1: 73–111.

Huber, John, and G. Bingham Powell, Jr. 1994. "Congruence between Citizens and Policy-Makers in Two Visions of Liberal Democracy." *World Politics* 46: 291–326.

Hug, Simon. 1995. "Third Parties in Equilibrium." *Public Choice* 82: 159–80.

Husted, T. A., Lawrence Kenny, and Rebecca B. Morton. 1995. "Constituent Errors in Assessing Their Senators." *Public Choice* 83: 251–71.

Ingberman, Daniel. 1992. "Incumbent Reputations and Ideological Campaign Contributions." *Mathematical and Computer Modeling* 16: 147–69.

Iversen, Torben. 1994a. "Political Leadership and Representation in Western European Democracies: A Test of Three Models of Voting." *American Journal of Political Science* 38: 45–74.

Iversen, Torben. 1994b. "The Logics of Electoral Politics: Spatial, Directional, and Mobilization Effects." *Comparative Political Studies* 27: 155–89.

Jackson, John E. 1975. "Issues, Party Choices, and Presidential Votes." *American Journal of Political Science* 19: 161–86.

Jackson, John E. 1997. "A Computational Model of Electoral Competition." Paper presented at the annual meeting of the American Political Science Association, Washington, DC, August 28–31.

Jennings, Kent, and Gregory Markus. 1984. "Partisan Orientations over the Long Haul." *American Political Science Review* 78: 1000–18.

Jennings, Kent, and Richard Niemi. 1981. *Generations and Politics*. Princeton, NJ: Princeton University Press.

Kavanaugh, Dennis. 2000. *British Politics: Continuities and Change*. New York: Oxford University Press.

Keane, Michael. 1992. "A Note on Identification in the Multinomial Probit Model." *Journal of Business and Economic Statistics* 10: 193–200.

Kedar, Orit. 2002. "Balancing the Seesaw: Rationality and Menu Dependence in Voter Behavior." Paper presented at the annual meeting of the Midwest Political Science Association, Chicago, IL, April 25–28.

Kenny, Lawrence, and Babak Lotfinia. Forthcoming. "Evidence on the Importance of Spatial Models in Presidential Nominations and Elections." *Public Choice*.

Kinder, Donald, and Roderick Kiewiet. 1981. "Sociotropic Voting: The American Case." *British Journal of Political Science* 11: 129–41.

Kollman, Kenneth, John Miller, and Scott Page. 1992. "Adaptive Parties in Spatial Elections." *American Political Science Review* 86: 929–37.

Kramer, Richard. 1977. "A Dynamic Model of Political Equilibrium." *Journal of Economic Theory* 16: 310–34.

Lacy, Dean, and Barry Burden. 1999. "The Vote-Stealing and Turnout Effects of Ross Perot in the 1992 United States Presidential Election." *American Journal of Political Science* 43: 233–55.

Lacy, Dean, and Philip Paolino. 1998. "Downsian Voting and Separation of Powers." *American Journal of Political Science* 42: 1180–99.

Lacy, Dean, and Philip Paolino. 2001. "Downsian Voting and Separation of Powers in the 1998 Texas and Ohio Gubernatorial Elections." Paper presented at the annual meeting of the Midwest Political Science Association, Chicago, IL, April 25–28.

Laver, Michael, and Ian, Budge, eds. 1992. *Party Policy and Government Coalitions in Western Europe*. London: Macmillan

Laver, Michael, and Norman Schofield. 1990. *Multiparty Governments: The Politics of Coalitions in Europe*. Oxford: Oxford University Press.

Laver, Michael, and Kenneth Shepsle. 1996. *Making and Breaking Governments: Cabinets and Legislatures in Parliamentary Democracies*. Cambridge: Cambridge University Press.

Lewis-Beck, Michael. 1988. *Economics and Elections*. Ann Arbor: University of Michigan Press.

Lewis-Beck, Michael, and Kevin Chlarson. 2002. "Party, Ideology, Institutions, and the 1995 French Presidential Election." *British Journal of Political Science* 32: 489–512.

Lewis-Beck, Michael, and Richard Nadeau. 2004. "Split-Ticket Voting: The Effects of Cognitive Madisonianism." *Journal of Politics* 66(1): 97–112.

Lijphart, Arend. 1984. *Democracies: Patterns of Majoritarian and Consensus Government in Twenty-One Countries*. New Haven, CT: Yale University Press.

Lijphart, Arend. 1994. *Electoral Systems and Party Systems: A Study of Twenty-Seven Democracies*. Oxford and New York: Oxford University Press.

Lijphart, Arend. 1997. "Unequal Participation: Democracy's Unresolved Dilemma." *American Political Science Review* 91: 1–14.

Lijphart, Arend. 1999. *Patterns of Democracy: Government Forms and Performance in Thirty-Six Countries*. New Haven, CT: Yale University Press.

Lin, Tse-min, James M. Enelow, and Han Dorussen. 1999. "Equilibrium in Multi-candidate Probabilistic Spatial Voting." *Public Choice* 98: 59–82.

Listhaug, O., S. E. Macdonald, and G. Rabinowitz. 1994a. Ideology and Party Support in Comparative Perspective." *European Journal of Political Research* 25: 111–49.

Lomborg, Bjorn. 1996. "Adaptive Parties in a Multiparty, Multidimensional System with Imperfect Information." Unpublished manuscript.

Londregan, John, and Thomas Romer. 1993. "Polarization, Incumbency, and the Personal Vote." In *Political Economy: Institutions, Competition, and Representation*, edited by William A. Barnett, Melvin Hinich, and Norman Schofield. New York: Cambridge University Press.

Macdonald, Stuart Elaine, and George Rabinowitz. 1998. "Solving the Paradox of Nonconvergence: Valence, Position, and Direction in Democratic Politics." *Electoral Studies* 17: 281–300.

Markus, Gregory A., and Philip E. Converse. 1979. "A Dynamic Simultaneous Equation Model of Electoral Choice." *American Political Science Review* 73: 1055–70.

Martin, Andrew, and Kevin Quinn. 2000. "An Integrated Computational Model of Multiparty Electoral Competition." Paper presented at the annual meeting of the American Political Science Association, Washington, DC, September 1–4.

McCuen, Brian, and Rebecca Morton. 2002. "Tactical Coalition Voting." Unpublished manuscript.

McGann, Anthony. 2002. "The Advantages of Ideological Cohesion: A Model of Constituency Representation and Electoral Competition in Multiparty Democracies." *Journal of Theoretical Politics* 14: 37–70.

McGann, Anthony, Bernard Grofman, and William Koetzle. 2003. "Why Party Leaders Are More Extreme Than Their Members: Modeling Sequential Elimination Elections in the United States House of Representatives." *Journal of Theoretical Politics* 15: 337–56.

McGann, Anthony, William Koetzle, and Bernard Grofman. 2002. "How an Ideologically Concentrated Minority Can Trump a Dispersed Majority: Non-Median Voter Results for Plurality, Runoff, and Sequential Elimination Elections." *American Journal of Political Science* 46: 134–48.

McKelvey, Richard. 1986. "Covering, Dominance, and Institution-Free Properties of Social Choice." *American Journal of Political Science* 30: 282–314.

Merrill, Samuel, III, and James Adams. 2001. "Computing Nash Equilibria in Probabilistic, Multiparty Spatial Models with Nonpolicy Components." *Political Analysis* 9: 347–61.

Merrill, Samuel, III, and James Adams. 2002. "Centrifugal Incentives in Multi-Candidate Elections." *Journal of Theoretical Politics* 14: 273–300.

Merrill, Samuel, III, and Bernard Grofman. 1997. "Directional and Proximity Spatial Models of Voter Utility and Choice: A New Synthesis and an Illustrative Test of Competing Models." *Journal of Theoretical Politics* 9: 25–48.

Merrill, Samuel, III, and Bernard Grofman. 1999. *A Unified Theory of Voting: Directional and Proximity Spatial Models.* Cambridge: Cambridge University Press.

Merrill, Samuel, III, Bernard Grofman, and James Adams. 2001. "Assimilation and Contrast Effects in Voter Projections of Party Locations: Evidence from Norway, France, and the United States." *European Journal of Political Research* 40: 199–223.

Miller, Gary, and Norman Schofield. 2003. "Activists and Partisan Realignment in the United States." *American Political Science Review* 97: 245–60.

Mitchell, D. W. 1987. "Candidate Behavior under Mixed Motives." *Social Choice and Welfare* 4: 153–60.

Moon, Woojin. In press. "Party Activists, Campaign Resources, and Candidate Position Taking in United States Senate Elections, 1974–2000: Theory and Tests." *British Journal of Political Science.*

Muller, Wolfgang, and Kaare Strom, eds. 1999. *Policy, Office, or Votes?* Cambridge: Cambridge University Press.

Nagel, Jack. 2001. "Center-Party Strength and Major-Party Polarization in Britain." Paper presented at the annual meeting of the American Political Science Association, San Francisco, CA, August 30–September 2.

Ordeshook, Peter. 1969. "Theory of Electoral Process." Ph. D. dissertation, University of Rochester.

Ortega, James M. 1972. *Numerical Analysis.* New York: Academic Press.

Owen, Guillermo, and Bernard Grofman. 1984. "Coalitions and Power in Political Situations." In *Coalitions and Collective Action,* edited by Manfred Holler. Wuerzburg: Physica-Verlag.

Owen, Guillermo, and Bernard Grofman. 1995. "Two-Stage Electoral Competition in Two-Party Contests: Persistent Divergence of Party Positions." Paper presented at the annual meeting of the Public Choice Society, Long Beach, CA, March 24–26.

Page, Benjamin. 1976. "The Theory of Political Ambiguity." *American Political Science Review* 70: 742–52.

Page, Benjamin, and Calvin Jones. 1979. "Reciprocal Effects of Policy Preferences, Party Loyalties, and the Vote." *American Political Science Review* 73: 1071–89.

Palfrey, Thomas. 1984. "Spatial Equilibrium with Entry." *Review of Economic Studies* 51: 139–56.

Parducci, Allen, and Louise M. Marshall. 1962. "Assimilation v. Contrast in the Anchoring of Perceptual Judgments of Weight." *Journal of Experimental Psychology* 63: 426–37.

Pierce, Roy. 1995. *Choosing the Chief: Presidential Elections in France and the United States.* Ann Arbor: University of Michigan Press.

Pierce, Roy. 1996. "French Presidential Election Study, 1988" [computer file]. ICPSR version. Ann Arbor, MI: Roy Pierce, University of Michigan [producer], 1995. Ann Arbor, MI: Inter-university Consortium for Political and Social Research [distributor], 1996.

Piven, Frances, and Richard Cloward. 1988. *Why Americans Don't Vote*. New York: Pantheon.

Polsby, Nelson. 1980. *Consequences of Party Reform*. New York: Oxford University Press.

Powell, G. Bingham. 1989. "Constitutional Design and Citizen Electoral Control." *Journal of Theoretical Politics* 1: 107–30.

Powell, G. Bingham. 2000. *Elections as Instruments of Democracy: Majoritarian and Proportional Visions*. New Haven, CT: Yale University Press.

Rabinowitz, George, and Stuart Macdonald. 1989. "A Directional Theory of Issue Voting." *American Political Science Review* 89: 93–121.

Rabinowitz, George, and Stuart Macdonald. 1998. "On Attempting to Rehabilitate the Proximity Model: Sometimes the Patient Just Can't Be Helped." *Journal of Politics* 60: 653–90.

Riker, William. 1986. *The Art of Political Manipulation*. New Haven, CT: Yale University Press.

Riker, William, and Peter Ordeshook. 1968. "A Theory of the Calculus of Voting." *American Political Science Review* 62: 25–42.

Riker, William, and Peter Ordeshook. 1973. *An Introduction to Positive Political Theory*. Englewood Cliffs, NJ: Prentice Hall.

Rivers, Douglas. 1988. "Heterogeneity in Models of Electoral Choice." *American Journal of Political Science* 32: 737–58.

Roemer, John. 2001. *Political Competition: Theory and Applications*. Cambridge, MA: Harvard University Press.

Rose, Richard, and Ian McAllister. 1990. *The Loyalties of Voters: A Lifetime Learning Model*. London: Sage.

Safran, William. 1998. *The French Polity*, 5th ed. White Plains, NY: Longman.

Sanders, Mitchell. 1998. "Unified Models of Turnout and Vote Choice for Two-Candidate and Three-Candidate Elections." *Political Analysis* 7: 89–116.

Sanders, Mitchell. 2001. "Uncertainty and Turnout." *Political Analysis* 9: 45–57.

Sartori, Giovanni. 1968. "Representational Systems." *International Encyclopedia of the Social Sciences* 13: 470–5.

Schofield, Norman. 1978. "Instability of Simple Dynamic Games." *Review of Economic Studies* 45: 575–94.

Schofield, Norman. 1996. "The Heart of a Polity." In *Collective Decision-Making: Social Choice and Political Economy*, edited by Norman Schofield. Boston: Kluwer.

Schofield, Norman. 2002. "Existence of a General Political Equilibrium." Unpublished manuscript.

Schofield, Norman. 2003. "Valence Competition in the Spatial Stochastic Model." *Journal of Theoretical Politics* 15: 371–84.

Schofield, Norman. 2004. "Equilibrium in the Spatial 'Valence' Model of Politics." *Journal of Theoretical Politics* 16: 447–81.

Schofield, Norman, Andrew Martin, Kevin Quinn, and Andrew Whitford. 1998. "Multiparty Electoral Competition in the Netherlands and Germany: A Model Based on Multinomial Probit." *Public Choice* 97: 257–93.

Schofield, Norman, and Itai Sened. 2003. "Multiparty Competition in Israel: 1992–1996." Unpublished manuscript.

Schofield, Norman, Itai Sened, and David Nixon. 1998. "Nash Equilibria in Multiparty Competition with 'Stochastic' Voters." *Annals of Operations Research* 84: 3–27.

Shepsle, Kenneth. 1991. *Models of Multiparty Electoral Competition*. London: Harwood Academic Publishers.

Sherif, M., and C. Hovland. 1961. *Social Judgment: Assimilation and Contrast Effects in Communication and Attitude Change*. New Haven, CT: Yale University Press.

Snyder, James, and Michael Chang. 2002. "An Informational Rationale for Political Parties." *American Journal of Political Science* 46: 9–110.

Stokes, Donald. 1963. "Spatial Models of Party Competition." *American Political Science Review* 57: 368–77.

Stokes, Susan. 1999. "What Do Policy Switches Tell Us about Democracy?" In *Democracy, Accountability, and Representation*, edited by Adam Przeworski, Susan Stokes, and Bernard Manin. Cambridge: Cambridge University Press.

Strøm, Kaare, and Lars Svåsand, eds. 1997. *Challenges to Political Parties: The Case of Norway*. Ann Arbor: University of Michigan Press.

Taagepera, Rein, and Matthew Shugart. 1989. *Seats and Votes: The Effects and Determinants of Electoral Systems*. New Haven, CT: Yale University Press.

Thurner, Paul, and Angelika Eymann. 2000. "Policy-Specific Alienation and Indifference in the Calculus of Voting: A Simultaneous Model of Party Choice and Abstention." *Public Choice* 102: 51–77.

Train, Kenneth. 1986. *Qualitative Choice Analysis*. Cambridge, MA: MIT Press.

Urwin, Derek. 1997. "The Norwegian Party System from the 1880s to the 1990s." In *Challenges to Political Parties: The Case of Norway*, edited by Kaare Strom and Lars Svasand. Ann Arbor: University of Michigan Press.

Valen, Henry. 1990. "The Storting Election of 1989: Polarization and Protest." *Scandinavian Political Studies* 3: 27–90.

van der Eijk, Cornelis, and Broer Niemöller. 1983. *Electoral Change in the Netherlands*. Amsterdam: CT Press.

Warwick, Paul. 2004. "Proximity, Directionality, and the Riddle of Relative Party Extremeness." *Journal of Theoretical Politics* 16: 263–87.

Weisberg, Herbert, and Bernard Grofman. 1981. "Candidate Evaluations and Turnout." *American Politics Quarterly* 9: 197–219.

Weissberg, Robert. 1978. "Collective vs. Dyadic Representation in Congress." *American Political Science Review* 72: 535–47.

Westholm, Anders. 1997. "Distance versus Direction: The Illusory Defeat of Proximity Theory." *American Political Science Review* 91: 865–83.

Wittman, Donald. 1973. "Parties as Utility Maximizers." *American Political Science Review* 67: 490–8.

Wittman, Donald. 1977. "Candidates with Policy Preferences: A Dynamic Model." *Journal of Economic Theory* 14: 180–9.

Wittman, Donald. 1983. "Candidate Motivation: A Synthesis of Alternatives." *American Political Science Review* 77: 142–57.

Wittman, Donald. 1990. "Spatial Strategies When Candidates Have Policy Preferences." In *Advances in the Spatial Theory of Voting*, edited by James Enelow and Melvin Hinich. Cambridge: Cambridge University Press.

Wolfinger, Raymond, and Steven Rosenstone. 1980. *Who Votes?* New Haven, CT: Yale University Press.

Wuffle, A., Scott Feld, and Guillermo Owen. 1989. "Finagle's Law and the Finagle Point: A New Solution Concept for Two-Candidate Competition in Spatial Voting Games." *American Journal of Political Science* 33: 348–75.

Zaller, John. 1992. *The Nature and Origins of Mass Opinion*. Cambridge: Cambridge University Press.

Index